COMPUTER PROGRAMMING
FUNDAMENTAL CONCEPTS
USING JAVA®

Rachel M. Jones

Y. Daniel Liang
Armstrong Atlantic State University

Pearson

Boston • Columbus • Indianapolis • New York • San Francisco • Amsterdam
Cape Town • Dubai • London • Madrid • Milan • Munich • Paris • Montréal • Toronto
Delhi • Mexico City • São Paulo • Sydney • Hong Kong • Seoul • Singapore • Taipei • Tokyo

Pearson

330 Hudson Street, New York, NY 10013
Hardcover ISBN 10: 0-13-467976-8
Hardcover ISBN 13: 978-0-13-467976-1

3 17

BRIEF CONTENTS

TABLE OF CONTENTS

CHAPTER 6

Using Loop Statements

CHAPTER 7

CHAPTER 8

CHAPTER 9

PREFACE

This book is an introduction to computer programming fundamentals. The intended audience of this book is students who desire a basic understanding of computer programming. It lays a foundation for more advanced courses at both the high school and college level, or for those seeking an entry-level position in the computer software industry.

The content begins by identifying expectations in the workplace, and the skills required of computer programmers. Students will learn about the differences between various programming languages and their common uses. An introduction to the software life-cycle approach to designing an application is also covered. The first step in learning computer programming is to understand how to analyze and solve problems in a logical way. Students will learn how to create algorithms to analyze and solve problems.

Basic programming concepts such as selection statements, looping, and array data structures are introduced using the Java programming language. Students gain hands on experience through examples and programming exercises throughout the book. The earlier chapters provide a solid foundation for the introduction of more advanced topics covered in chapters 8 and 9. These latter two chapters introduce modular, object-oriented programming. The final chapter provides a foundation for developing and implementing a risk assessment strategy, tactics for reducing security risks, and under-standing state and federal laws surrounding the industry. Several supplemental chapters are included. The intent of this supplemental material is to provide deeper understand-ing and advanced study at the discretion of both teachers and students. The supplements include topics such as algorithmic thinking, multi-dimensional arrays, variable scoping, and nested loops.

Much of the content is an adaptation from Y. Daniel Liang's *Introduction to Java Programming, Brief Version, Tenth Edition*. Additionally, adaptations of Lawrence Snyder's *Fluency 6 With Information Technology* is included in the algorithmic thinking and security sections of the book. It is with great admiration and appreciation for Professor Liang and Professor Snyder's groundwork that this book is created for you.

I would like to thank Felicia Carmouche of Katy, Texas Independent School District (KISD), Karen Misler, and Suzanne Weixel for their contributions to this book, and *Emergent Learning, LLC* for the opportunity to be involved in this project. I owe my deepest gratitude to Chuck, Robbi, and Chris for enduring the long hours in the "code cave" over the years.

It is our passion to encourage bright, young minds to enter into this fascinating and rewarding industry of software development. We hope this book lights a spark!

Sincerely,

Rachel M. Jones
twitter: @rachelmcjones

Pedagogical Features

The pedagogical approach is an introduction of topics through text narrative, coding examples, and case studies followed by hands-on coding exercises. Section assessments and end-of-chapter reviews provide additional learning reinforcement.

Objectives at the beginning of each chapter list what students should learn from the chapter. This will help them determine whether they have met the objectives after completing the chapter.

Key Points are included at the beginning of each section. Each key point highlights an important takeaway for the section.

Margin Terms provide a quick glance at key concepts. Readers can use the margin words as a reference locator of key concepts.

Section Assessments provide review questions to help students individually track their understanding of the material, or they can be used as assignments to measure student progress.

Case Studies and Examples highlight real-world application of the material and provide hands-on learning.

Notes, Tips, and Cautions are included throughout the book to offer valuable advice about computer programming, the work environment, and tools used in designing an application.

Chapter Review and Assessment sections at the end of each chapter include the following:

- **Key Terms** is a listing of important terms. The ability to describe the terms and apply them to exercises provides a minimal baseline metric for successful completion of the chapter.

- **Chapter Summary** reviews the important subjects that students should understand and remember. It helps them reinforce the key concepts they have learned in the chapter.

- **Programming Exercises** provide hands-on experience to apply the new skills learned. Answers to exercises are provided at the end of the Teacher's Edition, but are not included in the book.

- **Group exercises** are included in some chapters to emulate real-world experience of working on a team project.

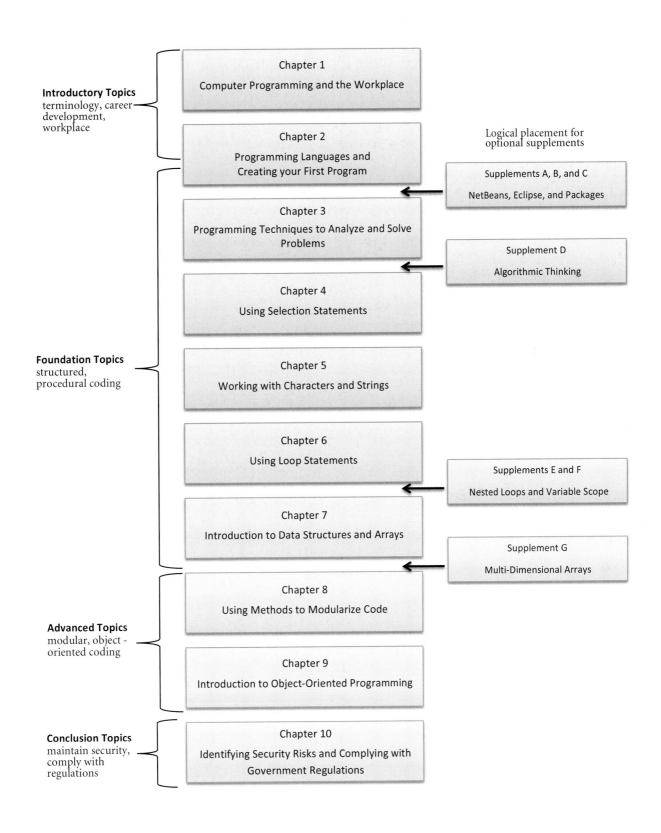

Introductory Topics
terminology, career development, workplace

Chapter 1
Computer Programming and the Workplace

Chapter 2
Programming Languages and Creating your First Program

Logical placement for optional supplements

Supplements A, B, and C
NetBeans, Eclipse, and Packages

Chapter 3
Programming Techniques to Analyze and Solve Problems

Supplement D
Algorithmic Thinking

Chapter 4
Using Selection Statements

Foundation Topics
structured, procedural coding

Chapter 5
Working with Characters and Strings

Chapter 6
Using Loop Statements

Supplements E and F
Nested Loops and Variable Scope

Chapter 7
Introduction to Data Structures and Arrays

Supplement G
Multi-Dimensional Arrays

Chapter 8
Using Methods to Modularize Code

Advanced Topics
modular, object - oriented coding

Chapter 9
Introduction to Object-Oriented Programming

Conclusion Topics
maintain security, comply with regulations

Chapter 10
Identifying Security Risks and Complying with Government Regulations

COMPUTER PROGRAMMING AND THE WORKPLACE

Objectives

- Understand basic computer terminology.

- Understand the basic *hardware and software components* of a computer.

- Identify *job opportunities* that require computer programming skills.

- Identify the necessary *skills* for a job in computer programming.

- Understand the *steps to problem solving*.

- Understand the definition of business *ethics*.

- Distinguish between *ethical and unethical business practices* in the information technology industry.

- Examine software *copyright* and *licensing* issues.

1.1 Concepts and Terminology of a Computer

Key Point

The central theme of this book is to learn how to solve problems by writing a program.

programming

program

This book is about programming. So, what is programming? The term *programming* means to create (or develop) software, which is also called a *program*. In basic terms, software contains the instructions that tell a computer—or a computerized device—what to do.

Software is all around you, even in devices that you might not think would need it. Of course, you expect to find and use software on a personal computer, but software also plays a role in running airplanes, cars, cell phones, and even toasters. On a personal computer, you use word processors to write documents, Web browsers to explore the Internet, and e-mail programs to send and receive messages. These programs are all examples of software. Software developers create software with the help of powerful tools called *programming languages.*

programming languages

This book teaches you how to create programs by using the Java programming language. There are many programming languages, some of which are decades old. Each language was invented for a specific purpose—to build on the strengths of a previous language, for example, or to give the programmer a new and unique set of tools. Knowing that there are so many programming languages available, it would be natural for you to wonder which one is best. But, in truth, there is no "best" language. Each one has its own strengths and weaknesses. Experienced programmers know that one language might work well in some situations, whereas a different language may be more appropriate in other situations. For this reason, seasoned programmers try to master as many different programming languages as they can, giving them access to a vast arsenal of software-development tools.

If you learn to program using one language, you should find it easy to pick up other languages. The key is to learn how to solve problems using a programming approach. That is the main theme of this book.

You are about to begin an exciting journey: learning how to program. At the outset, it is helpful to review computer basics, programs, and operating systems.

What Is a Computer?

Key Point

A computer is an electronic device that stores and processes data.

hardware

software

A computer includes both *hardware* and *software*. In general, hardware comprises the visible, physical elements of the computer, and software provides the invisible instructions that control the hardware and make it perform specific tasks. Knowing computer hardware isn't essential to learning a programming language, but it can help you better understand the effects that a program's instructions have on the computer and its components. This section introduces computer hardware components and their functions.

A computer consists of the following major hardware components (Figure 1.1):

- A central processing unit (CPU)

- Memory (main memory)

- Storage devices (such as disks and CDs)

- Input devices (such as the mouse and keyboard)

- Output devices (such as monitors and printers)

- Communication devices (such as modems and network interface cards)

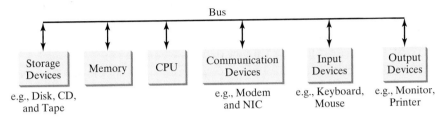

FIGURE 1.1 A computer consists of a CPU, memory, storage devices, input devices, output devices, and communication devices.

A computer's components are interconnected by a subsystem called a *bus*. You can think of a bus as a sort of system of roads running among the computer's components. Data and power travel along the bus from one part of the computer to another. In personal computers, the bus is built into the computer's *motherboard*, which is a circuit case that connects all of the parts of a computer together.

bus

motherboard

Central Processing Unit

The *central processing unit (CPU)* is the computer's brain. It retrieves instructions from memory and executes them. The CPU usually has two components: a *control unit* and an *arithmetic/logic unit*. The control unit controls and coordinates the actions of the other components. The arithmetic/logic unit performs numeric operations (addition, subtraction, multiplication, division) and logical operations (comparisons).

CPU

control unit
arithmetic/logic unit

Today's CPUs are built on small silicon semiconductor chips that contain millions of tiny electric switches, called *transistors*, for processing information.

transistors

Every computer has an internal clock, which emits electronic pulses at a constant rate. These pulses are used to control and synchronize the pace of operations. A higher clock *speed* enables more instructions to be executed in a given period of time. The unit of measurement of clock speed is the *hertz (Hz)*, with 1 hertz equaling 1 pulse per second. In the 1990s, computers measured clocked speed in *megahertz (MHz)*, but CPU speed has been improving continuously; the clock speed of a computer is now usually stated in *gigahertz (GHz)*. Intel's newest processors run at about 3 GHz.

speed

hertz

megahertz
gigahertz

CPUs were originally developed with only one core. The *core* is the part of the processor that performs the reading and executing of instructions. In order to increase CPU processing power, chip manufacturers are now producing CPUs that contain multiple cores. A multicore CPU is a single component with two or more independent cores. Today's consumer computers typically have two, three, and even four separate cores. Soon, CPUs with dozens or even hundreds of cores will be affordable.

core

Bits and Bytes

Before we discuss memory, let's look at how information (data and programs) are stored in a computer.

A computer is really nothing more than a series of switches. Each switch exists in two states: on or off. Storing information in a computer is simply a matter of setting a sequence of switches on or off. If the switch is on, its value is 1. If the switch is off, its value is 0. These 0s and 1s are interpreted as digits in the binary number system and are called *bits* (binary digits).

The minimum storage unit in a computer is a *byte*. A byte is composed of eight bits. A small number such as 3 can be stored as a single byte. To store a number that cannot fit into a single byte, the computer uses several bytes.

Data of various kinds, such as numbers and characters, are encoded as a series of bytes. As a programmer, you don't need to worry about the encoding and decoding of data, which the computer system performs automatically, based on the encoding scheme. An *encoding scheme* is a set of rules that govern how a computer translates characters, numbers, and symbols into data the computer can actually work with. Most schemes translate each character into a predetermined string of bits. In the popular ASCII encoding scheme, for example, the character C is represented as `01000011` in one byte.

A computer's storage capacity is measured in bytes and multiples of the byte, as follows:

- A *kilobyte (KB)* is about 1,000 bytes.
- A *megabyte (MB)* is about 1 million bytes.
- A *gigabyte (GB)* is about 1 billion bytes.
- A *terabyte (TB)* is about 1 trillion bytes.

A typical one-page word document might take 20 KB. Therefore, 1 MB can store 50 pages of documents and 1 GB can store 50,000 pages of documents. A typical two-hour high-resolution movie might take 8 GB, so it would require 160 GB to store 20 movies.

Memory

A computer's *memory* consists of an ordered sequence of bytes for storing programs as well as data that the program is working with. You can think of memory as the computer's work area for executing a program. A program and its data must be moved into the computer's memory before they can be executed by the CPU.

Every byte in the memory has a *unique address*, as shown in Figure 1.2. The address is used to locate the byte for storing and retrieving the data. Since the bytes in the memory can be accessed in any order, the memory is also referred to as *random-access memory (RAM)*.

Generally speaking, the more RAM a computer has, the faster it can operate, but there are limits to this simple rule of thumb.

A memory byte is never empty, but its initial content may be meaningless to your program. The current content of a memory byte is lost whenever new information is placed in it.

Margin notes:

bits
byte

encoding scheme

kilobyte (KB)

megabyte (MB)

gigabyte (GB)

terabyte (TB)

memory

unique address

RAM

Memory address Memory content

2000	01000011	Encoding for character 'C'
2001	01110010	Encoding for character 'r'
2002	01100101	Encoding for character 'e'
2003	01110111	Encoding for character 'w'
2004	00000011	Encoding for number 3

FIGURE 1.2 Memory stores data and program instructions in uniquely addressed memory locations.

Like the CPU, memory is built on silicon semiconductor chips that have millions of transistors embedded on their surface. Compared to CPU chips, memory chips are less complicated, slower, and less expensive.

Storage Devices

A computer's memory (RAM) is a volatile form of data storage: any information that has been stored in memory (i.e., saved) is lost when the system's power is turned off. Programs and data are permanently stored on *storage devices* and are moved, when the computer actually uses them, to memory, which operates at much faster speeds than permanent storage devices can.

storage devices

There are three main types of storage devices:

- Magnetic disk drives
- Optical disc drives (CD and DVD)
- USB flash drives

Drives are devices for operating a medium, such as disks and CDs. A storage medium physically stores data and program instructions. The drive reads data from the medium and writes data onto the medium.

drive

Disks

A computer usually has at least one hard disk drive. *Hard disks* are used for permanently storing data and programs. Newer computers have hard disks that can store from 500 gigabytes to several terabytes of data. Hard disk drives are usually encased inside the computer, but removable hard disks are also available.

hard disk

CDs and DVDs

CD stands for compact disc. There are two types of CD drives: CD-R and CD-RW. A *CD-R* is for read-only permanent storage; the user cannot modify its contents once they are recorded. A *CD-RW* can be used like a hard disk; that is, you can write data onto the disc, and then overwrite that data with new data.

CD-R
CD-RW

A single CD can hold up to 700 MB. Most new PCs are equipped with a CD-RW drive that can work with both CD-R and CD-RW discs.

DVD

DVD stands for digital versatile disc or digital video disc. DVDs and CDs look alike, and you can use either to store data. A DVD can hold more information than a CD. Like CDs, there are two types of DVDs: DVD-R (read-only) and DVD-RW (rewritable).

USB Flash Drives

Universal serial bus (USB) connectors allow the user to attach many kinds of peripheral devices to the computer. You can use a USB to connect a printer, digital camera, mouse, external hard disk drive, and other devices to the computer.

A USB *flash drive* is a device for storing and transporting data. A flash drive is small—about the size of a pack of gum. It acts like a portable hard drive that can be plugged into your computer's USB port.

Communication Devices

Computers can be networked through communication devices, such as a wired network interface card, or a wireless adapter.

network interface card (NIC)

local area network (LAN)

million bits per second (mbps)

- A *network interface card (NIC)* is a device that connects a computer to a *local area network (LAN)*. It requires the use of physical Ethernet wiring to connect and network two or more computers. A high-speed NIC called *1000BaseT* can transfer data at 1,000 *million bits per second (mbps)*.

- Wireless networking is now extremely popular in homes, businesses, and schools. Every laptop computer sold today is equipped with a wireless adapter that enables the computer to connect to a local area network and the Internet.

✓ Section 1.1 Assessment

1. What are hardware and software?
2. List five major hardware components of a computer.
3. What does the acronym "CPU" stand for?
4. What unit is used to measure CPU speed?
5. What is a bit? What is a byte?
6. What is memory for? What does RAM stand for? Why is memory called RAM?
7. What unit is used to measure memory size?
8. What unit is used to measure disk size?
9. What is the primary difference between memory and a storage device?

1.2 Exploring Careers and the Workplace

Careers in computer programming require problem-solving, time-management, teamwork, and leadership.

Key Point

A *career* is a chosen field of work in which you try to advance over time by gaining responsibility and earning more money. The career you choose has a major impact on the kind of life you will lead. It determines the type of training and education you will need. It might impact where you live and the type of lifestyle you achieve.

career

The U.S. Department of Education organizes careers into 16 clusters. A *cluster* is a group of similar items. Career clusters help you sort the career possibilities into 16 manageable groups. Within each of the 16 career clusters are related job, industry, and occupation types called pathways. Each pathway offers a variety of careers you might choose. Programming and software development is a pathway within the Information Technology career cluster. Careers in this pathway involve the design, development, implementation, and maintenance of computer systems and software.

cluster

Identifying Job Opportunities

Computer programmers create, test, and run the programs that make computer applications work. Some typical tasks include working alone or with others to write computer code, develop diagrams and flowcharts, document design and development procedures, and test systems to make sure they work as expected. Programmers must be detail-oriented, able to meet strict deadlines, and have strong teamwork, communications, and problem-solving skills.

Every industry that uses computer technology needs computer programmers. Examples include video game development, health care, financial institutions, and government agencies. There are also companies that exist to develop software. Some develop applications, while others develop system software. All of these companies need computer programmers.

Entry-level positions generally require a bachelor's degree. A master's degree may be required for advancement. According to the U.S. Bureau of Labor Statistics (BLS), in 2014 the median annual salary for computer programmers was about $77,500. Programmers usually work in an office but may be home-based.

A knowledge of computer programming can help you succeed in many careers. Even if you do not work as a programmer, the logic and problem-solving skills you learn by programming are highly valued by employers in many industries and will make you a strong candidate for other positions.

Teamwork and Leadership

A *team* is a group of two or more people who work together to achieve a common goal. When you are part of a team, you have access to all the knowledge, experience, and abilities of your teammates. Together you can have more ideas, achieve more goals, and solve more problems.

team

Most programming projects require teamwork. Depending on the project, programmers may work with a partner, or with a group of other programmers, usually under the direction of a team leader or project manager. But, no matter who is on the team and what the team is doing, the interactions between team members will be most productive if the members of the team:

■ Listen to each other

■ Respect each other's opinions

■ Recognize each other's skills and abilities

■ Share the work load

■ Share responsibility

leader

Even when all members of a team have an equal role in decision making and problem solving, it is important to have a leader. A *leader* is a type of manager who knows how to use available resources to help others achieve their goals.

Leaders exhibit positive qualities that other people respect, such as self-confidence, honesty, effective listening and speaking skills, decisiveness, respect for others, and open-mindedness. They are organized and supportive of the other team members.

Although you might have heard that someone is a "born leader," that's not usually the case. Becoming a leader takes time and patience. Leaders have to prove that they can make decisions, set goals, and solve problems. You can develop leadership characteristics by recognizing and modeling positive leadership qualities. One way to do this is by participating in student leadership and professional development opportunities. For example, you can join clubs and activities such as your school robotics team, and volunteer for leadership roles. You might also join a career technical student organization (CTSO) such as Technology Student Association (TSA) or SkillsUSA. CTSOs offer members a range of individual and group programs, activities, and competitions designed to build professional skills as well as leadership qualities.

While a strong leader is important to the success of a team, team members must also be committed to the group's success. An effective team member helps teammates if they need help, does not blame teammates for problems or mistakes, and offers ideas and suggestions instead of criticism. Effective team members use critical-thinking skills and interpersonal skills to identify and solve problems and achieve their goals.

You are a good team member if you are:

■ Open minded

■ Willing to compromise

■ Cooperative

■ Friendly

■ Trustworthy

Project Management

Employers value employees who know how to use planning and project management skills to make sure work is completed on time. *Project management* is a process used to take a project from conception to completion. There are four basic parts to the process:

- **Identifying measurable objectives.** An *objective* is a short-term goal used to keep a project on track for completion. A measurable objective can be evaluated by specific standards.

- **Identifying deliverables.** A *deliverable* is a product, or segment of a product, that can be provided to an employer, customer, or the public.

- **Setting a schedule.** The schedule should include a timeline with a final deadline, as well as milestones for achieving each objective. It involves setting *priorities*—which means deciding which tasks must be completed first.

- **Developing supporting plans.** Supporting plans usually specify items like how to allocate resources such as funds and technology, how to identify and manage risk, and methods for communication.

Many companies have project management software for scheduling, organizing, coordinating, and tracking project tasks. You can find basic project management templates in programs such as Microsoft Excel. There are also specific tools for project management, such as a *Gantt chart* (Figure 1.3a) and a PERT chart (Figure 1.3b). A Gantt chart, developed by Henry L. Gantt in 1917, is a horizontal bar chart that shows a graphical illustration of a schedule. A *PERT chart* (Program Evaluation Review Technique), developed by the U.S. Navy in the 1950s, shows project tasks, the order in which they must be completed, and the time requirements.

project management

objective

deliverable

priorities

Gantt chart

PERT chart

(a) (b)

Figure 1.3 (a) Gantt chart and (b) PERT chart

Time Management

Time management is a critical skill for both finding a career and succeeding at work. During a career search, you can use schedules and to-do lists to keep yourself organized and on-track. Combining goal-setting with time management is a

very effective way to make sure you get things done. Each time you set a goal, such as contacting a prospective employer or revising your resume, you can include a realistic time frame.

At work, you can use schedules and goal-setting to keep you focused on the tasks at hand. Computer programs can help you organize and meet your responsibilities.

- Set realistic and attainable goals using daily, weekly, and monthly schedules. Different schedules can help you identify tasks that must be accomplished within a specific timeframe.

- Make use of the calendar program on your computer or handheld device. You can enter schedules, phone calls, and appointments. Use the tasks list feature to record and prioritize the tasks you need to accomplish. Set the program to display a message or make a sound to remind you of deadlines.

It is also important to respect time in the workplace. It shows that you respect your co-workers. It also demonstrates to your employer that you take your responsibilities seriously and proves that you are ready for new challenges such as those that might come from a promotion.

To show that you respect time at work:

- Arrive on time.

- Notify your supervisor if you will be late.

- Take your lunch hour and other breaks at the designated time and return promptly.

- Do not leave until the end of the work day.

- Meet your deadlines.

- Do not conduct personal business during work hours.

 Key Point

1.3 Employability Skills

Employability means having and using skills and abilities to be hired and stay hired.

transferable skills

Employability skills include the knowledge for a specific career—such as writing and debugging computer code. They also include *transferable skills* that you can use in any career, such as the ability to solve problems, think critically, and communicate effectively.

Effective Communication

Communication is a process that involves an exchange of information between a sender and a recipient. The sender transmits the message with a specific intent. The recipient interprets the message and responds.

Effective communication occurs when the receiver interprets the message the way the sender intended. Ineffective communication occurs when the receiver misinterprets the message. Sometimes the sender thinks the message is clear, but in fact it might confuse or mislead the receiver.

In order to ensure effective communication:

- The message must be clear.

- The sender must be able to deliver the message in a concise and accurate manner.

- The receiver must be able to hear and receive the message.

- The receiver must be able to interpret the message correctly.

You can communicate effectively by using a six-step process:

1. **Be clear.** The receiver is more likely to get your message if you deliver it in a way he or she can understand. Speak slowly. Consider who he or she is. You probably use different language when you talk to a teacher than when you talk to a friend. You might even use a completely different type of communication —face-to-face instead of a social networking site.

2. **Be personal.** Use the other person's name—then he or she will know you are communicating with him or her. Use an "I" statement—a statement that starts with the word "I"—to frame the statement in terms of you and your goals. An "I" statement indicates that you are taking responsibility for your thoughts and feelings. It helps the receiver understand your point of view and respond to you, instead of focusing on himself or herself and how your statement affects him or her.

3. **Be positive.** Phrase your message in positive terms. Say what you want, not what you don't want.

4. **Get to the point.** Follow the "I" statement with an explanation of the message you are sending. Explain how or why you feel a certain way, or how or why you think a certain thing.

5. **Actively listen to the response.** Pay attention and make sure you hear the response.

6. **Think before you respond.** Make sure you understand the message. Repeat it, if necessary, and ask questions for clarification. Use critical thinking to make sure you are not letting emotions and preconceived ideas get in the way.

Verbal and Nonverbal Communications

Verbal communication is the exchange of messages by speaking, reading, or writing. For most of us, verbal communication is the most common way we stay in touch with other people in our lives. We talk face to face or on the phone. We send text messages, e-mails, and instant messages. We write blogs, tweet, pass notes, and send cards.

Talking is usually a very effective form of verbal communication. When you speak clearly and use language the receiver understands, he or she almost always gets the message the way you intend it.

Nonverbal communication helps put words into context. This form of communication includes visual messages that the receiver can see, such as a smile when you are talking. It also includes physical messages, such as a pat on the back.

During a conversation, the tone of your voice and the language you use combine to provide context for the words.

Writing is also verbal communication. Effective writing is simple, clear, and to the point. It is free from spelling and grammatical errors. Effective writing usually uses the *active voice* rather than the *passive voice*. In the active voice, the subject takes action. In the passive voice, the subject is acted upon. For example, *She threw the ball*, is in the active voice; *The ball was thrown by her*, is in the passive voice.

When you write, you lose some of the context, which can make the communication less effective. Exchanging written messages doesn't take place face to face. It might be across great distances. When the receiver can't hear your voice, he or she might misinterpret the message.

There are different ways to read, depending on what you are reading. Passive reading is the kind of reading you do for entertainment, such as when you read a magazine or a comic book. In this kind of reading, you are just taking in information or following the plot. When you read critically, you take time to really think about what is written and why. Critical reading happens when you are actively engaging the subject as you read.

Critical reading is essential for success. Following are three steps you can use to be sure you are reading critically:

- Determine the best reading strategy for the text. This means that you need to figure out whether to skim the text, read closely for detail, or read for meaning or critical analysis.

- As you read, stop and think about what is being said and try to put it in your own words, or rephrase it from your own point of view.

- Take notes while you are reading to make sure you are understanding and remembering the main points.

Active Listening

Active listening is an important part of effective communication. When you are an active listener, you pay attention to the speaker, and make sure you hear and understand the message.

Use these skills to be an active listener:

- Show interest using eye contact and positive nonverbal messages.

- Let the other person finish speaking before you respond.

- Ignore distractions such as cell phones and other people.

- Set your predetermined opinions and emotions aside.

- Repeat the message that you hear out loud, to make sure you received it correctly.

Active listening is a sign of respect. It shows you are willing to communicate and that you care about the speaker and the message. When you listen actively, the other person is more likely to listen when you speak, too.

Solving Problems

A *problem*—or challenge—is a difficulty that you must resolve before you can make progress. In other words, any barrier or obstacle between you and a goal is a problem. To overcome a problem, you can use a process to figure out the best solution:

1. **Identify the problem.** This is your chance to be honest, acknowledge the problem, and determine what goal it is blocking.

2. **Consider all possible solutions.** There may be one obvious solution, or there may be many possible solutions. Write down as many as you can think of. You will need to consider your values, standards, and resources, too. Some solutions might be harder to make happen, or take longer than others. Some might cost money and some might be free. Some might solve only part of the problem.

3. **Identify the consequences of each solution.** Like decisions, each solution will have consequences, and it is important to recognize how the consequences will affect you and others. Again, write them down.

4. **Select the best solution.** The best solution offers the best possible opportunity for you to continue your progress toward your goal.

5. **Make and implement a plan of action.** Recognizing and selecting a solution are only part of the process. You must take the necessary steps to make the solution real.

6. **Evaluate the solution, process, and outcome.** Did your solution work? Did you achieve your goal? Would you do anything differently if you had the same problem again?

Basically, computer programming is problem-solving. The programmer identifies the challenge—how to get the computer to perform a specific task—and then sets about identifying the best solution and writing the code to make it happen.

Thinking Critically

Critical thinking can help you evaluate your options in many situations. You can use it when you are making decisions, setting goals, and solving problems. When you think critically, you are honest, rational, and open-minded about your options. You try not to let emotions get in the way of choosing the best course of action.

- Being honest means acknowledging selfish feelings and preexisting opinions.
- Being rational means relying on reason and thought instead of on emotion or impulse.
- Being open-minded means being willing to evaluate all possible options—even those that are unpopular.

When you think critically, you consider all possible options and other points of view. You look objectively at information. *Objective* means fairly, without emotion or prejudice. Then, you use your values, standards, and ethics to interpret the information subjectively. *Subjective* means affected by existing opinions, feelings, and beliefs. Looking at things both objectively and subjectively can help you make choices that are right for you.

Thinking critically doesn't mean you should ignore emotions, or any other influence factors. It just means you should consider all possibilities before rushing to judgment.

You can think critically about a lot of things, not just decisions and problems. You don't have to believe everything you hear or read. You can question a news report or information you find on a Web site, look deeper into the meaning of a magazine article, or investigate the truth behind a rumor.

1.4 Ethical Responsibilities

 Key Point

Information technology professionals, including computer programmers, have many legal and ethical responsibilities.

ethics

work ethics

Ethics are a set of beliefs about what is right and what is wrong. *Work ethics* are moral principles, or beliefs and behaviors about what is right and wrong in a work environment. When you behave ethically at work, others will trust and respect you. Most work ethics are the same ethics from other areas of life that you apply to your workplace. Some typical business ethics are:

- Respect the rules and policies of your employer.

- Respect the authority of your supervisor.

- Respect your co-workers.

- Respect company property.

- Be honest.

- Obey the law.

Business Ethics

business ethics

Business ethics are moral principles applied to business issues and actions. When a company acts ethically, it treats employees, clients, and other businesses honestly and with respect. It obeys all laws and regulations governing its business. But, not all businesses behave ethically. They may use dishonest business practices to cheat clients, steal work from other companies or individuals, and advance their own interests. For example, a company might use someone else's copyrighted software code to develop its own product.

Unethical and dishonest business practices might seem to help a company in the short term, but in the long run the consequences can be severe. Businesses that do not obey laws and regulations might be forced to pay large fines and other penalties. They may be trapped in lengthy and expensive legal battles. In addition, the executives responsible for making the decisions that lead to illegal and unethical behavior may end up facing criminal charges.

Employees at companies that engage in unethical business practices often end up acting unethically in their own positions. They may believe that since the company is unethical, they can be, too. They may not respect their managers or the company executives. As a result, they may be less productive, causing the company to lose money. Clients and business partners may also lose respect for the unethical company, and make the decision to take their business elsewhere.

Copyright and Licensing

Federal laws that involve copyright protect individuals and companies from the theft or misuse of their intellectual property, such as creative, literary, or artistic work. This includes software code. Copyright exists as soon as a work is created, but the creator can register it with the U.S. Copyright Office. It is a crime to copy this kind of work without the permission of the person who owns the copyright to it. Penalties include paying a large fine and possibly jail time.

Copyright laws protect software developers from the misuse of their intellectual property by others. Someone who pretends that another person's work is his or her own has broken the law by committing copyright infringement. He or she has stolen another person's work. If you copy someone else's code and try to pass it off as your own, or use it in your own product, you are breaking the law. If you want to use content created by someone else, such as software code, you must obtain permission from the copyright holder.

Software must be legally licensed before it can be installed and used. A *software license* is a legally binding agreement between the software producer and the user. It specifies the terms of use and defines the rights of both the software producer and the user. The license permits the buyer to use and install the program, and sometimes entitles the buyer to receive free or reduced cost support and updates.

software license

Individuals might buy a single-user license for one copy of the program, or a single-seat license to install the program on a single computer. Organizations such as schools or businesses usually buy a volume or site license which lets them install on multiple systems or a network for multiple users. Network licensing generally costs less per user and allows users to share resources.

Creative Commons is a license that lets software copyright holders open some of their work for public use while letting them hold onto other parts of their work.

TABLE 1.1 Types of Software

Commercial software	Copyrighted software, also called proprietary software. The company, or individual, that developed the software owns the copyright. This means it is illegal for others to sell it, give it away, or even share it. When you buy commercial software, you are paying for the right to use the software, not necessarily for the right to the software's code. Software where the user doesn't gain access to the program's code is also called closed-source software.
Shareware	Copyrighted software that you can use on a try-before-you-buy basis. If you decide to keep it, you must pay a fee.
Freeware	Copyrighted software that the copyright owner gives away for free on the condition that users do not resell it.
Open-source software	A program, like proprietary software, and you may have to pay for it. Unlike proprietary software, it makes the source code available to the public. The idea is that the software will improve and benefit from the innovations of users, who troubleshoot weak points and expand features.
Public domain software	Software that the developers or authors allow others to use, copy, share, and even alter for free.

Legal and Ethical Responsibilities in Information Technology

Information technology professionals, including computer programmers, have many legal and ethical responsibilities. Some are the same as in any industry, such as treating co-workers and clients with respect, obeying all laws and regulations, and calling attention to negligent, illegal, unethical, abusive, or dangerous business practices. Some, however, are unique to IT.

One of the most significant legal and ethical responsibilities for an IT worker is to stop software piracy, which is the act of enabling access to software illegally. This is an area in which IT workers may be tempted to violate laws and policies for personal gain, but should also recognize the harm it does their own profession.

Another legal and ethical responsibility is to protect proprietary information. IT workers may have access to a company's trade secrets and other confidential information. In addition to legally protected information such as copyrighted code, it includes business information that is generally not available to the public, that has some degree of uniqueness, and that requires cost or effort to develop. Many companies require employees to sign a non-disclosure agreement that prohibits them from sharing proprietary information. However, there may be temptations for an employee to break that agreement. He or she may leave and start working at a competitor, or even be offered money to share the information.

Many IT workers also have access to employee and client personal information. It is imperative that they follow all security protocols to maintain an individual's right to privacy. Identity theft and fraud are serious crimes. IT workers may be responsible for protecting systems from security breaches which could compromise personal data.

To help IT professionals recognize and adhere to their legal and ethical responsibilities, some professional associations, including the Association of Information Technology Professionals (AITP) and the Association for Computing Machinery (ACM), have developed their own codes of ethics and professional conduct. These codes include standards such as the following:

- Not misrepresenting or withholding information concerning the capabilities of equipment, software, or systems

- Not using or taking credit for the work of others without specific acknowledgement and authorization

- Protecting the privacy and confidentiality of all information

- Not exploiting the weakness of a computer system for personal gain or personal satisfaction

Chapter 1 — Review and Assessment

KEY TERMS

bits 4
bus 3
business ethics 14
byte 4
career 7
central processing unit (CPU) 3
cluster 7
core 3
drive 5
encoding scheme 4
ethics 14
Gantt chart 9
gigabyte (GB) 4
gigahertz 3
hard disk 5
hardware 2
hertz 3
kilobyte (KB) 4
leader 8
local area network (LAN) 6
megabyte (MB) 4
megahertz 3
memory 4

million bits per second (mbps) 6
motherboard 3
network interface card (NIC) 6
objective 13
PERT chart 9
priorities 9
problem 13
program 2
programming 2
programming languages 2
project management 9
RAM 4
software 2
software license 15
speed 3
storage devices 5
subjective 13
team 7
terabyte (TB) 4
transistors 3
unique address 4
work ethics 14

CHAPTER SUMMARY

1. A computer is an electronic device that stores and processes data.

2. A computer includes both *hardware* and *software*.

3. Hardware is the physical aspect of the computer that can be touched.

4. Computer *programs*, known as *software*, are the invisible instructions that control the hardware and make it perform tasks.

5. Computer *programming* is the writing of instructions (i.e., code) for computers to perform.

6. The *central processing unit (CPU)* is a computer's brain. It retrieves instructions from *memory* and executes them.

7. Computers use zeros and ones because digital devices have two stable states, referred to by convention as zero and one.

8. A *bit* is a binary digit 0 or 1.

9. A *byte* is a sequence of 8 bits.

10. A *kilobyte* is about 1,000 bytes, a *megabyte* about 1 million bytes, a *gigabyte* about 1 billion bytes, and a *terabyte* about 1,000 gigabytes.

11. *Memory* stores data and program instructions for the CPU to execute.

12. A *memory unit* is an ordered sequence of bytes.

13. Memory is volatile, because information is lost when the power is turned off.

14. Programs and data are permanently stored on *storage devices* and are moved to memory when the computer actually uses them.

15. *Computer programmers* create, test, and run the programs that make computer applications work.

16. Every industry that uses computer technology needs computer programmers, and other industries seek employees with skills developed by learning computer programming.

17. Most programming projects require *teamwork*.

18. *Leaders* exhibit positive qualities that other people respect, such as self-confidence, honesty, effective listening and speaking skills, decisiveness, respect for others, and open-mindedness.

19. Planning and time management skills such as *project management* are critical for both finding a career and succeeding at work

20. *Employability skills* include effective reading and writing skills, as well as verbal and nonverbal communication skills.

21. Employers value employees who can *solve problems* and *think critically*.

22. *Business ethics* are moral principles applied to business issues and actions.

23. *Copyright laws* protect software developers from the misuse of their intellectual property by others.

24. Software must be *legally licensed* before it can be installed and used.

25. Information technology professionals, including computer programmers, have many legal and *ethical responsibilities*, including stopping software piracy, protecting confidential information, and protecting the privacy of others.

CHAPTER ASSESSMENT

1. List five major hardware components of a computer and explain their purpose.

2. Make a three column chart. In one column, list at least three jobs available in the programming and software development pathway. In the second column, list the type of business or industry in which that person might work. In the third column, list the job duties and tasks.

3. Define business ethics.

4. Explain the effects of unethical practices on a business.

5. Explain how copyright laws affect the software industry.

6. What is a software license? List at least three types of software licensing.

7. Explain the difference between honest and dishonest business practices. Give at least two examples of each.

8. Write a paragraph explaining legal and ethical responsibilities in relation to the field of information technology.

GROUP EXERCISE

Working in small teams, plan a presentation about legal and ethical responsibilities in relation to the field of information technology. Use problem-solving, planning, and time-management skills such as project management to organize the project. You may want to use a project management template in a program such as Excel. Take turns so each team member has the opportunity to demonstrate team leadership skills. Research the topic using effective reading skills. Use critical thinking to evaluate the information that you find, and only use content that is valid and accurate. Record and cite all source information. When your research is complete, compile the information into a presentation. Use effective writing skills to develop a script to accompany the slides. Take turns using verbal and nonverbal communications skills to read the script out loud and deliver the presentation.

CHAPTER 2

COMPARING PROGRAMMING LANGUAGES AND CREATING YOUR FIRST JAVA PROGRAM

Objectives

- Understand computer basics, programs, and operating systems.

- Understand differences of language styles, such as structured, procedural, event-driven, and object-oriented.

- Identify current programming languages and their uses.

- Practice writing an algorithm to explain the steps of a problem.

- Understand the meaning of Java language specification, API, JDK, and IDE.

- Write a simple Java program.

- Display output on the console.

- Explain the basic syntax of a Java program.

- Create, compile, and run Java programs.

- Learn to structure and document code with standard styling techniques.

- Explain the differences between syntax errors, runtime errors, and logic errors.

- Develop Java programs using NetBeans.

- Develop Java programs using Eclipse.

2.1 Types of Programming Languages and Their Uses

Key Point

Computer programs, known as software, are instructions that tell a computer what to do.

Computers do not understand human languages, so programs must be written in a language a computer can use. There are hundreds of programming languages, and they were developed to make the programming process easier for people. However, all programs must be converted into instructions the computer can execute.

Machine Language

machine language

A computer's native language, which differs among different types of computers, is its *machine language*—a set of built-in primitive instructions. These instructions are in the form of binary code, so if you want to give a computer an instruction in its native language, you have to enter the instruction as binary code. For example, to add two numbers, you might have to write an instruction in binary code, like this:

```
1101101010011010
```

Assembly Language

assembly language

Programming in machine language is a tedious process. Moreover, programs written in machine language are very difficult to read and modify. For this reason, *assembly language* was created in the early days of computing as an alternative to machine languages. Assembly language uses a short descriptive word, known as a *mnemonic*, to represent each of the machine-language instructions. For example, the mnemonic **add** typically means to add numbers and **sub** means to subtract numbers. To add the numbers **2** and **3** and get the result, you might write an instruction in assembly code like this:

```
add 2, 3, result
```

assembler

Assembly languages were developed to make programming easier. However, because the computer cannot execute assembly language, another program—called an *assembler*—is used to translate assembly-language programs into machine code, as shown in Figure 2.1.

low-level language

Writing code in assembly language is easier than in machine language. However, it is still tedious to write code in assembly language. An instruction in assembly language essentially corresponds to an instruction in machine code. Writing in assembly requires that you know how the CPU works. Assembly language is referred to as a *low-level language*, because assembly language is close in nature to machine language and is machine dependent.

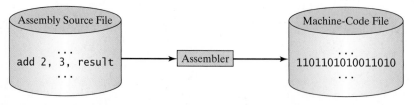

FIGURE 2.1 An assembler translates assembly-language instructions into machine code.

High-Level Language

In the 1950s, a new generation of programming languages known as *high-level languages* emerged. They are platform independent, which means that you can write a program in a high-level language and run it in different types of machines. High-level languages are English-like and easy to learn and use. The instructions in a high-level programming language are called *statements*. Here, for example, is a high-level language statement that computes the area of a circle with a radius of 5:

```
area = 5 * 5 * 3.14159;
```

There are many high-level programming languages, and each was designed for a specific purpose. Table 2.1 on the next page lists some popular ones and describes common environments for which they are used.

To execute any of the high-level programming languages listed in Table 2.1, an operating system must exist. The operating system (OS) is the most important program that runs on a computer. The OS manages and controls a computer's activities.

The popular *operating systems* for general-purpose computers are Microsoft Windows, Mac OS, and Linux. Application programs, such as a Web browser or a word processor, cannot run unless an operating system is installed and running on the computer.

A program written in a high-level language is called a *source program* or *source code*. Because a computer cannot execute a source program, a source program must be translated into machine code for execution. The translation can be done using another programming tool called an *interpreter* or a *compiler*.

high-level language

statement

operating system

source code
interpreter
compiler

- An interpreter reads one statement from the source code, translates it to the machine code or virtual machine code, and then executes it right away, as shown in Figure 2.2a. Note that a statement from the source code may be translated into several machine instructions.

- A compiler translates the entire source code into a machine-code file, and the machine-code file is then executed, as shown in Figure 2.2b.

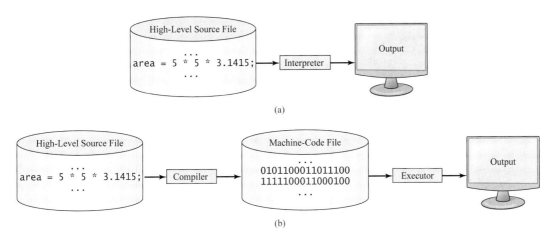

FIGURE 2.2 (a) An interpreter translates and executes a program one statement at a time. (b) A compiler translates the entire source program into a machine-language file for execution.

TABLE 2.1 Popular High-Level Programming Languages

Language	Description and Common Usage
BASIC	A **B**eginner's **A**ll-purpose **S**ymbolic **I**nstruction **C**ode. It was designed to be learned and used easily by beginners.
C	Developed at Bell Laboratories. C combines the power of an assembly language with the ease of use and portability of a high-level language. It is one of the oldest languages and is still used today when a lower-level language is required to program embedded devices. Examples of equipment that have embedded computer devices are heart rate monitors and ATM machines. Additionally, C is used to write some computer operating systems.
C++	Pronounced "cee plus plus." C++ is an object-oriented language, based on C.
C#	Pronounced "C Sharp." It is a hybrid of Java and C++ and was developed by Microsoft. C++ is often used to develop Windows platform applications.
COBOL	**CO**mmon **B**usiness **O**riented **L**anguage. Used for business applications and in financial institutions. Today, most programming in COBOL is done to maintain legacy applications. New applications are usually done in other more modern languages.
FORTRAN	**FOR**mula **TRAN**slation. Popular for scientific and mathematical applications. It was developed by IBM in the early 1950s. Although not as frequently used today, it is still used for applications that require intense numerical computations that require high performance.
Java	Developed by Sun Microsystems, now part of Oracle. It is widely used for developing platform-independent Internet applications. Java is the most widely used language and is used in many industries. You will learn how to program in Java in this course.
JavaScript	JavaScript is a popular scripting language that is used in many modern Web applications. It is used when developing HTML Web-based applications. Although it has a similar name to Java, it is an entirely different type of language and bears little similarity to the Java language. Popular sites today, such as Facebook, Yahoo, and Amazon, use JavaScript.
Pascal	Named for Blaise Pascal, who pioneered calculating machines in the seventeenth century. It is a simple, structured, general-purpose language primarily for teaching programming.
Python	A simple, general-purpose scripting language good for writing short programs.
Ruby	Ruby was developed in Japan and is one of the easiest programming languages to learn. It uses a syntax that is easy to read and write. Ruby is heavily used for Web programming.
Visual Basic	Visual Basic was developed by Microsoft and it enables programmers to rapidly develop graphical user interfaces.

✓ SECTION 2.1 ASSESSMENT

1. What language does the CPU understand?
2. What is an assembly language?
3. What is an interpreter?
4. What is a compiler?
5. What is the difference between an interpreted language and a compiled language?
6. Identify four current programming languages and the environment in which they are used.

2.2 Developing a Modular Design for Your Application

When you are writing an application, it is a good practice to separate the tasks into modules.

Key Point

Frequently, your application will be divided into a "*Front-End*" and a "*Back-End.*" The front-end portion of the application is the interface between the user and the data. It includes the screen designs of what the user sees. Common languages used to create the front-end of a Web-based application are HTML (Hypertext Markup Language) and JavaScript.

front-end

back-end

The back-end portion of an application handles the data and operations that communicate with the server. There is typically no user interface in this portion of an application. Compiled languages such as Java and C# are examples of languages used to create a back-end.

As an example, the front-end portion of an online store is the Web page(s) that allows a user to log in and then place an order. After the user enters his or her login information and presses the Login button, a back-end program module may perform the actions to check the user's credentials, perform the calculations to place the order, and store the information in a server database. Figure 2.3 illustrates this modular design.

Modular design is a concept we will use in later chapters. It is the practice of dividing your application into smaller, re-useable units that work together as a whole. The modules may be written in different languages. The technique of modular design is particularly helpful when working on a large project developed by a team of programmers.

modular design

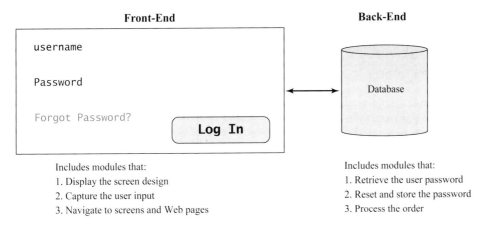

FIGURE 2.3 Example of a Simple Modular Design

✓ SECTION 2.2 ASSESSMENT

1. Explain the concept of modular design.

2. Give an example of a front-end section of a program.

3. Give an example of a back-end section of a program.

2.3 The Evolution of Programming Language Styles

 Key Point

Programming language styles have evolved over time. Sometimes you may hear this referred to as "Programming Paradigms."

Programming Paradigms

Unstructured Style

Unstructured Style

Earlier programming languages developed in the 1950s and early 1960s were of an *Unstructured Style*. This meant that the code was written in sequentially ordered lines and could include many GOTO statements. Because the code can be looped around in a meaningless order, it is sometimes referred to as "spaghetti code." Some of this code still exists today but new code is rarely written in such a manner. Today's standards consider this poor programming style.

pseudo-code

To demonstrate the evolution of programming styles, we will look at an example using pseudo-code. *Pseudo-code* is a set of instructions or algorithm that is written in an easily readable format and not in a particular programming language. If you were asked to write pseudo-code to bake a pie, an unstructured style might look like the following:

```
GOTO Pantry;
If ingredients are missing GOTO Store;
Get a mixing bowl;
GOTO MIXER;
Pour the ingredients in the pie shell;
Preheat the oven;
Place the pie in the oven;
Bake for 1 hour;
Remove and cool;
BREAK;
STORE: Buy Ingredients
RETURN;
MIXER: Add eggs;
Add milk;
Add sugar;
Add vanilla;
Add cherries;
RETURN;
PANTRY: Look for ingredients;
RETURN;
```

You may notice that this type of unstructured style of instructions is not easy to follow. This sample demonstrates why it is referred to as "spaghetti code"!

Structured Style

Structured Programming

In the late 1960s, *Structured Programming* style was developed in which code was written in a more meaningful order. Unstructured GOTO statements were eliminated. In a structured programming style, the programmer determines the sequential order in which the blocks of code will be executed.

A set of structured steps to bake a pie may look like the following:

```
01:   Walk to the Pantry;
02:   Look for Ingredients;
03:   If Ingredients are missing then
04:       go to the store;
05:   Get a mixing bowl;
06:   Add eggs;
07:   Add milk:
08:   Add sugar;
09:   Add vanilla;
10:   Add cherries;
11:   Pour the ingredients into the pie shell;
12:   Preheat the oven to 350˚;
13:   Place the pie in the oven;
14:   Bake for 1 hour;
15:   Remove and cool;
```

Procedural Style

Structured programming styles were improved upon with a new generation of languages called *Procedural Languages*. In a procedural language, units of code are grouped together into what is called a "procedure" or "function." These procedures and functions are retrieved or "*called*" from a main program when they need to be executed. Following is a set of instructions for baking a pie using a procedural paradigm:

Procedural Language

```
1. Perform the steps to: GetIngredients;
2. Perform the steps to: MixIngredients;
3. Perform the steps to: Bake;
```

```
GetIngredients:
Walk to the Pantry;
Look for ingredients;
If ingredients are missing then
   go to the store;
```

```
MixIngredients:
Get a mixing bowl;
Add eggs;
Add milk:
Add sugar;
Add vanilla;
Add cherries;
Pour ingredients into pie shell;
```

```
Bake:
Preheat the oven to 350˚;
Place the pie in the oven;
Bake for 1 hour;
Remove and cool;
```

Event-Driven Style

In the 1990s, a new paradigm called *Event-Driven Programming* became popular. With event-driven programming, code is still written in blocks of procedures and functional units. The difference is that these blocks of code are associated with particular events that may occur. Examples of events are: a click of a mouse; navigating to a new page; or rotating the position of a handheld computer device. When an event occurs, the associated block of code is executed. This programming style shifts the control of execution to the user. The user determines when he or she wants certain things to occur. For instance, the user determines when he or she is ready to place an order or open a new Web page. Additionally, the user can determine the order in which he or she chooses to execute the code. This type of programming style is particularly useful in developing front-end, user-interfaces. Two common programming languages that use event-driven programming are Javascript and Visual Basic. These are examples of languages used to develop front-end modules.

Expanding on the Procedural example above, event-driven instructions may be based around three actions or events: Prepare, Mix, and Bake. Envision a computer screen with three buttons, as illustrated in Figure 2.4. When a button is pressed, the associated steps for that action will be executed.

FIGURE 2.4 Example of user interface computer screen.

Object-Oriented Style

The most popular programming style today is *Object-Oriented Programming* (*OOP*). The OOP programming paradigm breaks down an application's design into logical units called *objects*. Each object has certain characteristics, attributes, and actions. As an example, a button on a web page is an object. Some characteristics, or properties, of the button are its size, color, and shape. An action it recognizes is a mouse-click or a double-finger tap.

In our example of baking a pie, our instructions would be centered around the objects we use. We have three objects: `Ingredients`, `Oven`, and `Pie`. Each of these objects has attributes and actions. Actions are also called *methods*.

The `Ingredients` object may have attributes such as *eggs*, *sugar*, and *cherries*. You may also perform actions to the ingredients, such as `add` and `mix`. If we want to perform an action (method) on an object, the code is usually specified in the following way: *ObjectName.MethodName*

Here are some examples:

```
Ingredients.Add;
Ingredients.Mix;
Oven.Preheat(350);
```

This is a simple introduction to Object-Oriented Programming style. Java is an example of an Object-Oriented Programming language. We will cover this topic further in Chapter 9. Java is a programming language that is mainly used to develop the back-end module of an application.

✓ Section 2.3 Assessment

1. Explain the basic principles of each type of programming style, such as procedural, object-oriented, and event-driven.

2. Write step-by-step instructions to wash a car. Use pseudo-code to write your instructions in a structured format. In other words, write an algorithm to describe the steps to wash a car.

2.4 Creating Your First Java Program

Java syntax is defined in the Java language specification, and the Java library is defined in the Java API. The JDK is the software for developing and running Java programs. An IDE is an integrated development environment for rapidly developing programs.

 Key Point

Computer languages have strict rules of usage. If you do not follow the rules when writing a program, the computer will not be able to understand it. The Java language specification and the Java API define the Java standards.

The *Java language specification* is a technical definition of the Java programming language's syntax and semantics. You can find the complete Java language specification at http://docs.oracle.com/javase/specs/.

Java language specification

The *application program interface (API)*, also known as *library*, contains predefined classes and interfaces for developing Java programs. The API is still expanding. You can view and download the latest version of the Java API at http://download. java.net/jdk8/docs/api/.

API

library

This book uses Java SE (Standard Edition) to introduce Java programming. Oracle releases each version with a *Java Development Toolkit (JDK)*. Your instructor may provide you with specific instructions on downloading the latest version of the Java SE and the JDK that comply with your school policies. You can also download the latest version from Oracle's official website.

Java Development Toolkit (JDK)

The JDK consists of a set of separate programs, each invoked from a command line, for developing and testing Java programs. Instead of using the JDK, you can use a Java development tool (e.g., NetBeans, Eclipse, and TextPad)—software that provides an *integrated development environment (IDE)* for developing Java programs quickly. Editing, compiling, building, debugging, and online help are integrated in one graphical user interface. You simply enter source code in one window or open an existing file in a window, and then click a button or menu item or press a function key to compile and run the program.

integrated development environment

A Simple Java Program

A Java program is executed from the **main** *method in the class.*

console
console input
console output

Let's begin with a simple Java program that displays the message `Welcome to Java!` on the console. (The word *console* is an old computer term that refers to the text entry and display device of a computer. *Console input* means to receive input from the keyboard, and *console output* means to display output on the monitor.) The program is shown in Listing 2.1.

class
main method
display message

LISTING 2.1 `Welcome.java`

```
1  public class Welcome {
2    public static void main(String[] args) {
3      // Display message Welcome to Java! on the console
4      System.out.println("Welcome to Java!");
5    }
6  }
```

Welcome to Java!

Note that the line numbers are for reference purposes only; they are not part of the program. So, don't type line numbers in your program.

class name

Line 1 defines a class. Every Java program must have at least one class. Each class has a name. By convention, class names start with an uppercase letter. In this example, the class name is `Welcome`.

main method

Line 2 defines the `main` method. The program is executed from the `main` method. A class may contain several methods. The `main` method is the entry point where the program begins execution.

string

A method is a construct that contains statements. The `main` method in this program contains the `System.out.println` statement. This statement displays the string `Welcome to Java!` on the console (line 4). *String* is a programming term meaning a sequence of characters. A string must be enclosed in double quotation marks. Every statement in Java ends with a semicolon (`;`), known as the *statement terminator*.

statement terminator
reserved word
keyword

Reserved words, or *keywords*, have a specific meaning to the compiler and cannot be used for other purposes in the program. For example, when the compiler sees the word `class`, it understands that the word after `class` is the name for the class. Other reserved words in this program are `public`, `static`, and `void`.

comment

Line 3 is a *comment* that documents what the program is and how it is constructed. Comments help programmers to communicate and understand the program. They are not programming statements and thus are ignored by the compiler. In Java, comments are preceded by two slashes (//) on a line, called a *line comment*, or enclosed between /* and */ on one or several lines, called a *block comment* or *paragraph comment*. When the compiler sees //, it ignores all text after // on the same line. When it sees /*, it scans for the next */ and ignores any text between /* and */. Here are examples of comments:

line comment
block comment

```
// This application program displays Welcome to Java!
/* This application program displays Welcome to Java! */
/* This application program
   displays Welcome to Java! */
```

A pair of curly braces in a program forms a *block* that groups the program's components. In Java, each block begins with an opening brace ({) and ends with a closing brace (}). Every class has a *class block* that groups the data and methods of the class. Similarly, every method has a *method block* that groups the statements in the method. Blocks can be *nested*, meaning that one block can be placed within another, as shown in the following code.

block

```
public class Welcome {
   public static void main(String[] args) {
      System.out.println("Welcome to Java!");
   }
}
```

Class block

Method block

Tip

An opening brace must be matched by a closing brace. Whenever you type an opening brace, immediately type a closing brace to prevent the missing-brace error. Most Java IDEs automatically insert the closing brace for each opening brace.

match braces

Caution

Java source programs are case sensitive. It would be wrong, for example, to replace `main` in the program with `Main`.

case sensitive

You have seen several special characters (e.g., { }, //, ;) in the program. They are used in almost every program. Table 2.2 summarizes their uses.

special characters

TABLE 2.2 Special Characters

Character	Name	Description
{}	Opening and closing braces	Denote a block to enclose statements.
()	Opening and closing parentheses	Used with methods.
[]	Opening and closing brackets	Denote an array.
//	Double slashes	Precede a comment line.
" "	Opening and closing quotation marks	Enclose a string (i.e., sequence of characters).
;	Semicolon	Mark the end of a statement.

The most common errors you will make as you learn to program will be syntax errors. Like any programming language, Java has its own syntax, and you need to write code that conforms to the *syntax rules*. If your program violates a rule—for example, if the semicolon is missing, a brace is missing, a quotation mark is missing, or a word is misspelled—the Java compiler will report syntax errors. Try to compile the program with these errors and see what the compiler reports.

common errors

syntax rules

Note

You are probably wondering why the `main` method is defined this way and why `System.out.println(...)` is used to display a message on the console. For the time being, simply accept that this is how things are done. Your questions will be fully answered in subsequent chapters.

The program in Listing 2.2 displays one message. Once you understand the program, it is easy to extend it to display more messages. For example, you can rewrite the program to display three messages, as shown in Listing 2.2.

LISTING 2.2 `WelcomeWithThreeMessages.java`

class

main method

display message

```
1  public class WelcomeWithThreeMessages {
2    public static void main(String[] args) {
3      System.out.println("Programming is fun!");
4      System.out.println("Fundamentals First");
5      System.out.println("Problem Driven");
6    }
7  }
```

```
Programming is fun!
Fundamentals First
Problem Driven
```

Further, you can perform mathematical computations and display the result on the console. Listing 2.3 gives an example of evaluating

LISTING 2.3 `ComputeExpression.java`

class

main method

compute expression

```
1  public class ComputeExpression {
2    public static void main(String[] args) {
3      System.out.println((10.5 + 2 * 3) / (45 - 3.5));
4    }
5  }
```

```
0.39759036144578314
```

The multiplication operator in Java is *. As you can see, it is a straightforward process to translate an arithmetic expression to a Java expression. We will discuss Java expressions further in Chapter 3.

✓ SECTION 2.4 ASSESSMENT

1. What does JDK stand for?
2. What does IDE stand for?
3. Are tools like Netbeans and Eclipse different languages from Java, or are they tools or extensions of Java?
4. What is a keyword? List some Java keywords.
5. Is Java case sensitive? What is the case for Java keywords?
6. What is a comment? Is the comment ignored by the compiler? How do you denote a comment line and a comment paragraph?
7. What is the statement to display a string on the console?
8. Show the output of the following code:

```
public class Test {
  public static void main(String[] args) {
    System.out.println("3.5 * 4 / 2 - 2.5 is ");
    System.out.println(3.5 * 4 / 2 - 2.5);
  }
}
```

2.5 Creating, Compiling, and Executing a Java Program

You save a Java program in a .java file and compile it into a .class file. The .class file is executed by the Java Virtual Machine.

Key Point

You have to create your program and compile it before it can be executed. This process is repetitive, as shown in Figure 2.5. If your program has compile errors, you have to modify the program to fix them, and then recompile it. If your program has runtime errors or does not produce the correct result, you have to modify the program, recompile it, and execute it again.

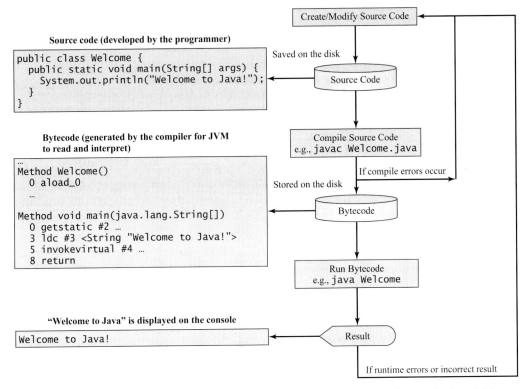

FIGURE 2.5 The Java program-development process consists of repeatedly creating/modifying source code, compiling, and executing programs.

command window

You can use any text editor or IDE to create and edit a Java source-code file. This section demonstrates how to create, compile, and run Java programs from a command window. Sections 2.8 and 2.9 will introduce developing Java programs using NetBeans and Eclipse. From the command window, you can use a text editor such as Notepad to create the Java source-code file, as shown in Figure 2.6.

```
Welcome.java - Notepad                          _ □ ×
File  Edit  Format  View  Help
public class Welcome {
  public static void main(String[] args) {
    System.out.println("Welcome to Java!");
  }
}
```

FIGURE 2.6 You can create a Java source file using Windows Notepad.

Note

The source file must end with the extension `.java` and must have the same exact name as the public class name. For example, the file for the source code in Listing 2.1 should be named **Welcome.java**, since the public class name is `Welcome`.

file name Welcome.java,

compile

A Java compiler translates a Java source file into a Java bytecode file. The following command compiles **Welcome.java**:

```
javac Welcome.java
```

Note

You must first install and configure the JDK before you can compile and run programs. Your teacher will provide you with the necessary instructions that adhere to your specific school policy on installing and configuring programs. Additionally, you can find instructions on the Web site from which you downloaded the JDK.

.class bytecode file

bytecode
Java Virtual Machine (JVM)

If there aren't any syntax errors, the *compiler* generates a bytecode file with a .class extension. Thus, the preceding command generates a file named **Welcome.class**, as shown in Figure 2.7a. The Java language is a high-level language, but Java bytecode is a low-level language. The *bytecode* is similar to machine instructions but is architecture neutral and can run on any platform that has a *Java Virtual Machine (JVM)*, as shown in Figure 2.7b. Rather than a physical machine, the virtual machine is a program that interprets Java bytecode. This is one of Java's primary advantages: *Java bytecode can run on a variety of hardware platforms and operating systems.* Java source code is compiled into Java bytecode and Java bytecode is interpreted by the JVM. Your Java code may use the code in the Java library. The JVM executes your code along with the code in the library.

interpret bytecode

To execute a Java program is to run the program's bytecode. You can execute the bytecode on any platform with a JVM, which is an interpreter. It translates the individual instructions in the bytecode into the target machine language code one at a time rather than the whole program as a single unit. Each step is executed immediately after it is translated.

run

The following command runs the bytecode for Listing 2.1:

```
java Welcome
```

javac command

java command

Figure 2.8 shows the `javac` command for compiling **Welcome.java**. The compiler generates the **Welcome.class** file, and this file is executed using the `java` command.

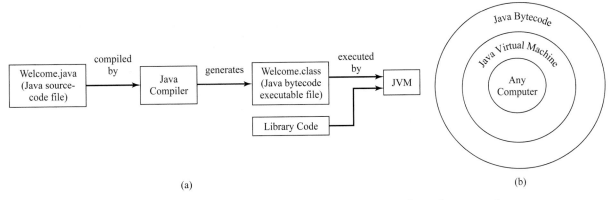

FIGURE 2.7 (a) Java source code is translated into bytecode. (b) Java bytecode can be executed on any computer with a Java Virtual Machine.

Note

For simplicity and consistency, all source-code and class files used in this book are placed under **c:\book** unless specified otherwise.

c:\book

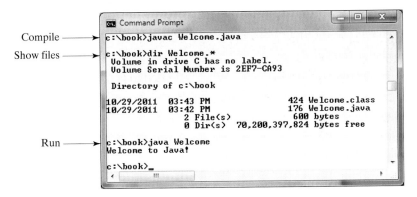

FIGURE 2.8 The output of Listing 2.1 displays the message "Welcome to Java!"

Caution

Do not use the extension `.class` in the command line when executing the program. Use `java ClassName` to run the program. If you use `java ClassName.class` in the command line, the system will attempt to fetch `ClassName.class.class`.

java ClassName

Tip

If you execute a class file that does not exist, a `NoClassDefFoundError` will occur. If you execute a class file that does not have a `main` method or you mistype the `main` method (e.g., by typing `Main` instead of `main`), a `NoSuchMethodError` will occur.

NoClassDefFoundError

NoSuchMethodError

class loader

bytecode verifier

Note

When executing a Java program, the JVM first loads the bytecode of the class to memory using a program called the *class loader*. If your program uses other classes, the class loader dynamically loads them just before they are needed. After a class is loaded, the JVM uses a program called the *bytecode verifier* to check the validity of the bytecode and to ensure that the bytecode does not violate Java's security restrictions. Java enforces strict security to make sure that Java class files are not tampered with and do not harm your computer.

Pedagogical Note

Your instructor may require you to use packages for organizing programs. For example, you may place all programs in this chapter in a package named *chapter1*. For instructions on how to use packages, see Supplement C, Using Packages to Organize Classes.

✓ SECTION 2.5 ASSESSMENT

1. What is the Java source filename extension, and what is the Java bytecode filename extension?

2. What are the input and output of a Java compiler?

3. What is the command to compile a Java program?

4. What is the command to run a Java program?

5. What is the JVM?

6. Can Java run on any machine? What is needed to run Java on a computer?

7. If a `NoClassDefFoundError` occurs when you run a program, what is the cause of the error?

8. If a `NoSuchMethodError` occurs when you run a program, what is the cause of the error?

2.6 Documenting your Program using a Defined Standard and Style

Key Point

A standard programming style and documentation should be implemented beginning with the initial design and throughout the development of your application.

programming style

documentation

Programming style deals with what programs look like. A program can compile and run properly even if written on only one line, but writing it all on one line would be bad programming style because it would be hard to read. *Documentation* is the body of explanatory remarks and comments pertaining to a program. Programming style and documentation are as important as coding. Good programming style and appropriate documentation reduce the chance of errors and make programs easy to read. This section gives several guidelines.

Appropriate Comments and Comment Styles

Include a summary at the beginning of the program that explains what the program does, its key features, and any unique techniques it uses. In a long program, you should also include comments that introduce each major step and explain

anything that is difficult to read. It is important to make comments concise so that they do not crowd the program or make it difficult to read.

In addition to line comments (beginning with //) and block comments (beginning with /*), Java supports comments of a special type, referred to as *javadoc comments.* javadoc comments begin with /** and end with */. They can be extracted into an HTML file using the JDK's `javadoc` command.

javadoc comment

Use javadoc comments (/** ... */) for commenting on an entire class or an entire method. These comments must precede the class or the method header in order to be extracted into a javadoc HTML file. For commenting on steps inside a method, use line comments (//).

Proper Indentation and Spacing

A consistent indentation style makes programs clear and easy to read, debug, and maintain. *Indentation* is used to illustrate the structural relationships between a program's components or statements. Java can read the program even if all of the statements are on the same long line, but humans find it easier to read and maintain code that is aligned properly. Indent each subcomponent or statement at least *two* spaces more than the construct within which it is nested.

indent code

A single space should be added on both sides of a binary operator, as shown in the following statement:

```
System.out.println(3+4*4);          Bad style

System.out.println(3 + 4 * 4);      Good style
```

Block Styles

A *block* is a group of statements surrounded by braces. There are two popular styles, *next-line* style and *end-of-line* style, as shown below.

```
public class Test
{
  public static void main(String[] args)
  {
    System.out.println("Block Styles");
  }
}
```
Next-line style

```
public class Test {
  public static void main(String[] args) {
    System.out.println("Block Styles");
  }
}
```
End-of-line style

The next-line style aligns braces vertically and makes programs easy to read, whereas the end-of-line style saves space and may help avoid some subtle programming errors. Both are acceptable block styles. The choice depends on personal or organizational preference. You should use a block style consistently—mixing styles is not recommended. This book uses the *end-of-line* style to be consistent with the Java API source code.

✓ SECTION 2.6 ASSESSMENT

1. Reformat the following program according to the programming style and documentation guidelines. Use the end-of-line brace style.

```
public class Test
{
  // Main method
  public static void main(String[] args) {
  /** Display output */
  System.out.println("Welcome to Java");
  }
}
```

2.7 Testing your Program and Understanding Programming Errors

Key Point

Programming errors can be categorized into three types: syntax errors, runtime errors, and logic errors.

Syntax Errors

syntax errors
compile errors

Errors that are detected by the compiler are called *syntax errors* or *compile errors.* Syntax errors result from errors in code construction, such as mistyping a keyword, omitting some necessary punctuation, or using an opening brace without a corresponding closing brace. These errors are usually easy to detect because the compiler tells you where they are and what caused them. For example, the program in Listing 2.4 has a syntax error, as shown in Figure 2.9.

LISTING 2.4 ShowSyntaxErrors.java

```
1  public class ShowSyntaxErrors {
2    public static main(String[] args) {
3      System.out.println("Welcome to Java);
4    }
5  }
```

Compile ⟶

```
c:\book>javac ShowSyntaxErrors.java
ShowSyntaxErrors.java:2: error: invalid method declaration; return type required
  public static main(String[] args) {
                ^
ShowSyntaxErrors.java:3: error: unclosed string literal
    System.out.println("Welcome to Java);
                       ^
ShowSyntaxErrors.java:3: error: ';' expected
    System.out.println("Welcome to Java);
                                         ^
ShowSyntaxErrors.java:5: error: reached end of file while parsing
}
 ^
4 errors

c:\book>
```

FIGURE 2.9 The compiler reports syntax errors.

Four errors are reported, but the program actually has two errors:

- The keyword `void` is missing before `main` in line 2.

- The string `Welcome to Java` should be closed with a closing quotation mark in line 3.

Since a single error will often display many lines of compile errors, it is a good practice to fix errors from the top line and work downward. Fixing errors that occur earlier in the program may also fix additional errors that occur later.

> **Tip**
> If you don't know how to correct it, compare your program closely, character by character, with similar examples in the text. In the first few weeks of this course, you will probably spend a lot of time fixing syntax errors. Soon you will be familiar with Java syntax and can quickly fix syntax errors.

Runtime Errors

Runtime errors are errors that cause a program to terminate abnormally. They occur while a program is running if the environment detects an operation that is impossible to carry out. Input mistakes typically cause runtime errors. An *input error* occurs when the program is waiting for the user to enter a value, but the user enters a value that the program cannot handle. For instance, if the program expects to read in a number, but instead the user enters a string, this causes a data-type mismatch and a runtime error occurs.

runtime errors

Another example of runtime errors is division by zero. This happens when the divisor is zero for integer divisions. For instance, the program in Listing 2.5 would cause a runtime error, as shown in Figure 2.10.

LISTING 2.5 ShowRuntimeErrors.java

```
1  public class ShowRuntimeErrors {
2    public static void main(String[] args) {
3      System.out.println(1 / 0);
4    }
5  }
```

runtime error

Run

FIGURE 2.10 The runtime error causes the program to terminate abnormally.

logic errors

Logic Errors

Logic errors occur when a program does not perform the way it was intended to. Errors of this kind occur for many different reasons. For example, suppose you wrote the program in Listing 2.6 to convert Celsius 35 degrees to a Fahrenheit degree:

LISTING 2.6 ShowLogicErrors.java

```
1  public class ShowLogicErrors {
2    public static void main(String[] args) {
3      System.out.println("Celsius 35 is Fahrenheit degree ");
4      System.out.println((9 / 5) * 35 + 32);
5    }
6  }
```

```
Celsius 35 is Fahrenheit degree
67
```

You will get Fahrenheit 67 degrees, which is wrong. It should be 95.0. In Java, the division for integers is the quotient—the fractional part is truncated—so in Java 9 / 5 is 1. To get the correct result, you need to use 9.0 / 5, which results in 1.8.

In general, syntax errors are easy to find and easy to correct because the compiler gives indications as to where the errors came from and why they are wrong. Runtime errors are not difficult to find, either, since the reasons and locations for the errors are displayed on the console when the program aborts. Finding logic errors, on the other hand, can be very challenging. In the upcoming chapters, you will learn the techniques of tracing programs and finding logic errors.

Common Errors

Missing a closing brace, missing a semicolon, missing quotation marks for strings, and misspelling names are common errors for new programmers.

Common Error 1: Missing Braces

The braces are used to denote a block in the program. Each opening brace must be matched by a closing brace. A common error is missing the closing brace. To avoid this error, type a closing brace whenever an opening brace is typed, as shown in the following example.

```
public class Welcome {

}  ←——Type this closing brace right away to match the opening brace
```

If you use an IDE such as NetBeans and Eclipse, the IDE automatically inserts a closing brace for each opening brace typed.

Common Error 2: Missing Semicolons

Each statement ends with a statement terminator (;). Often, a new programmer forgets to place a statement terminator for the last statement in a block, as shown in the following example.

```
public static void main(String[] args) {
  System.out.println("Programming is fun!");
  System.out.println("Fundamentals First");
  System.out.println("Problem Driven")
}
```
 ↑
 Missing a semicolon

Common Error 3: Missing Quotation Marks

A string must be placed inside the quotation marks. Often, a new programmer forgets to place a quotation mark at the end of a string, as shown in the following example.

```
System.out.println("Problem Driven );
```
 ↑
 Missing a quotation mark

If you use an IDE such as NetBeans and Eclipse, the IDE automatically inserts a closing quotation mark for each opening quotation mark typed.

Common Error 4: Misspelling Names

Java is case sensitive. Misspelling names is a common error for new programmers. For example, the word `main` is misspelled as `Main` and `String` is misspelled as `string` in the following code.

```
1  public class Test {
2    public static void Main(string[] args) {
3      System.out.println((10.5 + 2 * 3) / (45 - 3.5));
4    }
5  }
```

✓ SECTION 2.7 ASSESSMENT

1. What are syntax errors (compile errors), runtime errors, and logic errors?

2. Give examples of syntax errors, runtime errors, and logic errors.

3. If you forget to put a closing quotation mark on a string, what kind of error will be raised?

4. If your program needs to read integers, but the user entered strings, an error would occur when running this program. What kind of error is this?

5. Suppose you write a program for computing the perimeter of a rectangle and you mistakenly write your program so that it computes the area of a rectangle. What kind of error is this?

6. Identify and fix the errors in the following code:

```
1  public class Welcome {
2    public void Main(String[] args) {
3      System.out.println('Welcome to Java!);
4    }
5  }
```

2.8 Developing Java Programs Using NetBeans

Key
Point

You can edit, compile, run, and debug Java Programs using NetBeans.

NetBeans and Eclipse are two free popular integrated development environments for developing Java programs. They are easy to learn if you follow simple instructions. We recommend that you use either one for developing Java programs. This section gives the essential instructions to guide new users to create a project, create a class, compile, and run a class in NetBeans. The use of Eclipse will be introduced in the next section. For instructions on downloading and installing the latest version of NetBeans, see Supplement A.

Creating a Java Project

Before you can create Java programs, you need to first create a project. A project is like a folder to hold Java programs and all supporting files. You need to create a project only once. Here are the steps to create a Java project:

1. Choose *File*, *New Project* to display the New Project dialog box, as shown in Figure 2.11.

FIGURE 2.11 The New Project dialog is used to create a new project and specify a project type.

2. Select Java in the Categories section and Java Application in the Projects section and click *Next* to display the New Java Application dialog box, as shown in Figure 2.12.

3. Type `demo` in the Project Name field and `c:\michael` in Project Location field. Uncheck *Use Dedicated Folder for Storing Libraries* and uncheck *Create Main Class*.

4. Click *Finish* to create the project, as shown in Figure 2.13.

Creating a Java Class

After a project is created, you can create Java programs in the project using the following steps:

1. Right-click the demo node in the project pane to display a context menu. Choose *New*, *Java Class* to display the New Java Class dialog box, as shown in Figure 2.14.

FIGURE 2.12 The New Java Application dialog is for specifying a project name and location.

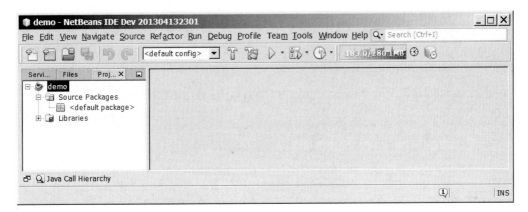

FIGURE 2.13 A New Java project named demo is created.

FIGURE 2.14 The New Java Class dialog box is used to create a new Java class.

2. Type `Welcome` in the Class Name field and select the Source Packages in the Location field. Leave the Package field blank. This will create a class in the default package.

3. Click *Finish* to create the Welcome class. The source code file Welcome.java is placed under the <default package> node.

4. Modify the code in the Welcome class to match Listing 2.1 in the text, as shown in Figure 2.15.

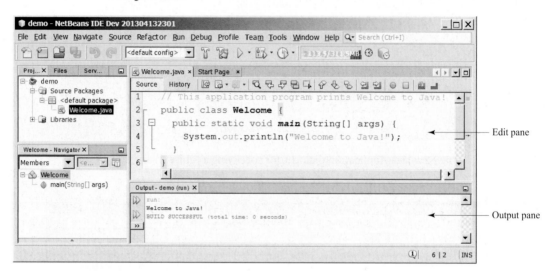

FIGURE 2.15 You can edit a program and run it in NetBeans.

Compiling and Running a Class

To run **Welcome.java**, right-click Welcome.java to display a context menu and choose *Run File*, or simply press the green arrow on the toolbar. The output is displayed in the Output pane, as shown in Figure 2.15. The *Run File* command automatically compiles the program if the program has been changed.

 Key Point

2.9 Developing Java Programs Using Eclipse

You can edit, compile, run, and debug Java Programs using Eclipse.

The preceding section introduced developing Java programs using NetBeans. You can also use Eclipse to develop Java programs. This section gives the essential instructions to guide new users to create a project, create a class, compile and run a class in Eclipse. All exercises in the book can be done in either NetBeans or Eclipse. Your teacher may make Section 2.9 optional, or provide you with further instructions on the IDE choice that aligns with the lab setup. Further instructions on installing and using Eclipse can be found in Supplement B at the back of the book.

Creating a Java Project

Before creating Java programs in Eclipse, you need to first create a project to hold all files. Here are the steps to create a Java project in Eclipse:

1. Choose *File, New, Java Project* to display the New Project wizard, as shown in Figure 2.16.

2. Type **demo** in the Project name field. As you type, the Location field is automatically set by default. You may customize the location for your project.

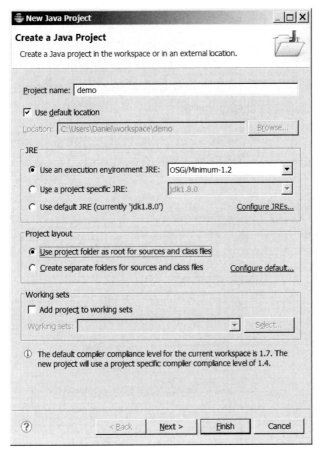

FIGURE 2.16 The New Java Project dialog is for specifying a project name and properties.

3. Make sure that you selected the options *Use project folder as root for sources and class files* so that the .java and .class files are in the same folder for easy access.

4. Click *Finish* to create the project, as shown in Figure 2.17.

FIGURE 2.17 A New Java project named demo is created.

Creating a Java Class

After a project is created, you can create Java programs in the project using the following steps:

1. Choose *File*, *New*, *Class* to display the New Java Class wizard.

2. Type `Welcome` in the Name field.

3. Check the option *public static void main(String[] args)*.

4. Click *Finish* to generate the template for the source code Welcome.java, as shown in Figure 2.18.

FIGURE 2.18 The New Java Class dialog box is used to create a new Java class.

Compiling and Running a Class

To run the program, right-click the class in the project to display a context menu. Choose *Run*, *Java Application* in the context menu to run the class. The output is displayed in the Console pane, as shown in Figure 2.19.

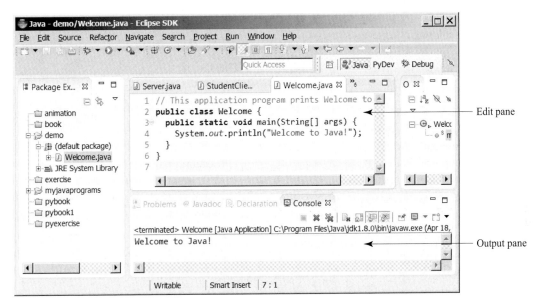

FIGURE 2.19 You can edit a program and run it in Eclipse.

Chapter 2 — Review and Assessment

KEY TERMS

Application Program Interface (API) 29
assembler 22
assembly language 22
back-end 25
block 31
bytecode 34
bytecode verifier 36
case sensitive 31
class loader 36
comment 30
compiler 23
console 30
event-driven programming 28
front-end 25
high-level language 23
integrated development environment
 (IDE) 29
interpreter 23
Java Development Toolkit (JDK) 29
Java Virtual Machine (JVM) 34
`javac` command 34

keyword (or reserved word) 30
library 29
logic error 40
low-level language 22
machine language 22
`main` method 30
modular design 25
Object-Oriented Programming
 (OOP) 28
operating system (OS) 23
Procedural Language 27
programming paradigm 26
programming style 36
runtime error 39
source code 23
statement 23
statement terminator 30
Structured Programming 26
syntax error 38
Unstructured Programming 26

CHAPTER SUMMARY

1. The *machine language* is a set of primitive instructions built into every computer.

2. *Assembly language* is a *low-level programming language* in which a mnemonic is used to represent each machine-language instruction.

3. *High-level languages* are English-like and easy to learn and program.

4. A program written in a high-level language is called a *source program*.

5. A *compiler* is a software program that translates the source program into a *machine-language program*.

6. The *operating system (OS)* is a program that manages and controls a computer's activities.

7. Java is platform independent, meaning that you can write a program once and run it on any computer.

8. Java programs can be embedded in HTML pages and downloaded by Web browsers to bring live animation and interaction to Web clients.

9. The Java source file name must match the public class name in the program. Java source code files must end with the `.java` extension.

10. Every class is compiled into a separate bytecode file that has the same name as the class and ends with the `.class` extension.

11. To compile a Java source-code file from the command line, use the **javac** command.

12. To run a Java class from the command line, use the **java** command.

13. Every Java program is a set of class definitions. The keyword `class` introduces a class definition. The contents of the class are included in a *block*.

14. A block begins with an opening brace ({) and ends with a closing brace (}).

15. Methods are contained in a class. To run a Java program, the program must have a `main` method. The `main` method is the entry point where the program starts when it is executed.

16. Every *statement* in Java ends with a semicolon (;), known as the *statement terminator.*

17. *Reserved words,* or *keywords,* have a specific meaning to the compiler and cannot be used for other purposes in the program.

18. In Java, comments are preceded by two slashes (//) on a line, called a *line comment,* or enclosed between /* and */ on one or several lines, called a *block comment* or *paragraph comment.* Comments are ignored by the compiler.

19. Java source programs are case sensitive.

20. Programming errors can be categorized into three types: *syntax errors, runtime errors,* and *logic errors.* Errors reported by a compiler are called syntax errors or *compile errors.* Runtime errors are errors that cause a program to terminate abnormally. Logic errors occur when a program does not perform the way it was intended to.

21. *Modular design* is the practice of dividing your application into smaller, reusable units that work together as a whole.

22. Programming languages have evolved over time. Types of language styles include *unstructured, structured, event-driven,* and *object-oriented.*

PROGRAMMING EXERCISES

1. (*Display three messages*) Write a program that displays `Welcome to Java`, `Welcome to Computer Science`, and `Programming is fun`.

2. (*Display five messages*) Write a program that displays `Welcome to Java` five times.

3. (*Print a table*) Write a program that displays the following table:

```
a        a^2     a^3
1        1       1
2        4       8
3        9       27
4        16      64
```

4. (*Compute expressions*) Write a program that displays the result of
$$\frac{9.5 \times 4.5 - 2.5 \times 3}{45.5 - 3.5}.$$

5. (*Summation of a series*) Write a program that displays the result of
$$1 + 2 + 3 + 4 + 5 + 6 + 7 + 8 + 9.$$

6. (*Approximate* π) π computed using the following formula:
$$\pi = 4 \times \left(1 - \frac{1}{3} + \frac{1}{5} - \frac{1}{7} + \frac{1}{9} - \frac{1}{11} + \cdots\right)$$

Write a program that displays the result of $4 \times \left(1 - \frac{1}{3} + \frac{1}{5} - \frac{1}{7} + \frac{1}{9} - \frac{1}{11}\right)$ and $4 \times \left(1 - \frac{1}{3} + \frac{1}{5} - \frac{1}{7} + \frac{1}{9} - \frac{1}{11} + \frac{1}{13}\right)$. Use `1.0` instead of `1` in your program.

7. (*Area and perimeter of a circle*) Write a program that displays the area and perimeter of a circle that has a radius of `5.5` using the following formula:
$$perimeter = 2 \times radius \times \pi$$
$$area = radius \times radius \times \pi$$

8. (*Area and perimeter of a rectangle*) Write a program that displays the area and perimeter of a rectangle with the width of `4.5` and height of `7.9` using the following formula:
$$area = radius \times radius \times \pi$$

9. (*Average speed in miles*) Assume a runner runs `14` kilometers in `45` minutes and `30` seconds. Write a program that displays the average speed in miles per hour. (Note that `1` mile is `1.6` kilometers.)

10. (*Average speed in kilometers*) Assume a runner runs `24` miles in `1` hour, `40` minutes, and `35` seconds. Write a program that displays the average speed in kilometers per hour. (Note that `1` mile is `1.6` kilometers.)

PROGRAMMING TECHNIQUES TO ANALYZE AND SOLVE PROBLEMS

Objectives

- Identify input that is required, and retrieve input using the Scanner class.

- Identify output that is required, and write it to the console.

- Write programming code using assignment statements and assignment expressions.

- Use constants to store permanent data.

- Use variable to store data.

- Use appropriate style and clarity when naming variables, constants, methods, and classes.

- Follow defined, standard procedures to document your project.

- Explore Java numeric primitive data types: byte, short, int, long, float, and double.

- Perform operations using operators +, -, *, /

- Describe the Software Development Life Cycle process.

- Design an application using a Software Development Life Cycle approach.

- Explain the quality assurance process.

- Test your application for quality assurance.

3.1 Introduction

The focus of this chapter is on learning beginning programming techniques to solve problems.

In Chapter 1 you learned how to create, compile, and run very basic Java programs. Now you will learn how to solve problems by writing programs. Through these problems, you will learn elementary programming using primitive data types, variables, constants, operators, expressions, and input and output.

Suppose, for example, that you need to take out a student loan. Given the loan amount, loan term, and annual interest rate, can you write a program to compute the monthly payment and total payment? This chapter shows you how to write programs like this. Along the way, you learn the basic steps that go into analyzing a problem, designing a solution, and implementing the solution by creating a program.

3.2 Writing a Simple Program

Writing a program involves designing a strategy for solving the problem and then using a programming language to implement that strategy.

Let's first consider the simple problem of computing the area of a circle. How do we write a program for solving this problem?

algorithm

Writing a program involves designing algorithms and translating algorithms into programming instructions, or code. An *algorithm* describes how a problem is solved by listing the actions that need to be taken and the order of their execution. Algorithms can help the programmer plan a program before writing it in a programming language. Algorithms can be described in natural languages

pseudocode

or in *pseudocode*. You may recall from Chapter 2 that pseudocode is a tool used to explain the logical steps of a program by using natural language mixed with some programming code. The algorithm for calculating the area of a circle can be described as follows:

1. Read in the circle's radius.

2. Compute the area using the following formula:

$$area = radius * radius * \pi$$

3. Display the result.

> **Tip**
> It's always good practice to outline your program (or its underlying problem) in the form of an algorithm before you begin coding.

When you *code*—that is, when you write a program—you translate an algorithm into a program. You already know that every Java program begins with a class definition in which the keyword `class` is followed by the class name. Assume that you have chosen `ComputeArea` as the class name. The outline of the program would look like this:

```
public class ComputeArea {
    // Details to be given later
}
```

As you know, every Java program must have a `main` method where program execution begins. The program is then expanded as follows:

```java
public class ComputeArea {
  public static void main(String[] args) {
    // Step 1: Read in radius

    // Step 2: Compute area
    // Step 3: Display the area
  }
}
```

Step 1 in the preceding code identifies the input requirements. The program needs to read the radius entered by the user from the keyboard. This raises two important issues:

- Reading the radius.

- Storing the radius in the program.

Let's address the second issue first. In order to store the radius, the program needs to declare a symbol called a *variable*. A variable represents a value stored in the computer's memory.

Rather than using `x` and `y` as variable names, choose descriptive names: in this case, `radius` for radius, and `area` for area. To let the compiler know what `radius` and `area` are, specify their data types. That is the kind of data stored in a variable, whether integer, real number, or something else. This is known as *declaring variables*. Java provides simple data types for representing integers, real numbers, characters, and Boolean types. These types are known as *primitive data types* or *fundamental types*.

Real numbers (i.e., numbers with a decimal point) are represented using a method known as *floating-point* in computers. So, the real numbers are also called *floating-point numbers*. In Java, you can use the keyword `double` to declare a floating-point variable. Declare `radius` and `area` as `double`. The program can be expanded as follows:

```java
public class ComputeArea {
  public static void main(String[] args) {
    double radius;
    double area;

    // Step 1: Read in radius

    // Step 2: Compute area

    // Step 3: Display the area
  }
}
```

The program declares `radius` and `area` as variables. The reserved word `double` indicates that `radius` and `area` are floating-point values stored in the computer.

The first step is to prompt the user to designate the circle's `radius`. You will soon learn how to prompt the user for information. For now, to learn how variables work, you can assign a fixed value to `radius` in the program as you write the code; later, you'll modify the program to prompt the user for this value.

Margin notes: variable · descriptive names · data type · declare variables · primitive data types · floating-point number

The second step is to compute `area` by assigning the result of the expression `radius * radius * 3.14159` to `area`.

The final step displays the output requirements. The program will display the value of `area` on the console by using the `System.out.println` method.

Listing 3.1 shows the complete program, and a sample run of the program is shown in Figure 3.1.

LISTING 3.1 ComputeArea.java

```
1  public class ComputeArea {
2    public static void main(String[] args) {
3      double radius; // Declare radius
4      double area; // Declare area
5
6      // Assign a radius
7      radius = 20; // radius is now 20
8
9      // Compute area
10     area = radius * radius * 3.14159;
11
12     // Display results
13     System.out.println("The area for the circle of radius " +
14       radius + " is " + area);
15   }
16 }
```

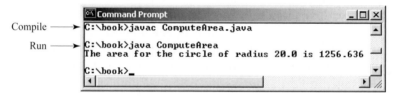

FIGURE 3.1 The program displays the area of a circle.

Variables such as `radius` and `area` correspond to memory locations. Every variable has a name, a type, a size, and a value. Line 3 declares that `radius` can store a `double` value. The value is not defined until you assign a value. Line 7 assigns 20 into variable `radius`. Similarly, line 4 declares variable `area`, and line 10 assigns a value into `area`. The following table shows the value in the memory for `area` and `radius` as the program is executed. Each row in the table shows the values of variables after the statement in the corresponding line in the program is executed. This method of reviewing how a program works is called *tracing a program*. Tracing programs are helpful for understanding how programs work, and they are useful tools for comparing actual results to anticipated results. As an example, at the execution of line 10 the *actual result* of the `area = 1256.636`.

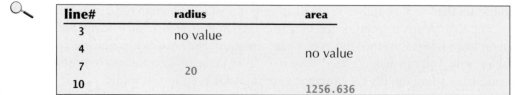

line#	radius	area
3	no value	
4		no value
7	20	
10		1256.636

You can determine the *anticipated result* of the area by using a calculator to multiply 20 * 20 * 3.14159. Insuring that *anticipated result = actual result* provides evidence that the program provides a correct solution.

The plus sign (+) has two meanings: one for addition and the other for concatenating (combining) strings. The plus sign (+) in lines 13–14 is called a *string concatenation operator*. It combines two strings into one. If a string is combined with a number, the number is converted into a string and concatenated with the other string. Therefore, the plus signs (+) in lines 13–14 concatenate strings into a longer string, which is then displayed in the output. Strings and string concatenation will be discussed further in Chapter 5.

concatenate strings

concatenate strings with numbers

> **Caution**
> A string cannot cross lines in the source code. Thus, the following statement would result in a compile error:
>
> ```
> System.out.println("Introduction to Computer Programming,
> by Pearson Publishing");
> ```
>
> To fix the error, break the string into separate substrings, and use the concatenation operator (+) to combine them:
>
> ```
> System.out.println("Introduction to Computer Programming, " +
> "by Pearson Publishing");
> ```

break a long string

✓ SECTION 3.2 ASSESSMENT

1. Identify and fix the errors in the following code:

```
1  public class Test {
2    public void main(string[] args) {
3      double i = 50.0;
4      double k = i + 50.0;
5      double j = k + 1;
6
7      System.out.println("j is " + j + " and
8        k is " + k);
9    }
10 }
```

2. In *Listing 3.1 ComputeArea.java*, which line of code provides the necessary output?

3.3 Identifying Input Requirements and Reading from the Console

Reading input from the console enables the program to accept input from the user.

Key Point

In Listing 3.1, the radius is fixed in the source code. However, the project requirements are to allow a user to input a different radius. To use a different radius, you have to modify the source code and recompile it. Obviously, this is not convenient, so instead you can use the **Scanner** class for console input.

Java uses `System.out` to refer to the standard output device and `System.in` to refer to the standard input device. By default, the output device is the display monitor and the input device is the keyboard. To perform console output, you simply use the `println` method to display a primitive value or a string to the console. Console input is not directly supported in Java, but you can use the `Scanner` class to create an object to read input from `System.in`, as follows:

```
Scanner input = new Scanner(System.in);
```

The syntax `new Scanner(System.in)` creates an object of the `Scanner` type. The syntax `Scanner input` declares that `input` is a variable whose type is `Scanner`. The whole line `Scanner input = new Scanner(System.in)` creates a `Scanner` object and assigns its reference to the variable `input`. An object may invoke its methods. To invoke a method on an object is to ask the object to perform a task. You can invoke the `nextDouble()` method to read a `double` value as follows:

```
double radius = input.nextDouble();
```

This statement reads a number from the keyboard and assigns the number to `radius`.

Listing 3.2 rewrites Listing 3.1 to prompt the user to enter a radius.

LISTING 3.2 ComputeAreaWithConsoleInput.java

import class
```
 1  import java.util.Scanner; // Scanner is in the java.util package
 2
 3  public class ComputeAreaWithConsoleInput {
 4    public static void main(String[] args) {
 5      // Create a Scanner object
 6      Scanner input = new Scanner(System.in);
 7
 8      // Prompt the user to enter a radius
 9      System.out.print("Enter a number for radius: ");
10      double radius = input.nextDouble();
11
12      // Compute area
13      double area = radius * radius * 3.14159;
14
15      // Display results
16      System.out.println("The area for the circle of radius " +
17        radius + " is " + area);
18    }
19  }
```

create a Scanner

read a double

```
Enter a number for radius:  2.5  ↵Enter
The area for the circle of radius 2.5 is 19.6349375
```

```
Enter a number for radius:  23  ↵Enter
The area for the circle of radius 23.0 is 1661.90111
```

prompt

Line 9 displays a string `"Enter a number for radius: "` to the console. This is known as a *prompt*, because it directs the user to enter an input. Your program should always tell the user what to enter when expecting input from the keyboard.

The `print` method in line 9

```
System.out.print("Enter a number for radius: ");
```

print vs. println

is identical to the `println` method except that `println` moves to the beginning of the next line after displaying the string, but `print` does not advance to the next line when completed.

Line 6 creates a `Scanner` object. The statement in line 10 reads input from the keyboard.

```
double radius = input.nextDouble();
```

After the user enters a number and presses the *Enter* key, the program reads the number and assigns it to `radius`.

More details on objects will be introduced in Chapter 9. For the time being, simply accept that this is how to obtain input from the console.

The `Scanner` class is in the `java.util` package. It is imported in line 1. There are two types of `import` statements: specific import and wildcard import. The *specific import* specifies a single class in the import statement. For example, the following statement imports `Scanner` from the package `java.util`.

specific import

```
import java.util.Scanner;
```

The *wildcard import* imports all the classes in a package by using the asterisk as the wildcard. For example, the following statement imports all the classes from the package `java.util`.

wildcard import

```
import java.util.*.;
```

The information for the classes in an imported package is not read in at compile time or runtime unless the class is used in the program. The import statement simply tells the compiler where to locate the classes. There is no performance difference between a specific import and a wildcard import declaration.

no performance difference

Listing 3.3 gives an example of reading multiple input from the keyboard. The program reads three numbers and displays their average.

LISTING 3.3 ComputeAverage.java

```
 1  import java.util.Scanner; // Scanner is in the java.util package
 2
 3  public class ComputeAverage {
 4    public static void main(String[] args) {
 5      // Create a Scanner object
 6      Scanner input = new Scanner(System.in);
 7
 8      // Prompt the user to enter three numbers
 9      System.out.print("Enter three numbers: ");
10      double number1 = input.nextDouble();
11      double number2 = input.nextDouble();
12      double number3 = input.nextDouble();
13
14      // Compute average
15      double average = (number1 + number2 + number3) / 3;
16
17      // Display results
18      System.out.println("The average of " + number1 + " " + number2
19        + " " + number3 + " is " + average);
20    }
21  }
```

import class

create a Scanner

read a double

enter input in one line

```
Enter three numbers: 1 2 3  ↵Enter
The average of 1.0 2.0 3.0 is 2.0
```

enter input in multiple lines

```
Enter three numbers: 10.5  ↵Enter
11  ↵Enter
11.5  ↵Enter
The average of 10.5 11.0 11.5 is 11.0
```

The code for importing the `Scanner` class (line 1) and creating a `Scanner` object (line 6) are the same as in the preceding example as well as in all new programs you will write for reading input from the keyboard.

Line 9 prompts the user to enter three numbers. The numbers are read in lines 10–13. You may enter three numbers separated by spaces, then press the *Enter* key, or enter each number followed by a press of the *Enter* key, as shown in the sample runs of this program.

If you entered an input other than a numeric value, a runtime error would occur.

IPO

Note
Most of the programs in the early chapters of this book perform three steps—input, process, and output—called *IPO*. Input is receiving input from the user; process is producing results using the input; and output is displaying the results.

Warning in IDE

Note
If you use an IDE such as Eclipse or NetBeans, you will get a warning to ask you to close the input to prevent a potential resource leak. Ignore the warning because the input is automatically closed when your program is terminated. In this case, there will be no resource leaking.

✓ SECTION 3.3 ASSESSMENT

1. Your software design requirements state that users must be allowed to input a double value from the keyboard. How do you write a statement to meet these requirements? What happens if you entered **5a** when executing the following code?

   ```
   double radius = input.nextDouble();
   ```

2. Are there any performance differences between the following two `import` statements?

   ```
   import java.util.Scanner;
   import java.util.*;
   ```

3.4 Identifiers

Identifiers are the names that identify the elements such as classes, methods, and variables in a program.

Key Point

As you see in Listing 3.3, `ComputeAverage`, `main`, `input`, `number1`, `number2`, `number3`, and so on are the names of things that appear in the program. In programming terminology, such names are called *identifiers*. All identifiers must obey the following rules:

identifiers

identifier naming rules

- An identifier is a sequence of characters that consists of letters, digits, underscores (_), and dollar signs ($).

- An identifier must start with a letter, an underscore (_), or a dollar sign ($). It cannot start with a digit.

- An identifier cannot be a reserved word. (See Appendix A for a list of reserved words.)

- An identifier cannot be `true`, `false`, or `null`.

- An identifier can be of any length.

For example, `$2`, `ComputeArea`, `area`, `radius`, and `print` are legal identifiers, whereas `2A` and `d+4` are not because they do not follow the rules. The Java compiler detects illegal identifiers and reports syntax errors.

Note
Since Java is case sensitive, `area`, `Area`, and `AREA` are all different identifiers.

case sensitive

Tip
Identifiers are for naming variables, methods, classes, and other items in a program. Descriptive identifiers make programs easy to read. Avoid using abbreviations for identifiers. Using complete words is more descriptive. For example, `numberOfStudents` is better than `numStuds`, `numOfStuds`, or `numOfStudents`. We use descriptive names for complete programs in the text. However, we will occasionally use variable names such as `i`, `j`, `k`, `x`, and `y` in the code snippets for brevity. These names also provide a generic tone to the code snippets.

descriptive names

Tip
Do not name identifiers with the `$` character. By convention, the `$` character should be used only in mechanically generated source code.

the $ character

✓ Section 3.4 Assessment

1. Which of the following identifiers are valid? Which are Java keywords?

 `miles`, `Test`, `a++`, `--a`, `4#R`, `$4`, `#44`, `apps`

 `class`, `public`, `int`, `x`, `y`, `radius`

**Key
Point**

3.5 Variables

Variables are used to represent values that may be changed in the program.

why called variables?

As you see from the programs in the preceding sections, variables are used to store values to be used later in a program. They are called variables because their values can be changed. In the program in Listing 3.2, `radius` and `area` are variables of the `double` type. You can assign any numerical value to `radius` and `area`, and the values of `radius` and `area` can be reassigned. For example, in the following code, `radius` is initially `1.0` (line 2) and then changed to `2.0` (line 7), and area is set to `3.14159` (line 3) and then reset to `12.56636` (line 8).

```
1  // Compute the first area
2  radius = 1.0;                                          radius: 1.0
3  area = radius * radius * 3.14159;                         area: 3.14159
4  System.out.println("The area is " + area + " for radius " + radius);
5
6  // Compute the second area
7  radius = 2.0;                                          radius: 2.0
8  area = radius * radius * 3.14159;                         area: 12.56636
9  System.out.println("The area is " + area + " for radius " + radius);
```

declare variable

Variables are for representing data of a certain type. To use a variable, you declare it by telling the compiler its name as well as what type of data it can store. The *variable declaration* tells the compiler to allocate appropriate memory space for the variable based on its data type. The syntax for declaring a variable is

```
datatype variableName;
```

Here are some examples of variable declarations:

```
int count;          // Declare count to be an integer variable
double radius;      // Declare radius to be a double variable
double interestRate; // Declare interestRate to be a double variable
```

These examples use the data types `int` and `double`. Later you will be introduced to additional data types, such as `byte`, `short`, `long`, `float`, `char`, and `boolean`.

If variables are of the same type, they can be declared together, as follows:

```
datatype variable1, variable2, ..., variablen;
```

The variables are separated by commas. For example,

```
int i, j, k; // Declare i, j, and k as int variables
```

initialize variables

Variables often have initial values. You can declare a variable and initialize it in one step. Consider, for instance, the following code:

```
int count = 1;
```

This is equivalent to the next two statements:

```
int count;
count = 1;
```

You can also use a shorthand form to declare and initialize variables of the same type together. For example,

```
int i = 1, j = 2;
```

Tip

A variable must be declared before it can be assigned a value. A variable declared in a method must be assigned a value before it can be used.

Whenever possible, declare a variable and assign its initial value in one step. This will make the program easy to read and avoid programming errors.

Every variable has a scope. The *scope of a variable* is the part of the program where the variable can be referenced. You can learn more about variable scope in Supplement E of this book. For now, all you need to know is that a variable must be declared and initialized before it can be used.

✓ SECTION 3.5 ASSESSMENT

1. Identify and fix the errors in the following code:

```
1  public class Test {
2    public static void main(String[] args) {
3      int i = k + 2;
4      System.out.println(i);
5    }
6  }
```

3.6 Assignment Statements and Assignment Expressions

An assignment statement designates a value for a variable. An assignment statement can be used as an expression in Java.

Key Point

After a variable is declared, you can assign a value to it by using an *assignment statement*. In Java, the equal sign (=) is used as the *assignment operator*. The syntax for assignment statements is as follows:

assignment statement

assignment operator

```
variable = expression;
```

An *expression* represents a computation involving values, variables, and operators that, taking them together, evaluates to a value. For example, consider the following code:

expression

```
int y = 1;              // Assign 1 to variable y
double radius = 1.0;    // Assign 1.0 to variable radius
int x = 5 * (3 / 2);    // Assign the value of the expression to x
x = y + 1;              // Assign the addition of y and 1 to x
double area = radius * radius * 3.14159; // Compute area
```

You can use a variable in an expression. A variable can also be used in both sides of the = operator. For example,

```
x = x + 1;
```

In this assignment statement, the result of x + 1 is assigned to x. If x is 1 before the statement is executed, then it becomes 2 after the statement is executed.

To assign a value to a variable, you must place the variable name to the left of the assignment operator. Thus, the following statement is wrong:

```
1 = x;   // Wrong
```

Note

In mathematics, x = 2 * x + 1 denotes an equation. However, in Java, x = 2 * x + 1 is an assignment statement that evaluates the expression 2 * x + 1 and assigns the result to x.

assignment expression

In Java, an assignment statement is essentially an expression that evaluates to the value to be assigned to the variable on the left side of the assignment operator. For this reason, an assignment statement is also known as an *assignment expression*. For example, the following statement is correct:

```
System.out.println(x = 1);
```

which is equivalent to

```
x = 1;
System.out.println(x);
```

If a value is assigned to multiple variables, you can use this syntax:

```
i = j = k = 1;
```

which is equivalent to

```
k = 1;
j = k;
i = j;
```

Note

In an assignment statement, the data type of the variable on the left must be compatible with the data type of the value on the right. For example, int x = 1.0 would be illegal, because the data type of x is int. You cannot assign a **double** value (1.0) to an **int** variable without using type casting. Type casting is introduced in Section 3.14.

✓ SECTION 3.6 ASSESSMENT

1. Identify and fix the errors in the following code:

```
1  public class Test {
2    public static void main(String[] args) {
3      int i = j = k = 2;
4      System.out.println(i + " " + j + " " + k);
5    }
6  }
```

3.7 Named Constants

**Key
Point**

A named constant is an identifier that represents a permanent value.

The value of a variable may change during the execution of a program, but a *named constant*, or simply *constant*, represents permanent data that never changes. In our `ComputeArea` program, π is constant. If you use it frequently, you don't want to keep typing `3.14159`; instead, you can declare a constant for π. Here is the syntax for declaring a constant:

constant

```
final datatype CONSTANTNAME = value;
```

A constant must be declared and initialized in the same statement. The word `final` is a Java keyword for declaring a constant. For example, you can declare π as a constant and rewrite Listing 3.1 as in Listing 3.4.

final keyword

LISTING 3.4 ComputeAreaWithConstant.java

```java
 1  import java.util.Scanner; // Scanner is in the java.util package
 2
 3  public class ComputeAreaWithConstant {
 4    public static void main(String[] args) {
 5      final double PI = 3.14159; // Declare a constant
 6
 7      // Create a Scanner object
 8      Scanner input = new Scanner(System.in);
 9
10      // Prompt the user to enter a radius
11      System.out.print("Enter a number for radius: ");
12      double radius = input.nextDouble();
13
14      // Compute area
15      double area = radius * radius * PI;
16
17      // Display result
18      System.out.println("The area for the circle of radius " +
19        radius + " is " + area);
20    }
21  }
```

There are three benefits of using constants:

benefits of constants

1. You don't have to repeatedly type the same value if it is used multiple times.

2. If you have to change the constant value (e.g., from `3.14` to `3.14159` for `PI`), you need to change it only in a single location in the source code.

3. A descriptive name for a constant makes the program easy to read.

3.8 Follow Defined Standards to Document Your Design

Key Point

Following common industry standards helps document your program design. Following the standard Java naming convention is a meaningful way to document your program. It makes your programs easy to read and avoids errors.

Make sure that you choose descriptive names with straightforward meanings for the variables, constants, classes, and methods in your program. As mentioned earlier, names are case sensitive. Listed below are the standard conventions for naming variables, methods, and classes.

name variables and methods

- Use lowercase for variables and methods. If a name consists of several words, concatenate them into one, making the first word lowercase and capitalizing the first letter of each subsequent word—for example, the variables `radius` and `area` and the method `print`.

name classes

- Capitalize the first letter of each word in a class name—for example, the class names `ComputeArea` and `System`.

name constants

- Capitalize every letter in a constant, and use underscores between words —for example, the constants `PI` and `MAX_VALUE`.

It is important to follow the naming conventions to make your programs easy to read.

Caution
Do not choose class names that are already used in the Java library. For example, since the `System` class is defined in Java, you should not name your class `System`.

name classes

✓ SECTION 3.8 ASSESSMENT

1. What are the benefits of using constants? Declare an `int` constant `SIZE` with value `20`.

2. What are the naming conventions for class names, method names, constants, and variables? Which of the following items can be a constant, a method, a variable, or a class according to the Java naming conventions?

 `MAX_VALUE`, `Test`, `read`, `readDouble`

3. Translate the following algorithm into Java code:

 Step 1: Declare a `double` variable named `miles` with initial value `100`.

 Step 2: Declare a `double` constant named `KILOMETERS_PER_MILE` with value `1.609`.

 Step 3: Declare a `double` variable named `kilometers`, multiply `miles` and `KILOMETERS_PER_MILE`, and assign the result to `kilometers`.

 Step 4: Display `kilometers` to the console.

 What is `kilometers` after Step 4?

3.9 Numeric Data Types and Operations

*Java has six numeric types for integers and floating-point numbers with operators +, -, *, /, and %.*

Key Point

Numeric Types

Every data type has a range of values. The compiler allocates memory space for each variable or constant according to its data type. Java provides eight primitive data types for numeric values, characters, and Boolean values. This section introduces numeric data types and operators.

Table 3.1 lists the six numeric data types, their ranges, and their storage sizes.

TABLE 3.1 Numeric Data Types

Name	Range	Storage Size	
byte	-2^7 to $2^7 - 1$ (-128 to 127)	8-bit signed	byte type
short	-2^{15} to $2^{15} - 1$ (-32768 to 32767)	16-bit signed	short type
int	-2^{31} to $2^{31} - 1$ (-2147483648 to 2147483647)	32-bit signed	int type
long	-2^{63} to $2^{63} - 1$ (i.e., -9223372036854775808 to 9223372036854775807)	64-bit signed	long type
float	Negative range: $-3.4028235E + 38$ to $-1.4E - 45$ Positive range: $1.4E - 45$ to $3.4028235E + 38$	32-bit IEEE 754	float type
double	Negative range: $-1.7976931348623157E + 308$ to $-4.9E - 324$ Positive range: $49E - 324$ to $1.7976931348623157E + 308$	64-bit IEEE 754	double type

Java uses four types for integers: byte, short, int, and long. Choose the type that is most appropriate for your variable. For example, if you know an integer stored in a variable is within a range of a byte, declare the variable as a byte. For simplicity and consistency, we will use int for integers most of the time in this book. *(integer types)*

Java uses two types for floating-point numbers: float and double. The double type is twice as big as float, so the double is known as *double precision* and float as *single precision*. Normally, you should use the double type, because it is more accurate than the float type. *(floating-point types)*

Reading Numbers from the Keyboard

You know how to use the nextDouble() method in the Scanner class to read a double value from the keyboard. You can also use the methods listed in Table 3.2 to read a number of the byte, short, int, long, and float type.

TABLE 3.2 Methods for Scanner Objects

Method	Description
nextByte()	reads an integer of the **byte** type.
nextShort()	reads an integer of the **short** type.
nextInt()	reads an integer of the **int** type.
nextLong()	reads an integer of the **long** type.
nextFloat()	reads a number of the **float** type.
nextDouble()	reads a number of the **double** type.

Here are examples for reading values of various types from the keyboard:

```
1   Scanner input = new Scanner(System.in);
2   System.out.print("Enter a byte value: ");
3   byte byteValue = input.nextByte();
4
5   System.out.print("Enter a short value: ");
6   short shortValue = input.nextShort();
7
8   System.out.print("Enter an int value: ");
9   int intValue = input.nextInt();
10
11  System.out.print("Enter a long value: ");
12  long longValue = input.nextLong();
13
14  System.out.print("Enter a float value: ");
15  float floatValue = input.nextFloat();
```

If you enter a value with an incorrect range or format, a runtime error would occur. For example, if you enter a value 128 for line 3, an error would occur because 128 is out of range for a **byte** type integer.

Numeric Operators

operators +, -, *, /, %

operand

The operators for numeric data types include the standard arithmetic operators: addition (+), subtraction (−), multiplication (*), division (/), and remainder (%), as shown in Table 3.3. The *operands* are the values operated by an operator.

TABLE 3.3 Numeric Operators

Name	Meaning	Example	Result
+	Addition	34 + 1	35
−	Subtraction	34.0 − 0.1	33.9
*	Multiplication	300 * 30	9000
/	Division	1.0 / 2.0	0.5
%	Remainder	20 % 3	2

When both operands of a division are integers, the result of the division is the quotient and the fractional part is truncated. For example, 5 / 2 yields 2, not 2.5, and -5 / 2 yields -2, not -2.5. To perform a float-point division, one of the operands must be a floating-point number. For example, 5.0 / 2 yields 2.5.

The % operator, known as *remainder* or *modulo* operator, yields the remainder after division. The operand on the left is the dividend and the operand on the right is the divisor. Therefore, 7 % 3 yields 1, 3 % 7 yields 3, 12 % 4 yields 0, 26 % 8 yields 2, and 20 % 13 yields 7.

```
    2          0          3          3              1  ←──── Quotient
  ┌───      ┌───      ┌───       ┌───            ┌───
3 │ 7      7 │ 3      4 │ 12     8 │ 26   Divisor ──→ 13 │ 20  ←──── Dividend
  ─6──       ─0──       ─12─      ─24─              ─13─
    1          3          0          2              7  ←──── Remainder
```

The % operator is often used for positive integers, but it can also be used with negative integers and floating-point values. The remainder is negative only if the dividend is negative. For example, -7 % 3 yields -1, -12 % 4 yields 0, -26 % -8 yields -2, and 20 % -13 yields 7.

✓ SECTION 3.9 ASSESSMENT

1. You are designing input requirements for an application. You need to store decimal numbers and ensure the highest accuracy. Which data type should you use?

2. You are designing input requirements for an application. What data type should you use to store a student's current age?

3. You are designing the output requirements for an application. What data type should you use to print a student ID ranging from 1000 - 100,000?

4. What is the output value of: 5 * 10 / 2 ?

3.10 Evaluating Expressions and Operator Precedence

Java expressions are evaluated in the same way as arithmetic expressions.

Key Point

In Java programming, operators contained within pairs of parentheses are evaluated first. Parentheses can be nested, in which case the expression in the inner parentheses is evaluated first. When more than one operator is used in an expression, the following operator precedence rule is used to determine the order of evaluation.

evaluating an expression

operator precedence rule

- Multiplication, division, and remainder operators are applied first. If an expression contains several multiplication, division, and remainder operators, they are applied from left to right.

- Addition and subtraction operators are applied last. If an expression contains several addition and subtraction operators, they are applied from left to right.

Here is an example of how an expression is evaluated:

```
3 + 4 * 4 + 5 * (4 + 3) - 1
                    ↑_____ (1) inside parentheses first
3 + 4 * 4 + 5 * 7 - 1
    ↑_____ (2) multiplication
3 + 16 + 5 * 7 - 1
            ↑_____ (3) multiplication
3 + 16 + 35 - 1
  ↑_____ (4) addition
19 + 35 - 1
   ↑_____ (5) addition
    54 - 1
       ↑_____ (6) subtraction
    53
```

Listing 3.5 gives a program that converts a Fahrenheit degree to Celsius using the formula celsius = ()(fahrenheit = 32).

LISTING 3.5 FahrenheitToCelsius.java

```java
1   import java.util.Scanner;
2
3   public class FahrenheitToCelsius {
4     public static void main(String[] args) {
5       Scanner input = new Scanner(System.in);
6
7       System.out.print("Enter a degree in Fahrenheit: ");
8       double fahrenheit = input.nextDouble();
9
10      // Convert Fahrenheit to Celsius
11      double celsius = (5.0 / 9) * (fahrenheit - 32);
12      System.out.println("Fahrenheit " + fahrenheit + " is " +
13        celsius + " in Celsius");
14    }
15  }
```

divide

```
Enter a degree in Fahrenheit: 100 ↵Enter
Fahrenheit 100.0 is 37.77777777777778 in Celsius
```

line#	fahrenheit	celsius
8	100	
11		37.77777777777778

integer vs. floating-point division

Be careful when applying division. Division of two integers yields an integer in Java. is translated to 5.0 / 9 instead of 5 / 9 in line 11, because 5 / 9 yields 0 in Java.

1. What is the output value of the following expressions?

   ```
   10 + 4 / 2
   10 * 3 *5 / 2 + 2
   10 * 3 * 5 / (2 + 2)
   ```

3.11 Case Study: Displaying the Current Time

Key Point

You can invoke `System.currentTimeMillis()` *to return the current time.*

The problem is to develop a program that displays the current time in GMT (Greenwich Mean Time) in the format hour:minute:second, such as 13:19:8.

The `currentTimeMillis` method in the `System` class returns the current time in milliseconds elapsed since midnight, January 1, 1970 GMT, as shown in Figure 3.2. This time is known as the *UNIX epoch*. The epoch is the point when time starts, and **1970** was the year when the UNIX operating system was formally introduced.

`currentTimeMillis`

UNIX epoch

FIGURE 3.2 The `System.currentTimeMillis()` returns the number of milliseconds since the UNIX epoch.

You can use this method to obtain the current time, and then compute the current second, minute, and hour as follows.

1. Obtain the total milliseconds since midnight, January 1, 1970, in `totalMilliseconds` by invoking `System.currentTimeMillis()` (e.g., **1203183068328** milliseconds).

2. Obtain the total seconds `totalSeconds` by dividing `totalMilliseconds` by **1000** (e.g., **1203183068328** milliseconds / **1000** = **1203183068** seconds).

3. Compute the current second from `totalSeconds % 60` (e.g., **1203183068** seconds % **60** = **8**, which is the current second).

4. Obtain the total minutes `totalMinutes` by dividing `totalSeconds` by **60** (e.g., **1203183068** seconds / **60** = **20053051** minutes).

5. Compute the current minute from `totalMinutes % 60` (e.g., **20053051** minutes % **60** = **31**, which is the current minute).

6. Obtain the total hours `totalHours` by dividing `totalMinutes` by **60** (e.g., **20053051** minutes / **60** = **334217** hours).

7. Compute the current hour from `totalHours % 24` (e.g., **334217** hours % **24** = **17**, which is the current hour).

Listing 3.6 gives the complete program.

LISTING 3.6 ShowCurrentTime.java

```
1  public class ShowCurrentTime {
2    public static void main(String[] args) {
3      // Obtain the total milliseconds since midnight, Jan 1, 1970
4      long totalMilliseconds = System.currentTimeMillis();
5
6      // Obtain the total seconds since midnight, Jan 1, 1970
7      long totalSeconds = totalMilliseconds / 1000;
8
9      // Compute the current second in the minute in the hour
10     long currentSecond = totalSeconds % 60;
11
12     // Obtain the total minutes
13     long totalMinutes = totalSeconds / 60;
14
15     // Compute the current minute in the hour
16     long currentMinute = totalMinutes % 60;
17
18     // Obtain the total hours
19     long totalHours = totalMinutes / 60;
20
21     // Compute the current hour
22     long currentHour = totalHours % 24;
23
24     // Display results
25     System.out.println("Current time is " + currentHour + ":"
26       + currentMinute + ":" + currentSecond + " GMT");
27   }
28 }
```

totalMilliseconds

totalSeconds

currentSecond

totalMinutes

currentMinute

totalHours

currentHour

preparing output

```
Current time is 17:31:8 GMT
```

Line 4 invokes `System.currentTimeMillis()` to obtain the current time in milliseconds as a `long` value. Thus, all the variables are declared as the long type in this program. The seconds, minutes, and hours are extracted from the current time using the / and % operators (lines 6–22).

Test the `ShowCurrentTime.java` program by comparing the anticipated results to the actual results. The following sample run shows the actual results. If the values between the anticipated and actual results differ, this indicates you may have an error in your code.

In the sample run, a single digit 8 is displayed for the second.

line# variables	4	7	10	13	16	19	22
totalMilliseconds	1203183068328						
totalSeconds		1203183068					
currentSecond			8				
totalMinutes				20053051			
currentMinute					31		
totalHours						334217	
currentHour							17

✓ Section 3.11 Assessment

1. How do you obtain the current second, minute, and hour?

3.12 Augmented Assignment Operators

*The operators +, -, *, /, and % can be combined with the assignment operator to form augmented operators.*

 Key Point

Very often the current value of a variable is used, modified, and then reassigned back to the same variable. For example, the following statement increases the variable **count** by 1:

```
count = count + 1;
```

Java allows you to combine assignment and addition operators using an augmented (or compound) assignment operator. For example, the preceding statement can be written as

```
count += 1;
```

The += is called the *addition assignment operator.* Table 3.4 shows other augmented assignment operators.

addition assignment operator

TABLE 3.4 Augmented Assignment Operators

Operator	Name	Example	Equivalent
+=	Addition assignment	i += 8	i = i + 8
-=	Subtraction assignment	i -= 8	i = i - 8
*=	Multiplication assignment	i *= 8	i = i * 8
/=	Division assignment	i /= 8	i = i / 8
%=	· Remainder assignment	i %= 8	i = i % 8

The augmented assignment operator is performed last after all the other operators in the expression are evaluated. For example,

```
x /= 4 + 5.5 * 1.5;
```

is same as

```
x = x / (4 + 5.5 * 1.5);
```

Caution
There are no spaces in the augmented assignment operators. For example, + = should be +=.

Note
Like the assignment operator (=), the operators (+=, -=, *=, /=, %=) can be used to form an assignment statement as well as an expression. For example, in the following code, x += 2 is a statement in the first line and an expression in the second line.
```
x += 2; // Statement
System.out.println(x += 2); // Expression
```

✓ SECTION 3.12 ASSESSMENT

1. Evaluate the following block of code and record the anticipated output. After recording the anticipated output, create a program by typing in the following code and run the program. Compare the actual results to the anticipated results. If the values are different, find and fix any errors, and re-run the program.

```
double a = 6.5;
a += a + 1;
System.out.println(a);
a = 6;
a /= 2;
System.out.println(a);
```

3.13 Increment and Decrement Operators

Key Point

The increment operator (++) and decrement operator (--) are for incrementing and decrementing a variable by 1.

increment operator (++)
decrement operator (--)

The ++ and -- are two shorthand operators for incrementing and decrementing a variable by 1. These are handy because that's often how much the value needs to be changed in many programming tasks. For example, the following code increments i by 1 and decrements j by 1.

```
int i = 3, j = 3;
i++; // i becomes 4
j--; // j becomes 2
```

postincrement
postdecrement

i++ is pronounced as i plus plus and i-- as i minus minus. These operators are known as *postfix increment* (or postincrement) and *postfix decrement* (or postdecrement), because the operators ++ and -- are placed after the variable. These operators can also be placed before the variable. For example,

```
int i = 3, j = 3;
++i;  // i becomes 4
--j; // j becomes 2
```

++i increments i by 1 and −−j decrements j by 1. These operators are known as *prefix increment* (or preincrement) and *prefix decrement* (or predecrement).

preincrement
predecrement

As you see, the effect of i++ and ++i or i−− and −−i are the same in the preceding examples. However, their effects are different when they are used in statements that do more than just increment and decrement. Table 3.5 describes their differences and gives examples.

TABLE 3.5 **Increment and Decrement Operators**

Operator	Name	Description	Example (assume i =1)
++var	preincrement	Increment var by 1, and use the new var value in the statement	`int j = ++i;` `// j is 2, i is 2`
var++	postincrement	Increment var by 1, but use the original var value in the statement	`int j = i++;` `// j is 1, i is 2`
−−var	predecrement	Decrement var by 1, and use the new var value in the statement	`int j = --i;` `// j is 0, i is 0`
var−−	postdecrement	Decrement var by 1, and use the original var value in the statement	`int j = i--;` `// j is 1, i is 0`

Here are additional examples to illustrate the differences between the prefix form of ++ (or −−) and the postfix form of ++ (or −−). Consider the following code:

```
int i = 10;
int newNum = 10 * i++;

System.out.print("i is " + i
  + ", newNum is " + newNum);
```

Same effect as →

```
int newNum = 10 * i;
i = i + 1;
```

```
i is 11, newNum is 100
```

In this case, i is incremented by 1, then the *old* value of i is used in the multiplication. So newNum becomes 100. If i++ is replaced by ++i as follows,

```
int i = 10;
int newNum = 10 * (++i);

System.out.print("i is " + i
  + ", newNum is " + newNum);
```

Same effect as →

```
i = i + 1;
int newNum = 10 * i;
```

```
i is 11, newNum is 110
```

i is incremented by 1, and the new value of i is used in the multiplication. Thus newNum becomes 110.

Here is another example:

```
double x = 1.0;
double y = 5.0;
double z = x-- + (++y);
```

After all three lines are executed, y becomes **6.0**, z becomes **7.0**, and x becomes **0.0**.

Tip
Using increment and decrement operators makes expressions short, but it also makes them complex and difficult to read. Avoid using these operators in expressions that modify multiple variables or the same variable multiple times, such as this one: `int k = ++i + i`.

✓ SECTION **3.13** ASSESSMENT

1. Which of these statements are true?

 a. Any expression can be used as a statement.

 b. The expression x++ can be used as a statement.

 c. The statement x = x + 5 is also an expression.

 d. The statement x = y = x = 0 is illegal.

2. Show the output of the following code:

```
int a = 6;
int b = a++;
System.out.println(a);
System.out.println(b);
a = 6;
b = ++a;
System.out.println(a);
System.out.println(b);
```

Key Point
3.14 Numeric Type Conversions

Floating-point numbers can be converted into integers using explicit casting.

Can you perform binary operations with two operands of different types? Yes. If an integer and a floating-point number are involved in a binary operation, Java automatically converts the integer to a floating-point value. So, 3 * 4.5 is the same as 3.0 * 4.5.

You can always assign a value to a numeric variable whose type supports a larger range of values; thus, for instance, you can assign a `long` value to a `float` variable. You cannot, however, assign a value to a variable of a type with a smaller range unless you use *type casting. Casting* is an operation that converts a value of one data type into a value of another data type. Casting a type with a small range to a type with a larger range is known as *widening a type.* Casting a type with a large range to a type with a smaller range is known as *narrowing a type.* Java will automatically widen a type, but you must narrow a type explicitly.

casting

widening a type

narrowing a type

The syntax for casting a type is to specify the target type in parentheses, followed by the variable's name or the value to be cast. For example, the following statement

```
System.out.println((int)1.7);
```

displays 1. When a `double` value is cast into an `int` value, the fractional part is truncated.

The following statement

```
System.out.println((double)1 / 2);
```

displays 0.5, because 1 is cast to 1.0 first, then 1.0 is divided by 2. However, the statement

```
System.out.println(1 / 2);
```

displays 0, because 1 and 2 are both integers and the resulting value should also be an integer.

Caution
Casting is necessary if you are assigning a value to a variable of a smaller type range, such as assigning a `double` value to an `int` variable. A compile error will occur if casting is not used in situations of this kind. However, be careful when using casting, as loss of information might lead to inaccurate results.

possible loss of precision

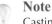
Note
Casting does not change the variable being cast. For example, `d` is not changed after casting in the following code:

```
double d = 4.5;
int i = (int)d;   // i becomes 4, but d is still 4.5
```

Note
In Java, an augmented expression of the form `x1 op= x2` is implemented as `x1 = (T)(x1 op x2)`, where T is the type for `x1`. Therefore, the following code is correct.

casting in an augmented expression

```
int sum = 0;
sum += 4.5; // sum becomes 4 after this statement
sum += 4.5 is equivalent to sum = (int)(sum + 4.5).
```

Note
To assign a variable of the `int` type to a variable of the `short` or `byte` type, explicit casting must be used. For example, the following statements have a compile error:

```
int i = 1;
byte b = i; // Error because explicit casting is required
```

However, so long as the integer literal is within the permissible range of the target variable, explicit casting is not needed to assign an integer literal to a variable of the `short` or `byte` type.

The program in Listing 3.7 displays the sales tax with two digits after the decimal point.

LISTING 3.7 SalesTax.java

```
1  import java.util.Scanner;
2
3  public class SalesTax {
4    public static void main(String[] args) {
5      Scanner input = new Scanner(System.in);
6
7      System.out.print("Enter purchase amount: ");
8      double purchaseAmount = input.nextDouble();
9
10     double tax = purchaseAmount * 0.06;
11     System.out.println("Sales tax is $" + (int)(tax * 100) / 100.0);
12   }
13 }
```

casting

```
Enter purchase amount: 197.55 ↵Enter
Sales tax is $11.85
```

line#	purchaseAmount	tax	output
8	197.55		
10		11.853	
11			11.85

formatting numbers

The variable **purchaseAmount** is **197.55** (line 8). The sales tax is **6%** of the purchase, so the **tax** is evaluated as **11.853** (line 10). Note that

```
tax * 100 is 1185.3
(int)(tax * 100) is 1185
(int)(tax * 100) / 100.0 is 11.85
```

So, the statement in line 11 displays the tax **11.85** with two digits after the decimal point.

✓ SECTION 3.14 ASSESSMENT

1. Can different types of numeric values be used together in a computation?

2. What does an explicit casting from a **double** to an **int** do with the fractional part of the **double** value? Does casting change the variable being cast?

3. Show the following output:
   ```
   float f = 12.5F;
   int i = (int)f;
   System.out.println("f is " + f);
   System.out.println("i is " + i);
   ```

4. If you change (int)(tax * 100) / 100.0 to (int)(tax * 100) / 100 in line 11 in Listing 3.7, what will be the output for the input purchase amount of **197.55**?

5. Show the output of the following code:

```java
double amount = 5;
System.out.println(amount / 2);
System.out.println(5 / 2);
```

3.15 Developing a Project Plan Using the Software Development Life Cycle Process

The software development life cycle is a multistage process that includes requirements specification, analysis, design, implementation, testing, deployment, and maintenance.

Key Point

software development life cycle

Developing a software product is an engineering process. Software products, no matter how large or how small, have the same life cycle: requirements specification, analysis, design, implementation, testing, deployment, and maintenance, as shown in Figure 3.3.

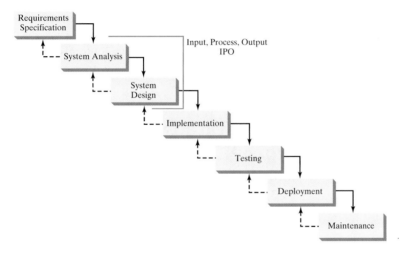

FIGURE 3.3 At any stage of the software development life cycle, it may be necessary to go back to a previous stage to correct errors or deal with other issues that might prevent the software from functioning as expected.

Requirements specification is the process of gathering data to identify the client and project requirements. It is a formal process that seeks to understand the problem that the software will address and to document in detail what the software system needs to do. This phase involves close interaction between users and developers. Most of the examples in this book are simple, and their requirements are clearly stated. In the real world, however, problems are not always well defined. Developers need to work closely with their customers (the individuals or organizations that will use the software) and study the problem carefully to identify what the software needs to do.

requirements specification

System analysis seeks to identify the data flow and input and output requirements. When you perform this analysis, it helps to identify what the output is first, and then figure out what input data you need in order to produce the output.

system analysis

input and output requirements

System design is the process of identifying the programming steps required to design the application. It involves using algorithms to describe the process for handling input, output, and identifies any issues you anticipate. Issues that you anticipate

system design

constraints

IPO
implementation

testing

deployment

maintenance

are called *constraints* and will be explored further in Chapter 5. This phase involves the use of many levels of abstraction to break down the problem into manageable components and design strategies for implementing each component. You can view each component as a subsystem that performs a specific function of the system. The essence of system analysis and design is input, process, and output (IPO).

Implementation involves translating the system design into programs. Separate programs are written for each component and then integrated to work together. This phase requires the use of a programming language such as Java. The implementation involves coding, self-testing, and debugging (that is, finding errors, called *bugs,* in the code).

Testing ensures that the code meets the requirements specification and weeds out bugs. Testing is generally an iterative process that is performed throughout the development of the project. In some cases, an independent team of software engineers not involved in the design and implementation of the product may conduct such testing.

Deployment makes the software available for use. Depending on the type of software, it may be installed on each user's machine or installed on a server accessible on the Internet.

Maintenance is concerned with updating and improving the product. A software product must continue to perform and improve in an ever-evolving environment. This requires periodic upgrades of the product to fix newly discovered bugs and incorporate changes.

3.16 Applying the Software Development Life Cycle Process

 Key Point

Applying a software development lifecyle process to your project helps maintain focus and clarity for project team members.

To see the software development process in action, we will now create a program that computes loan payments. The loan can be a car loan, a student loan, or a home mortgage loan. For an introductory programming course, we focus on requirements specification, analysis, design, implementation, and testing.

Stage 1: Requirements Specification— Identifying the Client and Project Needs
The program must satisfy the following requirements:

- It must let the user enter the interest rate, the loan amount, and the number of years for which payments will be made.

- It must compute and display the monthly payment and total payment amounts.

Stage 2: System Analysis—Identifying System Processing Requirements
The output is the monthly payment and total payment, which can be obtained using the following formulas:

So, the input needed for the program is the monthly interest rate, the length of the loan in years, and the loan amount.

Note

The requirements specification says that the user must enter the annual interest rate, the loan amount, and the number of years for which payments will be made. During analysis, however, it is possible that you may discover that input is not sufficient or that some values are unnecessary for the output. If this happens, you can go back and modify the requirements specification.

Note

In the real world, you will work with customers from all walks of life. You may develop software for chemists, physicists, engineers, economists, and psychologists, and of course you will not have (or need) complete knowledge of all these fields. Therefore, you don't have to know how formulas are derived, but given the monthly interest rate, the number of years, and the loan amount, you can compute the monthly payment in this program. You will, however, need to communicate with customers and understand how a mathematical model works for the system.

Stage 3: System Design—Identify the Software Process, Required Input/Output, and Possible Issues

During system design, you identify the steps in the program.

Step 1. Prompt the user to enter the annual interest rate, the number of years, and the loan amount.

(The interest rate is commonly expressed as a percentage of the principal for a period of one year. This is known as the *annual interest rate*.)

Step 2. The input for the annual interest rate is a number in percent format, such as 4.5%. The program needs to convert it into a decimal by dividing it by 100. To obtain the monthly interest rate from the annual interest rate, divide it by 12, since a year has 12 months. So, to obtain the monthly interest rate in decimal format, you need to divide the annual interest rate in percentage by 1200. For example, if the annual interest rate is 4.5%, then the monthly interest rate is 4.5/1200 = 0.00375.

Step 3. To avoid issues while performing calculations on numerical values, be sure to choose the most appropriate data type. Use *Casting* to help solve this issue. A limitation, or constraint of this application, is that the user must enter the values in the correct format.

Step 4. Compute the monthly payment using the preceding formula.

Step 5. Compute the total payment, which is the monthly payment multiplied by 12 and multiplied by the number of years.

Step 6. Display the monthly payment and total payment.

Stage 4: Implementation

Implementation is also known as *coding* (writing the code). In the formula, you have to compute $(1 + monthlyInterestRate)^{numberOfYears \times 12}$, which can be obtained using `Math.pow(1 + monthlyInterestRate, numberOfYears * 12)`.

Math.pow(a, b) method

Listing 3.8 gives the complete program.

LISTING 3.8 ComputeLoan.java

```java
 1  import java.util.Scanner;
 2
 3  public class ComputeLoan {
 4    public static void main(String[] args) {
 5      // Create a Scanner
 6      Scanner input = new Scanner(System.in);
 7
 8      // Enter annual interest rate in percentage, e.g., 7.25%
 9      System.out.print("Enter annual interest rate, e.g., 7.25%: ");
10      double annualInterestRate = input.nextDouble();
11
12      // Obtain monthly interest rate
13      double monthlyInterestRate = annualInterestRate / 1200;
14
15      // Enter number of years
16      System.out.print(
17        "Enter number of years as an integer, e.g., 5: ");
18      int numberOfYears = input.nextInt();
19
20      // Enter loan amount
21      System.out.print("Enter loan amount, e.g., 120000.95: ");
22      double loanAmount = input.nextDouble();
23
24      // Calculate payment
25      double monthlyPayment = loanAmount * monthlyInterestRate / (1
26        - 1 / Math.pow(1 + monthlyInterestRate, numberOfYears * 12));
27      double totalPayment = monthlyPayment * numberOfYears * 12;
28
29      // Display results
30      System.out.println("The monthly payment is $" +
31        (int)(monthlyPayment * 100) / 100.0);
32      System.out.println("The total payment is $" +
33        (int)(totalPayment * 100) / 100.0);
34    }
35  }
```

import class

create a Scanner

enter interest rate

enter years

enter loan amount

monthlyPayment

totalPayment

casting

casting

```
Enter annual interest rate, e.g., 5.75%: 5.75  ↵Enter
Enter number of years as an integer, e.g., 5: 15  ↵Enter
Enter loan amount, e.g., 120000.95: 250000  ↵Enter
The monthly payment is $2076.02
The total payment is $373684.53
```

Line 10 reads the annual interest rate, which is converted into the monthly interest rate in line 13.

Choose the most appropriate data type for the variable. For example, `numberOfYears` is best declared as an `int` (line 18), although it could be declared as a `long`, `float`, or `double`. Note that `byte` might be the most appropriate for `numberOfYears`. For simplicity, however, the examples in this book will use `int` for integer and `double` for floating-point values.

The formula for computing the monthly payment is translated into Java code in lines 25–27.

Casting is used in lines 31 and 33 to obtain a new `monthlyPayment` and `total-Payment` with two digits after the decimal points.

The program uses the `Scanner` class, imported in line 1. The program also uses the `Math` class, and you might be wondering why that class isn't imported into the program. The `Math` class is in the `java.lang` package, and all classes in the `java.lang` package are implicitly imported. Therefore, you don't need to explicitly import the `Math` class.

`java.lang` package

Stage 5: Testing—Assure Project Quality by Identifying Problems and Resolutions

Quality assurance is the process of monitoring a project to ensure the software design plan is followed and the expected results are achieved. Quality assurance reviews should occur throughout the project life cycle. Some of the techniques discussed in this chapter such as following a project plan, using standard coding practices, choosing standard and meaningful naming conventions, documenting your coding steps, and testing your code are all ways to maintain the quality of your project. Testing your application with some sample data and verifying the output is an important step in quality assurance.

quality assurance

✓ SECTION 3.16 ASSESSMENT

1. Explain the Software Development Life Cycle and identify the stages.
2. Explain the Quality Assurance process.
3. Create a quality assurance tracking table like the one that follows. Test and document the results of the **computeloan.java** example by filling in the results into the proper cell in the table.
 a. What is the value of *annualInterestRate* after line 10 is executed?
 b. What is the value of *monthlyInterestRate* after line 13 is executed?
 c. What is the value of *numberOfYears* after line 18 is executed?
 d. What is the value of *loanAmount* after line 22 is executed?
 e. What is the value of *monthlyPayment* after line 25 is executed?
 f. What is the value of totalPayment after line 27 is executed?

variables \ line#	10	13	18	22	25	27
annualInterestRate	_____					
monthlyInterestRate		_____				
numberOfYears			_____			
loanAmount				_____		
monthlyPayment					_____	
totalPayment						_____

3.17 Case Study: Counting Monetary Units

Key Point *This section presents a program that breaks a large amount of money into smaller units.*

Suppose you want to develop a program that changes a given amount of money into smaller monetary units. The program lets the user enter an amount as a `double` value representing a total in dollars and cents, and outputs a report listing the monetary equivalent in the maximum number of dollars, quarters, dimes, nickels, and pennies, in this order, to result in the minimum number of coins.

Here are the steps in developing the program:

1. Prompt the user to enter the amount as a decimal number, such as `11.56`.

2. Convert the amount (e.g., `11.56`) into cents (`1156`).

3. Divide the cents by `100` to find the number of dollars. Obtain the remaining cents using the cents remainder `100`.

4. Divide the remaining cents by `25` to find the number of quarters. Obtain the remaining cents using the remaining cents remainder `25`.

5. Divide the remaining cents by `10` to find the number of dimes. Obtain the remaining cents using the remaining cents remainder `10`.

6. Divide the remaining cents by `5` to find the number of nickels. Obtain the remaining cents using the remaining cents remainder `5`.

7. The remaining cents are the pennies.

8. Display the result.

The complete program is given in Listing 3.9.

LISTING 3.9 ComputeChange.java

```
1  import java.util.Scanner;                                              import class
2
3  public class ComputeChange {
4    public static void main(String[] args) {
5      // Create a Scanner
6      Scanner input = new Scanner(System.in);
7
8      // Receive the amount
9      System.out.print(
10        "Enter an amount in double, for example 11.56: ");
11      double amount = input.nextDouble();                              enter input
12
13      int remainingAmount = (int)(amount * 100);
14
15      // Find the number of one dollars
16      int numberOfOneDollars = remainingAmount / 100;                  dollars
17      remainingAmount = remainingAmount % 100;
18
19      // Find the number of quarters in the remaining amount
20      int numberOfQuarters = remainingAmount / 25;                     quarters
21      remainingAmount = remainingAmount % 25;
22
23      // Find the number of dimes in the remaining amount
24      int numberOfDimes = remainingAmount / 10;                        dimes
25      remainingAmount = remainingAmount % 10;
26
27      // Find the number of nickels in the remaining amount
28      int numberOfNickels = remainingAmount / 5;                       nickels
29      remainingAmount = remainingAmount % 5;
30
31      // Find the number of pennies in the remaining amount
32      int numberOfPennies = remainingAmount;                           pennies
33
34      // Display results
35      System.out.println("Your amount " + amount + " consists of");    output
36      System.out.println("    " + numberOfOneDollars + " dollars");
37      System.out.println("    " + numberOfQuarters + " quarters ");
38      System.out.println("    " + numberOfDimes + " dimes");
39      System.out.println("    " + numberOfNickels + " nickels");
40      System.out.println("    " + numberOfPennies + " pennies");
41    }
42  }
```

```
Enter an amount, for example, 11.56: 11.56 ↵Enter
Your amount 11.56 consists of
      11 dollars
      2 quarters
      0 dimes
      1 nickels
      1 pennies
```

line# variables	11	13	16	17	20	21	24	25	28	29	32
amount	11.56										
remainingAmount		1156		56		6		6		1	
numberOfOneDollars			11								
numberOfQuarters					2						
numberOfDimes							0				
numberOfNickels									1		
numberOfPennies											1

The variable `amount` stores the amount entered from the console (line 11). This variable is not changed, because the amount has to be used at the end of the program to display the results. The program introduces the variable `remainingAmount` (line 13) to store the changing remaining amount.

The variable `amount` is a `double` decimal representing dollars and cents. It is converted to an `int` variable `remainingAmount`, which represents all the cents. For instance, if `amount` is `11.56`, then the initial `remainingAmount` is `1156`. The division operator yields the integer part of the division, so `1156 / 100` is `11`. The remainder operator obtains the remainder of the division, so `1156 % 100` is `56`.

The program extracts the maximum number of singles from the remaining amount and obtains a new remaining amount in the variable `remainingAmount` (lines 16–17). It then extracts the maximum number of quarters from `remainingAmount` and obtains a new `remainingAmount` (lines 20–21). Continuing the same process, the program finds the maximum number of dimes, nickels, and pennies in the remaining amount.

loss of precision

One serious problem with this example is the possible loss of precision when casting a `double` amount to an `int remainingAmount`. This could lead to an inaccurate result. If you try to enter the amount `10.03`, `10.03 * 100` becomes `1002.999999999999`. You will find that the program displays `10` dollars and `2` pennies. To fix the problem, enter the amount as an integer value representing cents. As an example, `10.03` is represented as `1003` cents.

✓ Section 3.17 Assessment

1. Show the output with the input value `1.99`.

3.18 Testing Your Program for Common Errors and Pitfalls

When you are testing your application, you should start by looking for common errors. Common errors are often caused by undeclared variables, uninitialized variables, integer overflow, unintended integer division, and round-off errors.

Key
Point

Common Error 1: Undeclared/Uninitialized Variables and Unused Variables

A variable must be declared with a type and assigned a value before using it. A common error is not declaring a variable or initializing a variable. Consider the following code:

```
double interestRate = 0.05;
double interest = interestrate * 45;
```

This code is wrong, because `interestRate` is assigned a value `0.05`; but `interestrate` has not been declared and initialized. Java is case sensitive, so it considers `interestRate` and `interestrate` to be two different variables.

If a variable is declared, but not used in the program, it might be a potential programming error. So, you should remove the unused variable from your program. For example, in the following code, `taxRate` is never used. It should be removed from the code.

```
double interestRate = 0.05;
double taxRate = 0.05;
double interest = interestRate * 45;
System.out.println("Interest is " + interest);
```

If you use an IDE such as Eclipse and NetBeans, you will receive a warning on unused variables.

Common Error 2: Integer Overflow

Numbers are stored with a limited numbers of digits. When a variable is assigned a value that is too large (*in size*) to be stored, it causes *overflow*. For example, executing the following statement causes overflow, because the largest value that can be stored in a variable of the `int` type is `2147483647`. `2147483648` will be too large for an `int` value.

what is overflow?

```
int value = 2147483647 + 1;
// value will actually be -2147483648
```

Likewise, executing the following statement causes overflow, because the smallest value that can be stored in a variable of the `int` type is `-2147483648`. `-2147483649` is too large in size to be stored in an `int` variable.

```
int value = -2147483648 - 1;
// value will actually be 2147483647
```

Java does not report warnings or errors on overflow, so be careful when working with numbers close to the maximum or minimum range of a given type.

what is underflow?

When a floating-point number is too small (i.e., too close to zero) to be stored, it causes *underflow*. Java approximates it to zero, so normally you don't need to be concerned about underflow.

Common Error 3: Round-off Errors

round-off error

A *round-off error*, also called a *rounding error*, is the difference between the calculated approximation of a number and its exact mathematical value. For example, 1/3 is approximately 0.333 if you keep three decimal places, and is 0.3333333 if you keep seven decimal places. Since the number of digits that can be stored in a variable is limited, round-off errors are inevitable. Calculations involving floating-point numbers are approximated because these numbers are not stored with complete accuracy. For example,

```
System.out.println(1.0 - 0.1 - 0.1 - 0.1 - 0.1 - 0.1);
```

displays `0.5000000000000001`, not `0.5`, and

```
System.out.println(1.0 - 0.9);
```

displays `0.09999999999999998`, not `0.1`. Integers are stored precisely. Therefore, calculations with integers yield a precise integer result.

Common Error 4: Unintended Integer Division

Java uses the same divide operator, namely /, to perform both integer and floating-point division. When two operands are integers, the / operator performs an integer division. The result of the operation is an integer. The fractional part is truncated. To force two integers to perform a floating-point division, make one of the integers into a floating-point number. For example, the code in (a) displays that average is `1` and the code in (b) displays that average is `1.5`.

```
int number1 = 1;
int number2 = 2;
double average = (number1 + number2) / 2;
System.out.println(average);
```

(a)

```
int number1 = 1;
int number2 = 2;
double average = (number1 + number2) / 2.0;
System.out.println(average);
```

(b)

Common Pitfall 1: Redundant Input Objects

New programmers often write the code to create multiple input objects for each input. For example, the following code reads an integer and a double value.

```
Scanner input = new Scanner(System.in);
System.out.print("Enter an integer: ");
int v1 = input.nextInt();
```

```
Scanner input1 = new Scanner(System.in);      BAD CODE
System.out.print("Enter a double value: ");
double v2 = input1.nextDouble();
```

The code is not wrong, but inefficient. It creates two input objects unnecessarily and may lead to some subtle errors. You should rewrite the code as follows:

```
Scanner input = new Scanner(System.in);
System.out.print("Enter an integer: ");
int v1 = input.nextInt();
System.out.print("Enter a double value: ");
double v2 = input.nextDouble();
```

GOOD CODE

✓ SECTION 3.18 ASSESSMENT

1. Can you declare a variable as `int` and later redeclare it as `double`?

2. What is an integer overflow? Can floating-point operations cause overflow?

3. Will overflow cause a runtime error?

4. What is a round-off error? Can integer operations cause round-off errors? Can floating-point operations cause round-off errors?

Chapter 3 — Review and Assessment

KEY TERMS

algorithm 52
assignment operator (=) 61
assignment statement 61
byte type 65
casting 74
constant 63
data type 53
declare variables 53
decrement operator (--) 72
double type 65
expression 61
final keyword 63
float type 65
floating-point number 53
identifier 59
increment operator (++) 72
initialize variables 60
int type 65
integer overflow 85
IPO 58

long type 65
operators 66
postdecrement 72
postincrement 72
predecrement 72
preincrement 72
primitive data type 53
pseudocode 52
quality assurance 81
requirements specification 77
round-off error 86
short type 65
software development lifecycle 77
specific import 57
system analysis 77
system design 77
tracing program 54
UNIX epoch 69
variable 53
wildcard import 57

CHAPTER SUMMARY

1. *Identifiers* are names for naming elements such as variables, constants, methods, classes, packages in a program.

2. An identifier is a sequence of characters that consists of letters, digits, underscores (_), and dollar signs ($). An identifier must start with a letter or an underscore. It cannot start with a digit. An identifier cannot be a reserved word. An identifier can be of any length.

3. *Variables* are used to store data in a program. To declare a variable is to tell the compiler what type of data a variable can hold.

4. There are two types of import statements: *specific import* and *wildcard import*. The specific import specifies a single class in the import statement; the wildcard import imports all the classes in a package.

5. In Java, the equal sign (=) is used as the *assignment operator*.

6. A variable declared in a method must be assigned a value before it can be used.

7. A *named constant* (or simply a *constant*) represents permanent data that never changes.

8. A named constant is declared by using the keyword `final`.

9. Java provides four integer types (`byte`, `short`, `int`, and `long`) that represent integers of four different sizes.

10. Java provides two *floating-point types* (`float` and `double`) that represent floating-point numbers of two different precisions.

11. Java provides *operators* that perform numeric operations: + (addition), – (subtraction), * (multiplication), / (division), and % (remainder).

12. Integer arithmetic (/) yields an integer result.

13. The numeric operators in a Java expression are applied the same way as in an arithmetic expression.

14. Java provides the augmented assignment operators += (addition assignment), –= (subtraction assignment), *= (multiplication assignment), /= (division assignment), and %= (remainder assignment).

15. The *increment operator* (++) and the *decrement operator* (– –) increment or decrement a variable by 1.

16. When evaluating an expression with values of mixed types, Java automatically converts the operands to appropriate types.

17. You can explicitly convert a value from one type to another using the `(type)value` notation.

18. *Casting* a variable of a type with a small range to a variable of a type with a larger range is known as *widening a type.*

19. Casting a variable of a type with a large range to a variable of a type with a smaller range is known as *narrowing a type.*

20. Widening a type can be performed automatically without explicit casting. Narrowing a type must be performed explicitly.

21. In computer science, midnight of January 1, 1970, is known as the *UNIX epoch.*

22. *Quality assurance* is the process of monitoring a project throughout the software life-cycle process. Following standard coding practices and thoroughly testing the output of your project helps maintain quality. *Tracing* can be used to compare actual output with expected output.

PROGRAMMING EXERCISES

learn from examples

 Debugging TIP
The compiler usually gives a reason for a syntax error. If you don't know how to correct it, compare your program closely, character by character, with similar examples in the text.

document analysis and design

 Pedagogical Note
Your instructor may ask you to document your analysis and design for selected exercises. Use your own words to analyze the problem, including the input, output, and what needs to be computed, and describe how to solve the problem in pseudocode.

1. (*Convert Celsius to Fahrenheit*) Write a program that reads a Celsius degree in a **double** value from the console, then converts it to Fahrenheit and displays the result. The formula for the conversion is as follows:

fahrenheit = (9 / 5) * celsius + 32

Hint: In Java, 9 / 5 is 1, but 9.0 / 5 is 1.8.

Here is a sample run:

```
Enter a degree in Celsius: 43 ↵Enter
43 Celsius is 109.4 Fahrenheit
```

2. (*Compute the volume of a cylinder*) Write a program that reads in the radius and length of a cylinder and computes the area and volume using the following formulas:

area = radius * radius * π
volume = area * length

Here is a sample run:

```
Enter the radius and length of a cylinder: 5.5 12 ↵Enter
The area is 95.0331
The volume is 1140.4
```

3. (*Convert feet into meters*) Write a program that reads a number in feet, converts it to meters, and displays the result. One foot is 0.305 meter. Here is a sample run:

```
Enter a value for feet: 16.5 ↵Enter
16.5 feet is 5.0325 meters
```

4. (*Convert pounds into kilograms*) Write a program that converts pounds into kilograms. The program prompts the user to enter a number in pounds, converts it to kilograms, and displays the result. One pound is `0.454` kilograms. Here is a sample run:

```
Enter a number in pounds: 55.5 ↵Enter
55.5 pounds is 25.197 kilograms
```

5. (*Financial application: calculate tips*) Write a program that reads the subtotal and the gratuity rate, then computes the gratuity and total. For example, if the user enters `10` for subtotal and `15%` for gratuity rate, the program displays `$1.5` as gratuity and `$11.5` as total. Here is a sample run:

```
Enter the subtotal and a gratuity rate: 10 15 ↵Enter
The gratuity is $1.5 and total is $11.5
```

6. (*Physics: acceleration*) Average acceleration is defined as the change of velocity divided by the time taken to make the change, as shown in the following formula:

$$a = \frac{v_1 - v_0}{t}$$

Write a program that prompts the user to enter the starting velocity v_0 in meters/second, the ending velocity v_1 in meters/second, and the time span t in seconds, and displays the average acceleration. Here is a sample run:

```
Enter v0, v1, and t: 5.5 50.9 4.5 ↵Enter
The average acceleration is 10.0889
```

7. (*Science: calculating energy*) Write a program that calculates the energy needed to heat water from an initial temperature to a final temperature. Your program should prompt the user to enter the amount of water in kilograms and the initial and final temperatures of the water. The formula to compute the energy is

```
Q = M * (finalTemperature - initialTemperature) * 4184
```

where `M` is the weight of water in kilograms, temperatures are in degrees Celsius, and energy `Q` is measured in joules. Here is a sample run:

```
Enter the amount of water in kilograms: 55.5 ↵Enter
Enter the initial temperature: 3.5 ↵Enter
Enter the final temperature: 10.5 ↵Enter
The energy needed is 1625484.0
```

8. (*Physics: finding runway length*) Given an airplane's acceleration *a* and take-off speed *v*, you can compute the minimum runway length needed for an airplane to take off using the following formula:

$$\text{length} = \frac{v^2}{2a}$$

Write a program that prompts the user to enter *v* in meters/second (m/s) and the acceleration *a* in meters/second squared and displays the minimum runway length. Here is a sample run:

```
Enter speed and acceleration: 60 3.5  ↵Enter
The minimum runway length for this airplane is 514.286
```

CHAPTER
4

USING SELECTION STATEMENTS

Objectives

- Solve problems using structured coding.

- Declare `Boolean` variables and write Boolean expressions using relational operators.

- Design a flowchart to illustrate the logical design of an application.

- Implement selection control using one-way `if` statements.

- Implement selection control using two-way `if-else` statements.

- Implement selection control using nested `if` and multi-way `if` statements.

- Identify common errors and issues when writing `if` statements.

- Generate random numbers using the `Math.random()` method.

- Combine conditions using logical operators (`!`, `&&`, `||`, and `∧`).

- Program using selection statements with combined conditions (`LeapYear`, `Lottery`).

- Implement selection control using `switch` statements.

- Write expressions using the conditional expression.

- Examine the rules governing operator precedence and associativity.

- Apply common techniques to debug errors.

4.1 Introduction

Key Point

The program can decide which statements to execute based on a condition. Selection statements help create structured logical coding to solve problems. Selection statements are sometimes referred to as conditional structures.

problem
conditional structures

selection statements

If you enter a negative value for `radius` in Listing 3.2, ComputeAreaWithConsole-Input.java, the program displays an invalid result. If the radius is negative, you don't want the program to compute the area. How can you deal with this situation?

Like all high-level programming languages, Java provides *selection statements*: statements that let you choose actions with alternative courses. You can use the following selection statement to replace lines 12–17 in Listing 3.2:

```java
if (radius < 0) {
  System.out.println("Incorrect input");
}
else {
  area = radius * radius * 3.14159;
  System.out.println("Area is " + area);
}
```

Boolean expression
Boolean value

Selection statements use conditions that are Boolean expressions. A *Boolean expression* is an expression that evaluates to a *Boolean value*: `true` or `false`. We now introduce Boolean types and relational operators.

4.2 boolean Data Type

Key Point

The boolean data type declares a variable with the value either `true` or `false`.

`boolean` data type
relational operators

How do you compare two values, such as whether a radius is greater than 0, equal to 0, or less than 0? Java provides six *relational operators* (also known as *comparison operators*), shown in Table 4.1, which can be used to compare two values (assume radius is 5 in the table).

TABLE 4.1 Relational Operators

Java Operator	Mathematics Symbol	Name	Example (radius is 5)	Result
<	<	less than	`radius < 0`	`false`
<=	≤	less than or equal to	`radius <= 0`	`false`
>	>	greater than	`radius > 0`	`true`
>=	≥	greater than or equal to	`radius >= 0`	`true`
==	=	equal to	`radius == 0`	`false`
!=	≠	not equal to	`radius != 0`	`true`

`==` vs. `=`

Caution
The equality testing operator is two equal signs (==), not a single equal sign (=). The latter symbol is for assignment.

The result of the comparison is a Boolean value: `true` or `false`. For example, the following statement displays `true`:

```
double radius = 1;
System.out.println(radius > 0);
```

A variable that holds a Boolean value is known as a *Boolean variable*. The `boolean` data type is used to declare Boolean variables. A `boolean` variable can hold one of the two values: `true` or `false`. For example, the following statement assigns `true` to the variable `lightsOn`:

Boolean variable

```
boolean lightsOn = true;
```

`true` and `false` are treated as reserved words and cannot be used as identifiers in the program.

Suppose you want to develop a program to let a first-grader practice addition. The program randomly generates two single-digit integers, `number1` and `number2`, and displays to the student a question such as "What is 1 + 7?," as shown in the sample run in Listing 4.1. After the student types the answer, the program displays a message to indicate whether it is true or false.

Program addition quiz

There are several ways to generate random numbers. For now, generate the first integer using `System.currentTimeMillis() % 10` and the second using `System.currentTimeMillis() / 7 % 10`. Listing 4.1 gives the program. Lines 5–6 generate two numbers, `number1` and `number2`. Line 14 obtains an answer from the user. The answer is graded in line 18 using a Boolean expression `number1 + number2 == answer`.

LISTING 4.1 AdditionQuiz.java

```
1  import java.util.Scanner;
2
3  public class AdditionQuiz {
4    public static void main(String[] args) {
5      int number1 = (int)(System.currentTimeMillis() % 10);
6      int number2 = (int)(System.currentTimeMillis() / 7 % 10);
7
8      // Create a Scanner
9      Scanner input = new Scanner(System.in);
10
11     System.out.print(
12       "What is " + number1 + " + " + number2 + "? ");
13
14     int answer = input.nextInt();
15
16     System.out.println(
17       number1 + " + " + number2 + " = " + answer + " is " +
18       (number1 + number2 == answer));
19   }
20 }
```

generate number 1
generate number 2

show question

display result

```
What is 1 + 7? 8 ↵Enter
1 + 7 = 8 is true
```

```
What is 4 + 8? 9 [↵ Enter]
4 + 8 = 9 is false
```

line#	number1	number2	answer	output
5	4			
6		8		
14			9	
16				4 + 8 = 9 is false

✓ SECTION 4.2 ASSESSMENT

1. List six relational operators.

2. Assuming that `x is 1`, show the result of the following Boolean expressions:

    ```
    (x > 0)
    (x < 0)
    (x != 0)
    (x >= 0)
    (x != 1)
    ```

3. Can the following conversions involving casting be allowed? Write a test program to verify your answer.

    ```
    boolean b = true;
    i = (int)b;

    int i = 1;
    boolean b = (boolean)i;
    ```

4.3 if Statements

An if statement is a construct that enables a program to specify alternative paths of execution. Flowcharts are often used when designing if statements. A flowchart is a tool used to create the logical steps of an application.

Key Point

The preceding program displays a message such as "6 + 2 = 7 is false." If you wish the message to be "6 + 2 = 7 is incorrect," you have to use a selection statement to make this minor change.

why if statement?

Java has several types of selection statements: one-way `if` statements, two-way `if-else` statements, nested `if` statements, multi-way `if-else` statements, `switch` statements, and conditional expressions.

A one-way `if` statement executes an action if and only if the condition is `true`. The syntax for a one-way `if` statement is:

if statement

```
if (boolean-expression) {
   statement(s);
}
```

The flowchart in Figure 4.1a illustrates how Java executes the syntax of an `if` statement. A *flowchart* is a diagram that describes an algorithm or process, showing the steps as boxes of various kinds, and their order by connecting these with arrows. Process operations are represented in these boxes, and arrows connecting them represent the flow of control. A diamond box denotes a Boolean condition and a rectangle box represents statements.

flowchart

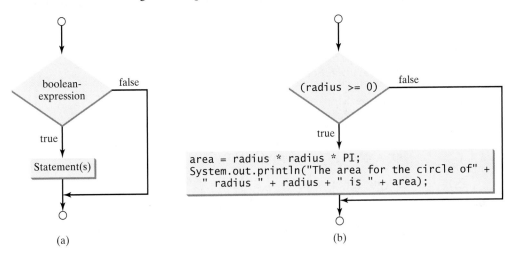

(a) (b)

FIGURE 4.1 An `if` statement executes statements if the `boolean-expression` evaluates to `true`.

If the `boolean-expression` evaluates to `true`, the statements in the block are executed. As an example, see the following code:

```java
if (radius >= 0) {
  area = radius * radius * PI;
  System.out.println("The area for the circle of radius " +
    radius + " is " + area);
}
```

The flowchart of the preceding statement is shown in Figure 4.1b. If the value of `radius` is greater than or equal to `0`, then the `area` is computed and the result is displayed; otherwise, the two statements in the block will not be executed.

The `boolean-expression` is enclosed in parentheses. For example, the code in (a) is wrong. It should be corrected, as shown in (b).

```java
if i > 0 {
  System.out.println("i is positive");
}
```
(a) Wrong

```java
if (i > 0) {
  System.out.println("i is positive");
}
```
(b) Correct

The block braces can be omitted if they enclose a single statement. For example, the following statements are equivalent.

```java
if (i > 0) {
  System.out.println("i is positive");
}
```
(a)

Equivalent

```java
if (i > 0)
  System.out.println("i is positive");
```
(b)

Omitting braces or not

 Note

Omitting braces makes the code shorter, but it is prone to errors. It is a common mistake to forget the braces when you go back to modify the code that omits the braces.

Listing 4.2 gives a program that prompts the user to enter an integer. If the number is a multiple of **5**, the program displays **HiFive**. If the number is divisible by **2**, it displays **HiEven**.

LISTING 4.2 SimpleIfDemo.java

enter input

check 5

check even

```
1  import java.util.Scanner;
2
3  public class SimpleIfDemo {
4    public static void main(String[] args) {
5      Scanner input = new Scanner(System.in);
6      System.out.println("Enter an integer: ");
7      int number = input.nextInt();
8
9      if (number % 5 == 0)
10       System.out.println("HiFive");
11
12     if (number % 2 == 0)
13       System.out.println("HiEven");
14   }
15 }
```

```
Enter an integer:    4  ↵Enter
HiEven
```

```
Enter an integer:    30  ↵Enter
HiFive
HiEven
```

The program prompts the user to enter an integer (lines 6–7) and displays **HiFive** if it is divisible by **5** (lines 9–10) and **HiEven** if it is divisible by **2** (lines 12–13).

✓ SECTION 4.3 ASSESSMENT

1. Write an **if** statement that assigns **1** to **x** if **y** is greater than **0**. Draw a flowchart of the code.

2. Write an **if** statement that increases pay by 3% if **score** is greater than **90**. Draw a flowchart of the code.

4.4 Two-Way `if-else` Statements

An `if-else` statement decides the execution path based on whether the condition is true or false.

A one-way `if` statement performs an action if the specified condition is `true`. If the condition is `false`, nothing is done. But what if you want to take alternative actions when the condition is `false`? You can use a two-way `if-else` statement. The actions that a two-way `if-else` statement specifies differ based on whether the condition is `true` or `false`.

Here is the syntax for a two-way `if-else` statement:

```
if (boolean-expression) {
   statement(s)-for-the-true-case;
}
else {
   statement(s)-for-the-false-case;
}
```

The flowchart of the statement is shown in Figure 4.2.

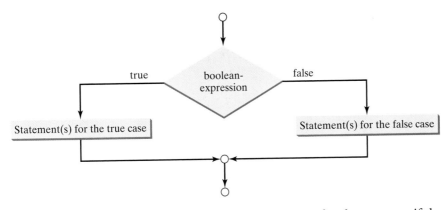

FIGURE 4.2 An `if-else` statement executes statements for the true case if the `Boolean-expression` evaluates to `true`; otherwise, statements for the false case are executed.

If the `boolean-expression` evaluates to `true`, the statement(s) for the true case are executed; otherwise, the statement(s) for the false case are executed. For example, consider the following code:

```
if (radius >= 0) {
   area = radius * radius * PI;
   System.out.println("The area for the circle of radius " +
     radius + " is " + area);
}
else {
   System.out.println("Negative input");
}
```

two-way `if-else` statement

If `radius >= 0` is `true`, `area` is computed and displayed; if it is `false`, the message `"Negative input"` is displayed.

As usual, the braces can be omitted if there is only one statement within them. The braces enclosing the `System.out.println("Negative input")` statement can therefore be omitted in the preceding example.

Here is another example of using the `if-else` statement. The example checks whether a number is even or odd, as follows:

```
if (number % 2 == 0)
   System.out.println(number + " is even.");
else
   System.out.println(number + " is odd.");
```

✓ SECTION 4.4 ASSESSMENT

1. Write an `if` statement that increases **pay** by 3% if **score** is greater than 90, otherwise increases **pay** by 1%.

2. What is the output of the code in (a) and (b) if **number** is 30? What if **number** is 35?

```
if (number % 2 == 0)
   System.out.println(number + " is even.");

System.out.println(number + " is odd.");
```
(a)

```
if (number % 2 == 0)
   System.out.println(number + " is even.");
else
   System.out.println(number + " is odd.");
```
(b)

4.5 Nested `if` and Multi-Way `if-else` Statements

Key Point

An `if` statement can be inside another `if` statement to form a nested `if` statement.

The statement in an `if` or `if-else` statement can be any legal Java statement, including another `if` or `if-else` statement. The inner `if` statement is said to be *nested* inside the outer `if` statement. The inner `if` statement can contain another `if` statement; in fact, there is no limit to the depth of the nesting. For example, the following is a nested `if` statement:

nested `if` statement

```
if (i > k) {
  if (j > k)
     System.out.println("i and j are greater than k");
}
else
   System.out.println("i is less than or equal to k");
```

The `if (j > k)` statement is nested inside the `if (i > k)` statement.

The nested `if` statement can be used to implement multiple alternatives. The statement given in Figure 4.3a, for instance, prints a letter grade according to the score, with multiple alternatives.

```
if (score >= 90.0)
  System.out.print("A");
else
  if (score >= 80.0)
    System.out.print("B");
  else
    if (score >= 70.0)
      System.out.print("C");
    else
      if (score >= 60.0)
        System.out.print("D");
      else
        System.out.print("F");
```
(a)

Equivalent

This is better

```
if (score >= 90.0)
  System.out.print("A");
else if (score >= 80.0)
  System.out.print("B");
else if (score >= 70.0)
  System.out.print("C");
else if (score >= 60.0)
  System.out.print("D");
else
  System.out.print("F");
```
(b)

FIGURE 4.3 A preferred format for multiple alternatives is shown in (b) using a multi-way if-else statement.

The execution of this if statement proceeds as shown in Figure 4.4. The first condition (score >= 90.0) is tested. If it is true, the grade is A. If it is false, the second condition (score >= 80.0) is tested. If the second condition is true, the grade is B. If that condition is false, the third condition and the rest of the conditions (if necessary) are tested until a condition is met or all of the conditions prove to be false. If all of the conditions are false, the grade is F. Note that a condition is tested only when all of the conditions that come before it are false.

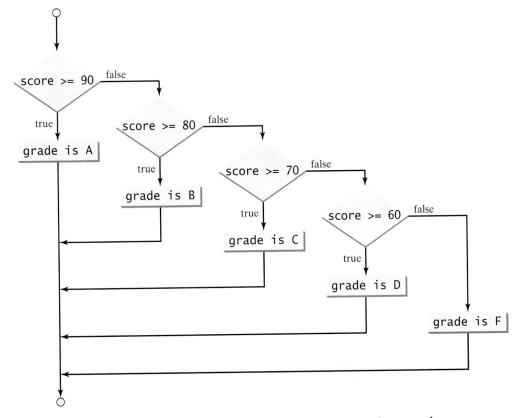

FIGURE 4.4 You can use a multi-way if-else statement to assign a grade.

The `if` statement in Figure 4.3a is equivalent to the `if` statement in Figure 4.3b. In fact, Figure 4.3b is the preferred coding style for multiple alternative `if` statements. This style, called *multi-way* `if-else` *statements*, avoids deep indentation and makes the program easy to read.

multi-way `if` statement

✓ Section 4.5 Assessment

1. Suppose x = 3 and y = 2; show the output, if any, of the following code. What is the output if x = 3 and y = 4? What is the output if x = 2 and y = 2? Draw a flowchart of the code.

```
if (x > 2) {
  if (y > 2) {
    z = x + y;
    System.out.println("z is " + z);
  }
}
else
  System.out.println("x is " + x);
```

2. Suppose x = 2 and y = 3. Show the output, if any, of the following code. What is the output if x = 3 and y = 2? What is the output if x = 3 and y = 3?

```
if (x > 2)
  if (y > 2) {
    int z = x + y;
    System.out.println("z is " + z);
  }
else
  System.out.println("x is " + x);
```

3. What is wrong in the following code?

```
if (score >= 60.0)
  System.out.println("D");
else if (score >= 70.0)
  System.out.println("C");
else if (score >= 80.0)
  System.out.println("B");
else if (score >= 90.0)
  System.out.println("A");
else
  System.out.println("F");
```

4.6 Identifying Common Software Development Issues and Errors

Key Point

Forgetting necessary braces, ending an `if` *statement in the wrong place, mistaking* `==` *for* `=`, *and dangling* `else` *clauses are common errors in selection statements. Duplicated statements in* `if-else` *statements and testing equality of double values are common mistakes that cause errors.*

The following errors and pitfalls are common among new programmers:

COMMON ERROR 1: **Forgetting Necessary Braces**

The braces can be omitted if the block contains a single statement. However, forgetting the braces when they are needed for grouping multiple statements is a common programming error. If you modify the code by adding new statements in an `if` statement without braces, you will have to insert the braces. For example, the following code in (a) is wrong. It should be written with braces to group multiple statements, as shown in (b).

```
if (radius >= 0)
  area = radius * radius * PI;
  System.out.println("The area "
    + " is " + area);
```
(a) Wrong

```
if (radius >= 0) {
  area = radius * radius * PI;
  System.out.println("The area "
    + " is " + area);
}
```
(b) Correct

COMMON ERROR 2: **Wrong Semicolon at the `if` Line**

Adding a semicolon at the end of an `if` line, as shown in (a) below, is a common mistake.

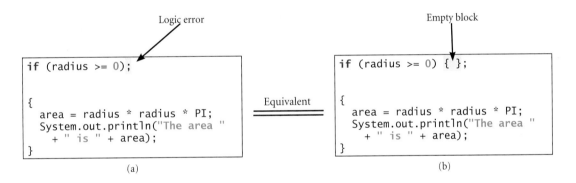

Logic error

```
if (radius >= 0);

{
  area = radius * radius * PI;
  System.out.println("The area "
    + " is " + area);
}
```
(a)

Equivalent

Empty block

```
if (radius >= 0) { };

{
  area = radius * radius * PI;
  System.out.println("The area "
    + " is " + area);
}
```
(b)

This mistake is hard to find, because it is neither a compile error nor a runtime error; it is a logic error. The code in (a) is equivalent to that in (b) with an empty block.

This error often occurs when you use the next-line block style. Using the end-of-line block style can help prevent this error.

COMMON ERROR 3: **Redundant Testing of Boolean Values**

To test whether a `boolean` variable is `true` or `false` in a test condition, it is redundant to use the equality testing operator like the code in (a):

```
if (even == true)
  System.out.println(
    "It is even.");
```
(a)

Equivalent

This is better

```
if (even)
  System.out.println(
    "It is even.");
```
(b)

Instead, it is better to test the `boolean` variable directly, as shown in (b). Another good reason for doing this is to avoid errors that are difficult to detect. Using the `=` operator instead of the `==` operator to compare the equality of two items in a test condition is a common error.

It could lead to the following erroneous statement:

```
if (even = true)
    System.out.println("It is even.");
```

This statement does not have compile errors. It assigns `true` to `even`, so that `even` is always `true`.

COMMON ERROR 4: Dangling `else` Ambiguity

dangling else ambiguity

The code in (a) below has two `if` clauses and one `else` clause. Which `if` clause is matched by the `else` clause? The indentation indicates that the `else` clause matches the first `if` clause. However, the `else` clause actually matches the second `if` clause. This situation is known as the *dangling else ambiguity*. The `else` clause always matches the most recent unmatched `if` clause in the same block. So, the statement in (a) is equivalent to the code in (b).

```
int i = 1, j = 2, k = 3;

if (i > j)
  if (i > k)
    System.out.println("A");
else
    System.out.println("B");
```
(a)

Equivalent — This is better with correct indentation

```
int i = 1, j = 2, k = 3;

if (i > j)
  if (i > k)
    System.out.println("A");
  else
    System.out.println("B");
```
(b)

Since `(i > j)` is false, nothing is displayed from the statements in (a) and (b). To force the `else` clause to match the first `if` clause, you must add a pair of braces:

```
int i = 1, j = 2, k = 3;

if (i > j) {
  if (i > k)
    System.out.println("A");
}
else
  System.out.println("B");
```

This statement displays `B`.

COMMON ERROR 5: Equality Test of Two Floating-Point Values

As discussed in Common Error 3 in Section 3.18, floating-point numbers have a limited precision and calculations; involving floating-point numbers can introduce round-off errors. So, equality test of two floating-point values is not reliable. For example, you expect the following code to display `true`, but surprisingly it displays `false`.

```
double x = 1.0 - 0.1 - 0.1 - 0.1 - 0.1 - 0.1;
System.out.println(x == 0.5);
```

Here, x is not exactly 0.5, but is 0.5000000000000001. You cannot reliably test equality of two floating-point values. However, you can compare whether they are close enough by testing whether the difference of the two numbers is less than some threshold. That is, two numbers x and y are very close if $|x-y| < \epsilon$ for a very small value, ϵ. ϵ, a Greek letter pronounced epsilon, is commonly used to denote a very small value. Normally, you set ϵ to 10^{-14} for comparing two values of the double type and to 10^{-7} for comparing two values of the float type. For example, the following code

```
final double EPSILON = 1E-14;
double x = 1.0 - 0.1 - 0.1 - 0.1 - 0.1 - 0.1;
if (Math.abs(x - 0.5) < EPSILON)
  System.out.println(x + " is approximately 0.5");
```

will display that

```
0.5000000000000001 is approximately 0.5
```

The `Math.abs(a)` method can be used to return the absolute value of `a`.

COMMON PITFALL 1: Simplifying Boolean Variable Assignment

Often, new programmers write the code that assigns a test condition to a boolean variable like the code in (a):

This is not an error, but it should be better written as shown in (b).

COMMON PITFALL 2: Avoiding Duplicate Code in Different Cases

Often, new programmers write the duplicate code in different cases that should be combined in one place. For example, the highlighted code in the following statement is duplicated.

```
if (inState) {
  tuition = 5000;
  System.out.println("The tuition is " + tuition);
}
else {
  tuition = 15000;
  System.out.println("The tuition is " + tuition);
}
```

This is not an error, but it should be better written as follows:

```
if (inState) {
  tuition = 5000;
}
else {
  tuition = 15000;
}
System.out.println("The tuition is " + tuition);
```

The new code removes the duplication and makes the code easy to maintain, because you only need to change in one place if the print statement is modified.

✓ SECTION 4.6 ASSESSMENT

1. Which of the following statements correctly indents code to add styling, readability, and clarity?

```
if (i > 0) if
(j > 0)
x = 0; else
if (k > 0) y = 0;
else z = 0;
```
(a)

```
if (i > 0) {
    if (j > 0)
        x = 0;
    else if (k > 0)
        y = 0;
}
else
    z = 0;
```
(b)

```
if (i > 0)
    if (j > 0)
        x = 0;
    else if (k > 0)
        y = 0;
    else
        z = 0;
```
(c)

```
if (i > 0)
    if (j > 0)
        x = 0;
    else if (k > 0)
        y = 0;
else
    z = 0;
```
(d)

2. Rewrite the following statement using a Boolean expression and proper indentation and styling:

```
if (count % 10 == 0)
    newLine = true;
else
    newLine = false;
```

3. Are the following statements correct? Which one is better?

```
if (age < 16)
    System.out.println
        ("Cannot get a driver's license");
if (age >= 16)
    System.out.println
        ("Can get a driver's license");
```
(a)

```
if (age < 16)
    System.out.println
        ("Cannot get a driver's license");
else
    System.out.println
        ("Can get a driver's license");
```
(b)

4. What is the output of the following code if number is 14, 15, or 30?

```
if (number % 2 == 0)
    System.out.println
        (number + " is even");
if (number % 5 == 0)
    System.out.println
        (number + " is multiple of 5");
```
(a)

```
if (number % 2 == 0)
    System.out.println
        (number + " is even");
else if (number % 5 == 0)
    System.out.println
        (number + " is multiple of 5");
```
(b)

4.7 Generating Random Numbers

You can use `Math.random()` *to obtain a random double value between* `0.0` *and* `1.0`, *excluding* `1.0`.

Key Point

Suppose you want to develop a program for a first-grader to practice subtraction. The program randomly generates two single-digit integers, `number1` and `number2`, with `number1 >= number2`, and it displays to the student a question such as "What is 9 – 2?" After the student enters the answer, the program displays a message indicating whether it is correct.

Program subtraction quiz

The previous programs generate random numbers using `System.current-TimeMillis()`. A better approach is to use the `random()` method in the `Math` class. Invoking this method returns a random double value `d` such that $0.0 \leq d < 1.0$. Thus, `(int)(Math.random() * 10)` returns a random single-digit integer (i.e., a number between `0` and `9`).

random() method

The program can work as follows:

1. Generate two single-digit integers into `number1` and `number2`.

2. If `number1 < number2`, swap `number1` with `number2`.

3. Prompt the student to answer, `"What is number1 - number2?"`

4. Check the student's answer and display whether the answer is correct.

The complete program is shown in Listing 4.3.

LISTING 4.3 `SubtractionQuiz.java`

```java
 1  import java.util.Scanner;
 2
 3  public class SubtractionQuiz {
 4    public static void main(String[] args) {
 5      // 1. Generate two random single-digit integers
 6      int number1 = (int)(Math.random() * 10);
 7      int number2 = (int)(Math.random() * 10);
 8
 9      // 2. If number1 < number2, swap number1 with number2
10      if (number1 < number2) {
11        int temp = number1;
12        number1 = number2;
13        number2 = temp;
14      }
15
16      // 3. Prompt the student to answer "What is number1 - number2?"
17      System.out.print
18        ("What is " + number1 + " - " + number2 + "? ");
19      Scanner input = new Scanner(System.in);
20      int answer = input.nextInt();
21
22      // 4. Grade the answer and display the result
23      if (number1 - number2 == answer)
24        System.out.println("You are correct!");
25      else {
26        System.out.println("Your answer is wrong.");
27        System.out.println(number1 + " - " + number2 +
28          " should be " + (number1 - number2));
```

random number

get answer

check the answer

```
29     }
30   }
31 }
```

```
What is 6 - 6?  0  ⏎Enter
You are correct!
```

```
What is 9 - 2?  5  ⏎Enter
Your answer is wrong
9 - 2 is 7
```

line#	number1	number2	temp	answer	output
6	2				
7		9			
11			2		
12	9				
13		2			
20				5	
26					Your answer is wrong 9 - 2 should be 7

To swap two variables `number1` and `number2`, a temporary variable `temp` (line 11) is used to first hold the value in `number1`. The value in `number2` is assigned to `number1` (line 12), and the value in `temp` is assigned to `number2` (line 13).

✓ SECTION 4.7 ASSESSMENT

1. Which of the following is a possible output from invoking `Math.random()`?

 `323.4, 0.5, 34, 1.0, 0.0, 0.234`

2. **a.** How do you generate a random integer `i` such that $0 \le i < 20$?

 b. How do you generate a random integer `i` such that $10 \le i < 20$?

 c. How do you generate a random integer `i` such that $10 \le i \le 50$?

 d. Write an expression that returns 0 or 1 randomly.

4.8 Case Study: Computing Body Mass Index

You can use nested if *statements to write a program that interprets body mass index.*

Key Point

Body Mass Index (BMI) is a measure of health based on height and weight. It can be calculated by taking your weight in kilograms and dividing it by the square of your height in meters. The interpretation of BMI for people 20 years or older is as follows:

BMI	Interpretation
BMI < 18.5	Underweight
$18.5 \leq$ BMI < 25.0	Normal
$25.0 \leq$ BMI < 30.0	Overweight
$30.0 \leq$ BMI	Obese

Write a program that prompts the user to enter a weight in pounds and height in inches and displays the BMI. Note that one pound is 0.45359237 kilograms and one inch is 0.0254 meters. Listing 4.4 gives the program.

LISTING 4.4 ComputeAndInterpretBMI.java

```java
 1  import java.util.Scanner;
 2
 3  public class ComputeAndInterpretBMI {
 4    public static void main(String[] args) {
 5      Scanner input = new Scanner(System.in);
 6
 7      // Prompt the user to enter weight in pounds
 8      System.out.print("Enter weight in pounds: ");
 9      double weight = input.nextDouble();                        input weight
10
11      // Prompt the user to enter height in inches
12      System.out.print("Enter height in inches: ");
13      double height = input.nextDouble();                        input height
14
15      final double KILOGRAMS_PER_POUND = 0.45359237; // Constant
16      final double METERS_PER_INCH = 0.0254; // Constant
17
18      // Compute BMI
19      double weightInKilograms = weight * KILOGRAMS_PER_POUND;
20      double heightInMeters = height * METERS_PER_INCH;
21      double bmi = weightInKilograms /                           compute bmi
22        (heightInMeters * heightInMeters);
23
24      // Display result
25      System.out.println("BMI is " + bmi);                       display output
26      if (bmi < 18.5)
27        System.out.println("Underweight");
28      else if (bmi < 25)
29        System.out.println("Normal");
30      else if (bmi < 30)
31        System.out.println("Overweight");
32      else
33        System.out.println("Obese");
34    }
35  }
```

```
Enter weight in pounds:  146  ↵Enter
Enter height in inches:   70  ↵Enter
BMI is 20.948603801493316
Normal
```

line#	weight	height	weightInKilograms	heightInMeters	bmi	output
9	146					
13		70				
19			66.22448602			
20				1.778		
21					20.9486	
25						BMI is 20.95
31						Normal

The constants KILOGRAMS_PER_POUND and METERS_PER_INCH are defined in lines 15–16. Using constants here makes programs easy to read.

test all cases

You should test the input that covers all possible cases for BMI to ensure that the program works for all cases.

Key Point

4.9 Case Study: Computing Taxes

You can use nested if statements to write a program for computing taxes.

Use multi-way if-else statements

The United States federal personal income tax is calculated based on filing status and taxable income. There are four filing statuses: single filers, married filing jointly or qualified widow(er), married filing separately, and head of household. The tax rates vary every year. Table 4.2 shows the rates for 2016. If you are, say, single with a taxable income of $10,000, the first $9,275 is taxed at 10% and the other $725 is taxed at 15%, so, your total tax is $1,036.25.

TABLE 4.2 2016 U.S. Federal Personal Tax Rates

Marginal Tax Rate	Single	Married Filing Jointly or Qualifying Widow(er)	Married Filing Separately	Head of Household
10%	$0 – $9,275	$0 – $18,550	$0 – $9,275	$0 – $13,250
15%	$9,276 – $37,650	$18,551 – $75,300	$9,276 – $37,650	$13,251 – $50,400
25%	$37,651 – $91,150	$75,301 – $151,900	$37,651 – $75,950	$50,401 – $130,150
28%	$91,151 – $190,150	$151,901 – $231,450	$75,951 – $115,725	$130,151 – $210,800
33%	$190,151 – $413,350	$231,451 – $413,350	$115,726 – $206,675	$210,801 – $413,350
35%	$413,351 – $415,050	$413,351 – $466,950	$206,676 – $233,475	$413,351 – $441,000
39.6%	$415,051+	$466,951+	$233,476+	$441,001+

You are to write a program to compute personal income tax. Your program should prompt the user to enter the filing status and taxable income and compute the tax. Enter 0 for single filers, 1 for married filing jointly or qualified widow(er), 2 for married filing separately, and 3 for head of household.

Your program computes the tax for the taxable income based on the filing status. The filing status can be determined using if statements outlined as follows:

```java
if (status == 0) {
  // Compute tax for single filers
}
else if (status == 1) {
  // Compute tax for married filing jointly or qualifying
widow(er)
}
else if (status == 2) {
  // Compute tax for married filing separately
}
else if (status == 3) {
  // Compute tax for head of household
}
else {
  // Display wrong status
}
```

For each filing status there are six tax rates. Each rate is applied to a certain amount of taxable income. For example, of a taxable income of \$400,000 for single filers, \$9,275 is taxed at 10%, (37,650 − 9,275) at 15%, (91,150 − 37,650) at 25%, (190,150 − 91,150) at 28%, and (400,000 − 190,150) at 33%.

Listing 4.5 gives the solution for computing taxes for single filers. The complete solution is left as an exercise.

LISTING 4.5 ComputeTax.java

```java
1  import java.util.Scanner;
2
3  public class ComputeTax {
4    public static void main(String[] args) {
5      // Create a Scanner
6      Scanner input = new Scanner(System.in);
7
8      // Prompt the user to enter filing status
9      System.out.print("(0-single filer, 1-married jointly or " +
10        "qualifying widow(er), 2-married separately, 3-head of " +
11        "household) Enter the filing status: ");
12
13      int status = input.nextInt();                              input status
14
15      // Prompt the user to enter taxable income
16      System.out.print("Enter the taxable income: ");
17      double income = input.nextDouble();                        input income
18
19      // Compute tax
20      double tax = 0;                                            compute tax
21
22 if (status == 0) { // Compute tax for single filers
23    if (income <= 9275)
24      tax = income * 0.10;
25    else if (income <= 37650)
```

```
26        tax = 9275 * 0.10 + (income - 9275) * 0.15;
27      else if (income <= 91150)
28        tax = 9275 * 0.10 + (37650 - 9275) * 0.15 +
29          (income - 37650) * 0.25;
30      else if (income <= 190150)
31        tax = 9275 * 0.10 + (37650 - 9275) * 0.15 +
32          (91150 - 37650) * 0.25 + (income - 91150) * 0.28;
33      else if (income <= 413350)
34        tax = 9275 * 0.10 + (37650 - 9275) * 0.15 +
35          (91150 - 37650) * 0.25 + (190150 - 91150) * 0.28 +
36          (income - 190150) * 0.33;
37      else if (income <= 415050)
38        tax = 9275 * 0.10 + (37650 - 9275) * 0.15 +
39          (91150 - 37650) * 0.25 + (190150 - 91150) * 0.28 +
40          (413350 - 190150) * 0.33 + (income - 413350) * 0.35;
41      else
42        tax = 9275 * 0.10 + (37650 - 9275) * 0.15 +
43          (91150 - 37650) * 0.25 + (190150 - 91150) * 0.28 +
44          (413350 - 190150) * 0.33 + (415050 - 413350) * 0.35 +
45          (income - 415050) * 0.396;
46    }
47    else if (status == 1) { // Left as an exercise
48      // Compute tax for married file jointly or qualifying widow(er)
49    }
50    else if (status == 2) { // Compute tax for married separately
51      // Left as an exercise
52    }
53    else if (status == 3) { // Compute tax for head of household
54      // Left as an exercise
55    }
56    else {
57      System.out.println("Error: invalid status");
58      System.exit(1);
59    }
60
61    // Display the result
62    System.out.println("Tax is " + (int)(tax * 100) / 100.0);
63  }
64 }
```

exit program

display output

```
(0-single filer, 1-married jointly or qualifying widow(er),
2-married separately, 3-head of household)
Enter the filing status:  0  ⏎Enter
Enter the taxable income:  400000  ⏎Enter
Tax is 117683.5
```

line#	status	income	tax	output
13	0			
17		400000		
20			0	
38			115529.25	
57				Tax is 115529.25

The program receives the filing status and taxable income. The multi-way `if-else` statements check the filing status and compute the tax based on the filing status.

`System.exit(status)` (line 58) is defined in the `System` class. Invoking this method terminates the program. The status `0` indicates that the program is terminated normally. A nonzero status code indicates abnormal termination.

System.exit(status)

An initial value of `0` is assigned to `tax` (line 20). A compile error would occur if it had no initial value, because all of the other statements that assign values to `tax` are within the `if` statement. The compiler thinks that these statements may not be executed and therefore reports a compile error.

To test a program, you should provide the input that covers all cases. For this program, your input should cover all statuses (`0`, `1`, `2`, `3`). For each status, test the tax for each of the six brackets. So, there are a total of 24 cases.

test all cases

Tip

For all programs, you should write a small amount of code and test it before moving on to add more code. This is called *incremental development and testing*. This approach makes testing easier, because the errors are likely in the new code you just added.

incremental development and testing

✓ SECTION 4.9 ASSESSMENT

1. Are the following two statements equivalent?

```
if (income <= 10000)
   tax = income * 0.1;
else if (income <= 20000)
   tax = 1000 +
     (income - 10000) * 0.15;
```

```
if (income <= 10000)
   tax = income * 0.1;
else if (income > 10000 &&
         income <= 20000)
   tax = 1000 +
     (income - 10000) * 0.15;
```

4.10 Logical Operators

The logical operators !, &&, ||, and ∧ can be used to create a compound Boolean expression.

Key Point

Sometimes, whether a statement is executed is determined by a combination of several conditions. You can use logical operators to combine these conditions to form a compound Boolean expression. *Logical operators*, also known as *Boolean operators*, operate on Boolean values to create a new Boolean value. Table 4.3 lists the Boolean operators. Table 4.4 defines the not (`!`) operator, which negates `true` to `false` and `false` to `true`. Table 4.5 defines the and (`&&`) operator. The and (`&&`) of two Boolean operands is `true` if and only if both operands are `true`. Table 4.6 defines the or (`||`) operator. The or (`||`) of two Boolean operands is `true` if at least one of the operands is `true`. Table 4.7 defines the exclusive or (`∧`) operator. The exclusive or (`∧`) of two Boolean operands is `true` if and only if the two operands have different Boolean values. Note that `p1 ∧ p2` is the same as `p1 != p2`.

logical operators

Boolean operators

TABLE 4.3 Boolean Operators

Operator	Name	Description
!	not	logical negation
&&	and	logical conjunction
\|\|	or	logical disjunction
^	exclusive or	logical exclusion

TABLE 4.4 Truth Table for Operator !

p	!p	Example (assume `age = 24, weight = 140`)
true	false	`!(age > 18)` is `false`, because `(age > 18)` is `true`.
false	true	`!(weight == 150)` is `true`, because `(weight == 150)` is `false`.

TABLE 4.5 Truth Table for Operator &&

p₁	p₂	p₁ && p₂	Example (assume `age = 24, weight = 140`)
false	false	false	
false	true	false	`(age > 28) && (weight <= 140)` is `true`, because `(age > 28)` is `false`.
true	false	false	
true	true	true	`(age > 18) && (weight >= 140)` is `true`, because `(age > 18)` and `(weight >= 140)` are both `true`.

TABLE 4.6 Truth Table for Operator ||

p₁	p₂	p₁ \|\| p₂	Example (assume `age = 24, weight = 140`)
false	false	false	`(age > 34) \|\| (weight >= 150)` is `false`, because `(age > 34)` and `(weight >= 150)` are both `false`.
false	true	true	
true	false	true	`(age > 18) \|\| (weight < 140)` is `true`, because `(age > 18)` is `true`.
true	true	true	

TABLE 4.7 Truth Table for Operator ∧

p₁	p₂	p₁ ∧ p₂	Example (assume **age = 24, weight = 140**)
false	false	false	(age > 34) ∧ (weight > 140) is false, because (age > 34) and (weight > 140) are both false.
false	true	true	(age > 34) ∧ (weight >= 140) is true, because (age > 34) is false but (weight >= 140) is true.
true	false	true	
true	true	false	

Listing 4.6 gives a program that checks whether a number is divisible by 2 and 3, by 2 or 3, and by 2 or 3 but not both:

LISTING 4.6 TestBooleanOperators.java

```
 1  import java.util.Scanner;                                        import class
 2
 3  public class TestBooleanOperators {
 4    public static void main(String[] args) {
 5      // Create a Scanner
 6      Scanner input = new Scanner(System.in);
 7
 8      // Receive an input
 9      System.out.print("Enter an integer: ");
10      int number = input.nextInt();                                input
11
12      if (number % 2 == 0 && number % 3 == 0)                      and
13        System.out.println(number + " is divisible by 2 and 3.");
14
15      if (number % 2 == 0 || number % 3 == 0)                      or
16        System.out.println(number + " is divisible by 2 or 3.");
17
18      if (number % 2 == 0 ^ number % 3 == 0)                       exclusive or
19        System.out.println(number +
20          " is divisible by 2 or 3, but not both.");
21    }
22  }
```

```
Enter an integer: 4 ↵Enter
4 is divisible by 2 or 3.
4 is divisible by 2 or 3, but not both.
```

```
Enter an integer: 18 ↵Enter
18 is divisible by 2 and 3.
18 is divisible by 2 or 3.
```

(`number % 2 == 0 && number % 3 == 0`) (line 12) checks whether the number is divisible by both 2 and 3. (`number % 2 == 0 || number % 3 == 0`) (line 15) checks whether the number is divisible by 2 or by 3. (`number % 2 == 0 ^ number % 3 == 0`) (line 18) checks whether the number is divisible by 2 or 3, but not both.

Caution

In mathematics, the expression

```
1 <= numberOfDaysInAMonth <= 31
```

is correct. However, it is incorrect in Java, because `1 <= number-OfDaysInAMonth` is evaluated to a `boolean` value, which cannot be compared with 31. Here, two operands (a `boolean` value and a numeric value) are *incompatible*. The correct expression in Java is

incompatible operands

```
(1 <= numberOfDaysInAMonth) && (numberOfDaysInAMonth <= 31)
```

Note

De Morgan's law

De Morgan's law, named after Indian-born British mathematician and logician Augustus De Morgan (1806–1871), can be used to simplify Boolean expressions. The law states:

```
!(condition1 && condition2) is the same as
   !condition1 || !condition2
!(condition1 || condition2) is the same as
   !condition1 && !condition2
```

For example,

```
! (number % 2 == 0 && number % 3 == 0)
```

can be simplified using an equivalent expression:

```
(number % 2 != 0 || number % 3 != 0)
```

As another example,

```
!(number == 2 || number == 3)
```

is better written as

```
number != 2 && number != 3
```

If one of the operands of an `&&` operator is `false`, the expression is `false`; if one of the operands of an `||` operator is `true`, the expression is `true`. Java uses these properties to improve the performance of these operators. When evaluating `p1 && p2`, Java first evaluates `p1` and then, if `p1` is `true`, evaluates `p2`; if `p1` is `false`, it does not evaluate `p2`. When evaluating `p1 || p2`, Java first evaluates `p1` and then, if `p1` is `false`, evaluates `p2`; if `p1` is `true`, it does not evaluate `p2`. In programming language terminology, `&&` and `||` are known as the *short-circuit* or *lazy* operators.

short-circuit operator
lazy operator

✓ SECTION 4.10 ASSESSMENT

1. Assuming that x is 1, show the result of the following Boolean expressions.

   ```
   (true) && (3 > 4)
   !(x > 0) && (x > 0)
   (x > 0) || (x < 0)

   (x != 0) || (x == 0)
   (x >= 0) || (x < 0)
   (x != 1) == !(x == 1)
   ```

2. (a) Write a Boolean expression that evaluates to **true** if a number stored in variable num is between 1 and 100. (b) Write a Boolean expression that evaluates to **true** if a number stored in variable num is between 1 and 100 or the number is negative.

3. (a) Write a Boolean expression for $|x - 5| < 4.5$. (b) Write a Boolean expression for $|x - 5| > 4.5$.

4. Assume that x and y are **int** type. Which of the following are legal Java expressions?

   ```
   x > y > 0
   x = y && y
   x /= y
   x or y
   x and y
   (x != 0) || (x = 0)
   ```

5. Are the following two expressions the same?

   ```
   a. x % 2 == 0 && x % 3 == 0
   b. x % 6 == 0
   ```

6. What is the value of the expression x >= 50 && x <= 100 if x is 45, 67, or 101?

7. Suppose, when you run the following program, you enter the input 2 3 6 from the console. What is the output?

   ```java
   public class Test {
     public static void main(String[] args) {
       java.util.Scanner input = new java.util.Scanner(System.in);
       double x = input.nextDouble();
       double y = input.nextDouble();
       double z = input.nextDouble();

       System.out.println("(x < y && y < z) is " + (x < y && y < z));
       System.out.println("(x < y || y < z) is " + (x < y || y < z));
       System.out.println("!(x < y) is " + !(x < y));
       System.out.println("(x + y < z) is " + (x + y < z));
       System.out.println("(x + y > z) is " + (x + y > z));
     }
   }
   ```

8. Write a Boolean expression that evaluates to **true** if age is greater than 13 and less than 18.

9. Write a Boolean expression that evaluates to `true` if `weight` is greater than **50** pounds or height is greater than **60** inches.

10. Write a Boolean expression that evaluates to `true` if `weight` is greater than **50** pounds and height is greater than **60** inches.

11. Write a Boolean expression that evaluates to `true` if either `weight` is greater than **50** pounds or height is greater than **60** inches, but not both.

Key Point

4.11 Case Study: Determining Leap Year

A year is a leap year if it is divisible by 4 but not by 100, or if it is divisible by 400.

You can use the following Boolean expressions to check whether a year is a leap year:

```
// A leap year is divisible by 4
boolean isLeapYear = (year % 4 == 0);

// A leap year is divisible by 4 but not by 100
isLeapYear = isLeapYear && (year % 100 != 0);

// A leap year is divisible by 4 but not by 100 or divisible by 400
isLeapYear = isLeapYear || (year % 400 == 0);
```

Or you can combine all these expressions into one like this:

```
isLeapYear = (year % 4 == 0 && year % 100 != 0) || (year % 400 == 0);
```

Listing 4.7 gives the program that lets the user enter a year and checks whether it is a leap year.

LISTING 4.7 LeapYear.java

```
 1  import java.util.Scanner;
 2
 3  public class LeapYear {
 4    public static void main(String[] args) {
 5      // Create a Scanner
 6      Scanner input = new Scanner(System.in);
 7      System.out.print("Enter a year: ");
 8      int year = input.nextInt();
 9
10      // Check if the year is a leap year
11      boolean isLeapYear =
12        (year % 4 == 0 && year % 100 != 0) || (year % 400 == 0);
13
14      // Display the result
15      System.out.println(year + " is a leap year? " + isLeapYear);
16    }
17  }
```

input

leap year?

display result

```
Enter a year:  2008 ↵Enter
2008 is a leap year? true
```

```
Enter a year:  1900 ↵Enter
1900 is a leap year? false
```

```
Enter a year: 2002  ↵Enter
2002 is a leap year? false
```

4.12 Case Study: Lottery

The lottery program involves generating random numbers, comparing digits, and using Boolean operators.

Suppose you want to develop a program to play lottery. The program randomly generates a lottery of a two-digit number, prompts the user to enter a two-digit number, and determines whether the user wins according to the following rules:

1. If the user input matches the lottery number in the exact order, the award is $10,000.

2. If all digits in the user input match all digits in the lottery number, the award is $3,000.

3. If one digit in the user input matches a digit in the lottery number, the award is $1,000.

Note that the digits of a two-digit number may be 0. If a number is less than 10, we assume the number is preceded by a 0 to form a two-digit number. For example, number 8 is treated as 08 and number 0 is treated as 00 in the program. Listing 4.8 gives the complete program.

LISTING 4.8 Lottery.java

```java
1  import java.util.Scanner;
2
3  public class Lottery {
4    public static void main(String[] args) {
5      // Generate a lottery number
6      int lottery = (int)(Math.random() * 100);              // generate a lottery number
7
8      // Prompt the user to enter a guess
9      Scanner input = new Scanner(System.in);
10     System.out.print("Enter your lottery pick (two digits): ");
11     int guess = input.nextInt();                           // enter a guess
12
13     // Get digits from lottery
14     int lotteryDigit1 = lottery / 10;
15     int lotteryDigit2 = lottery % 10;
16
17     // Get digits from guess
18     int guessDigit1 = guess / 10;
19     int guessDigit2 = guess % 10;
20
21     System.out.println("The lottery number is " + lottery);
22
23     // Check the guess
24     if (guess == lottery)                                  // exact match?
25       System.out.println("Exact match: you win $10,000");
26     else if (guessDigit2 == lotteryDigit1                  // match all digits?
27           && guessDigit1 == lotteryDigit2)
```

match one digit?

```
28              System.out.println("Match all digits: you win $3,000");
29         else if (guessDigit1 == lotteryDigit1
30                 || guessDigit1 == lotteryDigit2
31                 || guessDigit2 == lotteryDigit1
32                 || guessDigit2 == lotteryDigit2)
33           System.out.println("Match one digit: you win $1,000");
34         else
35           System.out.println("Sorry, no match");
36     }
37  }
```

```
Enter your lottery pick (two digits): 15 ↵Enter
The lottery number is 15
Exact match: you win $10,000
```

```
Enter your lottery pick (two digits): 45 ↵Enter
The lottery number is 54
Match all digits: you win $3,000
```

```
Enter your lottery pick:  23 ↵Enter
The lottery number is 34
Match one digit: you win $1,000
```

```
Enter your lottery pick: 23 ↵Enter
The lottery number is 14
Sorry: no match
```

line# variable	6	11	14	15	18	19	33
lottery	34						
guess		23					
lotteryDigit1			3				
lotteryDigit2				4			
guessDigit1					2		
guessDigit2						3	
Output							Match one digit: you win $1,000

The program generates a lottery using the `random()` method (line 6) and prompts the user to enter a guess (line 11). Note that `guess % 10` obtains the last digit from `guess` and `guess / 10` obtains the first digit from `guess`, since `guess` is a two-digit number (lines 18–19).

The program checks the guess against the lottery number in this order:

1. First, check whether the guess matches the lottery exactly (line 24).

2. If not, check whether the reversal of the guess matches the lottery (lines 26–27).

3. If not, check whether one digit is in the lottery (lines 29–32).

4. If not, nothing matches and display `"Sorry, no match"` (lines 34–35).

4.13 switch Statements

A `switch` *statement executes statements based on the value of a variable or an expression.*

Key Point

The `if` statement in Listing 4.5, ComputeTax.java, makes selections based on a single `true` or `false` condition. There are four cases for computing taxes, which depend on the value of `status`. To fully account for all the cases, nested `if` statements were used. Overuse of nested `if` statements makes a program difficult to read. Java provides a `switch` statement to simplify coding for multiple conditions. You can write the following `switch` statement to replace the nested `if` statement in Listing 4.5:

switch statement

```
switch (status) {
  case 0:  compute tax for single filers;
           break;
  case 1:  compute tax for married jointly or qualifying widow(er);
           break;
  case 2:  compute tax for married filing separately;
           break;
  case 3:  compute tax for head of household;
           break;
  default: System.out.println("Error: invalid status");
           System.exit(1);
}
```

The flowchart of the preceding `switch` statement is shown in Figure 4.5.

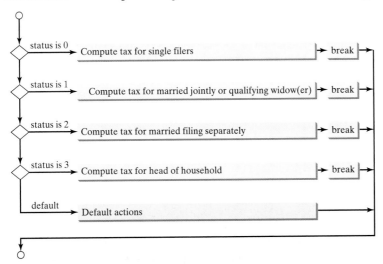

FIGURE 4.5 The `switch` statement checks all cases and executes the statements in the matched case.

This statement checks to see whether the status matches the value 0, 1, 2, or 3, in that order. If matched, the corresponding tax is computed; if not matched, a message is displayed. Here is the full syntax for the `switch` statement:

```
switch (switch-expression) {
  case value1: statement(s)1;
              break;
  case value2: statement(s)2;
              break;
  ...
  case valueN: statement(s)N;
              break;
  default:    statement(s)-for-default;
}
```

The `switch` statement observes the following rules:

■ The `switch-expression` must yield a value of `char`, `byte`, `short`, `int`, or `String` type and must always be enclosed in parentheses. (The `char` and `String` types will be introduced in the next chapter.)

■ The `value1,...`, and `valueN` must have the same data type as the value of the `switch-expression`. Note that `value1,...`, and `valueN` are constant expressions, meaning that they cannot contain variables, such as `1 + x`.

■ When the value in a `case` statement matches the value of the `switch-expression`, the statements *starting from this case* are executed until either a `break` statement or the end of the `switch` statement is reached.

■ The `default` case, which is optional, can be used to perform actions when none of the specified cases matches the `switch-expression`.

break

■ The keyword `break` is optional. The `break` statement immediately ends the `switch` statement.

without break

fall-through behavior

Caution

Do not forget to use a `break` statement when one is needed. Once a case is matched, the statements starting from the matched case are executed until a `break` statement or the end of the `switch` statement is reached. This is referred to as *fall-through* behavior. For example, the following code displays `Weekdays` for day of 1 to 5 and `Weekends` for day 0 and 6.

```
switch (day) {
  case 1:
  case 2:
  case 3:
  case 4:
  case 5: System.out.println("Weekday"); break;
  case 0:
  case 6: System.out.println("Weekend");
}
```

Tip

To avoid programming errors and improve code maintainability, it is a good idea to put a comment in a case clause if `break` is purposely omitted.

Now let us write a program to find out the Chinese Zodiac sign for a given year. The Chinese Zodiac is based on a twelve-year cycle, with each year represented by an animal—monkey, rooster, dog, pig, rat, ox, tiger, rabbit, dragon, snake, horse, or sheep—in this cycle, as shown in Figure 4.6.

Note that `year % 12` determines the Zodiac sign. 1900 is the year of the rat because `1900 % 12` is `4`. Listing 4.9 gives a program that prompts the user to enter a year and displays the animal for the year.

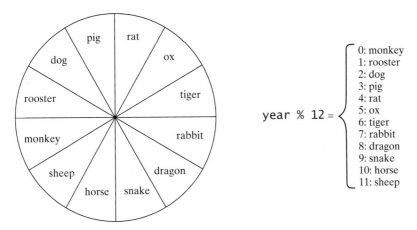

FIGURE 4.6 The Chinese Zodiac is based on a twelve-year cycle.

LISTING 4.9 `ChineseZodiac.java`

```java
 1  import java.util.Scanner;
 2
 3  public class ChineseZodiac {
 4    public static void main(String[] args) {
 5      Scanner input = new Scanner(System.in);
 6
 7      System.out.print("Enter a year: ");
 8      int year = input.nextInt();                          enter year
 9
10      switch (year % 12) {                                 determine Zodiac sign
11        case 0: System.out.println("monkey"); break;
12        case 1: System.out.println("rooster"); break;
13        case 2: System.out.println("dog"); break;
14        case 3: System.out.println("pig"); break;
15        case 4: System.out.println("rat"); break;
16        case 5: System.out.println("ox"); break;
17        case 6: System.out.println("tiger"); break;
18        case 7: System.out.println("rabbit"); break;
19        case 8: System.out.println("dragon"); break;
20        case 9: System.out.println("snake"); break;
21        case 10: System.out.println("horse"); break;
22        case 11: System.out.println("sheep");
23      }
24    }
25  }
```

```
Enter a year:   1963  ↵Enter
rabbit
```

```
Enter a year:   1877  ↵Enter
ox
```

✓ Section 4.13 Assessment

1. What data types are required for a `switch` variable? If the keyword `break` is not used after a case is processed, what is the next statement to be executed? Can you convert a `switch` statement to an equivalent `if` statement, or vice versa? What are the advantages of using a `switch` statement?

2. What is `y` after the following `switch` statement is executed? Rewrite the code using an `if-else` statement.

```
x = 3; y = 3;
switch (x + 3) {
  case 6:  y = 1;
  default: y += 1;
}
```

3. What is `x` after the following `if-else` statement is executed? Use a `switch` statement to rewrite it and draw the flowchart for the new `switch` statement.

```
int x = 1, a = 3;
if (a == 1)
    x += 5;
else if (a == 2)
    x += 10;
else if (a == 3)
    x += 16;
else if (a == 4)
    x += 34;
```

4. Write a `switch` statement that displays Sunday, Monday, Tuesday, Wednesday, Thursday, Friday, Saturday, if `day` is 0, 1, 2, 3, 4, 5, 6, accordingly.

4.14 Conditional Expressions

🔑 **Key Point**

A conditional expression evaluates an expression based on a condition.

You might want to assign a value to a variable that is restricted by certain conditions. For example, the following statement assigns 1 to `y` if `x` is greater than 0, and -1 to `y` if `x` is less than or equal to 0.

```
if (x > 0)
    y = 1;
else
    y = -1;
```

Alternatively, as in the following example, you can use a conditional expression to achieve the same result.

```
y = (x > 0) ? 1 : -1;
```

Conditional expressions are in a completely different style, with no explicit `if` in the statement. The syntax is:

conditional expression

```
boolean-expression ? expression1 : expression2;
```

The result of this conditional expression is `expression1` if `boolean-expression` is true; otherwise the result is `expression2`.

Suppose you want to assign the larger number of variable `num1` and `num2` to `max`. You can simply write a statement using the conditional expression:

```
max = (num1 > num2) ? num1 : num2;
```

For another example, the following statement displays the message "num is even" if `num` is even, and otherwise displays "num is odd."

```
System.out.println((num % 2 == 0) ? "num is even" : "num is odd");
```

As you can see from these examples, conditional expressions enable you to write short and concise code.

Note
The symbols `?` and `:` appear together in a conditional expression. They form a *conditional operator* and also called a *ternary operator* because it uses three operands. It is the only ternary operator in Java.

conditional operator
ternary operator

✓ SECTION 4.14 ASSESSMENT

1. Suppose that, when you run the following program, you enter the input `2 3 6` from the console. What is the output?

```
public class Test {
  public static void main(String[] args) {
    java.util.Scanner input = new java.util.Scanner(System.in);
    double x = input.nextDouble();
    double y = input.nextDouble();
    double z = input.nextDouble();

    System.out.println((x < y && y < z) ? "sorted" : "not sorted");
  }
}
```

2. Rewrite the following `if` statements using the conditional operator.

```
if (ages >= 16)
  ticketPrice = 20;
else
  ticketPrice = 10;
```

3. Rewrite the following conditional expressions using `if-else` statements.

a. `score = (x > 10) ? 3 * scale : 4 * scale;`

b. `tax = (income > 10000) ? income * 0.2 : income * 0.17 + 1000;`

c. `System.out.println((number % 3 == 0) ? i : j);`

4. Write conditional expression that returns -1 or 1 randomly.

4.15 Operator Precedence and Associativity

 Key Point

Operator precedence and associativity determine the order in which operators are evaluated.

Chapter 3 introduced operator precedence involving arithmetic operators. This section discusses operator precedence in more detail. Suppose that you have this expression:

```
3 + 4 * 4 > 5 * (4 + 3) - 1 && (4 - 3 > 5)
```

What is its value? What is the execution order of the operators?

The expression within parentheses is evaluated first. (Parentheses can be nested, in which case the expression within the inner parentheses is executed first.) When evaluating an expression without parentheses, the operators are applied according to the precedence rule and the associativity rule.

The precedence rule defines precedence for operators, as shown in Table 4.8, which contains the operators you have learned so far. Operators are listed in decreasing order of precedence from top to bottom. The logical operators have lower precedence than the relational operators and the relational operators have lower precedence than the arithmetic operators. Operators with the same precedence appear in the same group. (See Appendix C, *Operator Precedence Chart*, for a complete list of Java operators and their precedence.)

operator precedence

TABLE 4.8 Operator Precedence Chart

Precedence	Operator		
	`var++` and `var--` (Postfix)		
	`+, -` (Unary plus and minus), `++var` and `--var` (Prefix)		
	`(type)` (Casting)		
	`!` (Not)		
	`*, /, %` (Multiplication, division, and remainder)		
	`+, -` (Binary addition and subtraction)		
	`<, <=, >, >=` (Relational)		
	`==, !=` (Equality)		
	`^` (Exclusive OR)		
	`&&` (AND)		
	`		` (OR)
	`=, +=, -=, *=, /=, %=` (Assignment operator)		

If operators with the same precedence are next to each other, their *associativity* determines the order of evaluation. All binary operators except assignment operators are *left associative*. For example, since + and – are of the same precedence and are left associative, the expression

operator associativity

a - b + c - d is equivalent to ((a - b) + c) - d

Assignment operators are *right associative*. Therefore, the expression

a = b += c = 5 is equivalent to a = (b += (c = 5))

Suppose a, b, and c are 1 before the assignment; after the whole expression is evaluated, a becomes 6, b becomes 6, and c becomes 5. Note that left associativity for the assignment operator would not make sense.

✓ SECTION 4.15 ASSESSMENT

1. List the precedence order of the Boolean operators. Evaluate the following expressions:

```
true || true && false
true && true || false
```

2. True or false? All the binary operators except = are left associative.

3. Evaluate the following expressions:

```
2 * 2 - 3 > 2 && 4 - 2 > 5
2 * 2 - 3 > 2 || 4 - 2 > 5
```

4. Is $(x > 0 \text{ \&\& } x < 10)$ the same as $((x > 0) \text{ \&\& } (x < 10))$? Is $(x > 0 || x < 10)$ the same as $((x > 0) || (x < 10))$? Is $(x > 0 || x < 10 \text{ \&\& } y < 0)$ the same as $(x > 0 || (x < 10 \text{ \&\& } y < 0))$?

4.16 Troubleshooting Issues Using Debugging

Debugging is the process of finding and fixing errors in a program.

Key
Point

As mentioned in Chapter 2, Section 2.7, syntax errors are easy to find and easy to correct because the compiler gives indications as to where the errors came from and why they are there. Runtime errors are not difficult to find either, because the Java interpreter displays them on the console when the program aborts. Finding logic errors, on the other hand, can be very challenging.

Logic errors are called *bugs*. The process of finding and correcting errors is called *debugging*. A common approach to debugging is to use a combination of methods to help pinpoint the part of the program where the bug is located. You can *hand-trace* the program (i.e., catch errors by reading the program), or you can insert print statements in order to show the values of the variables or the execution

bugs

debugging

hand-traces

flow of the program. These approaches might work for debugging a short, simple program, but for a large, complex program, the most effective approach is to use a debugger utility.

JDK includes a command-line debugger, jdb, which is invoked with a class name. **jdb** is itself a Java program, running its own copy of Java interpreter. All the Java IDE tools, such as Eclipse and NetBeans, include integrated debuggers. The debugger utilities let you follow the execution of a program. They vary from one system to another, but they all support most of the following helpful features.

- **Executing a single statement at a time:** The debugger allows you to execute one statement at a time so that you can see the effect of each statement.

- **Tracing into or stepping over a method:** If a method is being executed, you can ask the debugger to enter the method and execute one statement at a time in the method, or you can ask it to step over the entire method. You should step over the entire method if you know that the method works. For example, always step over system-supplied methods, such as `System.out.println`.

- **Setting breakpoints:** You can also set a breakpoint at a specific statement. Your program pauses when it reaches a breakpoint. You can set as many breakpoints as you want. Breakpoints are particularly useful when you know where your programming error starts. You can set a breakpoint at that statement and have the program execute until it reaches the breakpoint.

- **Displaying variables:** The debugger lets you select several variables and display their values. As you trace through a program, the content of a variable is continuously updated.

- **Displaying call stacks:** The debugger lets you trace all of the method calls. This feature is helpful when you need to see a large picture of the program-execution flow.

- **Modifying variables:** Some debuggers enable you to modify the value of a variable when debugging. This is convenient when you want to test a program with different samples but do not want to leave the debugger.

debugging in IDE

Tip

If you use an IDE such as Eclipse or NetBeans, it is not necessary to use the jdb command line debugger. You can use the debugger built into the IDE. This is beyond the scope of this class. Your instructor may provide further steps or you can find information on https://netbeans.org.

Chapter 4 — Review and Assessment

KEY TERMS

boolean data type 94
Boolean expression 94
Boolean value 94
break 122
bugs 127
conditional operator 125
dangling else ambiguity 124
debugging 127
fall-through behavior 122

flowchart 97
if statement 96
lazy operator 116
operator associativity 127
operator precedence 126
relational operators 94
selection statement 94
short-circuit operator 116
switch statement 121

CHAPTER SUMMARY

1. A `boolean` type variable can store a `true` or `false` value.

2. The relational operators (`<`, `<=`, `==`, `!=`, `>`, `>=`) yield a Boolean value.

3. *Selection statements* are used for programming with alternative courses of actions. There are several types of selection statements: one-way `if` statements, two-way `if-else` statements, nested `if` statements, multi-way `if-else` statements, `switch` statements, and conditional expressions.

4. The various `if` statements all make control decisions based on a *Boolean expression*. Based on the `true` or `false` evaluation of the expression, these statements take one of two possible courses.

5. The Boolean operators `&&`, `||`, `!`, and `^` operate with Boolean values and variables.

6. When evaluating `p1 && p2`, Java first evaluates `p1` and then evaluates `p2` if `p1` is `true`; if `p1` is `false`, it does not evaluate `p2`. When evaluating `p1 || p2`, Java first evaluates `p1` and then evaluates `p2` if `p1` is `false`; if `p1` is `true`, it does not evaluate `p2`. Therefore, `&&` is referred to as the *conditional* or *short-circuit AND operator*, and `||` is referred to as the *conditional* or *short-circuit OR operator*.

7. The `switch` statement makes control decisions based on a switch expression of type `char`, `byte`, `short`, `int`, or `String`.

8. The keyword `break` is optional in a `switch` statement, but it is normally used at the end of each case in order to skip the remainder of the `switch` statement. If the `break` statement is not present, the next `case` statement will be executed.

9. The operators in expressions are evaluated in the order determined by the rules of parentheses, *operator precedence*, and *operator associativity*.

10. Parentheses can be used to force the order of evaluation to occur in any sequence.

11. Operators with higher precedence are evaluated earlier. For operators of the same precedence, their associativity determines the order of evaluation.

12. All binary operators except assignment operators are left-associative; assignment operators are right-associative.

13. Write code using a standard structured format that uses appropriate styling techniques such as indents and spacing. This provides clarity to you and your team members who read your code.

14. Debugging is the process of finding and fixing errors and technical issues with your program. Stepping through your code helps identify the point of failure.

PROGRAMMING EXERCISES

think before coding

> **Pedagogical Note**
> For each exercise, carefully analyze the problem requirements and design strategies for solving the problem before coding.

> **Debugging Tip**
> Before you ask for help, read and explain the program to yourself, and trace it using several representative inputs by hand or using an IDE debugger. You learn how to program by debugging your own mistakes.

learn from mistakes

> **Note**
> Exercises preceded by a star (*) are more challenging.

1. (*Game: add three numbers*) The program in Listing 4.1, AdditionQuiz.java, generates two integers and prompts the user to enter the sum of these two integers. Revise the program to generate three single-digit integers and prompt the user to enter the sum of these three integers.

*2. (*Find future dates*) Write a program that prompts the user to enter an integer for today's day of the week (Sunday is 0, Monday is 1, ..., and Saturday is 6). Also prompt the user to enter the number of days after today for a future day and display the future day of the week. Here is a sample run:

```
Enter today's day: 1 ↵Enter
Enter the number of days elapsed since today: 3 ↵Enter
Today is Monday and the future day is Thursday
```

```
Enter today's day: 0  ↵Enter
Enter the number of days elapsed since today: 31  ↵Enter
Today is Sunday and the future day is Wednesday
```

*3. (*Health application: BMI*) Revise Listing 4.4, ComputeAndInterpret-BMI.java, to let the user enter weight, feet, and inches. For example, if a person is 5 feet and 10 inches, you will enter 5 for feet and 10 for inches. Here is a sample run:

```
Enter weight in pounds: 140  ↵Enter
Enter feet: 5  ↵Enter
Enter inches: 10  ↵Enter
BMI is 20.087702275404553
Normal
```

4. (*Financial application: monetary units*) Modify Listing 3.9, ComputeChange.java, to display the nonzero denominations only, using singular words for single units such as 1 dollar and 1 penny, and plural words for more than one unit such as 2 dollars and 3 pennies.

*5. (*Sort three integers*) Write a program that prompts the user to enter three integers and display the integers in non-decreasing order.

6. (*Game: addition quiz*) Listing 4.3, SubtractionQuiz.java, randomly generates a subtraction question. Revise the program to randomly generate an addition question with two integers less than 100.

7. (*Palindrome number*) Write a program that prompts the user to enter a three-digit integer and determines whether it is a palindrome number. A number is palindrome if it reads the same from right to left and from left to right. Here is a sample run of this program:

```
Enter a three-digit integer: 121  ↵Enter
121 is a palindrome
```

```
Enter a three-digit integer: 123  ↵Enter
123 is not a palindrome
```

8. (*Game: heads or tails*) Write a program that lets the user guess whether the flip of a coin results in heads or tails. The program randomly generates an integer 0 or 1, which represents head or tail. The program prompts the user to enter a guess and reports whether the guess is correct or incorrect.

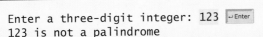

9. (*Random point*) Write a program that displays a random coordinate in a rectangle. The rectangle is centered at (0, 0) with width 100 and height 200.

*10. (*Game: scissor, rock, paper*) Write a program that plays the popular scissor-rock-paper game. (A scissor can cut a paper, a rock can knock a scissor, and a paper can wrap a rock.) The program randomly generates a number 0, 1, or 2 representing scissor, rock, and paper. The program prompts the user to enter a number 0, 1, or 2 and displays a message indicating whether the user or the computer wins, loses, or draws. Here are sample runs:

```
scissor (0), rock (1), paper (2): 1 ↵Enter
The computer is scissor. You are rock. You won
```

```
scissor (0), rock (1), paper (2): 2 ↵Enter
The computer is paper. You are paper too. It is a draw
```

*11. (*Cost of shipping*) A shipping company uses the following function to calculate the cost (in dollars) of shipping based on the weight of the package (in pounds).

$$c(w) = \begin{cases} 3.5, & \text{if } 0 < w <= 1 \\ 5.5, & \text{if } 1 < w <= 3 \\ 8.5, & \text{if } 3 < w <= 10 \\ 10.5, & \text{if } 10 < w <= 20 \end{cases}$$

Write a program that prompts the user to enter the weight of the package and display the shipping cost. If the weight is greater than 20, display a message "the package cannot be shipped."

CHAPTER

5

WORKING WITH CHARACTERS AND STRINGS

Objectives

- Use the `char` data type.
- Encode characters using ASCII and Unicode.
- Represent special characters using the escape sequences.
- Compare characters using methods in the `Character` class.
- Introduce objects and instance methods.
- Use the `string` object.
- Return the string length using the `length()` method.
- Return a character in the string using the `charAt(i)` method.
- Use the `+` operator to concatenate strings.
- Use `toUpperCase()` and `toLowerCase()` methods to return upper-case or lowercase strings.
- Use `trim()` method to remove whitespace characters.
- Read a character from the console.
- Compare strings using the `equals()` method and the `compareTo()` methods.
- Find a character or a substring in a string using the `indexOf()` method.
- Identify and document constraints of a software application.
- Format output using the `System.out.printf()` method.

5.1 Introduction

Key Point

The focus of this chapter is to introduce mathematical functions, characters, and string objects, and use them to develop programs.

Because strings are frequently used in programming, it is beneficial to introduce strings early so that you can begin to use them to develop useful programs. This chapter introduces character and string data types.

method

In addition, you will explore the use of methods to perform string manipulation. A *method* is a block of code that performs a specific task. Many methods are pre-written and are available for reuse within your code. These methods are stored in the Java Application Programming Interface (API) and are referred to as

pre-defined methods

pre-defined methods. You will use some of these pre-defined methods to perform string manipulation.

This chapter introduces methods. In Chapter 8, you will learn how to modularize code by writing your own custom methods.

5.2 Character Data Type and Operations

Key Point

A character data type represents a single character.

char type

In addition to processing numeric values, you can process characters in Java. The character data type, `char`, is used to represent a single character. A character literal is enclosed in single quotation marks. Consider the following code:

```
char letter = 'A';
char numChar = '4';
```

The first statement assigns character `A` to the `char` variable `letter`. The second statement assigns digit character `4` to the `char` variable `numChar`.

> **Caution**
>
char literal
> A string literal must be enclosed in quotation marks (`" "`). A character literal is a single character enclosed in single quotation marks (`' '`). Therefore, `"A"` is a string, but `'A'` is a character.

Unicode and ASCII Code

Computers use binary numbers internally. A character is stored in a computer as a sequence of 0s and 1s. Mapping a character to its binary representation is

encoding

called *encoding.* There are different ways to encode a character. How characters are encoded is defined by an *encoding scheme.*

Unicode

Java supports *Unicode,* an encoding scheme established by the Unicode Consortium to support the interchange, processing, and display of written texts in the

original Unicode

world's diverse languages. Unicode was originally designed as a 16-bit character encoding. The primitive data type `char` was intended to take advantage of this design by providing a simple data type that could hold any character. However, it turned out that the 65,536 characters possible in a 16-bit encoding are not sufficient to represent all the characters in the world. The Unicode standard therefore has been extended to allow up to 1,112,064 characters. Those characters that go

supplementary Unicode

beyond the original 16-bit limit are called *supplementary characters.* Java supports the supplementary characters. The processing and representing of supplementary

characters are beyond the scope of this book. For simplicity, this book considers only the original 16-bit Unicode characters. These characters can be stored in a char type variable.

A 16-bit Unicode takes two bytes, preceded by \u, expressed in four hexadecimal digits that run from \u0000 to \uFFFF. Hexadecimal numbers are introduced in Appendix D, Number Systems. For example, the English word welcome is translated into Chinese using two characters, 欢迎. The Unicodes of these two characters are \u6B22\u8FCE. The Unicodes for the Greek letters α β γ are \u03b1 \u03b2 \u03b4.

Most computers use *ASCII* (*American Standard Code for Information Interchange*), an 8-bit encoding scheme for representing all uppercase and lowercase letters, digits, punctuation marks, and control characters. Unicode includes ASCII code, with \u0000 to \u007F corresponding to the 128 ASCII characters. Table 5.1 shows the ASCII code for some commonly used characters. Appendix B, 'The ASCII Character Set,' gives a complete list of ASCII characters and their decimal and hexadecimal codes.

TABLE 5.1 **ASCII Code for Commonly Used Characters**

Characters	Code Value in Decimal	Unicode Value
'0' to '9'	48 to 57	\u0030 to \u0039
'A' to 'Z'	65 to 90	\u0041 to \u005A
'a' to 'z'	97 to 122	\u0061 to \u007A

You can use ASCII characters such as 'X', '1', and '$' in a Java program as well as Unicodes. Thus, for example, the following statements are equivalent:

ASCII

```
char letter = 'A';
char letter = '\u0041'; // Character A's Unicode is 0041
```

Both statements assign character A to the char variable letter.

Note

The increment and decrement operators can also be used on char variables to get the next or preceding Unicode character. For example, the following statements display character b.

char increment and decrement

```
char ch = 'a';
System.out.println(++ch);
```

Escape Sequences for Special Characters

Suppose you want to print a message with quotation marks in the output. Can you write a statement like this?

```
System.out.println("He said "Java is fun"");
```

No, this statement has a compile error. The compiler thinks the second quotation character is the end of the string and does not know what to do with the rest of the characters.

To overcome this problem, Java uses a special notation to represent special characters, as shown in Table 5.2. This special notation, called an *escape sequence*, consists of a backslash (\) followed by a character or a combination of digits. For example, \t is an escape sequence for the Tab character and an escape sequence such as \u03b1 is used to represent a Unicode. The symbols in an escape sequence are interpreted as a whole rather than individually. An escape sequence is considered as a single character.

So, now you can print the quoted message using the following statement:

```
System.out.println("He said \"Java is fun\"");
```

The output is

```
He said "Java is fun"
```

Note that the symbols \ and " together represent one character.

TABLE 5.2 **Escape Sequences**

Escape Sequence	Name	Unicode Code	Decimal Value
\b	Backspace	\u0008	8
\t	Tab	\u0009	9
\n	Linefeed	\u000A	10
\f	Formfeed	\u000C	12
\r	Carriage Return	\u000D	13
\\	Backslash	\u005C	92
\"	Double Quote	\u0022	34

The backslash \ is called an *escape character*. It is a special character. To display this character, you have to use an escape sequence \\. For example, the following code

```
System.out.println("\\t is a tab character");
```

displays

```
\t is a tab character
```

Comparing and Testing Characters

Two characters can be compared using the relational operators just like comparing two numbers. This is done by comparing the Unicodes of the two characters. For example,

'a' < 'b' is true because the Unicode for 'a' (97) is less than the Unicode for 'b' (98).

'a' < 'A' is false because the Unicode for 'a' (97) is greater than the Unicode for 'A' (65).

'1' < '8' is true because the Unicode for '1' (49) is less than the Unicode for '8' (56).

Often in the program, you need to test whether a character is a number, a letter, an uppercase letter, or a lowercase letter. As shown in Appendix B, the ASCII character set, the Unicodes for lowercase letters are consecutive integers starting from the Unicode for 'a', then for 'b', 'c', ..., and 'z'. The same is true for the uppercase letters and for numeric characters. This property can be used to write the code to test characters. For example, the following code tests whether a character ch is an uppercase letter, a lowercase letter, or a digital character.

```java
if (ch >= 'A' && ch <= 'Z')
  System.out.println(ch + " is an uppercase letter");
else if (ch >= 'a' && ch <= 'z')
  System.out.println(ch + " is a lowercase letter");
else if (ch >= '0' && ch <= '9')
  System.out.println(ch + " is a numeric character");
```

For convenience, Java provides the following pre-defined methods in the Character class for testing characters as shown in Table 5.3.

TABLE 5.3 Methods in the Character Class

Method	Description
isDigit(ch)	Returns true if the specified character is a digit.
isLetter(ch)	Returns true if the specified character is a letter.
isLetterOrDigit(ch)	Returns true if the specified character is a letter or digit.
isLowerCase(ch)	Returns true if the specified character is a lowercase letter.
isUpperCase(ch)	Returns true if the specified character is an uppercase letter.
toLowerCase(ch)	Returns the lowercase of the specified character.
toUpperCase(ch)	Returns the uppercase of the specified character.

For example,

```java
System.out.println("isDigit('a') is " + Character.isDigit('a'));
  System.out.println("isLetter('a') is " + Character.isLetter('a'));
  System.out.println("isLowerCase('a') is "
    + Character.isLowerCase('a'));
  System.out.println("isUpperCase('a') is "
    + Character.isUpperCase('a'));
  System.out.println("toLowerCase('T') is "
    + Character.toLowerCase('T'));
  System.out.println("toUpperCase('q') is "
    + Character.toUpperCase('q'));
```

displays

```
isDigit('a') is false
isLetter('a') is true
isLowerCase('a') is true
isUpperCase('a') is false
toLowerCase('T') is t
toUpperCase('q') is Q
```

✓ Section 5.2 Assessment

1. Give three examples of pre-defined methods included in the `Character` class? What are they used for?

2. Which of the following are correct literals for characters?

 `'1'`, `'\u345dE'`, `'\u3fFa'`, `'\b'`, `'\t'`

3. How do you display the characters \ and "?

4. Evaluate the following:

   ```
   int i = '1';
   int j = '1' + '2' * ('4' - '3') + 'b' / 'a';
   int k = 'a';
   char c = 90;
   ```

5. Show the output of the following program:

   ```
   public class Test {
     public static void main(String[] args) {
       char x = 'a';
       char y = 'c';
       System.out.println(++x);
       System.out.println(y++);
       System.out.println(x - y);
     }
   }
   ```

6. Show the output of the following statements:

   ```
   System.out.println('a' < 'b');
   System.out.println('a' <= 'A');
   System.out.println('a' > 'b');
   System.out.println('a' >= 'A');
   System.out.println('a' == 'a');
   System.out.println('a' != 'b');
   ```

Key Point

5.3 The String Type

A string is a sequence of characters.

The `char` type represents only one character. To represent a string of characters, use the data type called `String`. For example, the following code declares `message` to be a string with the value `"Welcome to Java"`.

```
String message = "Welcome to Java";
```

String

`String` is a predefined class in the Java library, just like the classes `System` and `Scanner`. The `String` type is not a primitive type. It is known as a *reference type*. A `String` is a series of characters (or `Char` types) that are stored together and referenced as one object.

In this chapter, you will learn how to declare a `String` variable, how to assign a string to the variable, and how to use the methods in the `String` class.

Table 5.4 lists the `String` methods for obtaining string length, for accessing characters in the string, for concatenating strings, for converting a string to upper or lowercases, and for trimming a string.

TABLE 5.4 Simple Methods for `String` Objects

Method	Description
`length()`	Returns the number of characters in this string.
`charAt(index)`	Returns the character at the specified index from this string.
`concat(s1)`	Returns a new string that concatenates this string with string s1.
`toUpperCase()`	Returns a new string with all letters in uppercase.
`toLowerCase()`	Returns a new string with all letters in lowercase
`trim()`	Returns a new string with whitespace characters trimmed on both sides.

Strings are objects in Java. The methods in Table 5.4 can only be invoked from a specific string instance. For this reason, these methods are called *instance methods*. A non-instance method is called a *static method*. A static method can be invoked without using an object. All the methods defined in the `Math` class are static methods. They are not tied to a specific object instance. The syntax to invoke an instance method is `referenceVariable.methodName(arguments)`. A method may have many arguments or no arguments. For example, the `charAt(index)` method has one argument, but the `length()` method has no arguments.

string object
instance method
static method

Getting String Length

You can use the `length()` method to return the number of characters in a string. For example, the following code

```
String message = "Welcome to Java";
System.out.println("The length of " + message + " is "
  + message.length());
```

displays

```
The length of Welcome to Java is 15
```

Note

When you use a string, you often know its literal value. For convenience, Java allows you to use the string literal to refer directly to strings without creating new variables. Thus, `"Welcome to Java".length()` is correct and returns 15. Note that `""` denotes an *empty string* and `"".length()` is 0.

string literal

empty string

Getting Characters from a String

The `s.charAt(index)` method can be used to retrieve a specific character in a string `s`, where the index is between `0` and `s.length()-1`. For example, `message.charAt(0)` returns the character `W`, as shown in Figure 5.1. Note that the index for the first character in the string is `0`.

charAt(index)

FIGURE 5.1 The characters in a `String` object can be accessed using its index.

string index range

 Caution

Attempting to access characters in a string `s` out of bounds is a common programming error. To avoid it, make sure that you do not use an index beyond `s.length() - 1`. For example, `s.charAt(s.length())` would cause a `StringIndexOutOfBoundsException`.

Concatenating Strings

concatenation

Concatenation is the process of joining two or more strings together. You can use the `concat` method to concatenate two strings. The statement shown below, for example, concatenates strings `s1` and `s2` into `s3`:

s1.concat(s2)

```
String s3 = s1.concat(s2);
```

Because string concatenation is heavily used in programming, Java provides a convenient way to accomplish it. You can use the plus (+) operator to concatenate two strings, so the previous statement is equivalent to

s1 + s2

```
String s3 = s1 + s2;
```

The following code combines the strings `message`, `" and "`, and `"HTML"` into one string:

```
String myString = message + " and " + "HTML";
```

concatenate strings and numbers

Recall that the + operator can also concatenate a number with a string. In this case, the number is converted into a string and then concatenated. Note that at least one of the operands must be a string in order for concatenation to take place. If one of the operands is a nonstring (e.g., a number), the nonstring value is converted into a string and concatenated with the other string. Here are some examples:

```
// Three strings are concatenated
String message = "Welcome " + "to " + "Java";

// String Chapter is concatenated with number 2
String s = "Chapter" + 2; // s becomes Chapter2

// String Supplement is concatenated with character B
String s1 = "Supplement" + 'B'; // s1 becomes SupplementB
```

If neither of the operands is a string, the plus sign (+) is the addition operator that adds two numbers.

The augmented += operator can also be used for string concatenation. For example, the following code appends the string `"and Java is fun"` with the string `"Welcome to Java"` in `message`.

```
message += " and Java is fun";
```

So the new `message` is `"Welcome to Java and Java is fun"`.
If `i = 1` and `j = 2`, what is the output of the following statement?

```
System.out.println("i + j is " + i + j);
```

The output is `"i + j is 12"` because `"i + j is "` is concatenated with the value of `i` first. To force `i + j` to be executed first, enclose `i + j` in the parentheses, as follows:

```
System.out.println("i + j is " + (i + j));
```

Converting Strings

The `toLowerCase()` method returns a new string with all lowercase letters and the `toUpperCase()` method returns a new string with all uppercase letters. For example,

`"Welcome".toLowerCase()` returns a new string `welcome`. `toLowerCase()`
`"Welcome".toUpperCase()` returns a new string `WELCOME`. `toUpperCase()`

The `trim()` method returns a new string by eliminating whitespace characters from both ends of the string. The characters `' '`, `\t`, `\f`, `\r`, or `\n` are known as *whitespace characters*. For example, whitespace character

`"\t Good Night \n".trim()` returns a new string `Good Night`. `trim()`

Reading a String from the Console

To read a string from the console, invoke the `next()` method on a `Scanner` object. For example, the following code reads three strings from the keyboard: read strings

```
Scanner input = new Scanner(System.in);
System.out.print("Enter three words separated by spaces: ");
String s1 = input.next();
String s2 = input.next();
String s3 = input.next();
System.out.println("s1 is " + s1);
System.out.println("s2 is " + s2);
System.out.println("s3 is " + s3);
```

```
Enter three words separated by spaces: Welcome to Java ⏎Enter
s1 is Welcome
s2 is to
s3 is Java
```

whitespace character

The `next()` method reads a string that ends with a whitespace character. You can use the `nextLine()` method to read an entire line of text. The `nextLine()` method reads a string that ends with the *Enter* key pressed. For example, the following statements read a line of text.

```
Scanner input = new Scanner(System.in);
System.out.println("Enter a line: ");
String s = input.nextLine();
System.out.println("The line entered is " + s);
```

```
Enter a line: Welcome to Java  ↵ Enter
The line entered is Welcome to Java
```

Reading a Character from the Console

To read a character from the console, use the `nextLine()` method to read a string and then invoke the `charAt(0)` method on the string to return a character. For example, the following code reads a character from the keyboard:

```
Scanner input = new Scanner(System.in);
System.out.print("Enter a character: ");
String s = input.nextLine();
char ch = s.charAt(0);
System.out.println("The character entered is " + ch);
```

Comparing Strings

The `String` class contains the methods as shown in Table 5.5 for comparing two strings.

TABLE 5.5 Comparison Methods for `String` Objects

Method	Description
`equals(s1)`	Returns true if this string is equal to string s1.
`equalsIgnoreCase(s1)`	Returns true if this string is equal to string s1; it is case insensitive.
`compareTo(s1)`	Returns an integer greater than 0, equal to 0, or less than 0 to indicate whether this string is greater than, equal to, or less than s1.
`compareToIgnoreCase(s1)`	Same as compareTo except that the comparison is case insensitive.
`startsWith(prefix)`	Returns true if this string starts with the specified prefix.
`endsWith(suffix)`	Returns true if this string ends with the specified suffix.
`contains(s1)`	Returns true if s1 is a substring in this string.

How do you compare the contents of two strings? You might attempt to use the
== operator, as follows:

```
if (string1 == string2)
  System.out.println("string1 and string2 are the same object");
else
  System.out.println("string1 and string2 are different objects");
```

==

However, the == operator checks only whether string1 and string2 refer to the
same object; it does not tell you whether they have the same contents. Therefore,
you cannot use the == operator to find out whether two string variables have the
same contents. Instead, you should use the equals method. The following code, for
instance, can be used to compare two strings:

```
if (string1.equals(string2))
  System.out.println("string1 and string2 have the same contents");
else
  System.out.println("string1 and string2 are not equal");
```

string1.equals(string2)

For example, the following statements display true and then false.

```
String s1 = "Welcome to Java";
String s2 = "Welcome to Java";
String s3 = "Welcome to C++";
System.out.println(s1.equals(s2)); // true
System.out.println(s1.equals(s3)); // false
```

The compareTo method can also be used to compare two strings. For example,
consider the following code:

```
s1.compareTo(s2)
```

s1.compareTo(s2)

The method returns the value 0 if s1 is equal to s2, a value less than 0 if s1
is lexicographically (i.e., in terms of Unicode ordering) less than s2, and a value
greater than 0 if s1 is lexicographically greater than s2.

The actual value returned from the compareTo method depends on the offset
of the first two distinct characters in s1 and s2 from left to right. For example,
suppose s1 is abc and s2 is abg, and s1.compareTo(s2) returns -4. The first two
characters (a vs. a) from s1 and s2 are compared. Because they are equal, the sec-
ond two characters (b vs. b) are compared. Because they are also equal, the third
two characters (c vs. g) are compared. Since the character c is 4 less than g, the
comparison returns -4.

> **Caution**
> Syntax errors will occur if you compare strings by using relational
> operators >, >=, <, or <=. Instead, you have to use s1.compareTo(s2).

> **Note**
> The equals method returns true if two strings are equal and false if
> they are not. The compareTo method returns 0, a positive integer, or a
> negative integer, depending on whether one string is equal to, greater
> than, or less than the other string.

The `String` class also provides the `equalsIgnoreCase` and `compareToIgnoreCase` methods for comparing strings. The `equalsIgnoreCase` and `compareToIgnoreCase` methods ignore the case of the letters when comparing two strings. You can also use `str.startsWith(prefix)` to check whether string `str` starts with a specified prefix, `str.endsWith(suffix)` to check whether string `str` ends with a specified suffix, and `str.contains(s1)` to check whether string `str` contains string `s1`. For example,

```
"Welcome to Java".startsWith("We") returns true.
"Welcome to Java".startsWith("we") returns false.
"Welcome to Java".endsWith("va") returns true.
"Welcome to Java".endsWith("v") returns false.
"Welcome to Java".contains("to") returns true.
"Welcome to Java".contains("To") returns false.
```

Listing 5.1 gives a program that prompts the user to enter two cities and displays them in alphabetical order.

LISTING 5.1 OrderTwoCities.java

```java
 1  import java.util.Scanner;
 2
 3  public class OrderTwoCities {
 4    public static void main(String[] args) {
 5      Scanner input = new Scanner(System.in);
 6
 7      // Prompt the user to enter two cities
 8      System.out.print("Enter the first city: ");
 9      String city1 = input.nextLine();
10      System.out.print("Enter the second city: ");
11      String city2 = input.nextLine();
12
13      if (city1.compareTo(city2) < 0)
14        System.out.println("The cities in alphabetical order are " +
15          city1 + " " + city2);
16      else
17        System.out.println("The cities in alphabetical order are " +
18          city2 + " " + city1);
19    }
20  }
```

input city1 — (line 9)

input city2 — (line 11)

compare two cities — (line 13)

```
Enter the first city: New York  ↵Enter
Enter the second city: Boston  ↵Enter
The cities in alphabetical order are Boston New York
```

The program reads two strings for two cities (lines 9, 11). If `input.nextLine()` is replaced by `input.next()` (line 9), you cannot enter a string with spaces for `city1`. Since a city name may contain multiple words separated by spaces, the program uses the `nextLine` method to read a string (lines 9, 11). Invoking `city1.compareTo(city2)` compares two strings `city1` with `city2` (line 13). A negative return value indicates that `city1` is less than `city2`.

Obtaining Substrings

You can obtain a single character from a string using the `charAt` method. You can also obtain a substring from a string using the `substring` method in the `String` class, as shown in Table 5.6.

For example,

```
String message = "Welcome to Java";
String message = message.substring(0, 11) + "HTML";
```

The string `message` now becomes `Welcome to HTML`.

TABLE 5.6 The `String` class contains the methods for obtaining substrings.

Method	Description
substring(beginIndex)	Returns this string's substring that begins with the character at the specified beginIndex and extends to the end of the string, as shown in Figure 5.2.
substring(beginIndex, endIndex)	Returns this string's substring that begins at the specified beginIndex and extends to the character at index endIndex - 1, as shown in Figure 5.2. Note that the character at endIndex is not part of the substring.

FIGURE 5.2 The `substring` method obtains a substring from a string.

Note
If `beginIndex` is `endIndex`, `substring(beginIndex, endIndex)` returns an empty string with length 0. If `beginIndex` > `endIndex`, it would be a runtime error.

beginIndex <= endIndex

Finding a Character or a Substring in a String

The `String` class provides several versions of `indexOf` and `lastIndexOf` methods to find a character or a substring in a string, as shown in Table 5.7.

TABLE 5.7 The `String` class contains the methods for finding substrings.

Method	Description
indexOf(ch)	Returns the index of the first occurrence of ch in the string. Returns –1 if not matched.
indexOf(ch, fromIndex)	Returns the index of the first occurrence of ch after fromIndex in the string. Returns –1 if not matched.
indexOf(s)	Returns the index of the first occurrence of string s in this string. Returns –1 if not matched.
indexOf(s, fromIndex)	Returns the index of the first occurrence of string s in this string after fromIndex. Returns –1 if not matched.
lastIndexOf(ch)	Returns the index of the last occurrence of ch in the string. Returns –1 if not matched.
lastIndexOf(ch, fromIndex)	Returns the index of the last occurrence of ch before fromIndex in this string. Returns –1 if not matched.
lastIndexOf(s)	Returns the index of the last occurrence of string s. Returns –1 if not matched.
lastIndexOf(s, fromIndex)	Returns the index of the last occurrence of string s before fromIndex. Returns –1 if not matched.

For example,

indexOf

"Welcome to Java".indexOf('W') returns 0.
"Welcome to Java".indexOf('o') returns 4.
"Welcome to Java".indexOf('o', 5) returns 9.
"Welcome to Java".indexOf("come") returns 3.
"Welcome to Java".indexOf("Java", 5) returns 11.
"Welcome to Java".indexOf("java", 5) returns -1.

lastIndexOf

"Welcome to Java".lastIndexOf('W') returns 0.
"Welcome to Java".lastIndexOf('o') returns 9.
"Welcome to Java".lastIndexOf('o', 5) returns 4.
"Welcome to Java".lastIndexOf("come") returns 3.
"Welcome to Java".lastIndexOf("Java", 5) returns -1.
"Welcome to Java".lastIndexOf("Java") returns 11.

Suppose a string s contains the first name and last name separated by a space. You can use the following code to extract the first name and last name from the string:

```java
int k = s.indexOf(' ');
String firstName = s.substring(0, k);
String lastName = s.substring(k + 1);
```

For example, if s is Kim Jones, the following diagram illustrates how the first name and last name are extracted.

Conversion between Strings and Numbers

Integer.parseInt method

You can convert a numeric string into a number. To convert a string into an int value, use the `Integer.parseInt` method, as follows:

```java
int intValue = Integer.parseInt(intString);
```

where `intString` is a numeric string such as "123".

Double.parseDouble method

To convert a string into a `double` value, use the `Double.parseDouble` method, as follows:

```java
double doubleValue = Double.parseDouble(doubleString);
```

where `doubleString` is a numeric string such as "123.45".

If the string is not a numeric string, the conversion would cause a runtime error. The `Integer` and `Double` classes are both included in the `java.lang` package, and thus they are automatically imported.

You can convert a number into a string, simply use the string concatenating operator as follows:

number to string

```java
String s = number + "";
```

✓ Section 5.3 Assessment

1. Suppose that s1, s2, and s3 are three strings, given as follows:

```
String s1 = "Welcome to Java";
String s2 = "Programming is fun";
String s3 = "Welcome to Java";
```

What are the results of the following expressions?

(a) s1 == s2

(b) s2 == s3

(c) s1.equals(s2)

(d) s1.equals(s3)

(e) s1.compareTo(s2)

(f) s2.compareTo(s3)

(g) s2.compareTo(s2)

(h) s1.charAt(0)

(i) s1.indexOf('j')

(j) s1.indexOf("to")

(k) s1.lastIndexOf('a')

(l) s1.lastIndexOf("o", 15)

(m) s1.length()

(n) s1.substring(5)

(o) s1.substring(5, 11)

(p) s1.startsWith("Wel")

(q) s1.endsWith("Java")

(r) s1.toLowerCase()

(s) s1.toUpperCase()

(t) s1.concat(s2)

(u) s1.contains(s2)

(v) "\t Wel \t".trim()

2. Suppose that s1 and s2 are two strings. Which of the following statements or expressions are incorrect?

```
String s = "Welcome to Java";
String s3 = s1 + s2;
String s3 = s1 - s2;
s1 == s2;
s1 >= s2;
s1.compareTo(s2);
int i = s1.length();
char c = s1(0);
char c = s1.charAt(s1.length());
```

3. Show the output of the following statements (write a program to verify your results):

```
System.out.println("1" + 1);
System.out.println('1' + 1);
System.out.println("1" + 1 + 1);
System.out.println("1" + (1 + 1));
System.out.println('1' + 1 + 1);
```

4. Evaluate the following expressions (write a program to verify your results):

```
1 + "Welcome " + 1 + 1
1 + "Welcome " + (1 + 1)
1 + "Welcome " + ('\u0001' + 1)
1 + "Welcome " + 'a' + 1
```

5. Let s1 be " Welcome " and s2 be " welcome ". Write the code for the following statements:

(a) Check whether s1 is equal to s2 and assign the result to a Boolean variable isEqual.

(b) Check whether s1 is equal to s2, ignoring case, and assign the result to a Boolean variable isEqual.

(c) Compare s1 with s2 and assign the result to an int variable x.

(d) Compare s1 with s2, ignoring case, and assign the result to an int variable x.

(e) Check whether s1 has the prefix AAA and assign the result to a Boolean variable b.

(f) Check whether s1 has the suffix AAA and assign the result to a Boolean variable b.

(g) Assign the length of s1 to an int variable x.

(h) Assign the first character of s1 to a char variable x.

(i) Create a new string s3 that combines s1 with s2.

(j) Create a substring of s1 starting from index 1.

(k) Create a substring of s1 from index 1 to index 4.

(l) Create a new string s3 that converts s1 to lowercase.

(m) Create a new string s3 that converts s1 to uppercase.

(n) Create a new string s3 that trims whitespace characters on both ends of s1.

(o) Assign the index of the first occurrence of the character e in s1 to an int variable x.

(p) Assign the index of the last occurrence of the string abc in s1 to an int variable x.

5.4 Identifying Software Application Constraints

 Key Point

A constraint is a limit or restriction of your application.

constraints

During the planning and design phase of a software application, project constraints should be identified. Most constraints fall into two categories: a business constraint or a technical constraint.

business constraints

Business constraints often involve project scheduling, budgeting, and security guidelines of the project. For example, if your project has a short deadline, it may prevent the completion of some enhanced features of the application. This is a business constraint.

technical constraints
environmental constraints

Technical constraints are sometimes called *environmental constraints*. They are often beyond the control of the programmer. For instance, a hardware or network configuration may place constraints on the application's performance. Consider an online store application. An example of an environmental constraint is that the application will work only if there is an established connection to the World Wide Web.

Software coding techniques can also impose technical constraints. Section 5.3 introduced the use of the `Char` data type. Using the `Char` data type creates a constraint in your application. Code that uses the `Char` data type is constrained to accept only the 16-bit original Unicode characters.

It is normal for software applications to have constraints. Part of the software design process includes identifying and documenting constraints.

✓ SECTION 5.4 ASSESSMENT

1. What is a constraint? During which phase of the software life cycle should you identify constraints?

2. You are designing an application that retrieves names from a dataset that begin with a particular letter of the alphabet. The user inputs the first letter of the names to be retrieved, and the value is stored in a `char` data type. Users must have login credentials, and company policy will not allow your application to reset passwords. Applications run slowly during a system backup performed every Sunday.

 List the constraints of the project and identify whether each is a business or a technical constraint.

5.5 Case Studies

Strings are fundamental in programming. The ability to write programs using strings is essential in learning Java programming.

 Key Point

You will frequently use strings to write useful programs. This section presents three examples of solving problems using strings.

Case Study: Converting a Hexadecimal Digit to a Decimal Value

The hexadecimal number system has 16 digits: 0–9, A–F. The letters A, B, C, D, E, and F correspond to the decimal numbers 10, 11, 12, 13, 14, and 15. We now write a program that prompts the user to enter a hex digit and display its corresponding decimal value, as shown in Listing 5.2.

LISTING 5.2 `HexDigit2Dec.java`

```
1  import java.util.Scanner;                                      convert hex to decimal
2
3  public class HexDigit2Dec {
4    public static void main(String[] args) {
5      Scanner input = new Scanner(System.in);
6      System.out.print("Enter a hex digit: ");
7      String hexString = input.nextLine();                       input string
8
9      // Check if the hex string has exactly one character        check length
10     if (hexString.length() != 1) {
11       System.out.println("You must enter exactly one character");
12       System.exit(1);
13     }
```

```
14
15        // Display decimal value for the hex digit
16        char ch = Character.toUpperCase(hexString.charAt(0));
17        if (ch <= 'F' && ch >= 'A') {
18          int value = ch - 'A' + 10;
19          System.out.println("The decimal value for hex digit "
20            + ch + " is " + value);
21        }
22        else if (Character.isDigit(ch)) {
23          System.out.println("The decimal value for hex digit "
24            + ch + " is " + ch);
25        }
26        else {
27          System.out.println(ch + " is an invalid input");
28        }
29      }
30    }
```

is 0-9?

```
Enter a hex digit: AB7C  ↵Enter
You must enter exactly one character
```

```
Enter a hex digit: B  ↵Enter
The decimal value for hex digit B is 11
```

```
Enter a hex digit: 8  ↵Enter
The decimal value for hex digit 8 is 8
```

```
Enter a hex digit: T  ↵Enter
T is an invalid input
```

The program reads a string from the console (line 7) and checks if the string contains a single character (line 10). If not, report an error and exit the program (line 12).

The program invokes the `Character.toUpperCase` method to obtain the character `ch` as an uppercase letter (line 16). If `ch` is between `'A'` and `'F'` (line 17), the corresponding decimal value is `ch - 'A' + 10` (line 18). Note that `ch - 'A'` is 0 if `ch` is `'A'`, `ch - 'A'` is 1 if `ch` is `'B'`, and so on. When two characters perform a numerical operation, the characters' Unicodes are used in the computation.

The program invokes the `Character.isDigit(ch)` method to check if `ch` is between `'0'` and `'9'` (line 22). If so, the corresponding decimal digit is the same as `ch` (lines 23–24).

If `ch` is not between `'A'` and `'F'` nor a digit character, the program displays an error message (line 27).

Case Study: Revising the Lottery Program Using Strings

The lottery program in Chapter 4, Listing 4.8, Lottery.java, generates a random two-digit number, prompts the user to enter a two-digit number, and determines whether the user wins according to the following rule:

1. If the user input matches the lottery number in the exact order, the award is $10,000.

2. If all the digits in the user input match all the digits in the lottery number, the award is $3,000.

3. If one digit in the user input matches a digit in the lottery number, the award is $1,000.

The program in Listing 4.8 uses an integer to store the number. Listing 5.3 gives a new program that generates a random two-digit string instead of a number and receives the user input as a string instead of a number.

LISTING 5.3 LotteryUsingStrings.java

```java
1  import java.util.Scanner;
2
3  public class LotteryUsingStrings {
4    public static void main(String[] args) {
5      // Generate a lottery as a two-digit string
6      String lottery = "" + (int)(Math.random() * 10)          generate a lottery
7        + (int)(Math.random() * 10);
8
9      // Prompt the user to enter a guess
10     Scanner input = new Scanner(System.in);
11     System.out.print("Enter your lottery pick (two digits): ");
12     String guess = input.nextLine();                          enter a guess
13
14     // Get digits from lottery
15     char lotteryDigit1 = lottery.charAt(0);
16     char lotteryDigit2 = lottery.charAt(1);
17
18     // Get digits from guess
19     char guessDigit1 = guess.charAt(0);
20     char guessDigit2 = guess.charAt(1);
21
22     System.out.println("The lottery number is " + lottery);
23
24     // Check the guess
25     if (guess.equals(lottery))                                exact match?
26       System.out.println("Exact match: you win $10,000");
27     else if (guessDigit2 == lotteryDigit1                     match all digits?
28         && guessDigit1 == lotteryDigit2)
29       System.out.println("Match all digits: you win $3,000");
30     else if (guessDigit1 == lotteryDigit1                     match one digit?
31         || guessDigit1 == lotteryDigit2
32         || guessDigit2 == lotteryDigit1
33         || guessDigit2 == lotteryDigit2)
34       System.out.println("Match one digit: you win $1,000");
35     else
36       System.out.println("Sorry, no match");
37   }
38 }
```

```
Enter your lottery pick (two digits): 00 [↵Enter]
The lottery number is 00
Exact match: you win $10,000
```

```
Enter your lottery pick (two digits): 45 [↵Enter]
The lottery number is 54
Match all digits: you win $3,000
```

```
Enter your lottery pick: 23 [↵Enter]
The lottery number is 34
Match one digit: you win $1,000
```

```
Enter your lottery pick: 23 [↵Enter]
The lottery number is 14
Sorry: no match
```

The program generates two random digits and concatenates them into the string `lottery` (lines 6–7). After this, `lottery` contains two random digits.

The program prompts the user to enter a guess as a two-digit string (line 12) and checks the guess against the lottery number in this order:

- First check whether the guess matches the lottery exactly (line 25).
- If not, check whether the reversal of the guess matches the lottery (line 27).
- If not, check whether one digit is in the lottery (lines 30–33).
- If not, nothing matches and display "Sorry, no match" (line 36).

Case Study: Guessing Birthdays

You can find out the date of the month when your friend was born by asking five questions. Each question asks whether the day is in one of the five sets of numbers.

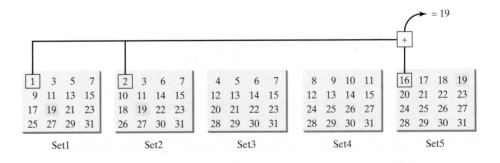

The birthday is the sum of the first numbers in the sets where the day appears. For example, if the birthday is 19, it appears in Set1, Set2, and Set5. The first numbers in these three sets are 1, 2, and 16. Their sum is 19.

Listing 5.4 gives a program that prompts the user to answer whether the day is in Set1 (lines 41–44), in Set2 (lines 50–53), in Set3 (lines 59–62), in Set4 (lines 68–71), and in Set5 (lines 77–80). If the number is in the set, the program adds the first number in the set to day (lines 47, 56, 65, 74, 83).

LISTING 5.4 GuessBirthday.java

```java
 1  import java.util.Scanner;
 2
 3  public class GuessBirthday {
 4    public static void main(String[] args) {
 5      String set1 =
 6        " 1  3  5  7\n" +
 7        " 9 11 13 15\n" +
 8        "17 19 21 23\n" +
 9        "25 27 29 31";
10
11      String set2 =
12        " 2  3  6  7\n" +
13        "10 11 14 15\n" +
14        "18 19 22 23\n" +
15        "26 27 30 31";
16
17      String set3 =
18        " 4  5  6  7\n" +
19        "12 13 14 15\n" +
20        "20 21 22 23\n" +
21        "28 29 30 31";
22
23      String set4 =
24        " 8  9 10 11\n" +
25        "12 13 14 15\n" +
26        "24 25 26 27\n" +
27        "28 29 30 31";
28
29      String set5 =
30        "16 17 18 19\n" +
31        "20 21 22 23\n" +
32        "24 25 26 27\n" +
33        "28 29 30 31";
34
35      int day = 0;                                           day to be determined
36
37      // Create a Scanner
38      Scanner input = new Scanner(System.in);
39
40      // Prompt the user to answer questions
41      System.out.print("Is your birthday in Set1?\n");
42      System.out.print(set1);
43      System.out.print("\nEnter 0 for No and 1 for Yes: ");
44      int answer = input.nextInt();
45
```

Page 154 Chapter 5 Working with Characters and Strings

in Set1?

```java
46     if (answer == 1)
47        day += 1;
48
49        // Prompt the user to answer questions
50        System.out.print("\nIs your birthday in Set2?\n");
51        System.out.print(set2);
52        System.out.print("\nEnter 0 for No and 1 for Yes: ");
53        answer = input.nextInt();
54
```

in Set2?

```java
55     if (answer == 1)
56        day += 2;
57
58        // Prompt the user to answer questions
59        System.out.print("Is your birthday in Set3?\n");
60        System.out.print(set3);
61        System.out.print("\nEnter 0 for No and 1 for Yes: ");
62        answer = input.nextInt();
63
```

in Set3?

```java
64     if (answer == 1)
65        day += 4;
66
67        // Prompt the user to answer questions
68        System.out.print("\nIs your birthday in Set4?\n");
69        System.out.print(set4);
70        System.out.print("\nEnter 0 for No and 1 for Yes: ");
71        answer = input.nextInt();
72
```

in Set4?

```java
73     if (answer == 1)
74        day += 8;
75
76        // Prompt the user to answer questions
77        System.out.print("\nIs your birthday in Set5?\n");
78        System.out.print(set5);
79        System.out.print("\nEnter 0 for No and 1 for Yes: ");
80        answer = input.nextInt();
81
```

in Set5?

```java
82     if (answer == 1)
83        day += 16;
84
85        System.out.println("\nYour birthday is " + day + "!");
86     }
87  }
```

```
Is your birthday in Set1?
 1   3   5   7
 9  11  13  15
17  19  21  23
25  27  29  31
Enter 0 for No and 1 for Yes: 1 ↵Enter

Is your birthday in Set2?
 2   3   6   7
10  11  14  15
18  19  22  23
26  27  30  31
Enter 0 for No and 1 for Yes: 1 ↵Enter

Is your birthday in Set3?
 4   5   6   7
12  13  14  15
20  21  22  23
28  29  30  31
Enter 0 for No and 1 for Yes: 0 ↵Enter

Is your birthday in Set4?
 8   9  10  11
12  13  14  15
24  25  26  27
28  29  30  31
Enter 0 for No and 1 for Yes: 0 ↵Enter

Is your birthday in Set5?
16  17  18  19
20  21  22  23
24  25  26  27
28  29  30  31
Enter 0 for No and 1 for Yes: 1 ↵Enter
Your birthday is 19!
```

line#	day	answer	output
35	0		
44		1	
47	1		
53		1	
56	3		
62		0	
71		0	
80		1	
83	19		
85			Your birthday is 19!

mathematics behind the game

This game is easy to program. You may wonder how the game was created. The mathematics behind the game is actually quite simple. The numbers are not grouped together by accident—the way they are placed in the five sets is deliberate. The starting numbers in the five sets are 1, 2, 4, 8, and 16, which correspond to 1, 10, 100, 1000, and 10000 in binary (binary numbers are introduced in Appendix D, Number Systems). A binary number for decimal integers between 1 and 31 has at most five digits, as shown in Figure 5.3a. Let it be Thus, as shown in Figure 5.3b. If a day's binary number has a digit 1 in the number should appear in Setk. For example, number 19 is binary 10011, so it appears in Set1, Set2, and Set5. It is binary 1 + 10 + 10000 = 10011 or decimal 1 + 2 + 16 = 19. Number 31 is binary 11111, so it appears in Set1, Set2, Set3, Set4, and Set5. It is binary 1 + 10 + 100 + 1000 + 10000 = 11111 or decimal 1 + 2 + 4 + 8 + 16 = 31.

FIGURE 5.3 (a) A number between 1 and 31 can be represented using a five-digit binary number. (b) A five-digit binary number can be obtained by adding binary numbers 1, 10, 100, 1000, or 10000.

✓ SECTION 5.5 ASSESSMENT

1. If you run Listing 5.4 GuessBirthday.java with input 1 for Set1, Set3, and Set4 and 0 for Set2 and Set5, what will be the birthday?

5.6 Formatting Console Output

You can use the `System.out.printf` *method to display formatted output on the console.*

Key Point

Often, it is desirable to display numbers in a certain format. For example, the following code computes interest, given the amount and the annual interest rate.

```
double amount = 12618.98;
double interestRate = 0.0013;
double interest = amount * interestRate;
System.out.println("Interest is $" + interest);
```

```
Interest is $16.404674
```

Because the interest amount is currency, it is desirable to display only two digits after the decimal point. To do this, you can write the code as follows:

```
double amount = 12618.98;
double interestRate = 0.0013;
double interest = amount * interestRate;
System.out.println("Interest is $"
  + (int)(interest * 100) / 100.0);
```

```
Interest is $16.4
```

However, the format is still not correct. There should be two digits after the decimal point: `16.40` rather than `16.4`. You can fix it by using the `printf` method, like this:

printf

```
double amount = 12618.98;
double interestRate = 0.0013;
double interest = amount * interestRate;
System.out.printf("Interest is $%4.2f",
  interest);
```

format specifier

field width · precision · conversion code

```
Interest is $16.40
```

The syntax to invoke this method is

```
System.out.printf(format, item1, item2, ..., itemk)
```

where `format` is a string that may consist of substrings and format specifiers.

A *format specifier* specifies how an item should be displayed. An item may be a numeric value, a character, a Boolean value, or a string. A simple format specifier consists of a percent sign (%) followed by a conversion code. Table 5.8 lists some frequently used simple format specifiers.

format specifier

TABLE 5.8 Frequently Used Format Specifiers

Format Specifier	Output	Example
%b	a Boolean value	true or false
%c	a character	'a'
%d	a decimal integer	200
%f	a floating-point number	45.460000
%e	a number in standard scientific notation	4.556000e+01
%s	a string	"Java is cool"

Here is an example:

```
int count = 5;
double amount = 45.56;
System.out.printf("count is %d and amount is %f", count, amount);
```

display count is 5 and amount is 45.560000

Items must match the format specifiers in order, in number, and in exact type. For example, the format specifier for `count` is `%d` and for `amount` is `%f`. By default, a floating-point value is displayed with six digits after the decimal point. You can specify the width and precision in a format specifier, as shown in the examples in Table 5.9.

TABLE 5.9 Examples of Specifying Width and Precision

Example	Output
%5c	Output the character and add four spaces before the character item, because the width is 5.
%6b	Output the Boolean value and add one space before the false value and two spaces before the true value.
%5d	Output the integer item with width at least 5. If the number of digits in the item is <5, add spaces before the number. If the number of digits in the item is >5, the width is automatically increased.
%10.2f	Output the floating-point item with width at least 10 including a decimal point and two digits after the point. Thus, there are 7 digits allocated before the decimal point. If the number of digits before the decimal point in the item is <7, add spaces before the number. If the number of digits before the decimal point in the item is >7, the width is automatically increased.
%10.2e	Output the floating-point item with width at least 10 including a decimal point, two digits after the point and the exponent part. If the displayed number in scientific notation has width less than 10, add spaces before the number.
%12s	Output the string with width at least 12 characters. If the string item has fewer than 12 characters, add spaces before the string. If the string item has more than 12 characters, the width is automatically increased.

If an item requires more spaces than the specified width, the width is automatically increased. For example, the following code

```
System.out.printf("%3d#%2s#%4.2f\n", 1234, "Java", 51.6653);
```

displays

```
1234#Java#51.67
```

The specified width for `int` item `1234` is `3`, which is smaller than its actual size `4`. The width is automatically increased to `4`. The specified width for string item `Java` is `2`, which is smaller than its actual size `4`. The width is automatically increased to `4`. The specified width for `double` item `51.6653` is `4`, but it needs width `5` to display 51.67, so the width is automatically increased to `5`.

By default, the output is right justified. You can put the minus sign (-) in the format specifier to specify that the item is left justified in the output within the specified field. For example, the following statements

right justify

left justify

```
System.out.printf("%8d%8s%8.1f\n", 1234, "Java", 5.63);
System.out.printf("%-8d%-8s%-8.1f \n", 1234, "Java", 5.63);
```

display

where the square box (□) denotes a blank space.

> **Caution**
> The items must match the format specifiers in exact type. The item for the format specifier %f or %e must be a floating-point type value such as 40.0, not 40. Thus, an `int` variable cannot match %f or %e.

> **Tip**
> The % sign denotes a format specifier. To output a literal % in the format string, use %%.

✓ SECTION 5.6 ASSESSMENT

1. What are the format specifiers for outputting a Boolean value, a character, a decimal integer, a floating-point number, and a string?

2. What is wrong in the following statements?

 (**a**) `System.out.printf("%5d %d", 1, 2, 3);`

 (**b**) `System.out.printf("%5d %f", 1);`

 (**c**) `System.out.printf("%5d %f", 1, 2);`

3. Show the output of the following statements.

(a) `System.out.printf("amount is %f %e\n", 32.32, 32.32);`

(b) `System.out.printf("amount is %5.2%% %5.4e\n", 32.327, 32.32);`

(c) `System.out.printf("%6b\n", (1 > 2));`

(d) `System.out.printf("%6s\n", "Java");`

(e) `System.out.printf("%-6b%s\n", (1 > 2), "Java");`

(f) `System.out.printf("%6b%-8s\n", (1 > 2), "Java");`

Chapter 5 — Review and Assessment

KEY TERMS

business constraints 148
char type 134
concatenation 140
constraints 148
encoding 134
escape character 136
escape sequence 136
format specifier 157
instance method 139

method 134
pre-defined method 134
static method 139
string object 139
supplementary Unicode 134
technical constraints 148
trim() method 141
Unicode 134

CHAPTER SUMMARY

1. The character type char represents a single character.

2. An escape sequence consists of a backslash (\) followed by a character or a combination of digits.

3. The character \ is called the escape character.

4. The characters ' ', \t, \f, \r, and \n are known as the whitespace characters.

5. Characters can be compared based on their Unicode using the relational operators.

6. The Character class contains the methods isDigit, isLetter, isLetterOrDigit, isLowerCase, isUpperCase for testing whether a character is a digit, letter, lowercase, and uppercase. It also contains the toLowerCase and toUpperCase methods for returning a lowercase or uppercase letter.

7. A *string* is a sequence of characters. A string value is enclosed in matching double quotes ("). A character value is enclosed in matching single quotes (').

8. Strings are objects in Java. A method that can only be invoked from a specific object is called an *instance method*. A non-instance method is called a static method, which can be invoked without using an object.

9. You can get the length of a string by invoking its length() method, retrieve a character at the specified index in the string using the charAt(index) method, and use the indexOf and lastIndexOf methods to find a character or a substring in a string.

10. You can use the `concat` method to concatenate two strings, or the plus (+) operator to concatenate two or more strings.

11. You can use the `substring` method to obtain a substring from the string.

12. You can use the `equals` and `compareTo` methods to compare strings. The `equals` method returns `true` if two strings are equal, and `false` if they are not equal. The `compareTo` method returns 0, a positive integer, or a negative integer, depending on whether one string is equal to, greater than, or less than the other string.

13. The `printf` method can be used to display a formatted output using format specifiers.

14. A *constraint* is a limit or restriction of your application. Constraints should be identified early in the software lifecycle during the design and planning stage.

PROGRAMMING EXERCISES

Note

Exercises preceded by a star (*) are more challenging.

*1. (*Find the character of an ASCII code*) Write a program that receives an ASCII code (an integer between 0 and 127) and displays its character. Here is a sample run:

```
Enter an ASCII code: 69  ↵Enter
The character for ASCII code 69 is E
```

*2. (*Find the Unicode of a character*) Write a program that receives a character and displays its Unicode. Here is a sample run:

```
Enter a character: E  ↵Enter
The Unicode for the character E is 69
```

*3. (*Guess birthday*) Rewrite Listing 5.4, GuessBirthday.java, to prompt the user to enter the character Y for Yes and N for No rather than entering 1 for Yes and 0 for No.

***4.** (*Decimal to hex*) Write a program that prompts the user to enter an integer between 0 and 15 and displays its corresponding hex number. Here are some sample runs:

```
Enter a decimal value (0 to 15): 11 ↵Enter
The hex value is B
```

```
Enter a decimal value (0 to 15): 5 ↵Enter
The hex value is 5
```

```
Enter a decimal value (0 to 15): 31 ↵Enter
31 is an invalid input
```

***5.** (*Hex to binary*) Write a program that prompts the user to enter a hex digit and displays its corresponding binary number. Here is a sample run:

```
Enter a hex digit: B ↵Enter
The binary value is 1011
```

```
Enter a hex digit: G ↵Enter
G is an invalid input
```

***6.** (*Vowel or consonant?*) Write a program that prompts the user to enter a letter and check whether the letter is a vowel or consonant. Here is a sample run:

```
Enter a letter: B ↵Enter
B is a consonant
```

```
Enter a letter grade: a ↵Enter
a is a vowel
```

```
Enter a letter grade: # ↵Enter
# is an invalid input
```

*7. (*Convert letter grade to number*) Write a program that prompts the user to enter a letter grade A, B, C, D, or F and displays its corresponding numeric value 4, 3, 2, 1, or 0. Here is a sample run:

```
Enter a letter grade: B  ↵Enter
The numeric value for grade B is 3
```

```
Enter a letter grade: T  ↵Enter
T is an invalid grade
```

*8. (*Phone key pads*) The international standard letter/number mapping found on the telephone is shown below:

Write a program that prompts the user to enter a letter and displays its corresponding number.

```
Enter a letter: A  ↵Enter
The corresponding number is 2
```

```
Enter a letter: a  ↵Enter
The corresponding number is 2
```

```
Enter a letter: +  ↵Enter
+ is an invalid input
```

9. (*Random character*) Write a program that displays a random uppercase letter using the `Math.random()` method.

10. (*Process a string*) Write a program that prompts the user to enter a string and displays its length and its first character.

11. (*Check substring*) Write a program that prompts the user to enter two strings and reports whether the second string is a substring of the first string.

```
Enter string s1: ABCD  ↵Enter
Enter string s2: BC  ↵Enter
BC is a substring of ABCD
```

```
Enter string s1: ABCD  ↵Enter
Enter string s2: BDC  ↵Enter
BDC is not a substring of ABCD
```

***12.** (*Order three cities*) Write a program that prompts the user to enter three cities and displays them in ascending order. Here is a sample run:

```
Enter the first city: Chicago  ↵Enter
Enter the second city: Los Angeles  ↵Enter
Enter the third city: Atlanta  ↵Enter
The three cities in alphabetical order are Atlanta Chicago Los
Angeles
```

USING LOOPING STATEMENTS

Objectives

- Write programs for executing statements repeatedly using a `while` loop.

- Apply algorithm strategies to design a loop.

- Control a loop with a sentinel value.

- Write loops using `do-while` statements.

- Write loops using `for` statements.

- Discover the similarities and differences of three types of loop statements.

- Implement program control with `break` and `continue`.

6.1 Introduction

A loop can be used to tell a program to execute statements repeatedly.

problem

Suppose that you need to display a string (e.g., `Welcome to Java!`) a hundred times. It would be tedious to have to write the following statement a hundred times:

100 times
```
System.out.println("Welcome to Java!");
System.out.println("Welcome to Java!");
...
System.out.println("Welcome to Java!");
```

So, how do you solve this problem?

loop

Java provides a powerful construct called a *loop* that controls how many times an operation or a sequence of operations is performed in succession. Using a loop statement, you simply tell the computer to display a string a hundred times without having to code the print statement a hundred times, as follows:

```
int count = 0;
while (count < 100) {
    System.out.println("Welcome to Java!");
    count++;
}
```

The variable `count` is initially 0. The loop checks whether `count < 100` is `true`. If so, it executes the loop body to display the message `Welcome to Java!` and increments `count` by 1. It repeatedly executes the loop body until `count < 100` becomes `false`. When `count < 100` is `false` (i.e., when `count` reaches 100), the loop terminates and the next statement after the loop statement is executed.

Loops are constructs that control repeated executions of a block of statements. The concept of looping is fundamental to programming. Java provides three types of loop statements: `while` loops, `do-while` loops, and `for` loops.

6.2 The `while` Loop

A `while` loop executes statements repeatedly while the condition is true.

The syntax for the `while` loop is:

while loop

```
while (loop-continuation-condition) {
    // Loop body
    Statement(s);
}
```

loop body

iteration

loop-continuation-
condition

Figure 6.1a shows the `while`-loop flowchart. The part of the loop that contains the statements to be repeated is called the *loop body*. A one-time execution of a loop body is referred to as an *iteration (or repetition) of the loop*. Each loop contains a *loop-continuation-condition,* a Boolean expression that controls the execution of the body. It is evaluated each time to determine if the loop body is executed. If its evaluation is `true`, the loop body is executed; if its evaluation is `false`, the entire loop terminates and the program control turns to the statement that follows the `while` loop.

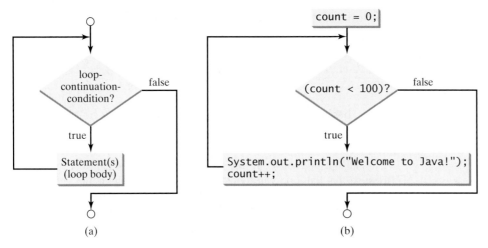

FIGURE 6.1 The `while` loop repeatedly executes the statements in the loop body when the `loop-continuation-condition` evaluates to `true`.

The loop for displaying `Welcome to Java!` a hundred times introduced in the preceding section is an example of a `while` loop. Its flowchart is shown in Figure 6.1b. The `loop-continuation-condition` is `count < 100` and the loop body contains the following two statements:

```java
                                  loop-continuation-condition
int count = 0;
while (count < 100)  {
   System.out.printIn("Welcome to Java!");   } loop body
   count++;
}
```

In this example, you know exactly how many times the loop body needs to be executed because the control variable `count` is used to count the number of executions. This type of loop is known as a *counter-controlled loop*.

counter-controlled loop

 Note
> The `loop-continuation-condition` must always appear inside the parentheses. The braces enclosing the loop body can be omitted only if the loop body contains one or no statement.

Here is another example to help understand how a loop works.

```java
int sum = 0, i = 1;
while (i < 10) {
   sum = sum + i;
   i++;
}
System.out.println("sum is " + sum); // sum is 45
```

If `i < 10` is `true`, the program adds `i` to `sum`. Variable `i` is initially set to 1, then is incremented to 2, 3, and up to 10. When `i` is 10, `i < 10` is `false`, so the loop exits. Therefore, the sum is 1 + 2 + 3 + ... + 9 = 45.

What happens if the loop is mistakenly written as follows?

```java
int sum = 0, i = 1;
while (i < 10) {
    sum = sum + i;
}
```

This loop is infinite, because i is always 1 and i < 10 will always be `true`.

Note

infinite loop

Make sure that the `loop-continuation-condition` eventually becomes `false` so that the loop will terminate. A common programming error involves *infinite loops* (i. e., the loop runs forever). If your program takes an unusually long time to run and does not stop, it may have an infinite loop. If you are running the program from the command window, press *CTRL+C* to stop it.

Caution

off-by-one error

Programmers often make the mistake of executing a loop one more or less time. This is commonly known as the *off-by-one error*. For example, the following loop displays `Welcome to Java` 101 times rather than 100 times. The error lies in the condition, which should be `count < 100` rather than `count <= 100`.

```java
int count = 0;
while (count <= 100) {
    System.out.println("Welcome to Java!");
    count++;
}
```

Recall that Listing 4.1, AdditionQuiz.java, gives a program that prompts the user to enter an answer for a question on addition of two single digits. Using a loop, you can now rewrite the program to let the user repeatedly enter a new answer until it is correct, as shown in Listing 6.1.

LISTING 6.1 RepeatAdditionQuiz.java

```java
 1  import java.util.Scanner;
 2
 3  public class RepeatAdditionQuiz {
 4    public static void main(String[] args) {
 5      int number1 = (int)(Math.random() * 10);
 6      int number2 = (int)(Math.random() * 10);
 7
 8      // Create a Scanner
 9      Scanner input = new Scanner(System.in);
10
11      System.out.print(
12        "What is " + number1 + " + " + number2 + "? ");
13      int answer = input.nextInt();
14
15      while (number1 + number2 != answer) {
16        System.out.print("Wrong answer. Try again. What is "
17          + number1 + " + " + number2 + "? ");
18        answer = input.nextInt();
19      }
20
```

generate number1 (line 5)
generate number2 (line 6)

show question (line 11)

get first answer (line 13)

check answer (line 15)

read an answer (line 18)

```
21        System.out.println("You got it!");
22    }
23 }
```

```
What is 5 + 9? 12 ↵Enter
Wrong answer. Try again. What is 5 + 9? 34 ↵Enter
Wrong answer. Try again. What is 5 + 9? 14 ↵Enter
You got it!
```

The loop in lines 15–19 repeatedly prompts the user to enter an `answer` when `number1 + number2 != answer` is `true`. Once `number1 + number2 != answer` is `false`, the loop exits.

Case Study: Guessing Numbers

The problem is to guess what number a computer has in mind. You will write a program that randomly generates an integer between `0` and `100`, inclusive. The program prompts the user to enter a number continuously until the number matches the randomly generated number. For each user input, the program tells the user whether the input is too low or too high, so the user can make the next guess intelligently. Here is a sample run:

Guess a number

```
Guess a magic number between 0 and 100
Enter your guess: 50 ↵Enter
Your guess is too high
Enter your guess: 25 ↵Enter
Your guess is too low
Enter your guess: 42 ↵Enter
Your guess is too high
Enter your guess: 39 ↵Enter
Yes, the number is 39
```

The magic number is between `0` and `100`. To minimize the number of guesses, enter `50` first. If your guess is too high, the magic number is between `0` and `49`. If your guess is too low, the magic number is between `51` and `100`. So, you can eliminate half of the numbers from further consideration after one guess.

intelligent guess

How do you write this program? Do you immediately begin coding? No. It is important to *think before coding*. Think how you would solve the problem without writing a program. You need first to generate a random number between `0` and `100`, inclusive, then to prompt the user to enter a guess, and then to compare the guess with the random number.

think before coding

It is a good practice to *code incrementally* one step at a time. For programs involving loops, if you don't know how to write a loop right away, you may first write the code for executing the loop one time, and then figure out how to repeatedly execute the code in a loop. For this program, you may create an initial draft, as shown in Listing 6.2.

code incrementally

LISTING 6.2 GuessNumberOneTime.java

```
 1  import java.util.Scanner;
 2
 3  public class GuessNumberOneTime {
 4    public static void main(String[] args) {
 5      // Generate a random number to be guessed
 6      int number = (int)(Math.random() * 101);
 7
 8      Scanner input = new Scanner(System.in);
 9      System.out.println("Guess a magic number between 0 and 100");
10
11      // Prompt the user to guess the number
12      System.out.print("\nEnter your guess: ");
13      int guess = input.nextInt();
14
15      if (guess == number)
16        System.out.println("Yes, the number is " + number);
17      else if (guess > number)
18        System.out.println("Your guess is too high");
19      else
20        System.out.println("Your guess is too low");
21    }
22  }
```

generate a number

enter a guess

correct guess?

too high?

too low?

When you run this program, it prompts the user to enter a guess only once. To let the user enter a guess repeatedly, you may wrap the code in lines 11–20 in a loop as follows:

```
while (true) {
  // Prompt the user to guess the number
  System.out.print("\nEnter your guess: ");
  guess = input.nextInt();

  if (guess == number)
    System.out.println("Yes, the number is " + number);
  else if (guess > number)
    System.out.println("Your guess is too high");
  else
    System.out.println("Your guess is too low");
} // End of loop
```

This loop repeatedly prompts the user to enter a guess. However, this loop is not correct, because it never terminates. When **guess** matches **number**, the loop should end. So, the loop can be revised as follows:

```
while (guess != number) {
  // Prompt the user to guess the number
  System.out.print("\nEnter your guess: ");
  guess = input.nextInt();

  if (guess == number)
    System.out.println("Yes, the number is " + number);
  else if (guess > number)
    System.out.println("Your guess is too high");
  else
    System.out.println("Your guess is too low");
} // End of loop
```

The complete code is given in Listing 6.3.

LISTING 6.3 GuessNumber.java

```java
1   import java.util.Scanner;
2
3   public class GuessNumber {
4     public static void main(String[] args) {
5       // Generate a random number to be guessed
6       int number = (int)(Math.random() * 101);
7
8       Scanner input = new Scanner(System.in);
9       System.out.println("Guess a magic number between 0 and 100");
10
11      int guess = -1;
12      while (guess != number) {
13        // Prompt the user to guess the number
14        System.out.print("\nEnter your guess: ");
15        guess = input.nextInt();
16
17        if (guess == number)
18          System.out.println("Yes, the number is " + number);
19        else if (guess > number)
20          System.out.println("Your guess is too high");
21        else
22          System.out.println("Your guess is too low");
23      } // End of loop
24    }
25  }
```

generate a number

enter a guess

too high?

too low?

	line#	number	guess	output
	6	39		
	11		-1	
iteration 1 {	15		50	
	20			Your guess is too high
iteration 2 {	15		25	
	22			Your guess is too low
iteration 3 {	15		42	
	20			Your guess is too high
iteration 4 {	15		39	
	18			Yes, the number is 39

The program generates the magic number in line 6 and prompts the user to enter a guess continuously in a loop (lines 12–23). For each guess, the program checks whether the guess is correct, too high, or too low (lines 17–22). When the guess is correct, the program exits the loop (line 12). Note that guess is initialized to -1. Initializing it to a value between 0 and 100 would be wrong, because that could be the number to be guessed.

Loop Design Strategies

Writing a correct loop is not an easy task for novice programmers. Before coding, it is helpful to plan out the steps and develop an algorithm. Consider three steps when writing a loop.

Step 1: Identify the statements that need to be repeated.

Step 2: Wrap these statements in a loop like this:

```java
while (true) {
  Statements;
}
```

Step 3: Code the `loop-continuation-condition` and add appropriate statements for controlling the loop.

```java
while (loop-continuation-condition) {
  Statements;
  Additional statements for controlling the loop;
}
```

Case Study: Multiple Subtraction Quiz

Multiple subtraction quiz

The Math subtraction learning tool program in Listing 4.3, SubtractionQuiz.java, generates just one question for each run. You can use a loop to generate questions repeatedly. How do you write the code to generate five questions? Follow the loop design strategy. First, identify the statements that need to be repeated. These are the statements for obtaining two random numbers, prompting the user with a subtraction question, and grading the question. Second, wrap the statements in a loop. Third, add a loop control variable and the `loop-continuation-condition` to execute the loop five times.

Listing 6.4 gives a program that generates five questions and, after a student answers all five, reports the number of correct answers. The program also displays the time spent on the test and lists all the questions.

LISTING 6.4 SubtractionQuizLoop.java

```java
 1  import java.util.Scanner;
 2
 3  public class SubtractionQuizLoop {
 4    public static void main(String[] args) {
 5      final int NUMBER_OF_QUESTIONS = 5; // Number of questions
 6      int correctCount = 0; // Count the number of correct answers
 7      int count = 0; // Count the number of questions
 8      long startTime = System.currentTimeMillis();
 9      String output = " "; // output string is initially empty
10      Scanner input = new Scanner(System.in);
11
12      while (count < NUMBER_OF_QUESTIONS) {
13        // 1. Generate two random single-digit integers
14        int number1 = (int)(Math.random() * 10);
15        int number2 = (int)(Math.random() * 10);
16
17        // 2. If number1 < number2, swap number1 with number2
18        if (number1 < number2) {
19          int temp = number1;
```

get start time

loop

```
20            number1 = number2;
21            number2 = temp;
22        }
23
24        // 3. Prompt the student to answer "What is number1 - number2?"
25        System.out.print(
26            "What is " + number1 + " - " + number2 + "? ");
27        int answer = input.nextInt();
28
29        // 4. Grade the answer and display the result
30        if (number1 - number2 == answer) {
31            System.out.println("You are correct!");
32            correctCount++; // Increase the correct answer count
33        }
34        else
35            System.out.println("Your answer is wrong.\n" + number1
36                + " - " + number2 + " should be " + (number1 - number2));
37
38        // Increase the question count
39        count++;
40
41        output += "\n" + number1 + "-" + number2 + "=" + answer +
42            ((number1 - number2 == answer) ? " correct" : " wrong");
43    }
44
45    long endTime = System.currentTimeMillis();
46    long testTime = endTime - startTime;
47
48    System.out.println("Correct count is " + correctCount +
49        "\nTest time is " + testTime / 1000 + " seconds\n" + output);
50    }
51 }
```

- display a question

- grade an answer

- increase correct count

- increase control variable

- prepare output

- end loop

- get end time
- test time

- display result

```
What is 9 - 2? 7 ↵Enter
You are correct!

What is 3 - 0? 3 ↵Enter
You are correct!

What is 3 - 2? 1 ↵Enter
You are correct!

What is 7 - 4? 4 ↵Enter
Your answer is wrong.
7 - 4 should be 3

What is 7 - 5? 4 ↵Enter
Your answer is wrong.
7 - 5 should be 2

Correct count is 3
Test time is 1021 seconds

9-2=7 correct
3-0=3 correct
3-2=1 correct
7-4=4 wrong
7-5=4 wrong
```

The program uses the control variable `count` to control the execution of the loop. `count` is initially `0` (line 7) and is increased by `1` in each iteration (line 39). A subtraction question is displayed and processed in each iteration. The program obtains the time before the test starts in line 8 and the time after the test ends in line 45, and computes the test time in line 46. The test time is in milliseconds and is converted to seconds in line 49.

Controlling a Loop with a Sentinel Value

sentinel value

sentinel-controlled loop

Another common technique for controlling a loop is to designate a special value when reading and processing a set of values. This special input value, known as a *sentinel value*, signifies the end of the input. A loop that uses a sentinel value to control its execution is called a *sentinel-controlled loop*.

Listing 6.5 writes a program that reads and calculates the sum of an unspecified number of integers. The input `0` signifies the end of the input. Do you need to declare a new variable for each input value? No. Just use one variable named `data` (line 12) to store the input value and use a variable named `sum` (line 15) to store the total. Whenever a value is read, assign it to `data` and, if it is not zero, add it to `sum` (line 17).

LISTING 6.5 SentinelValue.java

```
1  import java.util.Scanner;
2
3  public class SentinelValue {
4    /** Main method */
5    public static void main(String[] args) {
6      // Create a Scanner
7      Scanner input = new Scanner(System.in);
8
9      // Read an initial data
10     System.out.print(
11       "Enter an integer (the input ends if it is 0): ");
12     int data = input.nextInt();
13
14     // Keep reading data until the input is 0
15     int sum = 0;
16     while (data != 0) {
17       sum += data;
18
19       // Read the next data
20       System.out.print(
21         "Enter an integer (the input ends if it is 0): ");
22       data = input.nextInt();
23     }
24
25     System.out.println("The sum is " + sum);
26   }
27 }
```

input

loop

end of loop

display result

```
Enter an integer (the input ends if it is 0): 2 ⏎Enter
Enter an integer (the input ends if it is 0): 3 ⏎Enter
Enter an integer (the input ends if it is 0): 4 ⏎Enter
Enter an integer (the input ends if it is 0): 0 ⏎Enter
The sum is 9
```

	line#	Data	sum	output
	12	2		
	15		0	
iteration 1	17		2	
	22	3		
iteration 2	17		5	
	22	4		
iteration 3	17		9	
	22	0		
	25			The sum is 9

If `data` is not `0`, it is added to `sum` (line 17) and the next item of input data is read (lines 20–22). If `data` is `0`, the loop body is no longer executed and the `while` loop terminates. The input value `0` is the sentinel value for this loop. Note that if the first input read is `0`, the loop body never executes, and the resulting sum is `0`.

> **Caution**
>
> Don't use floating-point values for equality checking in a loop control. Because floating-point values are approximations for some values, using them could result in imprecise counter values and inaccurate results.
>
> Consider the following code for computing `1 + 0.9 + 0.8 + ... + 0.1`:
>
> ```
> double item = 1; double sum = 0;
> while (item != 0) { // No guarantee item will be 0
> sum += item;
> item -= 0.1;
> }
> System.out.println(sum);
> ```
>
> Variable `item` starts with `1` and is reduced by `0.1` every time the loop body is executed. The loop should terminate when `item` becomes `0`. However, there is no guarantee that item will be exactly `0`, because the floating-point arithmetic is approximated. This loop seems okay on the surface, but it is actually an infinite loop.

numeric error

✓ SECTION 6.2 ASSESSMENT

1. Analyze the following code. Is `count < 100` always `true`, always `false`, or sometimes `true` or sometimes `false` at Point A, Point B, and Point C?

```
int count = 0;
while (count < 100) {
  // Point A
  System.out.println("Welcome to Java!");
  count++;
  // Point B
}
// Point C
```

2. What is wrong if `guess` is initialized to `0` in line 11 in Listing 6.3?

3. How many times are the following loop bodies repeated? What is the output of each loop?

```
int i = 1;
while (i < 10)
  if (i % 2 == 0)
    System.out.println(i);
```
(a)

```
int i = 1;
while (i < 10)
  if (i % 2 == 0)
    System.out.println(i++);
```
(b)

```
int i = 1;
while (i < 10)
  if ((i++) % 2 == 0)
    System.out.println(i);
```
(c)

4. Suppose the input is `2  3  4  5  0`. What is the output of the following code?

```
import java.util.Scanner;

public class Test {
  public static void main(String[] args) {
    Scanner input = new Scanner(System.in);

    int number, max;
    number = input.nextInt();
    max = number;

    while (number != 0) {
      number = input.nextInt();
      if (number > max)
        max = number;
    }

    System.out.println("max is " + max);
    System.out.println("number " + number);
  }
}
```

5. What is the output of the following code? Explain the reason.

```
int x = 80000000;

while (x > 0)
  x++;

System.out.println("x is " + x);
```

6.3 The do-while Loop

A do-while *loop is the same as a* while *loop except that it executes the loop body first and then checks the loop continuation condition.*

The do-while loop is a variation of the while loop. Its syntax is:

do-while loop

```
do {
  // Loop body;
  Statement(s);
} while (loop-continuation-condition);
```

A flowchart tool is helpful to understand the logical steps. A do-while loop execution flowchart is shown in Figure 6.2.

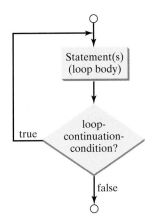

FIGURE 6.2 The do-while loop executes the loop body first, then checks the loop-continuation-condition to determine whether to continue or terminate the loop.

The loop body is executed first, and then the loop-continuation-condition is evaluated. If the evaluation is true, the loop body is executed again; if it is false, the do-while loop terminates. The difference between a while loop and a do-while loop is the order in which the loop-continuation-condition is evaluated and the loop body executed. You can write a loop using either the while loop or the do-while loop. Sometimes one is a more convenient choice than the other. For example, you can rewrite the while loop in Listing 6.5 using a do-while loop, as shown in Listing 6.6.

LISTING 6.6 TestDoWhile.java

```
 1  import java.util.Scanner;
 2
 3  public class TestDoWhile {
 4    /** Main method */
 5    public static void main(String[] args) {
 6      int data;
 7      int sum = 0;
 8
 9      // Create a Scanner
10      Scanner input = new Scanner(System.in);
```

loop

end loop

```
11
12    // Keep reading data until the input is 0
13    do {
14      // Read the next data
15      System.out.print(
16        "Enter an integer (the input ends if it is 0): ");
17      data = input.nextInt();
18
19      sum += data;
20    } while (data != 0);
21
22    System.out.println("The sum is " + sum);
23    }
24 }
```

```
Enter an integer (the input ends if it is 0): 3  ⏎Enter
Enter an integer (the input ends if it is 0): 5  ⏎Enter
Enter an integer (the input ends if it is 0): 6  ⏎Enter
Enter an integer (the input ends if it is 0): 0  ⏎Enter
The sum is 14
```

Tip

Use a do-while loop if you have statements inside the loop that must be executed *at least once*, as in the case of the do-while loop in the preceding TestDoWhile program. These statements must appear before the loop as well as inside it if you use a while loop.

✓ SECTION 6.3 ASSESSMENT

1. Suppose the input is 2 3 4 5 0. What is the output of the following code?

```
import java.util.Scanner;

public class Test {
  public static void main(String[] args) {
    Scanner input = new Scanner(System.in);

    int number, max;
    number = input.nextInt();
    max = number;

    do {
      number = input.nextInt();
      if (number > max)
        max = number;
    } while (number != 0);

    System.out.println("max is " + max);
    System.out.println("number " + number);
  }
}
```

2. What are the differences between a `while` loop and a `do-while` loop?
Convert the following `while` loop into a `do-while` loop.

```
Scanner input = new Scanner(System.in);
int sum = 0;
System.out.println("Enter an integer " +
  "(the input ends if it is 0)");
int number = input.nextInt();
while (number != 0) {
  sum += number;
  System.out.println("Enter an integer " +
    "(the input ends if it is 0)");
  number = input.nextInt();
}
```

6.4 The for Loop

Key
Point

A for loop has a concise syntax for writing loops.

Often you write a loop in the following common form:

```
i = initialValue;  // Initialize loop control variable
while (i < endValue)
  // Loop body
  ...
  i++; // Adjust loop control variable
}
```

A `for` loop can be used to simplify the preceding loop as:

```
for (i = initialValue; i < endValue; i++)
  // Loop body
  ...
}
```

In general, the syntax of a `for` loop is:

```
for (initial-action; loop-continuation-condition;
    action-after-each-iteration) {
  // Loop body;
  Statement(s);
}
```

for loop

The flowchart of the `for` loop is shown in Figure 6.3a.

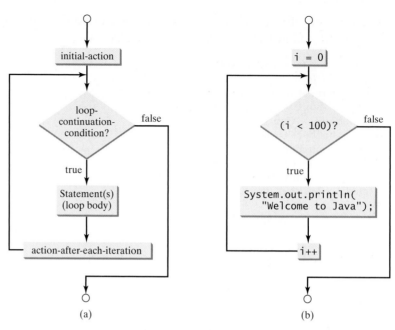

FIGURE 6.3 A `for` loop performs an initial action once, then repeatedly executes the statements in the loop body, and performs an action after an iteration when the `loop-continuation-condition` evaluates to `true`.

The `for` loop statement starts with the keyword `for`, followed by a pair of parentheses enclosing the control structure of the loop. This structure consists of `initial-action`, `loop-continuation-condition`, and `action-after-each-iteration`. The control structure is followed by the loop body enclosed inside braces. The `initial-action`, `loop-continuation-condition`, and `action-after-each-iteration` are separated by semicolons.

control variable

A `for` loop generally uses a variable to control how many times the loop body is executed and when the loop terminates. This variable is referred to as a *control variable*. The `initial-action` often initializes a control variable, the `action-after-each-iteration` usually increments or decrements the control variable, and the `loop-continuation-condition` tests whether the control variable has reached a termination value. For example, the following `for` loop prints `Welcome to Java!` a hundred times:

```
int i;
for (i = 0; i < 100; i++) {
  System.out.println("Welcome to Java!");
}
```

The flowchart of the statement is shown in Figure 6.3b. The `for` loop initializes `i` to `0`, then repeatedly executes the `println` statement and evaluates `i++` while `i` is less than `100`.

initial-action

The `initial-action`, `i = 0`, initializes the control variable, `i`. The `loop-continuation-condition`, `i < 100`, is a Boolean expression. The expression is evaluated right after the initialization and at the beginning of each iteration. If this condition is `true`, the loop body is executed. If it is `false`, the loop terminates and the program control turns to the line following the loop.

The `action-after-each-iteration`, i++, is a statement that adjusts the control variable. This statement is executed after each iteration and increments the control variable. Eventually, the value of the control variable should force the `loop-continuation-condition` to become `false`; otherwise, the loop is infinite.

The loop control variable can be declared and initialized in the `for` loop. Here is an example:

```
for (int i = 0; i < 100; i++) {
  System.out.println("Welcome to Java!");
}
```

If there is only one statement in the loop body, as in this example, the braces can be omitted.

Tip
The control variable must be declared inside the control structure of the loop or before the loop. If the loop control variable is used only in the loop, and not elsewhere, it is a good programming practice to declare it in the `initial-action` of the `for` loop. If the variable is declared inside the loop control structure, it cannot be referenced outside the loop. In the preceding code, for example, you cannot reference i outside the `for` loop, because it is declared inside the `for` loop.

Note
The `initial-action` in a `for` loop can be a list of zero or more comma-separated variable declaration statements or assignment expressions. For example:

```
for (int i = 0, j = 0; i + j < 10; i++, j++) {
  // Do something
}
```

The `action-after-each-iteration` in a `for` loop can be a list of zero or more comma-separated statements. For example:

```
for (int i = 1; i < 100; System.out.println(i), i++);
```

This example is correct, but it is a bad example, because it makes the code difficult to read. Normally, you declare and initialize a control variable as an initial action and increment or decrement the control variable as an action after each iteration.

Note
If the `loop-continuation-condition` in a `for` loop is omitted, it is implicitly `true`. Thus the statement given below in (a), which is an infinite loop, is the same as in (b). To avoid confusion, though, it is better to use the equivalent loop in (c).

action-after-each-iteration

omitting braces

declare control variable

for loop variations

✓ Section 6.4 Assessment

1. Do the following two loops result in the same value in sum?

```
for (int i = 0; i < 10; ++i) {
   sum += i;
}
```
(a)

```
for (int i = 0; i < 10; i++) {
   sum += i;
}
```
(b)

2. What are the three parts of a for loop control? Write a for loop that prints the numbers from 1 to 100.

3. Suppose the input is 2 3 4 5 0. What is the output of the following code?

```java
import java.util.Scanner;

public class Test {
   public static void main(String[] args) {
      Scanner input = new Scanner(System.in);

      int number, sum = 0, count;

      for (count = 0; count < 5; count++) {
         number = input.nextInt();
         sum += number;
      }

      System.out.println("sum is " + sum);
      System.out.println("count is " + count);
   }
}
```

4. What does the following statement do?

```java
for ( ; ; ) {
   // Do something
}
```

5. If a variable is declared in a for loop control, can it be used after the loop exits?

6. Convert the following for loop statement to a while loop and to a do-while loop:

```java
long sum = 0;
for (int i = 0; i <= 1000; i++)
   sum = sum + i;
```

7. Count the number of iterations in the following loops.

```
int count = 0;
while (count < n) {
  count++;
}
```
(a)

```
for (int count = 0;
     count <= n; count++) {
}
```
(b)

```
int count = 5;
while (count < n) {
  count++;
}
```
(c)

```
int count = 5;
while (count < n) {
  count = count + 3;
}
```
(d)

6.5 Which Loop to Use?

You can use a for *loop, a* while *loop, or a* do-while *loop, whichever is convenient.*

Key Point

The while loop and for loop are called *pretest loops* because the continuation condition is checked before the loop body is executed. The do-while loop is called a *posttest loop* because the condition is checked after the loop body is executed. The three forms of loop statements—while, do-while, and for—are expressively equivalent; that is, you can write a loop in any of these three forms. For example, a while loop in (a) in the following figure can always be converted into the for loop in (b).

pretest loop

posttest loop

```
while (loop-continuation-condition) {
  // Loop body
}
```
(a)

Equivalent

```
for ( ; loop-continuation-condition; ) {
  // Loop body
}
```
(b)

A for loop in (a) in the next figure can generally be converted into the while loop in (b) except in certain special cases (see Section 6.7 Assessment Question #2 for such a case).

```
for (initial-action;
     loop-continuation-condition;
     action-after-each-iteration) {
  // Loop body;
}
```
(a)

Equivalent

```
initial-action;
while (loop-continuation-condition) {
  // Loop body;
  action-after-each-iteration;
}
```
(b)

Use the loop statement that is most intuitive and comfortable for you. In general, a for loop may be used if the number of repetitions is known in advance, as, for example, when you need to display a message a hundred times. A while loop may be used if the number of repetitions is not fixed, as in the case of reading the numbers until the input is 0. A do-while loop can be used to replace a while loop if the loop body has to be executed before the continuation condition is tested.

Caution

Adding a semicolon at the end of the **for** clause before the loop body is a common mistake, as shown below in (a). In (a), the semicolon signifies the end of the loop prematurely. The loop body is actually empty, as shown in (b). (a) and (b) are equivalent. Both are incorrect.

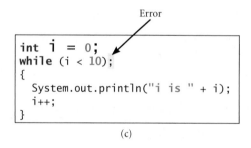

```
for (int i = 0; i < 10; i++);
{
  System.out.println("i is " + i);
}
```
(a)

```
for (int i = 0; i < 10; i++) { };
{
  System.out.println("i is " + i);
}
```
(b)

Similarly, the loop in (c) is also wrong. (c) is equivalent to (d). Both are incorrect.

```
int i = 0;
while (i < 10);
{
  System.out.println("i is " + i);
  i++;
}
```
(c)

```
int i = 0;
while (i < 10) { };
{
  System.out.println("i is " + i);
  i++;
}
```
(d)

These errors often occur when you use the next-line block style. Using the end-of-line block style can avoid errors of this type.

In the case of the **do-while** loop, the semicolon is needed to end the loop.

```
int i = 0;
do {
  System.out.println("i is " + i);
  i++;
} while (i < 10);
```

Correct

✓ SECTION 6.5 ASSESSMENT

1. Can you convert a **for** loop to a **while** loop? List the advantages of using **for** loops.

2. Explain the difference between a **while** loop, a **do-while** loop, and a **for** loop. Create a flowchart diagram for each type.

3. Identify and fix the errors in the following code:

```
1  public class Test {
2    public void main(String[] args) {
3      for (int i = 0; i < 10; i++);
4        sum += i;
```

```
 5
 6        if (i < j);
 7           System.out.println(i)
 8        else
 9           System.out.println(j);
10
11        while (j < 10);
12        {
13           j++;
14        }
15
16        do {
17           j++;
18        } while (j < 10)
19     }
20  }
```

4. What is wrong with the following programs?

```
 1 public class ShowErrors {
 2   public static void main(String[] args) {
 3     int i = 0;
 4     do {
 5        System.out.println(i + 4);
 6        i++;
 7     }
 8     while (i < 10)
 9   }
10 }
```
(a)

```
 1 public class ShowErrors {
 2     public static void main(String[]
 args) {
 3        for (int i = 0; i < 10; i++);
 4           System.out.println(i + 4);
 5     }
 6 }
```
(b)

6.6 Case Studies

Loops are fundamental in programming. The ability to write loops is essential in learning Java programming.

Key Point

If you can write programs using loops, you know how to program! This section presents two additional examples of solving problems using loops.

Case Study: Finding the Greatest Common Divisor

The greatest common divisor (gcd) of the two integers 4 and 2 is 2. The greatest common divisor of the two integers 16 and 24 is 8. How would you write this program to find the greatest common divisor? Would you immediately begin to write the code? No. It is important to *think before you code*. Thinking enables you to generate a logical solution for the problem without concern about how to write the code.

gcd

think before you code

Let the two input integers be n1 and n2. You know that number 1 is a common divisor, but it may not be the greatest common divisor. So, you can check whether k (for k 2, 3, 4, and so on) is a common divisor for n1 and n2, until k is greater than n1 or n2. Store the common divisor in a variable named gcd. Initially, gcd is 1. Whenever a new common divisor is found, it becomes the new gcd. When you have checked all the possible common divisors from 2 up to n1 or n2, the value in variable gcd is the greatest common divisor. Once you have a logical solution, type the code to translate the solution into a Java program as follows:

logical solution

```
int gcd = 1; // Initial gcd is 1
int k = 2; // Possible gcd

while (k <= n1 && k <= n2) {
  if (n1 % k == 0 && n2 % k == 0)
    gcd = k; // Update gcd
  k++; // Next possible gcd
}

// After the loop, gcd is the greatest common divisor for n1 and n2
```

Listing 6.7 presents the program that prompts the user to enter two positive integers and finds their greatest common divisor.

LISTING 6.7 GreatestCommonDivisor.java

```
 1  import java.util.Scanner;
 2
 3  public class GreatestCommonDivisor {
 4    /** Main method */
 5    public static void main(String[] args) {
 6      // Create a Scanner
 7      Scanner input = new Scanner(System.in);
 8
 9      // Prompt the user to enter two integers
10      System.out.print("Enter first integer: ");
11      int n1 = input.nextInt();
12      System.out.print("Enter second integer: ");
13      int n2 = input.nextInt();
14
15      int gcd = 1; // Initial gcd is 1
16      int k = 2; // Possible gcd
17      while (k <= n1 && k <= n2) {
18        if (n1 % k == 0 && n2 % k == 0)
19          gcd = k; // Update gcd
20        k++;
21      }
22
23      System.out.println("The greatest common divisor for " + n1 +
24        " and " + n2 + " is " + gcd);
25    }
26  }
```

input *(line 11)*

input *(line 13)*

gcd *(line 15)*

check divisor *(line 18)*

output *(line 23)*

```
Enter first integer: 125  ↵Enter
Enter second integer: 2525  ↵Enter
The greatest common divisor for 125 and 2525 is 25
```

mulitple solutions

Translating a logical solution to Java code is not unique. A problem can often be solved in many ways. For example, you could use a **for** loop to rewrite the code as follows:

```
for (int k = 2; k <= n1 && k <= n2; k++) {
  if (n1 % k == 0 && n2 % k == 0)
    gcd = k;
}
```

Case Study: Predicting Future Tuition

Suppose that the tuition for a university is $10,000 this year and tuition increases 7% every year. In how many years will the tuition be doubled?

Before you can write a program to solve this problem, first consider how to solve it by hand. The tuition for the second year is the tuition for the first year * 1.07. The tuition for a future year is the tuition of its preceding year * 1.07. Thus, the tuition for each year can be computed as follows:

think before you code

```
double tuition = 10000;   int year = 0;  // Year 0
tuition = tuition * 1.07; year++;        // Year 1
tuition = tuition * 1.07; year++;        // Year 2
tuition = tuition * 1.07; year++;        // Year 3
...
```

Keep computing the tuition for a new year until it is at least 20000. By then you will know how many years it will take for the tuition to be doubled. You can now translate the logic into the following loop:

```
double tuition = 10000;   // Year 0
int year = 0;
while (tuition < 20000) {
  tuition = tuition * 1.07;
  year++;
}
```

The complete program is shown in Listing 6.8.

LISTING 6.8 FutureTuition.java

```
 1  public class FutureTuition {
 2    public static void main(String[] args) {
 3      double tuition = 10000;   // Year 0
 4      int year = 0;
 5      while (tuition < 20000) {
 6        tuition = tuition * 1.07;
 7        year++;
 8      }
 9
10      System.out.println("Tuition will be doubled in "
11        + year + " years");
12      System.out.printf("Tuition will be $%.2f in %1d years",
13        tuition, year);
14    }
15  }
```

loop
next year's tuition

```
Tuition will be doubled in 11 years
Tuition will be $21048.52 in 11 years
```

The while loop (lines 5–8) is used to repeatedly compute the tuition for a new year. The loop terminates when the tuition is greater than or equal to 20000.

6.7 Keywords break and continue

The break and continue keywords provide additional controls in a loop.

Key
Point

> **Pedagogical Note**
> Two keywords, break and continue, can be used in loop statements
> to provide additional controls. Using break and continue can simplify
> programming in some cases. Overusing or improperly using them, how-
> ever, can make programs difficult to read and debug.

break statement

You have used the keyword break in a switch statement. You can also use break
in a loop to immediately terminate the loop. Listing 6.9 presents a program to
demonstrate the effect of using break in a loop.

LISTING 6.9 TestBreak.java

break

```
 1  public class TestBreak {
 2    public static void main(String[] args) {
 3      int sum = 0;
 4      int number = 0;
 5
 6      while (number < 20) {
 7        number++;
 8        sum += number;
 9        if (sum >= 100)
10          break;
11      }
12
13      System.out.println("The number is " + number);
14      System.out.println("The sum is " + sum);
15    }
16  }
```

```
The number is 14
The sum is 105
```

The program in Listing 6.9 adds integers from 1 to 20 in this order to sum until
sum is greater than or equal to 100. Without the if statement (line 9), the program
calculates the sum of the numbers from 1 to 20. But with the if statement, the loop
terminates when sum becomes greater than or equal to 100. Without the if state-
ment, the output would be:

```
The number is 20
The sum is 210
```

continue statement

You can also use the continue keyword in a loop. When it is encountered, it
ends the current iteration and program control goes to the end of the loop body.
In other words, continue breaks out of an iteration while the break keyword
breaks out of a loop. Listing 6.10 presents a program to demonstrate the effect of
using continue in a loop.

LISTING 6.10 `TestContinue.java`

```java
 1  public class TestContinue {
 2    public static void main(String[] args) {
 3      int sum = 0;
 4      int number = 0;
 5
 6      while (number < 20) {
 7        number++;
 8        if (number ==10 || number == 11)
 9          continue;
10        sum += number;
11      }
12
13      System.out.println("The sum is " + sum);
14    }
15  }
```

continue

```
The sum is 189
```

The program in Listing 6.10 adds integers from 1 to 20 except 10 and 11 to sum. With the `if` statement in the program (line 8), the `continue` statement is executed when `number` becomes 10 or 11. The `continue` statement ends the current iteration so that the rest of the statement in the loop body is not executed; therefore, `number` is not added to `sum` when it is 10 or 11. Without the `if` statement in the program, the output would be as follows:

```
The sum is 210
```

In this case, all of the numbers are added to `sum`, even when `number` is 10 or 11. Therefore, the result is 210, which is 21 more than it was with the `if` statement.

> **Note**
> The `continue` statement is always inside a loop. In the `while` and `do-while` loops, the `loop-continuation-condition` is evaluated immediately after the `continue` statement. In the `for` loop, the `action-after-each-iteration` is performed, then the `loop-continuation-condition` is evaluated, immediately after the `continue` statement.

You can always write a program without using `break` or `continue` in a loop (see Section 6.7 Assessment, Question 3). In general, though, using `break` and `continue` is appropriate if it simplifies coding and makes programs easier to read.

Suppose you need to write a program to find the smallest factor other than 1 for an integer n (assume n `>=` 2). You can write a simple and intuitive code using the `break` statement as follows:

```
int factor = 2;
while (factor <= n) {
  if (n % factor == 0)
    break;
  factor++;
}
System.out.println("The smallest factor other than 1 for "
  + n + " is " + factor);
```

You may rewrite the code without using break as follows:

```
boolean found = false;
int factor = 2;
while (factor <= n && !found) {
  if (n % factor == 0)
    found = true;
  else
    factor++;
}
System.out.println("The smallest factor other than 1 for "
  + n + " is " + factor);
```

Obviously, the break statement makes this program simpler and easier to read in this case. However, you should use break and continue with caution. Too many break and continue statements will produce a loop with many exit points and make the program difficult to read.

goto

Note

Some programming languages have a goto statement. The goto statement indiscriminately transfers control to any statement in the program and executes it. This makes your program vulnerable to errors. The break and continue statements in Java are different from goto statements. They operate only in a loop or a switch statement. The break statement breaks out of the loop, and the continue statement breaks out of the current iteration in the loop.

Note

Programming is a creative endeavor. There are many different ways to write code. In fact, you can find a smallest factor using a rather simple code as follows:

```
int factor = 2;
while (factor <= n && n % factor != 0)
  factor++;
```

✓ SECTION 6.7 ASSESSMENT

1. What is the keyword break for? What is the keyword continue for? Will the following programs terminate? If so, give the output.

```
int balance = 10;
while (true) {
  if (balance < 9)
    break;
  balance = balance - 9;
}

System.out.println("Balance is "
  + balance);
```
(a)

```
int balance = 10;
while (true) {
  if (balance < 9)
    continue;
  balance = balance - 9;
}

System.out.println("Balance is "
  + balance);
```
(b)

2. The for loop on the left is converted into the while loop on the right. What is wrong? Correct it.

```
int sum = 0;
for (int i = 0; i < 4; i++) {
  if (i % 3 == 0) continue;
  sum += i;
}
```

Converted ⟶ Wrong conversion

```
int i = 0, sum = 0;
while (i < 4) {
  if (i % 3 == 0) continue;
  sum += i;
  i++;
}
```

3. Rewrite the programs TestBreak and TestContinue in Listings 6.9 and 6.10 without using break and continue.

4. After the break statement in (a) is executed in the following loop, which statement is executed? Show the output. After the continue statement in (b) is executed in the following loop, which statement is executed? Show the output.

```
for (int i = 1; i < 4; i++) {
  for (int j = 1; j < 4; j++) {
    if (i * j > 2)
      break;

    System.out.println(i * j);
  }

  System.out.println(i);
}
```
(a)

```
for (int i = 1; i < 4; i++) {
  for (int j = 1; j < 4; j++) {
    if (i * j > 2)
      continue;

    System.out.println(i * j);
  }

  System.out.println(i);
}
```
(b)

6.8 Case Study: Checking Palindromes

This section presents a program that checks whether a string is a palindrome.

A string is a palindrome if it reads the same forward and backward. The words "mom," "dad," and "noon," for instance, are all palindromes.

The problem is to write a program that prompts the user to enter a string and reports whether the string is a palindrome. One solution is to check whether the first character in the string is the same as the last character. If so, check whether the second character is the same as the second-to-last character. This process continues until a mismatch is found or all the characters in the string are checked, except for the middle character if the string has an odd number of characters.

think before you code

Listing 6.11 gives the program.

LISTING 6.11 Palindrome.java

```java
1  import java.util.Scanner;
2
3  public class Palindrome {
4    /** Main method */
5    public static void main(String[] args) {
6      // Create a Scanner
7      Scanner input = new Scanner(System.in);
8
9      // Prompt the user to enter a string
10     System.out.print("Enter a string: ");
11     String s = input.nextLine();
12
13     // The index of the first character in the string
14     int low = 0;
15
16     // The index of the last character in the string
17     int high = s.length() - 1;
18
19     boolean isPalindrome = true;
20     while (low < high) {
21       if (s.charAt(low) != s.charAt(high)) {
22         isPalindrome = false;
23         break;
24       }
25
26       low++;
27       high--;
28     }
29
30     if (isPalindrome)
31       System.out.println(s + " is a palindrome");
32     else
33       System.out.println(s + " is not a palindrome");
34   }
35 }
```

input string

low index

high index

update indices

```
Enter a string: noon ⏎Enter
noon is a palindrome
```

```
Enter a string: moon  ↵Enter
moon is not a palindrome
```

The program uses two variables, `low` and `high`, to denote the position of the two characters at the beginning and the end in a string `s` (lines 14, 17). Initially, `low` is 0 and `high` is `s.length()` - 1. If the two characters at these positions match, increment `low` by 1 and decrement `high` by 1 (lines 26–27). This process continues until (`low >= high`) or a mismatch is found (line 21).

The program uses a `boolean` variable `isPalindrome` to denote whether the string `s` is a palindrome. Initially, it is set to `true` (line 19). When a mismatch is discovered (line 21), `isPalindrome` is set to `false` (line 22) and the loop is terminated with a break statement (line 23).

6.9 Case Study: Displaying Prime Numbers

This section presents a program that displays the first fifty prime numbers in five lines, each containing ten numbers.

Key
Point

An integer greater than 1 is *prime* if its only positive divisor is 1 or itself. For example, 2, 3, 5, and 7 are prime numbers, but 4, 6, 8, and 9 are not.

The problem is to display the first 50 prime numbers in five lines, each of which contains ten numbers. The problem can be broken into the following tasks:

- Determine whether a given number is prime.

- For `number` 2, 3, 4, 5, 6, ..., test whether it is prime.

- Count the prime numbers.

- Display each prime number, and display ten numbers per line.

Obviously, you need to write a loop and repeatedly test whether a new `number` is prime. If the `number` is prime, increase the count by 1. The `count` is 0 initially. When it reaches 50, the loop terminates.

Here is the algorithm for the problem:

```
Set the number of prime numbers to be printed as
  a constant NUMBER_OF_PRIMES;
Use count to track the number of prime numbers and
  set an initial count to 0;
Set an initial number to 2;

while (count < NUMBER_OF_PRIMES) {
  Test whether number is prime;

  if number is prime {
    Display the prime number and increase the count;
  }

  Increment number by 1;
}
```

To test whether a number is prime, check whether it is divisible by 2, 3, 4, and so on up to number/2. If a divisor is found, the number is not a prime. The algorithm can be described as follows:

```
Use a boolean variable isPrime to denote whether
  the number is prime; Set isPrime to true initially;

for (int divisor = 2; divisor <= number / 2; divisor++) {
  if (number % divisor == 0) {
    Set isPrime to false
    Exit the loop;
  }
}
```

The complete program is given in Listing 6.12.

LISTING 6.12 PrimeNumber.java

```
 1  public class PrimeNumber {
 2    public static void main(String[] args) {
 3      final int NUMBER_OF_PRIMES = 50; // Number of primes to display
 4      final int NUMBER_OF_PRIMES_PER_LINE = 10; // Display 10 per line
 5      int count = 0; // Count the number of prime numbers
 6      int number = 2; // A number to be tested for primeness
 7
 8      System.out.println("The first 50 prime numbers are \n");
 9
10      // Repeatedly find prime numbers
11      while (count < NUMBER_OF_PRIMES) {
12        // Assume the number is prime
13        boolean isPrime = true; // Is the current number prime?
14
15        // Test whether number is prime
16        for (int divisor = 2; divisor <= number / 2; divisor++) {
17          if (number % divisor == 0) { // If true, number is not prime
18            isPrime = false; // Set isPrime to false
19            break; // Exit the for loop
20          }
21        }
22
23        // Display the prime number and increase the count
24        if (isPrime) {
25          count++; // Increase the count
26
27          if (count % NUMBER_OF_PRIMES_PER_LINE == 0) {
28            // Display the number and advance to the new line
29            System.out.println(number);
30          }
31          else
32            System.out.print(number + " ");
33        }
34
35        // Check if the next number is prime
36        number++;
37      }
38    }
39  }
```

count prime numbers — line 11

check primeness — line 16

exit loop — line 19

display if prime — line 24

```
The first 50 prime numbers are
2 3 5 7 11 13 17 19 23 29
31 37 41 43 47 53 59 61 67 71
73 79 83 89 97 101 103 107 109 113
127 131 137 139 149 151 157 163 167 173
179 181 191 193 197 199 211 223 227 229
```

This is a complex program for novice programmers. The key to developing a programmatic solution for this problem, and for many other problems, is to break it into subproblems and develop solutions for each of them in turn. Do not attempt to develop a complete solution in the first trial. Instead, begin by writing the code to determine whether a given number is prime, then expand the program to test whether other numbers are prime in a loop.

subproblem

To determine whether a number is prime, check whether it is divisible by a number between 2 and number/2 inclusive (lines 16–21). If so, it is not a prime number (line 18); otherwise, it is a prime number. For a prime number, display it. If the count is divisible by 10 (lines 27–30), advance to a new line. The program ends when the count reaches 50.

The program uses the **break** statement in line 19 to exit the **for** loop as soon as the number is found to be a nonprime. You can rewrite the loop (lines 16–21) without using the **break** statement, as follows:

```
for (int divisor = 2; divisor <= number / 2 && isPrime;
    divisor++) {
  // If true, the number is not prime
  if (number % divisor == 0) {
    // Set isPrime to false, if the number is not prime
    isPrime = false;
  }
}
```

However, using the **break** statement makes the program simpler and easier to read in this case.

Chapter 6 — Review and Assessment

KEY TERMS

break statement 190
continue statement 191
do-while loop 179
for loop 181
infinite loop 170
iteration 168
loop 168

loop body 168
off-by-one error 170
posttest loop 185
pretest loop 185
sentinel value 176
while loop 168

CHAPTER SUMMARY

1. There are three types of repetition statements: the while loop, the do-while loop, and the for loop.

2. The part of the loop that contains the statements to be repeated is called the *loop body.*

3. A one-time execution of a loop body is referred to as an *iteration of the loop.*

4. An *infinite loop* is a loop statement that executes infinitely.

5. In designing loops, you need to consider both the *loop control structure* and the loop body.

6. The while loop checks the loop-continuation-condition first. If the condition is true, the loop body is executed; if it is false, the loop terminates.

7. The do-while loop is similar to the while loop, except that the do-while loop executes the loop body first and then checks the loop-continuation-condition to decide whether to continue or to terminate.

8. The while loop and the do-while loop often are used when the number of repetitions is not predetermined.

9. A *sentinel value* is a special value that signifies the end of the loop.

10. The for loop generally is used to execute a loop body a fixed number of times.

11. The for loop control has three parts. The first part is an initial action that often initializes a control variable. The second part, the loop-continuation-condition, determines whether the loop body is to be executed. The third part is executed after each iteration and is often used to adjust the control variable. Usually, the loop control variables are initialized and changed in the control structure.

12. The `while` loop and `for` loop are called *pretest loops* because the continuation condition is checked before the loop body is executed.

13. The `do-while` loop is called a *posttest loop* because the condition is checked after the loop body is executed.

14. Two keywords, `break` and `continue`, can be used in a loop.

15. The `break` keyword immediately ends the innermost loop, which contains the break.

16. The `continue` keyword only ends the current iteration.

PROGRAMMING EXERCISES

Pedagogical Note
Read each problem several times until you understand it. Think how to solve the problem before starting to write code. Translate your logic into a program.

read and think before coding

A problem often can be solved in many different ways. Students are encouraged to explore various solutions.

explore solutions

***1.** (*Count positive and negative numbers and compute the average of numbers*) Write a program that reads an unspecified number of integers, determines how many positive and negative values have been read, and computes the total and average of the input values (not counting zeros). Your program ends with the input `0`. Display the average as a floating-point number. Here is a sample run:

```
Enter an integer, the input ends if it is 0: 1 2 -1 3 0 ↵Enter
The number of positives is 3
The number of negatives is 1
The total is 5.0
The average is 1.25
```

```
Enter an integer, the input ends if it is 0: 0 ↵Enter
No numbers are entered except 0
```

2. (*Repeat additions*) Listing 6.4, SubtractionQuizLoop.java, generates five random subtraction questions. Revise the program to generate ten random addition questions for two integers between `1` and `15`. Display the correct count and test time.

3. (*Conversion from kilograms to pounds*) Write a program that displays the following table (note that 1 kilogram is 2.2 pounds):

```
Kilograms      Pounds
1                 2.2
3                 6.6
...
197             433.4
199             437.8
```

4. (*Conversion from miles to kilometers*) Write a program that displays the following table (note that 1 mile is 1.609 kilometers):

```
Miles         Kilometers
1              1.609
2              3.218
...
9             14.481
10            16.090
```

5. (*Conversion from kilograms to pounds and pounds to kilograms*) Write a program that displays the following two tables side by side:

```
Kilograms  Pounds   |    Pounds    Kilograms
1            2.2     |    20           9.09
3            6.6     |    25          11.36
...
197        433.4     |    510        231.82
199        437.8     |    515        234.09
```

6. (*Conversion from miles to kilometers*) Write a program that displays the following two tables side by side:

```
Miles      Kilometers  | Kilometers    Miles
1           1.609       | 20          12.430
2           3.218       | 25          15.538
...
9          14.481       | 60          37.290
10         16.090       | 65          40.398
```

7. (*Find the highest score*) Write a program that prompts the user to enter the number of students and each student's name and score, and finally displays the name of the student with the highest score.

8. (*Find numbers divisible by 5 and 6*) Write a program that displays all the numbers from 100 to 1,000, ten per line, that are divisible by 5 and 6. Numbers are separated by exactly one space.

9. (*Find numbers divisible by 5 or 6, but not both*) Write a program that displays all the numbers from 100 to 200, ten per line, that are divisible by 5 or 6, but not both. Numbers are separated by exactly one space.

INTRODUCTION TO DATA STRUCTURES AND ARRAYS

Objectives

- Describe data structure concepts.

- Explain why data structures are necessary in programming.

- Differentiate between concepts of data represented as a single-dimensional or two-dimensional structure.

- Apply data structure concepts by using arrays to solve problems.

- Access array elements using indexes.

- Declare, create, and initialize an array using an array initializer.

- Simplify programming using a `foreach` loop.

- Apply arrays in application development (`AnalyzeNumbers`, `DeckOfCards`)

- Use the methods in the `java.util.Arrays` class.

7.1 Introduction to Data Structures

Key Point *A data structure is a grouping of data organized in a particular way and used to store data in computer memory.*

data structure

Several types of data structures are used in computer programming. *Arrays* are a common type of data structure. This chapter introduces the concept of data structures by exploring the use of arrays in your programming design.

single-dimensional array

A *single-dimensional array* is a common data structure that organizes data into a single row or column. There are a fixed number of items, or *elements*, in the array. The data is stored sequentially and is retrieved by accessing the particular location in the array. This location is referred to as the *index*.

index

Visualize six names of fruit listed in a row as shown in the following:

```
Fruit [apple, banana, orange, pear, peach, mango]
```

Apple is stored at location 0.
Banana is stored at location 1.
Orange is stored at location 2.
Pear is stored at location 3.
Peach is stored at location 4.
Mango is stored at location 5.

To access banana in the Fruit array, reference the corresponding location, or index. Thus, the value stored in location: Fruit[1] is banana. Notice the index begins at 0, and not at 1.

two-dimensional array

Arrays can also be multi-dimensional. Consider a spreadsheet with columns and rows. This is an example of a two-dimensional array. A *two-dimensional array* is a data structure where information is organized in columns *and* rows. Data in a two-dimensional structure is stored and retrieved by specifying *both* the row and column. As an example, to store data in column A and row 1 of a spreadsheet, you reference the location as [A1]. Detailed information on two-dimensional and multi-dimensional arrays can be found in Supplement G. In this chapter, we will cover single-dimensional arrays.

Arrays are helpful to store a large number of values during the execution of a program. Suppose that you need to read 100 numbers and compute their average. You also need to determine how many numbers are above the average. To solve this problem, your program first reads the numbers and computes their average, then compares each number with the average to determine if it is above the average. In order to accomplish this task, the numbers must all be stored in variables. You have to declare 100 numeric variables and repeatedly write almost identical code 100 times. Writing a program this way would be impractical.

A more efficient way to accomplish this task is by creating a one-dimensional array with a fixed size to hold 100 numeric values. You can store and retrieve values in the array by using looping statements to iterate through the array.

In this chapter, you will learn how to apply data structure concepts by using arrays.

✓ SECTION 7.1 ASSESSMENT

1. What is a data structure? When is it beneficial to use a data structure?

2. Write pseudocode to describe a single-dimensional array that holds the days of the week. Sunday is the first element in the array. Name the array: `weekDays`.

3. Using the `weekDays` array created in question 2, what is the value of x in the following expression? x = `weekDays`[4];

4. Draw two illustrations, representing data as a single-dimensional and a two-dimensional array. Explain the difference.

7.2 Array Basics

Once an array is created, its size is fixed. An array reference variable is used to access the elements in an array using an index.

 Key Point

An array is used to store a collection of data, but often we find it more useful to think of an array as a collection of variables of the same type. Instead of declaring individual variables, such as `number0`, `number1`, ..., and `number99`, you declare one array variable such as `numbers` and use `numbers[0]`, `numbers[1]`, ..., and `numbers[99]` to represent individual variables. This section introduces how to declare array variables, create arrays, and process arrays using indexes.

Declaring Array Variables

To use an array in a program, you must declare a variable to reference the array and specify the array's *element type*. Here is the syntax for declaring an array variable:

```
elementType[] arrayRefVar;
```

element type

The `elementType` can be any data type, and all elements in the array will have the same data type. For example, the following code declares a variable `myList` that references an array of double elements.

```
double[] myList;
```

> **Note**
> You can also use `elementType arrayRefVar[]` to declare an array variable. This style comes from the C/C++ language and was adopted in Java to accommodate C/C++ programmers. The style `elementType[] arrayRefVar` is preferred.

Creating Arrays

Unlike declarations for primitive data type variables, the declaration of an array variable does not allocate any space in memory for the array. It creates only a storage location for the reference to an array. If a variable does not contain a reference to an array, the value of the variable is `null`. You cannot assign elements to an array unless it has already been created. After an array variable is declared, you can create an array by using the `new` operator and assign its reference to the variable with the following syntax:

```
arrayRefVar = new elementType[arraySize];
```

null

new operator

This statement does two things:

1. It creates an array using `new elementType[arraySize]`.

2. It assigns the reference of the newly created array to the variable `arrayRefVar`.

Declaring an array variable, creating an array, and assigning the reference of the array to the variable can be combined in one statement as:

```
elementType[] arrayRefVar = new elementType[arraySize];
```

or

```
elementType arrayRefVar[] = new elementType[arraySize];
```

Here is an example of such a statement:

```
double[] myList = new double[10];
```

This statement declares an array variable, `myList`, creates an array of ten elements of `double` type, and assigns its reference to `myList`. To assign values to the elements, use the syntax:

```
arrayRefVar[index] = value;
```

For example, the following code initializes the array.

```
myList[0] = 5.6;
myList[1] = 4.5;
myList[2] = 3.3;
myList[3] = 13.2;
myList[4] = 4.0;
myList[5] = 34.33;
myList[6] = 34.0;
myList[7] = 45.45;
myList[8] = 99.993;
myList[9] = 11123;
```

This array is illustrated in Figure 7.1.

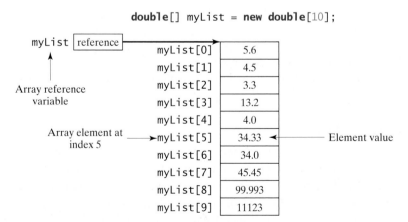

FIGURE 7.1 The array `myList` has ten elements of `double` type and `int` indices from 0 to 9.

array vs. array variable

> **Note**
> An array variable that appears to hold an array actually contains a reference to that array. Strictly speaking, an array variable and an array are different, but most of the time the distinction can be ignored. Thus it is all right to say, for simplicity, that `myList` is an array, instead of stating, at greater length, that `myList` is a variable that contains a reference to an array of ten double elements.

Array Size and Default Values

When space for an array is allocated, the array size must be given, specifying the number of elements that can be stored in it. The size of an array cannot be changed after the array is created. Size can be obtained using `arrayRefVar.length`. For example, `myList.length` is 10.

array length

When an array is created, its elements are assigned the default value of 0 for the numeric primitive data types, `\u0000` for `char` types, and `false` for `boolean` types.

default values

Accessing Array Elements

The array elements are accessed through the index. As discussed in Section 7.1, array indices are 0 based; that is, they range from 0 to `arrayRefVar.length-1`. In the example in Figure 7.1, `myList` holds ten `double` values, and the indices are from 0 to 9.

0 based

Each element in the array is represented using the following syntax, known as an *indexed variable*:

indexed variable

```
arrayRefVar[index];
```

For example, `myList[9]` represents the last element in the array `myList`.

> **Caution**
> Some programming languages use parentheses to reference an array element, as in `myList(9)`, but Java uses brackets, as in `myList[9]`.

The following code adds the values in `myList[0]` and `myList[1]` to `myList[2]`.

```
myList[2] = myList[0] + myList[1];
```

The following loop assigns 0 to `myList[0]`, 1 to `myList[1]`, ..., and 9 to `myList[9]`:

```
for (int i = 0; i < myList.length; i++) {
  myList[i] = i;
}
```

Array Initializers

Java has a shorthand notation, known as the *array initializer*, which combines the declaration, creation, and initialization of an array in one statement using the following syntax:

array initializer

```
elementType[] arrayRefVar = {value0, value1, ..., valuek};
```

For example, the statement

```
double[] myList = {1.9, 2.9, 3.4, 3.5};
```

declares, creates, and initializes the array `myList` with four elements, which is equivalent to the following statements:

```
double[] myList = new double[4];
myList[0] = 1.9;
myList[1] = 2.9;
myList[2] = 3.4;
myList[3] = 3.5;
```

 Caution

The `new` operator is not used in the array-initializer syntax. Using an array initializer, you have to declare, create, and initialize the array all in one statement. Splitting it would cause a syntax error. Thus, the next statement is wrong:

```
double[] myList;
myList = {1.9, 2.9, 3.4, 3.5};
```

Processing Arrays

When processing array elements, you will often use a `for` loop—for two reasons:

- All of the elements in an array are of the same type. They are evenly processed in the same fashion repeatedly using a loop.

- Since the size of the array is known, it is natural to use a `for` loop.

Assume the array is created as follows:

```
double[] myList = new double[10];
```

The following are some examples of processing arrays:

1. *Initializing arrays with input values:* The following loop initializes the array `myList` with user input values.

   ```
   java.util.Scanner input = new java.util.Scanner(System.in);
   System.out.print("Enter " + myList.length + " values: ");
   for (int i = 0; i < myList.length; i++)
     myList[i] = input.nextDouble();
   ```

2. *Initializing arrays with random values:* The following loop initializes the array `myList` with random values between `0.0` and `100.0`, but less than `100.0`.

   ```
   for (int i = 0; i < myList.length; i++) {
     myList[i] = Math.random() * 100;
   }
   ```

3. *Displaying arrays:* To print an array, you have to print each element in the array using a loop like the following:

```
for (int i = 0; i < myList.length; i++) {
   System.out.print(myList[i] + " ");
}
```

 Tip

For an array of the `char[]` type, it can be printed using one print state-
ment. For example, the following code displays `Dallas`:

print character array

```
char[] city = {'D', 'a', 'l', 'l', 'a', 's'};
System.out.println(city);
```

4. *Summing all elements:* Use a variable named `total` to store the sum. Initially `total` is 0. Add each element in the array to `total` using a loop like this:

```
double total = 0;
for (int i = 0; i < myList.length; i++) {
   total += myList[i];
}
```

5. *Finding the largest element:* Use a variable named `max` to store the largest ele-
ment. Initially `max` is `myList[0]`. To find the largest element in the array
`myList`, compare each element with `max`, and update `max` if the element is
greater than `max`.

```
double max = myList[0];
for (int i = 1; i < myList.length; i++) {
   if (myList[i] > max) max = myList[i];
}
```

6. *Finding the smallest index of the largest element:* Often you need to locate the
largest element in an array. If an array has multiple elements with the same
largest value, find the smallest index of such an element. Suppose the array
`myList` is {1, 5, 3, 4, 5, 5}. The largest element is 5 and the smallest index for
5 is 1. Use a variable named `max` to store the largest element and a variable
named `indexOfMax` to denote the index of the largest element. Initially `max` is
`myList[0]`, and `indexOfMax` is 0. Compare each element in `myList` with `max`,
and update `max` and `indexOfMax` if the element is greater than `max`.

```
double max = myList[0];
int indexOfMax = 0;
for (int i = 1; i < myList.length; i++) {
   if (myList[i] > max) {
      max = myList[i];
      indexOfMax = i;
   }
}
```

7. *Random shuffling:* In many applications, you need to randomly reorder the elements in an array. This is called *shuffling.* To accomplish this, for each element `myList[i]`, randomly generate an index `j` and swap `myList[i]` with `myList[j]`, as follows:

```
for (int i = myList.length - 1; i > 0; i--) {
    // Generate an index j randomly with 0 <= j <= i
    int j = (int)(Math.random()
        * (i + 1));

    // Swap myList[i] with myList[j]
    double temp = myList[i];
    myList[i] = myList[j];
    myList[j] = temp;
}
```

8. *Shifting elements:* Sometimes you need to shift the elements left or right. Here is an example of shifting the elements one position to the left and filling the last element with the first element:

```
double temp = myList[0]; // Retain the first element

// Shift elements left
for (int i = 1; i < myList.length; i++) {
    myList[i - 1] = myList[i];
}

// Move the first element to fill in the last position
myList[myList.length - 1] = temp;
```

9. *Simplifying coding:* Arrays can be used to greatly simplify coding for certain tasks. For example, suppose you wish to obtain the English name of a given month by its number. If the month names are stored in an array, the month name for a given month can be accessed simply via the index. The following code prompts the user to enter a month number and displays its month name:

```
String[] months = {"January", "February", ..., "December"};
System.out.print("Enter a month number (1 to 12): ");
int monthNumber = input.nextInt();
System.out.println("The month is " + months[monthNumber - 1]);
```

If you didn't use the `months` array, you would have to determine the month name using a lengthy multi-way `if-else` statement as follows:

```
if (monthNumber == 1)
    System.out.println("The month is January");
else if (monthNumber == 2)
    System.out.println("The month is February");
...
else
    System.out.println("The month is December");
```

Foreach Loops

Java supports a convenient `for` loop, known as a *foreach loop*, which enables you to traverse the array sequentially without using an index variable. For example, the following code displays all the elements in the array `myList`:

```java
for (double e: myList) {
   System.out.println(e);
}
```

You can read the code as "for each element `e` in `myList`, do the following." Note that the variable, `e`, must be declared as the same type as the elements in `myList`.

In general, the syntax for a foreach loop is

```java
for (elementType element: arrayRefVar) {
   // Process the element
}
```

You still have to use an index variable if you wish to traverse the array in a different order or change the elements in the array.

Caution

Accessing an array out of bounds is a common programming error that throws a runtime `ArrayIndexOutOfBoundsException`. To avoid it, make sure that you do not use an index beyond `arrayRefVar.length - 1`.

ArrayIndexOutOfBounds–
 Exception

Programmers often mistakenly reference the first element in an array with index `1`, but it should be `0`. This is called the *off-by-one error*. Another common off-by-one error in a loop is using `<=` where `<` should be used. For example, the following loop is wrong.

off-by-one error

```java
for (int i = 0; i <= list.length; i++)
   System.out.print(list[i] + " ");
```

The `<=` should be replaced by `<`.

✓ SECTION 7.2 ASSESSMENT

1. How do you declare an array reference variable and how do you create an array?

2. When is the memory allocated for an array?

3. What is the output of the following code?

```java
int x = 30;
int[] numbers = new int[x];
x = 60;
System.out.println("x is " + x);
System.out.println("The size of numbers is " + numbers.
length);
```

4. Indicate `true` or `false` for the following statements:

 ■ Every element in an array has the same type.

 ■ The array size is fixed after an array reference variable is declared.

 ■ The array size is fixed after it is created.

 ■ The elements in an array must be a primitive data type.

5. Which of the following statements are valid?

   ```
   int i = new int(30);
   double d[] = new double[30];
   char[] r = new char(1..30);
   int i[] = (3, 4, 3, 2);
   float f[] = {2.3, 4.5, 6.6};
   char[] c = new char();
   ```

6. How do you access elements in an array?

7. What is the array index type? What is the lowest index? What is the representation of the third element in an array named a?

8. Write statements to do the following:

 a. Create an array to hold **10** double values.

 b. Assign the value **5.5** to the last element in the array.

 c. Display the sum of the first two elements.

 d. Write a loop that computes the sum of all elements in the array.

 e. Write a loop that finds the minimum element in the array.

 f. Randomly generate an index and display the element of this index in the array.

 g. Use an array initializer to create another array with the initial values 3.5, 5.5, 4.52, and 5.6.

9. What happens when your program attempts to access an array element with an invalid index?

10. Identify and fix the errors in the following code:

    ```
    1  public class Test {
    2    public static void main(String[] args) {
    3      double[100] r;
    4
    5      for (int i = 0; i < r.length(); i++);
    6        r(i) = Math.random * 100;
    7    }
    8  }
    ```

11. What is the output of the following code?

    ```
    1  public class Test {
    2    public static void main(String[] args) {
    3      int list[] = {1, 2, 3, 4, 5, 6};
    4      for (int i = 1; i < list.length; i++)
    5        list[i] = list[i - 1];
    6
    7      for (int i = 0; i < list.length; i++)
    ```

```
 8        System.out.print(list[i] + " ");
 9      }
10  }
```

7.3 Case Study: Analyzing Numbers

The problem is to write a program that finds the number of items above the average of all items.

Key
Point

Now you can write a program using arrays to solve the problem proposed at the beginning of this chapter in Section 7.1. The problem is to read 100 numbers, get the average of these numbers, and find the number of the items greater than the average. To be flexible for handling any number of input, we will let the user enter the number of input, rather than fixing it to 100. Listing 7.1 gives a solution.

LISTING 7.1 AnalyzeNumbers.java

```
 1  public class AnalyzeNumbers {
 2    public static void main(String[] args) {
 3      java.util.Scanner input = new java.util.Scanner(System.in);
 4      System.out.print("Enter the number of items: ");
 5      int n = input.nextInt();
 6      double [] numbers = new double[n];
 7      double sum = 0;
 8
 9      System.out.print("Enter the numbers: ");
10      for (int i = 0; i < n; i++) {
11        numbers[i] = input.nextDouble();
12        sum += numbers[i];
13      }
14
15      double average = sum / n;
16
17      int count = 0; // The number of elements above average
18      for (int i = 0; i < n; i++)
19        if (numbers[i] > average)
20          count++;
21
22      System.out.println("Average is " + average);
23      System.out.println("Number of elements above the average is "
24        + count);
25    }
26  }
```

numbers[0]:
numbers[1]:
numbers[2]:

create array

.
.
numbers[i]: .

numbers[n - 3]:
numbers[n - 2]: store number
numbers[n - 1]: in array

get average

above
average?

```
Enter the number of items: 10 ⏎Enter
Enter the numbers: 3.4 5 6 1 6.5 7.8 3.5 8.5 6.3 9.5 ⏎Enter
Average is 5.75
Number of elements above the average is 6
```

The program prompts the user to enter the array size (line 5) and creates an array with the specified size (line 6). The program reads the input, stores numbers into the array (line 11), adds each number to sum in line 11, and obtains the average (line 15). It then compares each number in the array with the average to count the number of values above the average (lines 17–20).

7.4 Case Study: Deck of Cards

Key Point

The problem is to create a program that will randomly select four cards from a deck of cards.

Say you want to write a program that will pick four cards at random from a deck of **52** cards. All the cards can be represented using an array named **deck**, filled with initial values **0** to **51**, as follows:

```
int[] deck = new int[52];

// Initialize cards
for (int i = 0; i < deck.length; i++)
  deck[i] = i;
```

Card numbers **0** to **12**, **13** to **25**, **26** to **38**, and **39** to **51** represent 13 Spades, 13 Hearts, 13 Diamonds, and 13 Clubs, respectively, as shown in Figure 7.2. `cardNumber / 13` determines the suit of the card and `cardNumber % 13` determines the rank of the card, as shown in Figure 7.3. After shuffling the array **deck**, pick the first four cards from **deck**. The program displays the cards from these four card numbers.

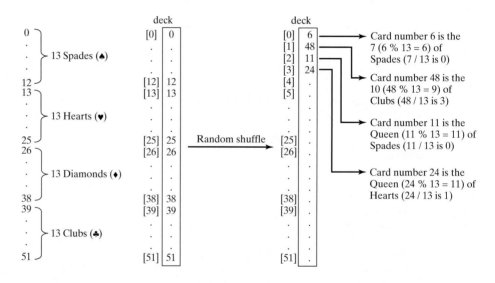

FIGURE 7.2 52 cards are stored in an array named **deck**.

FIGURE 7.3 `CardNumber` identifies a card's suit and rank number.

Listing 7.2 gives the solution to the problem.

LISTING 7.2 DeckOfCards.java

```
 1  public class DeckOfCards {
 2    public static void main(String[] args) {
 3      int[] deck = new int[52];                                       create array deck
 4      String[] suits = {"Spades", "Hearts", "Diamonds", "Clubs"};     array of strings
 5      String[] ranks = {"Ace", "2", "3", "4", "5", "6", "7", "8", "9", array of strings
 6        "10", "Jack", "Queen", "King"};
 7
 8      // Initialize the cards
 9      for (int i = 0; i < deck.length; i++)                            initialize deck
10        deck[i] = i;
11
12      // Shuffle the cards
13      for (int i = 0; i < deck.length; i++) {                         shuffle deck
14        // Generate an index randomly
15        int index = (int)(Math.random() * deck.length);
16        int temp = deck[i];
17        deck[i] = deck[index];
18        deck[index] = temp;
19      }
20
21      // Display the first four cards
22      for (int i = 0; i < 4; i++) {
23        String suit = suits[deck[i] / 13];                            suit of a card
24        String rank = ranks[deck[i] % 13];                            rank of a card
25        System.out.println("Card number " + deck[i] + ": "
26          + rank + " of " + suit);
27      }
28    }
29  }
```

```
Card number 6: 7 of Spades
Card number 48: 10 of Clubs
Card number 11: Queen of Spades
Card number 24: Queen of Hearts
```

The program creates an array suits for four suits (line 4) and an array ranks for 13 cards in a suit (lines 5–6). Each element in these arrays is a string.

The program initializes deck with values 0 to 51 in lines 9–10. The deck value 0 represents the card Ace of Spades, 1 represents the card 2 of Spades, 13 represents the card Ace of Hearts, and 14 represents the card 2 of Hearts.

Lines 13–19 randomly shuffle the deck. After a deck is shuffled, deck[i] contains an arbitrary value. deck[i] / 13 is 0, 1, 2, or 3, which determines the suit (line 23). deck[i] % 13 is a value between 0 and 12, which determines the rank (line 24). If the suits array is not defined, you would have to determine the suit using a lengthy multi-way if-else statement as follows:

```
if (deck[i] / 13 == 0)
  System.out.print("suit is Spades");
else if (deck[i] / 13 == 1)
  System.out.print("suit is Hearts");
else if (deck[i] / 13 == 2)
```

```
        System.out.print("suit is Diamonds");
      else
        System.out.print("suit is Clubs");
```

With `suits = {"Spades", "Hearts", "Diamonds", "Clubs"}` created in an array, `suits[deck / 13]` gives the suit for the `deck`. Using arrays greatly simplifies the solution for this program.

7.5 The Arrays Class

 Key Point

The java.util.Arrays class contains useful methods for common array operations such as sorting and searching.

The `java.util.Arrays` class contains various static methods for sorting and searching arrays, comparing arrays, filling array elements, and returning a string representation of the array.

parallelSort
sort

You can use the `sort` or `parallelSort` method to sort a whole array or a partial array. For example, the following code sorts an array of numbers and an array of characters.

```
double[] numbers = {6.0, 4.4, 1.9, 2.9, 3.4, 3.5};
java.util.Arrays.sort(numbers); // Sort the whole array
java.util.Arrays.parallelSort(numbers); // Sort the whole array

char[] chars = {'a', 'A', '4', 'F', 'D', 'P'};
java.util.Arrays.sort(chars, 1, 3); // Sort part of the array
java.util.Arrays.parallelSort(chars, 1, 3); // Sort part of the array
```

Invoking `sort(numbers)` sorts the whole array `numbers`. Invoking `sort(chars, 1, 3)` sorts a partial array from `chars[1]` to `chars[3-1]`. `parallelSort` is more efficient if your computer has multiple processors.

binarySearch

You can use the `binarySearch` method to search for a key in an array. The array must be presorted in increasing order. If the key is not in the array, the method returns `-(insertionIndex + 1)`. For example, the following code searches the keys in an array of integers and an array of characters.

```
int[] list = {2, 4, 7, 10, 11, 45, 50, 59, 60, 66, 69, 70, 79};
System.out.println("1. Index is " +
    java.util.Arrays.binarySearch(list, 11));
System.out.println("2. Index is " +
    java.util.Arrays.binarySearch(list, 12));

char[] chars = {'a', 'c', 'g', 'x', 'y', 'z'};
System.out.println("3. Index is " +
    java.util.Arrays.binarySearch(chars, 'a'));
System.out.println("4. Index is " +
    java.util.Arrays.binarySearch(chars, 't'));
```

The output of the preceding code is

1. Index is 4

2. Index is

3. Index is 0

4. Index is

You can use the `equals` method to check whether two arrays are strictly equal. Two arrays are strictly equal if their corresponding elements are the same. In the following code, `list1` and `list2` are equal, but `list2` and `list3` are not.

equals

```
int[] list1 = {2, 4, 7, 10};
int[] list2 = {2, 4, 7, 10};
int[] list3 = {4, 2, 7, 10};
System.out.println(java.util.Arrays.equals(list1, list2)); // true
System.out.println(java.util.Arrays.equals(list2, list3)); // false
```

You can use the `fill` method to fill in all or part of the array. For example, the following code fills `list1` with 5 and fills 8 into elements `list2[1]` through `list2[5-1]`.

fill

```
int[] list1 = {2, 4, 7, 10};
int[] list2 = {2, 4, 7, 7, 7, 10};
java.util.Arrays.fill(list1, 5); // Fill 5 to the whole array
java.util.Arrays.fill(list2, 1, 5, 8); // Fill 8 to a partial array
```

You can also use the `toString` method to return a string that represents all elements in the array. This is a quick and simple way to display all elements in the array. For example, the following code

toString

```
int[] list = {2, 4, 7, 10};
System.out.println(Arrays.toString(list));
```

displays `[2, 4, 7, 10]`.

✓ Section 7.5 Assessment

1. What two methods from the `java.util.Arrays.sort` class can you use to sort a whole or partial array?

2. To apply `java.util.Arrays.binarySearch(array, key)`, should the array be sorted in increasing order, in decreasing order, or neither?

3. Show the output of the following code:

```
int[] list1 = {2, 4, 7, 10};
java.util.Arrays.fill(list1, 7);
System.out.println(java.util.Arrays.toString(list1));
```

```
int[] list2 = {2, 4, 7, 10};
System.out.println(java.util.Arrays.toString(list2));
System.out.print(java.util.Arrays.equals(list1, list2));
```

Chapter 7 — Review and Assessment

KEY TERMS

0 based 205
data structure 202
index 202
indexed variable 205
`java.util.Arrays.parallelSort` 214
`java.util.Arrays.sort` 214

`new` operator 203
null 203
off-by-one error 209
single-dimensional array 202
two-dimensional array 202

CHAPTER SUMMARY

1. A *data structure* is a collection of data organized in a particular way, and used to store data in computer memory. An *array* is a commonly used type of data structure.

2. When designing your application, consider using a data structure if you have a large amount of data to store and process during program execution. It is important to note that data structures store data in RAM memory while your program is running.

3. A *single-dimensional array* organizes data into a sequential, single row or column. There are a fixed number of *elements* in an array.

4. An example of a *two-dimensional array* is a spreadsheet where data is stored and retrieved by the location of both a column and a row.

5. Unlike declarations for primitive data type variables, the declaration of an array variable does not allocate any space in memory for the array. An array variable is not a primitive data type variable. An array variable contains a reference to an array.

6. You cannot assign elements to an array unless it has already been created. You can create an array by using the `new` operator with the following syntax: `new elementType[arraySize]`.

7. Each element in the array is represented using the syntax `arrayRefVar[index]`. An *index* must be an integer or an integer expression.

8. After an array is created, its size becomes permanent and can be obtained using `arrayRefVar.length`. Since the index of an array always begins with 0, the last index is always `arrayRefVar.length - 1`. An *out-of-bounds error* will occur if you attempt to reference elements beyond the bounds of an array.

9. Programmers often mistakenly reference the first element in an array with index 1, but it should be 0. This is called the index *off-by-one error*.

10. When an array is created, its elements are assigned the default value of 0 for the numeric primitive data types, `\u0000` for char types, and `false` for `boolean` types.

11. Java has a shorthand notation, known as the *array initializer*, which combines declaring an array, creating an array, and initializing an array in one statement, using the syntax `elementType[] arrayRefVar = {value0, value1, ..., valuek}`.

PROGRAMMING EXERCISES

Note

Exercises preceded by a star (*) are more challenging.

***1.** (*Assign grades*) Write a program that reads student scores, gets the best score, and then assigns grades based on the following scheme:

Grade is A if score isbest

Grade is B if score isbest

Grade is C if score isbest

Grade is D if score isbest

Grade is F otherwise.

The program prompts the user to enter the total number of students, then prompts the user to enter all of the scores, and concludes by displaying the grades. Here is a sample run:

```
Enter the number of students: 4 ↵Enter
Enter 4 scores: 40 55 70 58 ↵Enter
Student 0 score is 40 and grade is C
Student 1 score is 55 and grade is B
Student 2 score is 70 and grade is A
Student 3 score is 58 and grade is B
```

2. (*Reverse the numbers entered*) Write a program that reads ten integers and displays them in the reverse of the order in which they were read.

3. (*Analyze scores*) Write a program that reads an unspecified number of scores and determines how many scores are above or equal to the average and how many scores are below the average. Enter a negative number to signify the end of the input. Assume that the maximum number of scores is 100.

*4. (*Revise Listing 6.12, PrimeNumber.java*) Listing 6.12 determines whether a number n is prime by checking whether 2, 3, 4, 5, 6, ..., n/2 is a divisor. If a divisor is found, n is not prime. A more efficient approach is to check whether any of the prime numbers less than or equal to can divide n evenly. If not, n is prime. Rewrite Listing 6.12 to display the first 50 prime numbers using this approach. You need to use an array to store the prime numbers and later use them to check whether they are possible divisors for n.

*5. (*Count single digits*) Write a program that generates 100 random integers between 0 and 9 and displays the count for each number. (*Hint*: Use an array of ten integers, say `counts`, to store the counts for the number of 0s, 1s, ..., 9s.)

USING METHODS TO MODULARIZE CODE

Objectives

- Construct a method definition.

- Explain the principles of *modular* software system design.

- Invoke methods with parameters.

- Define methods with a return value.

- Define methods without a return value.

- Develop reusable code that is modular, easy to read, easy to debug, and easy to maintain.

- Compare a *procedural* vs. a *modular* programming style.

- Design methods using a stepwise refinement (*abstraction*) strategy.

- Identify program *constraints*.

- Identify and track potential issues and resolutions.

8.1 Introduction

Key
Point

Methods can be used to define reusable code and organize and simplify coding. Using methods in the application design is an effective way to modularize code and distribute programming efforts across a team.

Suppose that you need to find the sum of integers from 1 to 10, from 20 to 37, and from 35 to 49, respectively. You may write the code as follows:

```java
int sum = 0;
for (int i = 1; i <= 10; i++)
  sum += i;
System.out.println("Sum from 1 to 10 is " + sum);

sum = 0;
for (int i = 20; i <= 37; i++)
  sum += i;
System.out.println("Sum from 20 to 37 is " + sum);

sum = 0;
for (int i = 35; i <= 49; i++)
  sum += i;
System.out.println("Sum from 35 to 49 is " + sum);
```

You may have observed that computing these sums from 1 to 10, from 20 to 37, and from 35 to 49 are very similar except that the starting and ending integers are different. Wouldn't it be nice if we could write the common code once and reuse it? We can do so by defining a method and invoking it.

The preceding code can be simplified as follows:

```java
1  public static int sum(int i1, int i2) {
2    int result = 0;
3    for (int i = i1; i <= i2; i++)
4      result += i;
5
6    return result;
7  }
8
9  public static void main(String[] args) {
10   System.out.println("Sum from 1 to 10 is " + sum(1, 10));
11   System.out.println("Sum from 20 to 37 is " + sum(20, 37));
12   System.out.println("Sum from 35 to 49 is " + sum(35, 49));
13 }
```

why methods?

define sum method

main method
invoke sum

Lines 1–7 define the method named `sum` with two parameters `i1` and `i2`. The statements in the `main` method invoke `sum(1, 10)` to compute the sum from 1 to 10, `sum(20, 37)` to compute the sum from 20 to 37, and `sum(35, 49)` to compute the sum from 35 to 49.

method

A *method* is a collection of statements grouped together to perform an operation. In earlier chapters you have used predefined methods such as `System.out.println`, `System.exit`, and `Math.random`. These methods are defined in the Java library. In this chapter, you will learn how to define your own methods and apply method abstraction to solve complex problems.

8.2 Defining a Method

A method definition consists of its method name, parameters, return value type, and body.

Key Point

The syntax for defining a method is as follows:

```
modifier returnValueType methodName(list of parameters) {
   // Method body;
}
```

Let's look at a method defined to find the larger between two integers. This method, named `max`, has two `int` parameters, `num1` and `num2`, the larger of which is returned by the method. Figure 8.1 illustrates the components of this method.

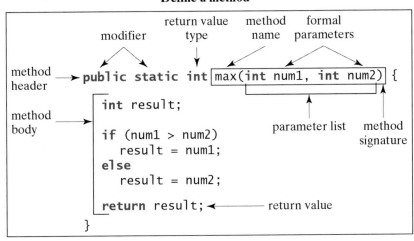

FIGURE 8.1 A method definition consists of a method header and a method body.

The *method header* specifies the *modifiers, return value type, method name,* and *parameters* of the method. The `static` modifier is used for all the methods in this chapter.

method header
modifier

A method may return a value. The `returnValueType` is the data type of the value the method returns. Some methods perform desired operations without returning a value. In this case, the `returnValueType` is the keyword `void`. For example, the `returnValueType` is `void` in the `main` method, as well as in `System. exit`, and `System.out.println`. If a method returns a value, it is called a *value-returning method;* otherwise it is called a *void method.*

value-returning method
void method

The variables defined in the method header are known as *formal parameters* or simply *parameters.* A parameter is like a placeholder: when a method is invoked, you pass a value to the parameter. This value is referred to as an *actual parameter* or *argument.* The *parameter list* refers to the method's type, order, and number of the parameters. The method name and the parameter list together constitute the *method signature.* Parameters are optional; that is, a method may contain no parameters. For example, the `Math.random()` method has no parameters.

parameter
argument
parameter list

method signature

The method body contains a collection of statements that implement the method. The method body of the `max` method uses an `if` statement to determine which number is larger and return the value of that number. In order for a value-returning method to return a result, a return statement using the keyword `return` is *required*. The method terminates when a return statement is executed.

Note
Some programming languages refer to methods as *procedures* and *functions*. In those languages, a value-returning method is called a *function* and a void method is called a *procedure*.

Caution
In the method header, you need to declare each parameter separately. For instance, `max(int num1, int num2)` is correct, but `max(int num1, num2)` is wrong.

Note
We say "*define* a method" and "*declare* a variable." We are making a subtle distinction here. A definition defines what the defined item is, but a declaration usually involves allocating memory to store data for the declared item.

define vs. declare

8.3 Calling a Method

Calling a method executes the code in the method.

In a method definition, you define what the method is to do. To execute the method, you have to *call* or *invoke* it. Figure 8.2 illustrates what the code would look like to invoke the method in Figure 8.1.

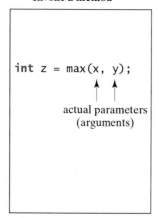

FIGURE 8.2 Example code for invoking a method.

There are two ways to call a method, depending on whether or not the method returns a value.

A value is returned.

If a method returns a value, a call to the method is usually treated as a value. For example,

```java
int larger = max(3, 4);
```

calls `max(3, 4)` and assigns the result of the method to the variable `larger`. Another example of a call that is treated as a value is

```java
System.out.println(max(3, 4));
```

which prints the return value of the method call `max(3, 4)`.

No value is returned.

A method that does not return a value is called a `void` method. If a method returns `void`, a call to the method must be a statement. For example, the method `println` returns `void`. The following call is a statement:

```java
System.out.println("Welcome to Java!");
```

>
> **Note**
> A value-returning method can also be invoked as a statement in Java. In this case, the caller simply ignores the return value. This is not often done, but it is permissible if the caller is not interested in the return value.

When a program calls a method, program control is transferred to the called method. A called method returns control to the caller when its return statement is executed or when its method-ending closing brace is reached.

Listing 8.1 shows a complete program that is used to test the `max` method.

LISTING 8.1 TestMax.java

```java
 1  public class TestMax {
 2    /** Main method */
 3    public static void main(String[] args) {          main method
 4      int i = 5;
 5      int j = 2;
 6      int k = max(i, j);                                invoke max
 7      System.out.println("The maximum of " + i +
 8        " and " + j + " is " + k);
 9    }
10
11    /** Return the max of two numbers */
12    public static int max(int num1, int num2) {        define method
13      int result;
14
15      if (num1 > num2)
16        result = num1;
17      else
18        result = num2;
19
20      return result;
21    }
22  }
```

```
The maximum of 5 and 2 is 5
```

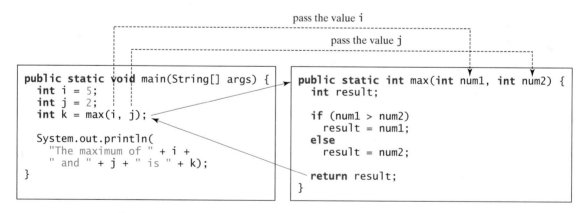

line#	i	j	k	num1	num2	result
4	5					
5		2				
12				5	2	
13						undefined
16						5
6			5			

Invoking max { 12, 13, 16 }

main method

This program contains the `main` method and the `max` method. The `main` method is just like any other method except that it is invoked by the JVM to start the program.

The `main` method's header is always the same. Like the one in this example, it includes the modifiers `public` and `static`, return value type `void`, method name `main`, and a parameter of the `String[]` type. `String[]` indicates that the parameter is an array of `String`, a subject addressed in Chapter 7.

The statements in `main` may invoke other methods that are defined in the class that contains the `main` method or in other classes. In this example, the `main` method invokes `max(i, j)`, which is defined in the same class with the `main` method.

max method

When the `max` method is invoked (line 6), variable `i`'s value 5 is passed to `num1`, and variable `j`'s value 2 is passed to `num2` in the `max` method. The flow of control transfers to the `max` method, and the `max` method is executed. When the `return` statement in the `max` method is executed, the `max` method returns the control to its caller (in this case the caller is the `main` method). This process is illustrated in Figure 8.3.

pass the value i

pass the value j

```
public static void main(String[] args) {
    int i = 5;
    int j = 2;
    int k = max(i, j);

    System.out.println(
        "The maximum of " + i +
        " and " + j + " is " + k);
}
```

```
public static int max(int num1, int num2) {
    int result;

    if (num1 > num2)
        result = num1;
    else
        result = num2;

    return result;
}
```

FIGURE 8.3 When the `max` method is invoked, the flow of control transfers to it. Once the `max` method is finished, it returns control back to the caller.

Caution

A `return` statement is required for a value-returning method. The method shown in part (a) of the following figure is logically correct, but it has a compile error because the Java compiler thinks that this method might not return a value.

```
public static int sign(int n) {
  if (n > 0)
    return 1;
  else if (n == 0)
    return 0;
  else if (n < 0)
    return -1;
}
```
(a)

Should be ⟶

```
public static int sign(int n) {
  if (n > 0)
    return 1;
  else if (n == 0)
    return 0;
  else
    return -1;
}
```
(b)

To fix this problem, delete `if (n < 0)` in (a), so the compiler will see a `return` statement to be reached regardless of how the `if` statement is evaluated.

 Note

Methods enable code sharing and reuse. The `max` method can be invoked from any class, not just `TestMax`. If you create a new class, you can invoke the `max` method using `ClassName.methodName` (i.e., `TestMax.max`).

code sharing and reuse

8.4 void Method Example

 Key Point

*A **void** method does not return a value.*

The preceding section gives an example of a value-returning method. This section shows how to define and invoke a **void** method. Listing 8.2 gives a program that defines a method named `printGrade` and invokes it to print the grade for a given score.

void method

LISTING 8.2 TestVoidMethod.java

```
 1  public class TestVoidMethod {
 2    public static void main(String[] args) {
 3      System.out.print("The grade is ");
 4      printGrade(78.5);
 5
 6      System.out.print("The grade is ");
 7      printGrade(59.5);
 8    }
 9
10    public static void printGrade(double score) {
11      if (score >= 90.0) {
12        System.out.println('A');
13      }
14      else if (score >= 80.0) {
15        System.out.println('B');
16      }
17      else if (score >= 70.0) {
18        System.out.println('C');
19      }
20      else if (score >= 60.0) {
21        System.out.println('D');
22      }
23      else {
24        System.out.println('F');
25      }
26    }
27  }
```

main method

invoke printGrade

printGrade method

```
The grade is C
The grade is F
```

The `printGrade` method is a `void` method because it does not return any value.
A call to a `void` method must be a statement. Therefore, it is invoked as a state-
ment in line 4 in the `main` method. Like any Java statement, it is terminated with
a semicolon.

void vs. value-returned

To see the differences between a void and value-returning method, let's rede-
sign the `printGrade` method to return a value. The new method, which we call
`getGrade`, returns the grade as shown in Listing 8.3.

LISTING 8.3 TestReturnGradeMethod.java

main method

invoke getGrade

getGrade method

```
 1  public class TestReturnGradeMethod {
 2    public static void main(String[] args) {
 3      System.out.print("The grade is " + getGrade(78.5));
 4      System.out.print("\nThe grade is " + getGrade(59.5));
 5    }
 6
 7    public static char getGrade(double score) {
 8      if (score >= 90.0)
 9        return 'A';
10      else if (score >= 80.0)
11        return 'B';
12      else if (score >= 70.0)
13        return 'C';
14      else if (score >= 60.0)
15        return 'D';
16      else
17        return 'F';
18    }
19  }
```

```
The grade is C
The grade is F
```

The `getGrade` method defined in lines 7–18 returns a character grade based on
the numeric score value. The caller invokes this method in lines 3–4.

The `getGrade` method can be invoked by a caller wherever a character may
appear. The `printGrade` method does not return any value, so it must be invoked
as a statement.

return in void method

Note

A `return` statement is not needed for a `void` method, but it can be used
for terminating the method and returning to the method's caller. The
syntax is simply

return;

This is not often done, but sometimes it is useful for circumventing the
normal flow of control in a `void` method. For example, the following code
has a return statement to terminate the method when the score is invalid.

```
public static void printGrade(double score) {
  if (score < 0 || score > 100) {
    System.out.println("Invalid score");
    return;
  }

  if (score >= 90.0) {
    System.out.println('A');
  }
  else if (score >= 80.0) {
    System.out.println('B');
  }
  else if (score >= 70.0) {
    System.out.println('C');
  }
  else if (score >= 60.0) {
    System.out.println('D');
  }
  else {
    System.out.println('F');
  }
}
```

✓ Section 8.4 Assessment

1. What are the benefits of using a method?

2. How do you define a method? How do you invoke a method?

3. How do you simplify the `max` method in Listing 8.1 using the conditional operator?

4. True or false? A call to a method with a `void` return type is always a statement itself, but a call to a value-returning method cannot be a statement by itself.

5. What is the `return` type of a `main` method?

6. What would be wrong with not writing a `return` statement in a value-returning method? Can you have a `return` statement in a `void` method? Does the `return` statement in the following method cause syntax errors?

```
public static void xMethod(double x, double y) {
  System.out.println(x + y);
  return x + y;
}
```

7. Define the terms parameter, argument, and method signature.

8. Write method headers (not the bodies) for the following methods:

 a. Return a sales commission, given the sales amount and the commission rate.

 b. Display the calendar for a month, given the month and year.

 c. Test whether a number is even, and returning `true` if it is.

 d. Display a message a specified number of times.

9. Identify and correct the errors in the following program:

```
1  public class Test {
2    public static method1(int n, m) {
3      n += m;
4      method2(3.4);
5    }
6
7    public static int method2(int n) {
8      if (n > 0) return 1;
9      else if (n == 0) return 0;
10     else if (n < 0) return -1;
11   }
12 }
```

10. Reformat the following program according to the programming style and documentation guidelines proposed in Section 2.7, Programming Style and Documentation. Use the next-line brace style.

```
public class Test {
  public static double method(double i, double j)
  {
  while (i < j) {
     j--;
  }

  return j;
  }
}
```

8.5 Passing Arguments by Values

The arguments are passed by value to parameters when invoking a method.

The power of a method is its ability to work with parameters. You can use `println` to print any string and `max` to find the maximum of any two `int` values. When calling a method, you need to provide arguments, which must be given in the same order as their respective parameters in the method signature. This is known as *parameter order association*. For example, the following method prints a message n times:

parameter order association

```
public static void nPrintln(String message, int n) {
  for (int i = 0; i < n; i++)
    System.out.println(message);
}
```

You can use `nPrintln("Hello",   3)` to print `Hello` three times. The `nPrintln("Hello",   3)` statement passes the actual string parameter `Hello` to the parameter `message`, passes `3` to `n`, and prints `Hello` three times. However, the statement `nPrintln(3,  "Hello")` would be wrong. The data type of `3` does not match the data type for the first parameter, `message`, nor does the second argument, `Hello`, match the second parameter, `n`.

> **Caution**
> The arguments must match the parameters in *order, number,* and *compatible type,* as defined in the method signature. Compatible type means that you can pass an argument to a parameter without explicit casting, such as passing an **int** value argument to a **double** value parameter.

When you invoke a method with an argument, the value of the argument is passed to the parameter. This is referred to as *pass-by-value.* If the argument is a variable rather than a fixed value, the value of the variable is passed to the parameter. The variable is not affected, regardless of the changes made to the parameter inside the method. As shown in Listing 8.4, the value of x (1) is passed to the parameter n to invoke the **increment** method (line 5). The parameter n is incremented by 1 in the method (line 10), but x is not changed no matter what the method does.

pass-by-value

LISTING 8.4 Increment.java

```
1  public class Increment {
2    public static void main(String[] args) {
3      int x = 1;
4      System.out.println("Before the call, x is " + x);
5      increment(x);
6      System.out.println("After the call, x is " + x);
7    }
8
9    public static void increment(int n) {
10     n++;
11     System.out.println("n inside the method is " + n);
12   }
13 }
```

invoke increment

increment n

```
Before the call, x is 1
n inside the method is 2
After the call, x is 1
```

✓ SECTION 8.5 ASSESSMENT

1. How is an argument passed to a method? Can the argument have the same name as its parameter?

2. Identify and correct the errors in the following program:

```
1  public class Test {
2    public static void main(String[] args) {
3      nPrintln(5, "Welcome to Java!");
4    }
5
6    public static void nPrintln(String message, int n) {
7      int n = 1;
8      for (int i = 0; i < n; i++)
9        System.out.println(message);
10   }
11 }
```

8.6 Modularizing Code

Key Point

Writing code in a modular format is an important design concept. Modular code makes the code easy to maintain, debug, and reuse.

modular code

Methods can be used to reduce redundant code and enable code reuse. Methods can also be used to modularize code and improve the quality of the program.

Listing 6.7 gives a program that prompts the user to enter two integers and displays their greatest common divisor. You can rewrite the program using a method, as shown in Listing 8.5.

LISTING 8.5 GreatestCommonDivisorMethod.java

```java
 1  import java.util.Scanner;
 2
 3  public class GreatestCommonDivisorMethod {
 4    /** Main method */
 5    public static void main(String[] args) {
 6      // Create a Scanner
 7      Scanner input = new Scanner(System.in);
 8
 9      // Prompt the user to enter two integers
10      System.out.print("Enter first integer: ");
11      int n1 = input.nextInt();
12      System.out.print("Enter second integer: ");
13      int n2 = input.nextInt();
14
15      System.out.println("The greatest common divisor for " + n1 +
16        " and " + n2 + " is " + gcd(n1, n2));
17    }
18
19    /** Return the gcd of two integers */
20    public static int gcd(int n1, int n2) {
21      int gcd = 1; // Initial gcd is 1
22      int k = 2;   // Possible gcd
23
24      while (k <= n1 && k <= n2) {
25        if (n1 % k == 0 && n2 % k == 0)
26          gcd = k; // Update gcd
27        k++;
28      }
29
30      return gcd; // Return gcd
31    }
32  }
```

invoke gcd

compute gcd

return gcd

```
Enter first integer: 45 ⏎Enter
Enter second integer: 75 ⏎Enter
The greatest common divisor for 45 and 75 is 15
```

By encapsulating the code for obtaining the gcd in a method, this program has several advantages:

1. It isolates the problem for computing the gcd from the rest of the code in the main method. Thus, the logic becomes clear and the program is easier to read.

2. The errors on computing the gcd are confined in the gcd method, which narrows the scope of debugging.

3. The gcd method now can be reused by other programs.

Listing 8.6 applies the concept of code modularization to improve Listing 6.12, PrimeNumber.java.

LISTING 8.6 `PrimeNumberMethod.java`

```
 1  public class PrimeNumberMethod {
 2    public static void main(String[] args) {
 3      System.out.println("The first 50 prime numbers are \n");
 4      printPrimeNumbers(50);                                              invoke printPrimeNumbers
 5    }
 6
 7    public static void printPrimeNumbers(int numberOfPrimes) {            printPrimeNumbers
 8      final int NUMBER_OF_PRIMES_PER_LINE = 10; // Display 10 per line    method
 9      int count = 0; // Count the number of prime numbers
10      int number = 2; // A number to be tested for primeness
11
12      // Repeatedly find prime numbers
13      while (count < numberOfPrimes) {
14        // Print the prime number and increase the count
15        if (isPrime(number)) {                                           invoke isPrime
16          count++; // Increase the count
17
18          if (count % NUMBER_OF_PRIMES_PER_LINE == 0) {
19            // Print the number and advance to the new line
20            System.out.printf("%-5s\n", number);
21          }
22          else
23            System.out.printf("%-5s", number);
24        }
25
26        // Check whether the next number is prime
27        number++;
28      }
29    }
30
31    /** Check whether number is prime */
32    public static boolean isPrime(int number) {                          isPrime method
33      for (int divisor = 2; divisor <= number / 2; divisor++) {
34        if (number % divisor == 0) { // If true, number is not prime
35          return false; // Number is not a prime
36        }
37      }
38
39      return true; // Number is prime
40    }
41  }
```

```
The first 50 prime numbers are
2    3    5    7    11   13   17   19   23   29
31   37   41   43   47   53   59   61   67   71
73   79   83   89   97   101  103  107  109  113
127  131  137  139  149  151  157  163  167  173
179  181  191  193  197  199  211  223  227  229
```

We divided a large problem into two subproblems: determining whether a number is a prime and printing the prime numbers. As a result, the new program is easier to read and easier to debug. Moreover, the methods `printPrimeNumbers` and `isPrime` can be reused by other programs.

✓ SECTION 8.6 ASSESSMENT

1. Identify the concepts of modular code design. Why is it used?

8.7 Case Study: Converting Hexadecimals to Decimals

Key Point

This section presents a program that converts a hexadecimal number into a decimal number.

Chapter 5, Listing 5.4 is an example of converting a hex number into a decimal using a *procedural coding style*. The case study in Listing 8.7 looks at solving the same problem using a *modular, object-oriented coding style*. Programming logic for converting a value from hexadecimal to decimal is removed from the main body of code, and grouped together in a method. Grouping and modularizing the code into independent units is a common design concept. Designing code into modular units lays the foundation for object-oriented design. You will learn more about object-oriented design in the next chapter.

Given a hexadecimal number $h_n h_{n-1} h_{n-2} \ldots h_2 h_1 h_0$ the equivalent decimal value is

$$h_n \times 16^n + h_{n-1} \times 16^{n-1} + h_{n-2} \times 16^{n-2} + \ldots$$
$$+ h_2 \times 16^2 + h_1 \times 16^1 + h_0 \times 16^0$$

For example, the hex number AB8C is

$$10 \times 16^3 + 11 \times 16^2 + 8 \times 16^1 + 12 \times 16^0 = 43916$$

Our program will prompt the user to enter a hex number as a string and convert it into a decimal using the following method:

```
public static int hexToDecimal(String hex)
```

A brute-force approach is to convert each hex character into a decimal number, multiply it by for a hex digit at the i's position, and then add all the items together to obtain the equivalent decimal value for the hex number.

Note that

$$h_n \times 16^n + h_{n-1} \times 16^{n-1} + h_{n-2} \times 16^{n-2} + \ldots + h_1 \times 16^1 + h_0 \times 16^0$$
$$= (\ldots ((h_n \times 16 + h_n - 1) \times 16 + h_n - 2) \times 16 + \ldots + h_1) \times 16 + h_0$$

This observation, known as the Horner's algorithm, leads to the following efficient code for converting a hex string to a decimal number:

```
int decimalValue = 0;
for (int i = 0; i < hex.length(); i++) {
  char hexChar = hex.charAt(i);
  decimalValue = decimalValue * 16 + hexCharToDecimal(hexChar);
}
```

Here is a trace of the algorithm for hex number AB8C:

	i	hexChar	hexCharToDecimal (hexChar)	decimalValue
before the loop				0
after the 1st iteration	0	A	10	10
after the 2nd iteration	1	B	11	10 * 16 + 11
after the 3rd iteration	2	8	8	(10 * 16 + 11) * 16 + 8
after the 4th iteration	3	C	12	((10 * 16 + 11) * 16 + 8) * 16 + 12

Listing 8.7 gives the complete program.

LISTING 8.7 Hex2Dec.java

```
1  import java.util.Scanner;
2
3  public class Hex2Dec {
4    /** Main method */
5    public static void main(String[] args) {
6      // Create a Scanner
7      Scanner input = new Scanner(System.in);
8
9      // Prompt the user to enter a string
10     System.out.print("Enter a hex number: ");
11     String hex = input.nextLine();
12
13     System.out.println("The decimal value for hex number "
14       + hex + " is " + hexToDecimal(hex.toUpperCase()));
15   }
16
```

input string

hex to decimal

```
17    public static int hexToDecimal(String hex) {
18      int decimalValue = 0;
19      for (int i = 0; i < hex.length(); i++) {
20        char hexChar = hex.charAt(i);
21        decimalValue = decimalValue * 16 + hexCharToDecimal(hexChar);
22      }
23
24      return decimalValue;
25    }
26
27    public static int hexCharToDecimal(char ch) {
28      if (ch >= 'A' && ch <= 'F')
29        return 10 + ch - 'A';
30      else // ch is '0', '1', ..., or '9'
31        return ch - '0';
32    }
33  }
```

hex char to decimal
check uppercase

```
Enter a hex number: AB8C  ⏎Enter
The decimal value for hex number AB8C is 43916
```

```
Enter a hex number: af71  ⏎Enter
The decimal value for hex number af71 is 44913
```

The program reads a string from the console (line 11), and invokes the `hexToDecimal` method to convert a hex string to decimal number (line 14). The characters can be in either lowercase or uppercase. They are converted to uppercase before invoking the `hexToDecimal` method.

The `hexToDecimal` method is defined in lines 17–25 to return an integer. The length of the string is determined by invoking `hex.length()` in line 19.

The `hexCharToDecimal` method is defined in lines 27–32 to return a decimal value for a hex character. The character can be in either lowercase or uppercase. Recall that to subtract two characters is to subtract their Unicodes. For example, `'5' - '0'` is 5.

✓ SECTION 8.7 ASSESSMENT

1. Compare the code design in Listing 5.4 and Listing 8.7. Explain the difference between the two programming styles.

8.8 Software Design Strategies using Abstraction and Stepwise Refinement

The key to developing software is to apply the concept of abstraction.

You will learn many levels of abstraction from this book. *Method abstraction* is achieved by separating the use of a method from its implementation. The client can use a method without knowing how it is implemented. The details of the implementation are encapsulated in the method and hidden from the client who invokes the method. This is also known as *information hiding* or *encapsulation*. If you decide to change the implementation, the client program will not be affected, provided that you do not change the method signature. The implementation of the method is hidden from the client in a "black box," as shown in Figure 8.4.

method abstraction

information hiding

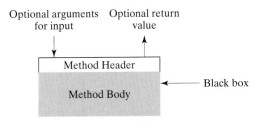

FIGURE 8.4 The method body can be thought of as a black box that contains the detailed implementation for the method.

You have already used the `System.out.print` method to display a string and the `max` method to find the maximum number. You know how to write the code to invoke these methods in your program, but as a user of these methods, you are not required to know how they are implemented.

The concept of method abstraction can be applied to the process of developing programs. When writing a large program, you can use the *divide-and-conquer* strategy, also known as *stepwise refinement*, to decompose it into subproblems. The subproblems can be further decomposed into smaller, more manageable problems.

divide and conquer

stepwise refinement

Suppose you write a program that displays the calendar for a given month of the year. The program prompts the user to enter the year and the month, then displays the entire calendar for the month, as shown in the following sample run.

Let us use this example to demonstrate the divide-and-conquer approach.

Top-Down Design

How would you get started on such a program? Would you immediately start coding? Beginning programmers often start by trying to work out the solution to every detail. Although details are important in the final program, concern for detail in the early stages may block the problem-solving process. To make problem solving flow as smoothly as possible, this example begins by using method abstraction to isolate details from design and only later implements the details.

For this example, the problem is first broken into two subproblems: get input from the user and print the calendar for the month. At this stage, you should be concerned with what the subproblems will achieve, not with how to get input and print the calendar for the month. You can draw a structure chart to help visualize the decomposition of the problem (see Figure 8.5a).

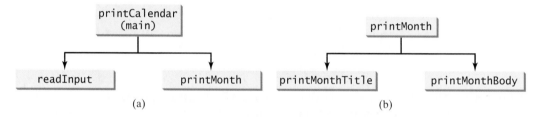

(a) (b)

FIGURE 8.5 The structure chart shows that the `printCalendar` problem is divided into two subproblems, `readInput` and `printMonth` in (a), and that `printMonth` is divided into two smaller subproblems, `printMonthTitle` and `printMonthBody` in (b).

You can use **Scanner** to read input for the year and the month. The problem of printing the calendar for a given month can be broken into two subproblems: print the month title and print the month body, as shown in Figure 8.5b. The month title consists of three lines: month and year, a dashed line, and the names of the seven days of the week. You need to get the month name (e.g., January) from the numeric month (e.g., 1). This is accomplished in **getMonthName** (see Figure 8.6a).

In order to print the month body, you need to know which day of the week is the first day of the month (**getStartDay**) and how many days the month has (**getNumberOfDaysInMonth**), as shown in Figure 8.6b. For example, December 2013 has 31 days, and December 1, 2013, is a Sunday.

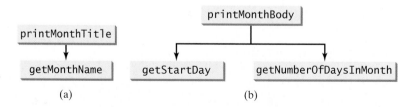

(a) (b)

FIGURE 8.6 (a) To `printMonthTitle`, you need `getMonthName`.
(b) The `printMonthBody` problem is refined into several smaller problems.

How would you get the start day for the first date in a month? There are several ways to do so. For now, we'll use an alternative approach. Assume you know that the start day for January 1, 1800, was a Wednesday (`START_DAY_FOR_JAN_1_1800` = 3). You could compute the total number of days (`totalNumberOfDays`) between January 1, 1800, and the first date of the calendar month. The start day for the calendar month is (`totalNumberOfDays` + `START_DAY_FOR_JAN_1_1800`) % 7, since every week has seven days. Thus, the `getStartDay` problem can be further refined as `getTotalNumberOfDays`, as shown in Figure 8.7a.

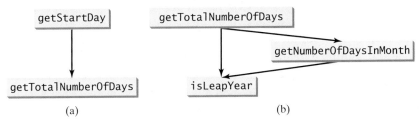

(a) (b)

FIGURE 8.7 (a) To `getStartDay`, you need `getTotalNumberOfDays`. (b) The `getTotalNumberOfDays` problem is refined into two smaller problems.

To get the total number of days, you need to know whether the year is a leap year and the number of days in each month. Thus, `getTotalNumberOfDays` can be further refined into two subproblems: `isLeapYear` and `getNumberOfDaysInMonth`, as shown in Figure 8.7b. The complete structure chart is shown in Figure 8.8.

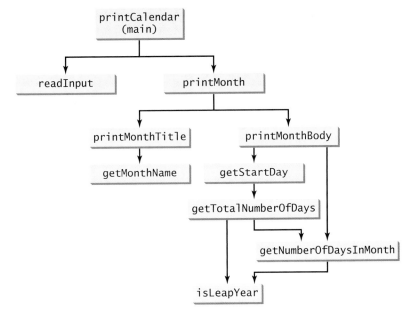

FIGURE 8.8 The structure chart shows the hierarchical relationship of the subproblems in the program.

Top-Down and/or Bottom-Up Implementation

Now we turn our attention to implementation. In general, a subproblem corresponds to a method in the implementation, although some are so simple that this is unnecessary. You would need to decide which modules to implement as methods and which to combine with other methods. Decisions of this kind should be based on whether the overall program will be easier to read as a result of your choice. In this example, the subproblem `readInput` can be simply implemented in the `main` method.

top-down approach

stub

You can use either a "top-down" or a "bottom-up" approach. The top-down approach implements one method in the structure chart at a time from the top to the bottom. *Stubs*—a simple but incomplete version of a method—can be used for the methods waiting to be implemented. The use of stubs enables you to quickly build the framework of the program. Implement the `main` method first, and then use a stub for the `printMonth` method. For example, let `printMonth` display the year and the month in the stub. Thus, your program may begin like this:

```java
public class PrintCalendar {
  /** Main method */
  public static void main(String[] args) {
    Scanner input = new Scanner(System.in);

    // Prompt the user to enter year
    System.out.print("Enter full year (e.g., 2012): ");
    int year = input.nextInt();

    // Prompt the user to enter month
    System.out.print("Enter month as a number between 1 and 12: ");
    int month = input.nextInt();

    // Print calendar for the month of the year
    printMonth(year, month);
  }

  /** A stub for printMonth may look like this */
  public static void printMonth(int year, int month){
    System.out.print(month + " " + year);
  }

  /** A stub for printMonthTitle may look like this */
  public static void printMonthTitle(int year, int month){
  }

  /** A stub for getMonthBody may look like this */
  public static void printMonthBody(int year, int month){
  }

  /** A stub for getMonthName may look like this */
  public static String getMonthName(int month) {
    return "January"; // A dummy value
  }

  /** A stub for getStartDay may look like this */
  public static int getStartDay(int year, int month) {
    return 1; // A dummy value
  }
}
```

```
/** A stub for getTotalNumberOfDays may look like this */
public static int getTotalNumberOfDays(int year, int month) {
  return 10000; // A dummy value
}

/** A stub for getNumberOfDaysInMonth may look like this */
public static int getNumberOfDaysInMonth(int year, int month) {
  return 31; // A dummy value
}

/** A stub for isLeapYear may look like this */
public static boolean isLeapYear(int year) {
  return true; // A dummy value
}
}
```

Compile and test the program, and fix any errors. You can now implement the
`printMonth` method. For methods invoked from the `printMonth` method, you
can again use stubs.

The bottom-up approach implements one method in the structure chart at a
time from the bottom to the top. For each method implemented, write a test program, known as the *driver*, to test it. The top-down and bottom-up approaches are
equally good: Both approaches implement methods incrementally, help to isolate
programming errors, and make debugging easy. They can be used together. Breaking down the steps into units makes it easy to identify all the processes required
to solve a problem.

bottom-up approach

driver

identify processes

Implementation Details

The `isLeapYear(int year)` method can be implemented using the following
code from Section 4.11:

```
return year % 400 == 0 || (year % 4 == 0 && year % 100 != 0);
```

Use the following facts to implement `getTotalNumberOfDaysInMonth(int year,
int month)`:

- January, March, May, July, August, October, and December have 31 days.

- April, June, September, and November have 30 days.

- February has 28 days during a regular year and 29 days during a leap year.
 A regular year, therefore, has 365 days, a leap year 366 days.

To implement `getTotalNumberOfDays(int year, int month)`, you need to compute the total number of days (`totalNumberOfDays`) between January 1, 1800,
and the first day of the calendar month. You could find the total number of days
between the year 1800 and the calendar year and then figure out the total number
of days prior to the calendar month in the calendar year. The sum of these two
totals is `totalNumberOfDays`.

To print a body, first pad some space before the start day and then print the
lines for every week.

The complete program is given in Listing 8.8.

LISTING 8.8 PrintCalendar.java

```java
1  import java.util.Scanner;
2
3  public class PrintCalendar {
4    /** Main method */
5    public static void main(String[] args) {
6      Scanner input = new Scanner(System.in);
7
8      // Prompt the user to enter year
9      System.out.print("Enter full year (e.g., 2012): ");
10     int year = input.nextInt();
11
12     // Prompt the user to enter month
13     System.out.print("Enter month as a number between 1 and 12: ");
14     int month = input.nextInt();
15
16     // Print calendar for the month of the year
17     printMonth(year, month);
18   }
19
20   /** Print the calendar for a month in a year */
21   public static void printMonth(int year, int month) {
22     // Print the headings of the calendar
23     printMonthTitle(year, month);
24
25     // Print the body of the calendar
26     printMonthBody(year, month);
27   }
28
29   /** Print the month title, e.g., March 2012 */
30   public static void printMonthTitle(int year, int month) {
31     System.out.println("            " + getMonthName(month)
32       + " " + year);
33     System.out.println("-----------------------------");
34     System.out.println(" Sun Mon Tue Wed Thu Fri Sat");
35   }
36
37   /** Get the English name for the month */
38   public static String getMonthName(int month) {
39     String monthName = "";
40     switch (month) {
41       case 1: monthName = "January"; break;
42       case 2: monthName = "February"; break;
43       case 3: monthName = "March"; break;
44       case 4: monthName = "April"; break;
45       case 5: monthName = "May"; break;
46       case 6: monthName = "June"; break;
47       case 7: monthName = "July"; break;
48       case 8: monthName = "August"; break;
49       case 9: monthName = "September"; break;
50       case 10: monthName = "October"; break;
51       case 11: monthName = "November"; break;
52       case 12: monthName = "December";
53     }
54
55     return monthName;
56   }
57
```

printMonth

printMonthTitle

getMonthName

```
58    /** Print month body */
59    public static void printMonthBody(int year, int month) {          printMonthBody
60      // Get start day of the week for the first date in the month
61      int startDay = getStartDay(year, month)
62
63      // Get number of days in the month
64      int numberOfDaysInMonth = getNumberOfDaysInMonth(year, month);
65
66      // Pad space before the first day of the month
67      int i = 0;
68      for (i = 0; i < startDay; i++)
69        System.out.print("    ");
70
71      for (i = 1; i <= numberOfDaysInMonth; i++) {
72        System.out.printf("%4d", i);
73
74        if ((i + startDay) % 7 == 0)
75          System.out.println();
76      }
77
78      System.out.println();
79    }
80
81    /** Get the start day of month/1/year */
82    public static int getStartDay(int year, int month) {              getStartDay
83      final int START_DAY_FOR_JAN_1_1800 = 3;
84      // Get total number of days from 1/1/1800 to month/1/year
85      int totalNumberOfDays = getTotalNumberOfDays(year, month);
86
87      // Return the start day for month/1/year
88      return (totalNumberOfDays + START_DAY_FOR_JAN_1_1800) % 7;
89    }
90
91    /** Get the total number of days since January 1, 1800 */
92    public static int getTotalNumberOfDays(int year, int month) {     getTotalNumberOfDays
93      int total = 0;
94
95      // Get the total days from 1800 to 1/1/year
96      for (int i = 1800; i < year; i++)
97        if (isLeapYear(i))
98          total = total + 366;
99        else
100         total = total + 365;
101
102     // Add days from Jan to the month prior to the calendar month
103     for (int i = 1; i < month; i++)
104       total = total + getNumberOfDaysInMonth(year, i);
105
106     return total;
107   }
108
109   /** Get the number of days in a month */
110   public static int getNumberOfDaysInMonth(int year, int month) {   getNumberOfDaysInMonth
111     if (month == 1 || month == 3 || month == 5 || month == 7 ||
112       month == 8 || month == 10 || month == 12)
113       return 31;
114
115     if (month == 4 || month == 6 || month == 9 || month == 11)
116       return 30;
```

isLeapYear

```
117
118      if (month == 2) return isLeapYear(year) ? 29 : 28;
119
120      return 0; // If month is incorrect
121    }
122
123    /** Determine if it is a leap year */
124    public static boolean isLeapYear(int year) {
125      return year % 400 == 0 || (year % 4 == 0 && year % 100 != 0);
126    }
127 }
```

Benefits of Stepwise Refinement

Stepwise refinement breaks a large problem into smaller manageable subproblems. Each subproblem can be implemented using a method. This approach makes the program easier to write, reuse, debug, test, modify, and maintain.

Simpler Program

The print calendar program is long. Rather than writing a long sequence of statements in one method, stepwise refinement breaks it into smaller methods. This simplifies the program and makes the whole program easier to read and understand.

Reusing Methods

Stepwise refinement promotes code reuse within a program. The isLeapYear method is defined once and invoked from the getTotalNumberOfDays and getNumberOfDaysInMonth methods. This reduces redundant code.

Easier Developing, Debugging, and Testing

Since each subproblem is solved in a method, a method can be developed, debugged, and tested individually. This isolates the errors and makes developing, debugging, and testing easier.

incremental development and testing

When implementing a large program, use the top-down and/or bottom-up approach. Do not write the entire program at once. Using these approaches seems to take more development time (because you repeatedly compile and run the program), but it actually saves time and makes debugging easier.

Better Facilitating Teamwork

When a large problem is divided into subprograms, subproblems can be assigned to different programmers. This makes it easier for programmers to work in teams.

✓ SECTION 8.8 ASSESSMENT

1. Explain the principles of *abstraction*. What are the benefits of this system design strategy?

8.9 Evaluating and Documenting the Design

Key Point

Follow quality assurance procedures to track and solve issues.

Documenting Constraints

When designing an application, it is important to identify limitations, or *constraints*. For instance, the program design of Listing 8.8 *PrintCalendar.java*, is limited to printing a calendar for a time span of one month. Additionally, it cannot print calendars for dates before 1800. Adjustments can be made to remove these limitations but time constraints and budget may dictate otherwise. Designing a project requires a balancing of needs, time, and budget. Constraints that cannot be solved within the budget and time allotment are documented in the project documentation.

constraints

Identifying Problems and Tracking Resolutions

Evaluating and testing code helps identify potential problems. As an example, the code in Listing 8.8 does not validate user input. The program returns an incorrect value if the user enters a month not in the range between 1 and 12 or a year before 1800.

identify problems

If you are working on a large project, it is helpful to use an *issue tracking system* to log issues. Documenting issues and resolutions help manage the progress of the project. The tracking system can be as simple as a spreadsheet, or an integrated development environment (IDE) that includes project management features.

issue tracking system

✓ Section 8.9 Assessment

1. Identify and document the constraints of the program in Listing 8.8 *PrintCalendar.java* program.

2. Why is it important to log potential problems and resolutions? How is this helpful in a team project?

3. You work on a team project and are responsible for *testing* and *logging* issues into a tracking system. While testing Listing 8.8 *PrintCalendar.java* program, you enter a month outside of the range of 1 through 12. This causes incorrect output. Write a tracking system logging statement that explains the issue.

4. You work on a team and are responsible for *finding solutions* to problems identified in the issue tracking system. What code can you add to the *PrintCalendar.java* program to solve the issue presented in question 3? Write a statement for the tracking system that explains how you resolved the problem.

Chapter 8 — Review and Assessment

KEY TERMS

argument 221
constraints 243
divide and conquer 235
identify problems 243
identify processes 239
incremental development and testing 242
information hiding 235
issue tracking system 243
method 220

method abstraction 235
method signature 221
modular code 230
parameter 221
stepwise refinement 235
stub 238
value-returning method 221
`void` method 221

CHAPTER SUMMARY

1. Making programs modular and reusable is one of the central goals in software engineering. Java provides many powerful constructs that help to achieve this goal. *Methods* are one such construct.

2. The method header specifies the *modifiers, return value type, method name,* and *parameters* of the method. The `static` modifier is used for all the methods in this chapter.

3. A method may return a value. The `returnValueType` is the data type of the value the method returns. If the method does not return a value, the `returnValueType` is the keyword `void`.

4. The *parameter list* refers to the type, order, and number of a method's parameters. The method name and the parameter list together constitute the *method signature*. Parameters are optional; that is, a method doesn't need to contain any parameters.

5. A return statement can also be used in a `void` method for terminating the method and returning to the method's caller. This is useful occasionally for circumventing the normal flow of control in a method.

6. The arguments that are passed to a method should have the same number, type, and order as the parameters in the method signature.

7. *Method abstraction* is achieved by separating the use of a method from its implementation. The client can use a method without knowing how it is implemented. The details of the implementation are encapsulated in the method and hidden from the client who invokes the method. This is known as *information hiding* or *encapsulation.*

8. Method abstraction modularizes programs in a neat, hierarchical manner. Programs written as collections of concise methods are easier to write, debug, maintain, and modify than would otherwise be the case. This writing style also promotes method reusability.

9. When implementing a large program, use the top-down and/or bottom-up coding approach. Do not write the entire program at once. This approach may seem to take more time for coding (because you are repeatedly compiling and running the program), but it actually saves time and makes debugging easier.

10. Part of the project planning and design process includes identifying constraints and documenting them in the project specifications.

11. Throughout the project lifecycle, problems are evaluated through standard testing procedures and logged into an issue tracking system. Additionally, resolutions to problems are documented. A project management tracking system is particularly helpful in large, team projects.

PROGRAMMING EXERCISES

 Note
Exercises preceded by a star (*) are more challenging.

1. (*Math: pentagonal numbers*) A pentagonal number is defined as $n(3n–1)/2$ for . . ., and so on. Therefore, the first few numbers are 1, 5, 12, 22, Write a method with the following header that returns a pentagonal number:

   ```
   public static int getPentagonalNumber(int n)
   ```

 Write a test program that uses this method to display the first 100 pentagonal numbers with 10 numbers on each line.

*2. (*Display an integer reversed*) Write a method with the following header to display an integer in reverse order:

   ```
   public static void reverse(int number)
   ```

 For example, `reverse(3456)` displays `6543`. Write a test program that prompts the user to enter an integer and displays its reversal.

*3. (*Sort three numbers*) Write a method with the following header to display three numbers in increasing order:

   ```
   public static void displaySortedNumbers(
      double num1, double num2, double num3)
   ```

 Write a test program that prompts the user to enter three numbers and invokes the method to display them in increasing order.

*4. (*Display patterns*) Write a method to display a pattern as follows:

```
        1
      2 1
    3 2 1
 ...
n n-1 ... 3 2 1
```

The method header is

public static void displayPattern(**int** n)

5. (*Conversions between Celsius and Fahrenheit*) Write a class that contains the following two methods:

```
/** Convert from Celsius to Fahrenheit */
public static double celsiusToFahrenheit(double celsius)
```

```
/** Convert from Fahrenheit to Celsius */
public static double fahrenheitToCelsius(double fahrenheit)
```

The formula for the conversion is:

```
fahrenheit = (9.0 / 5) * celsius + 32
celsius = (5.0 / 9) * (fahrenheit - 32)
```

Write a test program that invokes these methods to display the following tables:

Celsius	Fahrenheit		Fahrenheit	Celsius
40.0	104.0		120.0	48.89
39.0	102.2		110.0	43.33
...				
32.0	89.6		40.0	4.44
31.0	87.8		30.0	-1.11

6. (*Conversions between feet and meters*) Write a class that contains the following two methods:

```
/** Convert from feet to meters */
public static double footToMeter(double foot)
```

```
/** Convert from meters to feet */
public static double meterToFoot(double meter)
```

The formula for the conversion is:

```
meter = 0.305 * foot
foot = 3.279 * meter
```

Write a test program that invokes these methods to display the following tables:

Feet	Meters		Meters	Feet
1.0	0.305	\|	20.0	65.574
2.0	0.610	\|	25.0	81.967
...				
9.0	2.745	\|	60.0	196.721
10.0	3.050	\|	65.0	213.115

7. (*Use the* `isPrime` *Method*) Listing 8.6, PrimeNumberMethod.java, provides the `isPrime(int number)` method for testing whether a number is prime. Use this method to find the number of prime numbers less than `10000`.

8. (*Display characters*) Write a method that prints characters using the following header:

```
public static void printChars(char ch1, char ch2, int
    numberPerLine)
```

This method prints the characters between `ch1` and `ch2` with the specified numbers per line. Write a test program that prints ten characters per line from `1` to `Z`. Characters are separated by exactly one space.

***9.** (*Number of days in a year*) Write a method that returns the number of days in a year using the following header:

```
public static int numberOfDaysInAYear(int year)
```

Write a test program that displays the number of days in year from 2000 to 2020.

***10.** (*Display matrix of 0s and 1s*) Write a method that displays an *n*-by-*n* matrix using the following header:

```
public static void printMatrix(int n)
```

Each element is 0 or 1, which is generated randomly. Write a test program that prompts the user to enter `n` and displays an *n*-by-*n* matrix. Here is a sample run:

```
Enter n: 3  ↵Enter
0 1 0
0 0 0
1 1 1
```

***11.** (*The* `MyTriangle` *class*) Create a class named `MyTriangle` that contains the following two methods:

```
/** Return true if the sum of any two sides is
 *   greater than the third side. */
public static boolean isValid(
   double side1, double side2, double side3)

/** Return the area of the triangle. */
public static double area(
   double side1, double side2, double side3)
```

Write a test program that reads three sides for a triangle and computes the area if the input is valid. Otherwise, it displays that the input is invalid. The formula for computing the area of a triangle is:

$$s = (side1 + side2 + side3)/2;$$

$$area = \sqrt{s(s - side1)(s - side2)(s - side3)}$$

***12.** (*Count the letters in a string*) Write a method that counts the number of letters in a string using the following header:

```
public static int countLetters(String s)
```

Write a test program that prompts the user to enter a string and displays the number of letters in the string.

***13.** (*Phone keypads*) The international standard letter/number mapping for telephones is shown in Chapter 5, Programming Exercise 8. Write a method that returns a number, given an uppercase letter, as follows:

```
int getNumber(char uppercaseLetter)
```

Write a test program that prompts the user to enter a phone number as a string. The input number may contain letters. The program translates a letter (uppercase or lowercase) to a digit and leaves all other characters intact. Here is a sample run of the program:

```
Enter a string: 1-800-Flowers  Enter
1-800-3569377
```

```
Enter a string: 1800flowers  Enter
18003569377
```

14. (*Geometry: area of a pentagon*) The area of a pentagon can be computed using the following formula:

$$Area = \frac{5 \times s^2}{4 \times \tan\left(\dfrac{\pi}{5}\right)}$$

Write a method that returns the area of a pentagon using the following header:

```
public static double area(double side)
```

Write a main method that prompts the user to enter the side of a pentagon and displays its area. Here is a sample run:

```
Enter the side: 5.5  ↵Enter
The area of the pentagon is 52.04444136781625
```

15. (*Format an integer*) Write a method with the following header to format the integer with the specified width.

```
public static String format(int number, int width)
```

The method returns a string for the number with one or more prefix 0s. The size of the string is the width. For example, `format(34, 4)` returns 0034 and `format(34, 5)` returns 00034. If the number is longer than the width, the method returns the string representation for the number. For example, `format(34, 1)` returns 34.

Write a test program that prompts the user to enter a number and its width and displays a string returned by invoking `format(number, width)`.

INTRODUCTION TO OBJECT-ORIENTED PROGRAMMING

Objectives

- Explain the principles of *object-oriented programming* (*OOP*).

- Describe the concept of a *class* and an *object* using real-world analogies.

- Create a class design using *Unified Object Modeling* (*UML*) tool.

- Write object-oriented code and use standard programming practices that make your code easy to understand.

- Demonstrate how to define classes and create objects.

- Use the *dot operator* (.) to reference an object's members.

- Use the `Date` and `Random` Java library classes.

9.1 Introduction

Key Point

Object-oriented programming enables you to develop large-scale software applications. It is the programming paradigm used most often today to build new applications.

Having learned the material in the preceding chapters, you are able to solve many programming problems using selections, loops, and arrays. These are all structured programming constructs used in everyday programming. However, these programming features are not sufficient for large-scale software systems, and for applications developed by a team of programmers.

why oop?

As your project grows in size and complexity, your code should be modular in design and reusable. To create modular, reusable code, you must learn object-oriented programming. Your code should also be well-commented and follow a consistent styling technique. This helps programmers work together in understanding the entire team project.

The basic concept of Object-Oriented Programming (OOP) was introduced in Section 2.3. This chapter will explore OOP in further detail. Consider the classic example of a house. A house is an *object* built from a template, or blueprint. A blueprint provides the foundation to build the house. To build a second, similar house, it is more efficient to use the same blueprint rather than start over from the beginning. Both houses *inherit* all the basic features provided in the template, such as the square footage and floor plan. You, as the developer, can *override* basic

override

features of the template. For instance, the basic design may call for a wood exterior. You can override this feature with a brick exterior. Additionally, the template can be *extended*. For instance, a house can include an additional sunroom. The con-

inheritance

cepts of *inheritance*, *overriding*, and *extensibility* are all important principles of

extensibility

OOP. It is important to have a basic understanding of these principles as you begin to learn OOP programming. You will explore these concepts further in other advanced computer programming courses.

Suppose you want to develop a graphical user interface (GUI, pronounced *goo-ee*). The design includes two buttons (OK and Cancel) as shown in Figure 9.1. Both buttons are objects. Each button has properties such as size and shape. Buttons recognize certain actions such as a *click* action. Code is written to establish these properties and functionality. Rather than rewriting this code every time a button is added to the GUI, you create a button based upon an existing button template.

button class

This template is called a *button class*. When a button is added to the GUI, an instance of the button object is created. The new button inherits basic characteristics and functionality from the base button class. This saves much programming time and effort.

FIGURE 9.1 The GUI objects are created from classes.

In addition to using classes already established, such as the button class, you can create your own classes. These classes can be reused within your application, other applications, or by other programmers.

This chapter explores classes and objects. These are two building blocks for creating modular, object-oriented code.

✓ SECTION 9.1 ASSESSMENT

1. a) Use a pie recipe to explain the principles of object-oriented design. Create a template, or class, for the pie recipe and list four properties or attributes you might include in the class. Name your class `pieRecipe`.

 b) Create a pie object based on the `pieRecipe` class. Identify properties you might inherit, override, and extend from the base class. Articulate the design in a paragraph and draw a picture to illustrate the design.

2. You are required to name your class `pieRecipe` in Question 1. What other names could you have used? Why is it important to follow an appropriate style when naming objects?

9.2 Defining Classes for Objects

A class defines the properties and behaviors for objects.

Key Point

Object-oriented programming (OOP) involves programming using objects. An *object* represents an entity in the real world that can be distinctly identified. For example, a student, a desk, a circle, a button, and even a loan can all be viewed as objects. An object has a unique identity, state, and behavior.

object-oriented programming (OOP)

object

properties

attributes

- Objects have *properties* or *attributes*. A circle object, for example, has a `radius` property. A rectangle object has a `width` and a `height` property. Properties are stored in a *data field*.

data field

- The *behavior* of an object (also known as its *actions*) is defined by methods. To invoke a method on an object is to ask the object to perform an action. For example, you may define methods named `getArea()` and `getPerimeter()` for circle objects. A circle object may invoke `getArea()` to return its area and `getPerimeter()` to return its perimeter. You may also define the `setRadius(radius)` method. A circle object can invoke this method to change its radius.

actions

Objects of the same type are defined using a common class. A *class* is a template, blueprint, or *contract* that defines what an object's data fields and methods will be. An object is an instance of a class. You can create many instances of a class. Creating an instance is referred to as *instantiation*. The terms *object* and *instance* are often interchangeable. The relationship between classes and objects is analogous to that between an apple-pie recipe and apple pies: You can make as many apple pies as you want from a single recipe. Figure 9.2 shows a class named `Circle` and its three objects.

class

contract

instantiation

instance

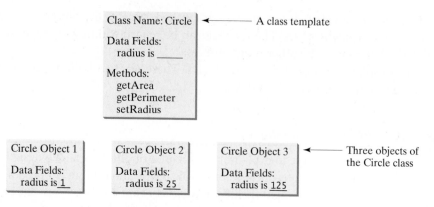

FIGURE 9.2 A class is a template for creating objects.

A Java class uses variables to define data fields and methods to define actions. Additionally, a class provides methods of a special type, known as *constructors*, which are used to create a new object. A constructor can perform any action, but constructors are designed to perform initializing actions, such as initializing the data fields of objects. Figure 9.3 shows an example of a class for a circle.

method

constructors

```java
class Circle {
  /** The radius of this circle */
  double radius = 1;                             ← ———————— Data field

  /** Construct a circle object */
  Circle() {
  }                                              ┐
                                                 │
  /** Construct a circle object */               ├ ← ———— Constructors
  Circle(double newRadius) {                     │
    radius = newRadius;                          │
  }                                              ┘

  /** Return the area of this circle */          ┐
  double getArea() {                             │
    return radius * radius * Math.PI;            │
  }                                              │
                                                 │
  /** Return the perimeter of this circle */     │
  double getPerimeter() {                        ├ ← ———— Method
    return 2 * radius * Math.PI;                 │
  }                                              │
                                                 │
  /** Set new radius for this circle */          │
  void setRadius(double newRadius) {             │
    radius = newRadius;                          │
  }                                              ┘
}
```

FIGURE 9.3 A class is a construct that defines objects of the same type.

The `Circle` class is different from all of the other classes you have seen thus far. It does not have a `main` method and therefore cannot be run; it is merely a definition for circle objects. The class that contains the `main` method will be referred to in this book, for convenience, as the *main class*.

main class

In Section 9.1 Assessment, you created an illustration that depicted the Pie class. It may have looked similar to Figure 9.2. Creating a diagram is a popular way to describe the steps of a program design. There is a standard tool used to illustrate the design of class templates and objects. It is known as *Unified Modeling Language (UML)* notation. If we translate Figure 9.3 into standard UML, it will resemble the illustration in Figure 9.4. This UML class diagram is simply called a *class diagram*. In the class diagram, the data field is denoted as

Unified Modeling Language (UML)

class diagram

```
dataFieldName: dataFieldType
```

The constructor is denoted as

```
ClassName(parameterName: parameterType)
```

The method is denoted as

```
methodName(parameterName: parameterType): returnType
```

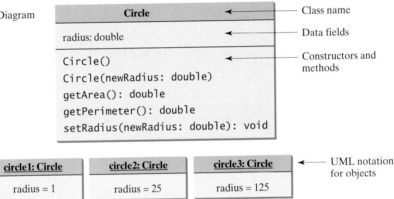

FIGURE 9.4 Classes and objects can be represented using UML notation.

9.3 Example: Defining Classes and Creating Objects

Classes are definitions for objects and objects are created from classes.

Key Point

This section gives two examples of defining classes and uses the classes to create objects. Listing 9.1 is a program that defines the `Circle` class and uses it to create objects. The program constructs three circle objects with radius 1, 25, and 125 and displays the radius and area of each of the three circles. It then changes the radius of the second object to 100 and displays its new radius and area.

Note
To avoid a naming conflict with several enhanced versions of the `Circle` class introduced later in the chapter, the `Circle` class in this example is named `SimpleCircle`. For simplicity, we will still refer to the class in the text as `Circle`.

avoid naming conflicts

LISTING 9.1 TestSimpleCircle.java

main class	
main method	
create object	
create object	
create object	
class SimpleCircle	
data field	
no-arg constructor	
second constructor	
getArea	
getPerimeter	
setRadius	

```java
 1  public class TestSimpleCircle {
 2    /** Main method */
 3    public static void main(String[] args) {
 4      // Create a circle with radius 1
 5      SimpleCircle circle1 = new SimpleCircle();
 6      System.out.println("The area of the circle of radius "
 7        + circle1.radius + " is " + circle1.getArea());
 8
 9      // Create a circle with radius 25
10      SimpleCircle circle2 = new SimpleCircle(25);
11      System.out.println("The area of the circle of radius "
12        + circle2.radius + " is " + circle2.getArea());
13
14      // Create a circle with radius 125
15      SimpleCircle circle3 = new SimpleCircle(125);
16      System.out.println("The area of the circle of radius "
17        + circle3.radius + " is " + circle3.getArea());
18
19      // Modify circle radius
20      circle2.radius = 100; // or circle2.setRadius(100)
21      System.out.println("The area of the circle of radius "
22        + circle2.radius + " is " + circle2.getArea());
23    }
24  }
25
26  // Define the circle class with two constructors
27  class SimpleCircle {
28    double radius;
29
30    /** Construct a circle with radius 1 */
31    SimpleCircle() {
32      radius = 1;
33    }
34
35    /** Construct a circle with a specified radius */
36    SimpleCircle(double newRadius) {
37      radius = newRadius;
38    }
39
40    /** Return the area of this circle */
41    double getArea() {
42      return radius * radius * Math.PI;
43    }
44
45    /** Return the perimeter of this circle */
46    double getPerimeter() {
47      return 2 * radius * Math.PI;
48    }
49
50    /** Set a new radius for this circle */
51    void setRadius(double newRadius) {
52      radius = newRadius;
53    }
54  }
```

```
The area of the circle of radius 1.0 is 3.141592653589793
The area of the circle of radius 25.0 is 1963.4954084936207
The area of the circle of radius 125.0 is 49087.385212340516
The area of the circle of radius 100.0 is 31415.926535897932
```

The program contains two classes. The first of these, `TestSimpleCircle`, is the main class. Its sole purpose is to test the second class, `SimpleCircle`. Such a program that uses the class is often referred to as a *client* of the class. When you run the program, the Java runtime system invokes the `main` method in the main class.

client

You can put the two classes into one file, but only one class in the file can be a *public class*. Furthermore, the public class must have the same name as the file name. Therefore, the file name is **TestSimpleCircle.java**, since `TestSimpleCircle` is public. Each class in the source code is compiled into a **.class** file. When you compile **TestSimpleCircle.java**, two class files **TestSimpleCircle.class** and **SimpleCircle.class** are generated, as shown in Figure 9.5.

public class

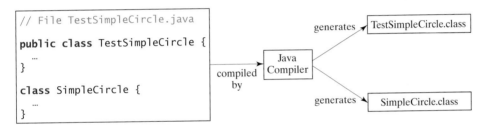

FIGURE 9.5 Each class in the source code file is compiled into a **.class** file.

The main class contains the `main` method (line 3) that creates three objects. As in creating an array, the `new` operator is used to create an object from the constructor: `new SimpleCircle()` creates an object with radius `1` (line 5), `new SimpleCircle(25)` creates an object with radius `25` (line 10), and `new SimpleCircle(125)` creates an object with radius `125` (line 15).

These three objects (referenced by `circle1`, `circle2`, and `circle3`) have different data but the same methods. Therefore, you can compute their respective areas by using the `getArea()` method. The data fields can be accessed via the reference of the object using `circle1.radius`, `circle2.radius`, and `circle3.radius`, respectively. The object can invoke its method via the reference of the object using `circle1.getArea()`, `circle2.getArea()`, and `circle3.getArea()`, respectively.

These three objects are independent. The radius of `circle2` is changed to `100` in line 20. The object's new radius and area are displayed in lines 21–22.

There are many ways to write Java programs. For instance, you can combine the two classes in the example into one, as shown in Listing 9.2.

LISTING 9.2 SimpleCircle.java

```java
 1  public class SimpleCircle {
 2    /** Main method */
 3    public static void main(String[] args) {
 4      // Create a circle with radius 1
 5      SimpleCircle circle1 = new SimpleCircle();
 6      System.out.println("The area of the circle of radius "
 7        + circle1.radius + " is " + circle1.getArea());
 8
 9      // Create a circle with radius 25
10      SimpleCircle circle2 = new SimpleCircle(25);
11      System.out.println("The area of the circle of radius "
12        + circle2.radius + " is " + circle2.getArea());
13
14      // Create a circle with radius 125
15      SimpleCircle circle3 = new SimpleCircle(125);
16      System.out.println("The area of the circle of radius "
17        + circle3.radius + " is " + circle3.getArea());
18
19      // Modify circle radius
20      circle2.radius = 100;
21      System.out.println("The area of the circle of radius "
22        + circle2.radius + " is " + circle2.getArea());
23    }
24
25    double radius;
26
27    /** Construct a circle with radius 1 */
28    SimpleCircle() {
29      radius = 1;
30    }
31
32    /** Construct a circle with a specified radius */
33    SimpleCircle(double newRadius) {
34      radius = newRadius;
35    }
36
37    /** Return the area of this circle */
38    double getArea() {
39      return radius * radius * Math.PI;
40    }
41
42    /** Return the perimeter of this circle */
43    double getPerimeter() {
44      return 2 * radius * Math.PI;
45    }
46
47    /** Set a new radius for this circle */
48    void setRadius(double newRadius) {
49      radius = newRadius;
50    }
51  }
```

Margin notes:
main method (line 3)
data field (line 25)
no-arg constructor (line 28)
second constructor (line 33)
method (line 38)

Since the combined class has a `main` method, it can be executed by the Java interpreter. The `main` method is the same as that in Listing 9.1. This demonstrates that you can test a class by simply adding a `main` method in the same class.

As another example, consider television sets. Each TV is an object with states (current channel, current volume level, power on or off) and behaviors (change channels, adjust volume, turn on/off). You can use a class to model TV sets. The UML diagram for the class is shown in Figure 9.6.

The + sign indicates public modifier

FIGURE 9.6 The TV class models TV sets.

Listing 9.3 gives a program that defines the TV class.

LISTING 9.3 TV.java

```
 1  public class TV {
 2    int channel = 1; // Default channel is 1              data fields
 3    int volumeLevel = 1; // Default volume level is 1
 4    boolean on = false; // TV is off
 5
 6    public TV() {                                          constructor
 7    }
 8
 9    public void turnOn() {                                 turn on TV
10      on = true;
11    }
12
13    public void turnOff() {                                turn off TV
14      on = false;
15    }
16
17    public void setChannel(int newChannel) {               set a new channel
18      if (on && newChannel >= 1 && newChannel <= 120)
19        channel = newChannel;
20    }
21
22    public void setVolume(int newVolumeLevel) {            set a new volume
23      if (on && newVolumeLevel >= 1 && newVolumeLevel <= 7)
24        volumeLevel = newVolumeLevel;
25    }
26
27    public void channelUp() {                              increase channel
28      if (on && channel < 120)
```

```
29          channel++;
30      }
31
32      public void channelDown() {
33        if (on && channel > 1)
34          channel--;
35      }
36
37      public void volumeUp() {
38        if (on && volumeLevel < 7)
39          volumeLevel++;
40      }
41
42      public void volumeDown() {
43        if (on && volumeLevel > 1)
44          volumeLevel--;
45      }
46    }
```

decrease channel *(margin note, line 32)*

increase volume *(margin note, line 37)*

decrease volume *(margin note, line 42)*

The constructor and methods in the TV class are defined public so they can be accessed from other classes. Note that the channel and volume level are not changed if the TV is not on. Before either of these is changed, its current value is checked to ensure that it is within the correct range.

Listing 9.4 gives a program that uses the TV class to create two objects.

LISTING 9.4 TestTV.java

main method *(margin note, line 2)*
create a TV *(margin note, line 3)*
turn on *(margin note, line 4)*
set a new channel *(margin note, line 5)*
set a new volume *(margin note, line 6)*

create a TV *(margin note, line 8)*
turn on *(margin note, line 9)*
increase channel *(margin note, line 10)*

increase volume *(margin note, line 12)*

display state *(margin note, line 14)*

```
1  public class TestTV {
2    public static void main(String[] args) {
3      TV tv1 = new TV();
4      tv1.turnOn();
5      tv1.setChannel(30);
6      tv1.setVolume(3);
7
8      TV tv2 = new TV();
9      tv2.turnOn();
10     tv2.channelUp();
11     tv2.channelUp();
12     tv2.volumeUp();
13
14     System.out.println("tv1's channel is " + tv1.channel
15       + " and volume level is " + tv1.volumeLevel);
16     System.out.println("tv2's channel is " + tv2.channel
17       + " and volume level is " + tv2.volumeLevel);
18   }
19 }
```

```
tv1's channel is 30 and volume level is 3
tv2's channel is 3 and volume level is 2
```

The program creates two objects in lines 3 and 8 and invokes the methods on the objects to perform actions for setting channels and volume levels and for increasing channels and volumes. The program displays the state of the objects in lines 14–17. The methods are invoked using syntax such as **tv1.turnOn()** (line 4). The data fields are accessed using syntax such as **tv1.channel** (line 14).

These examples have given you a glimpse of classes and objects. You may have many questions regarding constructors, objects, reference variables, accessing data fields, and invoking object's methods. The sections that follow discuss these issues in detail.

✓ SECTION 9.3 ASSESSMENT

1. Describe the relationship between an object and its defining class.
2. How do you define a class?
3. How do you declare an object's reference variable?
4. How do you create an object?

9.4 Constructing Objects Using Constructors

A constructor is invoked to create an object using the **new** *operator.*

Key Point

Constructors are a special kind of method. They have three peculiarities:

- A constructor must have the same name as the class itself. | constructor's name
- Constructors do not have a return type—not even **void**. | no return type
- Constructors are invoked using the **new** operator when an object is created. Constructors play the role of initializing objects. | new operator

The constructor has exactly the same name as its defining class. Like regular methods, constructors can be overloaded (i.e., multiple constructors can have the same name but different signatures), making it easy to construct objects with different initial data values.

It is a common mistake to put the void keyword in front of a constructor. For example,

```
public void Circle() {
}
```
no void

In this case, `Circle()` is a method, not a constructor.

Constructors are used to construct objects. To construct an object from a class, | constructing objects
invoke a constructor of the class using the new operator, as follows:

```
new ClassName(arguments);
```

For example, `new Circle()` creates an object of the `Circle` class using the first constructor defined in the `Circle` class, and `new Circle(25)` creates an object using the second constructor defined in the `Circle` class.

A class normally provides a constructor without arguments (e.g., `Circle()`). Such a constructor is referred to as a *no-arg* or *no-argument constructor*. | no-arg constructor

A class may be defined without constructors. In this case, a public no-arg constructor with an empty body is implicitly defined in the class. This constructor, called a *default constructor*, is provided automatically *only if no constructors are explicitly defined in the class.* | default constructor

✓ **SECTION 9.4 ASSESSMENT**

1. What are the differences between constructors and methods?
2. When will a class have a default constructor?

9.5 Instantiating an Object and Accessing its Members

Use the **new** *keyword to create an instance of an object. Once the object is created, you can access its data members.*

When variables are created, a *type* is specified. Earlier chapters covered primitive types such as `int`, `byte`, and `boolean`. Primitive variable types are value types. A *value type* stores a variable's values in physical memory. For instance, in the line of code: x = 5, 5 is stored in a memory slot.

value type

Class variables are *reference types*. An object can be very large. Rather than storing the entire object in memory, a reference pointer to the object is stored in memory. During program execution, the pointer locates and retrieves the object when needed. *Declaring* the object simply means to declare the need for space to store the reference pointer in memory. Memory space must be allocated to store the object reference.

reference type

declare an object

The following code declares an object and assigns it the name of `myCircle`. The object is a `Circle` type.

```
Circle myCircle;
```

Now that the object is declared, the next step is to instantiate the object. To *instantiate* an object is to create the reference to the newly created object. The **new** keyword is used to instantiate reference types.

```
myCircle = new Circle();
```

You can write a single statement that combines the two lines of code above into one line:

```
Circle myCircle = new Circle();
```

Once the object is created, its data members can be accessed. In OOP terminology, an object's members are its data fields and methods. The syntax used to invoke a member is the *dot operator* (.). The following lines of code are examples of using the dot operator to access an object's members.

dot operator (.)

```
myCircle.radius references the radius data field.
myCircle.radius = 4 assigns the value of 4 to the radius data field.
myCircle.getArea() references the getArea method of the object.
System.out.printIn("Area is " + myCircle.getArea()); writes the
area of myCircle to the console.
```

✓ SECTION 9.5 ASSESSMENT

1. Define reference type. Compare reference types to primitive types.

2. A base class named Animal exists. Write a single statement that declares and instantiates an object based on the animal class. Use standard naming convention to name the class.

3. Using Listing 9.3 TV.java class, write object-oriented program code to:

 • Declare and instantiate a new TV object.

 • Turn on the TV.

 • Set the volume level to 15.

 Write your code using an appropriate naming convention style. Use structure and clarity in your code by indenting where appropriate and add comments to explain each step.

9.6 Using Classes from the Java Library

The Java API contains a rich set of classes for developing Java programs.

 Key Point

Listing 9.1 defined the `SimpleCircle` class and created objects from the class. You will frequently use the classes in the Java library to develop programs. This section gives some examples of the classes in the Java library.

The Date Class

The built-in `java.util.Date` class, as shown in Figure 9.7, provides functionality in working with date and time values. The details of how the functions are performed are encapsulated inside the class. The concept of *encapsulation* is important in object-oriented programming and was introduced in Chapter 8. *Encapsulating*, or hiding the details of a class, helps programmers develop applications faster. Understanding the details of the class is not necessary to use the class. For instance, the `Date` class includes a method that calculates the milliseconds between two date values. It is not important to understand the detailed steps of the calculation to use the method. The dot operator(.) is used to invoke the method.

java.util.Date class

encapsulation

java.util.Date	
+Date()	Constructs a `Date` object for the current time.
+Date(elapseTime: long)	Constructs a `Date` object for a given time in milliseconds elapsed since January 1, 1970, GMT.
+toString(): String	Returns a string representing the date and time.
+getTime(): long	Returns the number of milliseconds since January 1, 1970, GMT.
+setTime(elapseTime: long): void	Sets a new elapse time in the object.

FIGURE 9.7 A `Date` object represents a specific date and time.

You can use the no-arg constructor in the `Date` class to create an instance for the current date and time, the `getTime()` method to return the elapsed time since January 1, 1970, GMT, and the `toString()` method to return the date and time as a string. For example, the following code

create object

get elapsed time
invoke toString

```
java.util.Date date = new java.util.Date();
System.out.println("The elapsed time since Jan 1, 1970 is " +
  date.getTime() + " milliseconds");
System.out.println(date.toString());
```

displays the output like this:

```
The elapsed time since Jan 1, 1970 is 1324903419651 milliseconds
Mon Dec 26 07:43:39 EST 2011
```

The `Date` class has another constructor, `Date(long elapseTime)`, which can be used to construct a `Date` object for a given time in milliseconds elapsed since January 1, 1970, GMT.

The Random Class

You have used `Math.random()` to obtain a random `double` value between `0.0` and `1.0` (excluding `1.0`). Another way to generate random numbers is to use the `java.util.Random` class, as shown in Figure 9.8, which can generate a random `int`, `long`, `double`, `float`, and `boolean` value.

java.util.Random	
+Random()	Constructs a Random object with the current time as its seed.
+Random(seed: long)	Constructs a Random object with a specified seed.
+nextInt(): int	Returns a random int value.
+nextInt(n: int): int	Returns a random int value between 0 and n (excluding n).
+nextLong(): long	Returns a random long value.
+nextDouble(): double	Returns a random double value between 0.0 and 1.0 (excluding 1.0).
+nextFloat(): float	Returns a random float value between 0.0F and 1.0F (excluding 1.0F).
+nextBoolean(): boolean	Returns a random boolean value.

FIGURE 9.8 A Random object can be used to generate random values.

When you create a `Random` object, you have to specify a seed or use the default seed. A seed is a number used to initialize a random number generator. The no-arg constructor creates a `Random` object using the current elapsed time as its seed. If two `Random` objects have the same seed, they will generate identical sequences of numbers. For example, the following code creates two `Random` objects with the same seed, 3.

```
Random random1 = new Random(3);
System.out.print("From random1: ");
for (int i = 0; i < 10; i++)
  System.out.print(random1.nextInt(1000) + " ");

Random random2 = new Random(3);
System.out.print("\nFrom random2: ");
for (int i = 0; i < 10; i++)
  System.out.print(random2.nextInt(1000) + " ");
```

The code generates the same sequence of random `int` values:

```
From random1: 734 660 210 581 128 202 549 564 459 961
From random2: 734 660 210 581 128 202 549 564 459 961
```

✓ SECTION 9.6 ASSESSMENT

1. What method can you use from the `Date` class to retrieve the current time?

2. Explain the principle of encapsulation in an OOP design. How does it benefit the programmer?

Chapter 9 — Review and Assessment

KEY TERMS

action 253	inheritance 252
attribute 253	instantiation 253
class 253	no-arg constructor 261
class diagram 255	object 253
constructor 254	object-oriented programming (OOP) 253
data field 253	override 252
default constructor 261	property 253
dot operator 262	reference type 262
encapsulation 263	Unified Modeling Language (UML) 255
extensibility 252	value type 262

CHAPTER SUMMARY

1. As your project grows in size and complexity, it is important to develop well-commented and structured code that follows a consistent styling technique.

2. *Object-Oriented Programming* (*OOP*) is the most common programming style used today. OOP is particularly helpful in designing large-scale applications requiring a team of programmers.

3. Classes and objects are two basic building blocks in creating object-oriented code.

4. A *class* is a template for objects. One or more objects can be created, or *instantiated*, from a class.

5. The concepts of *inheritance, overriding, extensibility,* and *encapsulation* are important principles of OOP design. Objects can *inherit* members from a class. The details of the class are hidden, or *encapsulated.* Inherited members can be changed, or *overridden.* You can *extend* an object by adding additional members or functionality.

6. An object is an instance of a class. Use the `new` keyword to create an object, and the dot operator (.) to access members of the object.

7. Objects have *properties* or *attributes.* A circle object, for example, has a `radius` property. A rectangle object has a `width` and a `height` property. Properties are stored in a *data field.*

8. The *behavior* of an object (also known as its *actions*) is defined by methods.

9. Class variables are *reference* types. An object can be very large. Rather than storing the entire object in memory, a reference pointer to the object is stored in memory. When the object is needed during program execution, the pointer is used to retrieve the object. Space must be reserved in memory to store the object reference.

10. *Unified Modeling Language (UML)* is a standard tool used to illustrate the design of class templates and objects.

11. There are classes available for re-use in the Java library. Two examples of Java library classes are `Date` class and `Random` class.

PROGRAMMING EXERCISES

Note

Exercises preceded by a star (*) are more challenging.

1. (*The `Rectangle` class*) Following the example of the `Circle` class in Section 9.2, design a class named `Rectangle` to represent a rectangle. The class contains:

 ■ Two `double` data fields named `width` and `height` that specify the width and height of the rectangle. The default values are `1` for both `width` and `height`.
 ■ A no-arg constructor that creates a default rectangle.
 ■ A constructor that creates a rectangle with the specified `width` and `height`.
 ■ A method named `getArea()` that returns the area of this rectangle.
 ■ A method named `getPerimeter()` that returns the perimeter.

 Draw the UML diagram for the class and then implement the class. Write a test program that creates two `Rectangle` objects—one with width `4` and height `40` and the other with width `3.5` and height `35.9`. Display the width, height, area, and perimeter of each rectangle in this order. Write your code using standard naming convention. Comment your code and use proper spacing and indents for clarity and readability.

2. (*The `Stock` class*) Following the example of the `Circle` class in Section 9.2, design a class named `Stock` that contains:

 ■ A string data field named `symbol` for the stock's symbol.
 ■ A string data field named `name` for the stock's name.
 ■ A `double` data field named `previousClosingPrice` that stores the stock price for the previous day.
 ■ A `double` data field named `currentPrice` that stores the stock price for the current time.

- A constructor that creates a stock with the specified symbol and name.
- A method named getChangePercent() that returns the percentage changed from previousClosingPrice to currentPrice.

Draw the UML diagram for the class and then implement the class. Write a test program that creates a Stock object with the stock symbol ORCL, the name Oracle Corporation, and the previous closing price of 34.5. Set a new current price to 34.35 and display the price-change percentage.

*3. (*Use the Date class*) Write a program that creates a Date object, sets its elapsed time to 10000, 100000, 1000000, 10000000, 100000000, 1000000000, 10000000000, and 100000000000, and displays the date and time using the toString() method, respectively.

*4. (*Use the Random class*) Write a program that creates a Random object with seed 1000 and displays the first 50 random integers between 0 and 100 using the nextInt(100) method.

CHAPTER 10

IDENTIFYING SECURITY RISKS AND COMPLYING WITH GOVERNMENT REGULATIONS

Objectives

- Define *risk assessment*.

- Identify the steps to *risk assessment*.

- Identify the computer system components that are subject to *security risks*.

- Describe potential risks to each computer system component.

- Identify and select the correct procedures to reduce security risks.

- Describe ways to recover from a security failure.

- Understand *data encryption*.

- Identify types of *malware* and ways to recover from malware infection.

- Describe the purpose of *cookies*.

- Differentiate between types of *computer crimes*.

- Describe *state and federal laws* that pertain to computer crimes.

10.1 Security Risk Assessment

Key Point

Maintaining a secure computer system spans a wide range of job roles. Everyone on the team plays a part. The information technology (IT) administrator, database (DB) administrator, software developer, and security analyst all play a role in keeping a computer information system safe. According to the U.S. Bureau of Labor Statistics, demand for jobs in computer security continues to rise.

After an application is developed, the project team's job does not stop there. Software applications require installations, user training, and ongoing support and maintenance. Part of the design and ongoing maintenance of an application includes the evaluation of potential security risks. A *security risk* is a person, object, or situation that poses a threat to the safety of something. Anything that negatively affects your computer system is considered a security risk. Protecting your software system not only includes managing malicious attacks, but also protection from accidental incidents.

security risk

There are three main goals to maintaining a secure computer system:

1. Keeping sensitive data *confidential.*

2. Maintaining the *integrity* of data.

3. Insuring the *availability* of data when and where it is needed.

These three goals of *Confidentiality*, *Integrity*, and *Availability* are often referred to as the *CIA Triad* principle. To achieve these goals, you must first identify and assess potential risks.

CIA Triad

A *risk assessment* is the process of identifying and planning for factors that can negatively affect the security of a system. A risk assessment includes the following five stages:

risk assessment

Step 1: Identify potential risks.

Identify the potential for both malicious and accidental risks. An example of a malicious attack may be the intrusion of a virus or a burglary of the premises. Examples of accidental risks are damage caused by a natural disaster, or hard drive failure.

Step 2: Quantify the risk.

Quantifying risks is the process of estimating the likelihood of a specific risk. A numerical value or percentage is assigned to each risk reflecting the possibility of the risk occurring. Assigning a value helps rank and prioritize risks. As an example, the likelihood of a hurricane would be far less likely to occur in an interior region of a country. However, the same location may be near a fault-line where earthquakes occur regularly. In this scenario, you would assign a higher risk factor to an earthquake risk than a hurricane risk.

Step 3: Develop a plan.

After identifying and quantifying the risks, create a written plan documenting the findings. There is usually more than one solution to handling security issues. Several factors, such as time and budget, help determine the best plan of action. Management and decision makers use the plan to determine the actions required.

Step 4: Implement a plan.

Once decisions are finalized, the plan is put into place. Prevention is always the "best medicine" when tackling security issues. Implementing the plan involves several members of a team. Those responsible for both hardware and software work together to secure the system.

Step 5: Monitor and evaluate the plan.

A security analyst's job is never done. A good risk assessment plan includes continuous monitoring and evaluation of the plan. Adjustments are made as the project components, usage, and physical location change. Figure 10.1 illustrates the stages involved in a risk assessment. The arrows represent the ongoing process of evaluation.

FIGURE 10.1 Steps to security risk assessment.

✓ SECTION 10.1 ASSESSMENT

1. Define risk assessment. List the stages of a risk assessment plan and identify the order in which they should occur.

2. What does the CIA triad principle stand for?

3. Who is responsible for the security of a computer system?

4. Why is a security analyst's job never done?

10.2 Identify Risks to Computer Systems

Key Point

It is impossible to have 100% assurance that you are protected from a security failure. However, a good risk management plan will identify potential risks, implement tactics to minimize their possibility, and develop a recovery plan in the event of a security breach.

The following components of a computer information system may be at risk:

- Physical facilities of the application servers
- Hardware components of your application
- Network and data communications system
- Software components

Physical Facilities

physical facilities

cloud storage

Physical facilities include the building structure in which the software application servers reside. This may be onsite or in a cloud storage facility. Today many software applications reside in cloud storage. *Cloud storage* is a storage system in which data is stored across multiple servers and various locations. The data can be shared across multiple devices. A third party often hosts the cloud system. Some hosting companies charge a fee, but there are many services available free of charge. Even with cloud storage, a physical location exists and therefore a risk assessment is necessary.

Types of risks that can negatively affect the physical facility are the following:

- Terrorist attack
- Burglary and sabotage
- Acts of nature such as fire, earthquake, lightning strike

After potential risks are identified, the next step is to explore ways to reduce the risk. Installing a security system or hiring security guards are ways to secure your building from burglary, sabotage, or terrorist attacks. Installing proper locks on entryways is a simple but overlooked way to secure a building. Additionally, you need to establish a policy to determine what hours of the day the door should remain locked. Consider the example of your home. Most people have locks on exterior doors, but many robberies occur simply because the door is left unlocked. Even the most sophisticated locking system will be ineffective if it is not used. Requiring proper identification before entering the building insures that only approved personnel are allowed inside.

biometrics

smart chip ID

Security is an ever-increasing concern for both private businesses and government facilities. New technologies such as biometric devices and smart chip ID systems are becoming popular. *Biometrics* is the process of measuring a person's biological features for the purpose of identification. Examples are fingerprint scanners, retina scanners, voice recognition, or facial recognition. *Smart chip ID* cards and badges include a computerized chip that holds credentials and are read by a computer device to determine security clearance.

Keeping your system secure goes beyond keeping predators out. It also means making sure the computer system is available when needed. Natural disasters may strike at any time and are often out of your control. However, having a plan in place to deal with them reduces the effects. For example, installing sprinkler systems and alarms can minimize damage. Additionally, having removable hard drives that can be taken off premise or a backup to a cloud storage location is an important part of planning for natural disasters.

Hardware Components

The hardware components are the physical parts of the computer system. They include computer monitors, keyboards, pointing devices, hard drives, CPUs, memory boards, and other computer parts.

hardware components

The types of risks hardware components are susceptible to include the following:

- Hardware malfunction

- Natural disasters

- Computer theft or vandalism

- Lost or misplaced mobile devices

Hardware malfunctions, such as a hard drive failure, are typically due to aging hardware. Implementing a regular backup plan of your data is critical. Having spare parts on hand to fix hardware issues helps minimize the downtime and loss of productivity.

Natural disasters can damage hardware. Although natural disasters are often uncontrollable, a proper risk plan can reduce the impact. Using the proper equipment is important. For instance, in areas where lightning strikes are prevalent, using fiber optic cable over Ethernet wiring is a logical choice. *Fiber optic* cabling is made up of tiny, glass threads where data is transmitted through light pulses. *Ethernet* cabling is the older of the two technologies; it transmits data through electrical pulses over thin strands of copper wiring. Fiber optic cabling is more expensive than traditional Ethernet cabling, but it is less susceptible to lightning strikes.

fiber optic

Ethernet

Keeping copies of backup data offsite is also important. If a disaster hits, the hardware may not be recoverable, but the data can be retrieved from the offsite location.

Computer theft and vandalism can be costly. Sensitive data may also be at risk. One way to reduce the risk of computer theft is to have an inventory-tracking plan in place. This helps identify the location of equipment at all times. Other tactics include: implementing a check-in/check-out system for mobile devices; installing a locking system on devices so that they cannot leave the premises; requiring identification to enter the premises; and installing an alarm system. If these preventative measures fail and computer theft occurs, plan ahead to have the ability to remotely delete sensitive data from any stolen device.

Computer theft continues to rise, as devices get smaller and are more accessible to thieves. However, when a computer is missing from inventory, it is often due to

the carelessness and unintentional acts of employees. Lost or misplaced laptops cost companies millions of dollars each year. When a device is lost, the cost not only involves the replacement of the device itself, but also the cost of preventing information from falling into the wrong hands. Oftentimes, individuals store sensitive company data on the device. The device may also allow access into company networks. The highest cost of keeping computer systems secure is usually due to careless acts of employees, rather than from malicious attacks. Ways to reduce the risk include implementing stringent rules for passwords, keeping sensitive data centralized and off of mobile device hard drives, and having the ability to remotely delete data from missing devices.

Data Communication System

data communication
system

The *data communication system* is the structure that communicates and transmits data back and forth from client to server. It includes internal company-wide *networks*, Internet policy and *settings*, and *wireless communication*. A company's data communication system is a common doorway into a company for a malicious attack.

A data communication system is susceptible to the following risks:

- Network breach or failure

- Website or Internet breach

- Wireless router breach or failure

firewall

To protect a network, install a firewall. The firewall blocks unknown users from gaining access to a computer system. A *firewall* can be either a piece of hardware or software that controls the incoming and outgoing traffic to a computer system. Additionally, tracking and logging network activity can help you identify any suspicious activity.

To prevent a security breach through the Internet, regulate and restrict harmful Internet traffic. This helps keep your computer virus-free. Adjust Internet browser settings to block users from visiting untrusted sites that are known to cause threats to security. Figure 10.2 is an example of a security settings page for a popular Web browser.

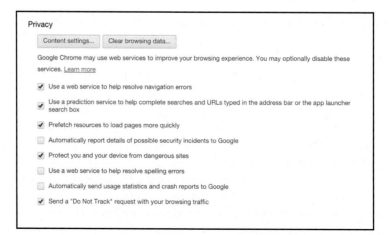

FIGURE 10.2 Example of a security settings page for a popular Web browser.

Implementing a training and education plan for employees can go a long way toward preventing security breaches. Oftentimes, viruses can be avoided by following a few simple rules when browsing the Internet and opening email. Web browsing safety tips will be covered in more detail in Section 10.5.

A wireless communication system transmits data over electromagnetic waves through the air. As a result, wireless communication systems are particularly at risk for a security breach. A wired setting, such as Ethernet cabling, offers a private communication medium. Wireless communication, on the other hand, uses a public wave frequency. Two methods used to implement security in a wireless environment are authentication and encryption. *Authentication* is the process of identifying a user who wishes to access the computer system. Requiring a network password is a way of authenticating a user. *Data encryption* is the process of applying an algorithm to convert data into an unreadable form during data transmission. When the data is retrieved, it is then decrypted, or converted back to readable form. This process reduces the chance of personal data being stolen during transmission. This process is also referred to as *encoding* and *decoding* of data. There are three basic types of data encryption algorithms for securing a wireless network:

authentication

data encryption

data decryption

- **Wired Equivalent Privacy (WEP)** is the oldest of the three types of wireless encryption. Although it is widely used, it provides the least amount of security.

 Wired Equivalent Privacy (WEP)

- **Wi-Fi Protected Access (WPA)** was formerly adopted by the industry as a standard in 2003 and was meant to improve the older WEP encryption policy.

 Wi-Fi Protected Access (WPA)

- **Wi-Fi Protected Access II (WPA2)** provides the highest security and was adopted as an industry standard in 2006.

 Wi-Fi Protected Access II (WPA2)

 Note

Wireless communication is sometimes referred to as *Wi-Fi*. It stands for *Wireless Fidelity*. Because this method of data transmission occurs over a public frequency, standards for security and transmission must be set and shared across the industry. Standards are based on a protocol called *IEEE 802.11* that is governed by the Institute of Electrical and Electronics Engineers (IEEE).

wireless communication

Software System

In addition to your software application, the software components include the operating system, databases, and security software installed on your computers.

software components

A software system is susceptible to the following risks:

- Data corruption

- Virus attacks

- Data theft

Data corruption can be caused by a malicious attack or by a hardware or communication failure. As an example, if a hard drive fails, data could be lost or corrupted. If the network goes down in the middle of a data transfer, data can become corrupted. Performing regular backups reduces the risk of data loss.

Your devices can be infiltrated with a virus through email, Internet sites, or the sharing of unlicensed software. Install virus and malware protection software and keep it up-to-date. Keep your operating system up-to-date, as latest version releases often include security patches.

Data theft is on the rise. Massive amounts of digital data are being collected and stored at exponential rates. The large amounts of data collected and digitally stored are called "*big data*." This prolific amount of digital data storage provides hackers with data at their fingertips. Ways to keep intruders away include installing firewalls and implementing a stringent password policy. Like home invasions, data thieves work when no one else is watching. Disabling logons during non-work hours can keep predators out of your data. If you suspect someone is stealing sensitive data, a *keylogger* can be installed on your computer device. A keylogger is a piece of software or hardware that tracks and logs the activity on a computer. Be mindful of sending and receiving sensitive data across a network, Wi-Fi, or the Internet. Data can be intercepted during data transmission. Transmitting your data in an unreadable, encrypted format can protect your data. This is discussed in the next section.

big data

keylogger

✓ Section 10.2 Assessment

1. List four computer components that are susceptible to security risks.
2. Define *firewall* and explain why it is used.
3. Describe *biometrics*. Give an example of when you have witnessed the use of biometrics in everyday life.
4. Name the three types of Wi-Fi security. Which one offers the highest level of protection?
5. Open a Web browser. Locate the security section under the *Tools* menu. It may look similar to Figure 10.2. Write a set of instructions that explains how to navigate to the settings.

10.3 How Encryption Works

 Key Point

Encryption is the process of encoding and decoding data. It is a common technique used to keep data private. Data encryption can be traced back to the days of Julius Caesar.

encryption
Caesar Cipher

The idea of encrypting a message by shifting its letters a fixed amount in the alphabet is called a *Caesar Cipher*, named after Julius Caesar. Julius Caesar encrypted messages by shifting by three letters.

In your daily computing, say when you're at a coffee shop surfing the Web, you would prefer that your activities be private, or shared only with the person sitting next to you. But, your wireless is using a radio to send your keystrokes and mouse clicks to the shop's hotspot. Every computer in the room receives those signals, and if the communication wasn't encrypted—that is, recoded to hide its true meaning—everyone could follow your whole session. So, it's obvious you need encryption. But, how does it work?

The Key to Encryption

A key component of encryption is the key. And it comes in two forms: private and public.

Keys

In encryption, a *key* is a "magic number" used to transform text, called *cleartext*, into gibberish, called a *ciphertext*. Both the sender and receiver—the two ends of the communication—must agree on the key, because it will be used to encode the cleartext, and decode the ciphertext back to cleartext.

key
cleartext
ciphertext

If the two communicators have agreed on a key, then the basic process is a five-step algorithm:

1. The sender breaks the message into groups of letters.

2. "Multiply" each group of letters (the bits are just treated as a number) times the key.

3. Send the "products"—the results from the "multiplications"—to the receiver.

4. The receiver "divides" the "products" by the key to recreate the groups.

5. Assemble the groups into the message.

This works because of a fact you know: Multiplying any number by another number, and then dividing the result by the same number gives the original number back. Right?

6 × 4 = 24

24 / 4 = 6

Such facts provide the "reversibility" of encryption that makes them 2-way ciphers. Because only the sender and receiver know the key (in this case, 4), the products are just useless numbers to anyone snooping the transmission.

2-way ciphers

What's happening in the five-step algorithm is a *secure communication* (see Figure 10.3 for a schematic of the idea). The sender takes the cleartext and encrypts it using the key, making it into gibberish or ciphertext (Steps 1 and 2). The ciphertext is transmitted (Step 3). The receiver gets the gibberish, and reverses the transformation, that is, decrypts it, to recreate cleartext (Steps 4 and 5).

secure communication

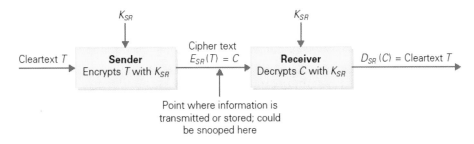

FIGURE 10.3 Schematic of a cryptosystem. The sender encrypts the cleartext information to produce a ciphertext, and the receiver decrypts the ciphertext to recover the cleartext. In the middle, where the content is exposed and can be snooped, it is unintelligible.

Encrypting Example

To see the encryption/decryption algorithm in action, let's work a small example. Suppose the message we want to send is MEET @ 9 and the key is 13. Here's how it works:

1. Visiting www.branah.com/ascii-converter and typing in MEET @ 9, we learn that these eight letters (blanks are letters, too!) in ASCII have the decimal values:

 77 69 69 84 32 64 32 57

2. Grouping the decimal values into pairs, we "multiply" each pair by the key, 13:

 $7769 \times 13 = 100997$

 $6984 \times 13 = 090792$

 $3264 \times 13 = 042432$

 $3257 \times 13 = 042341$

 (The "leading zeros" make all numbers six digits.)

3. Send the "products"—100997 090792 042432 042341—to the receiver.

4. The receiver "divides" by the key, 13:

 $100997/13 = 7769$

 $090792/13 = 6984$

 $042432/13 = 3264$

 $042341/13 = 3257$

 and types in the digits 77 69 69 84 32 64 32 57 to the www.branah.com/asciiconverter program to get the ASCII: M E E T @ 9.

5. Reassembling the message, MEET @ 9.

So, in the privacy of her own computer, the sender converted her message MEET @ 9 to 100997 090792 042432 042341. The public could see those numbers when she sent them, but they looked like gibberish. Then, in the privacy of his own computer, the receiver converted them to the message, MEET @ 9. The message was in cleartext only when it was private.

Private Key Encryption

private key encryption

symmetric key cryptography

The technique just explained is called *private key encryption*, or *symmetric key cryptography*. The example, to be simple enough for us to study, is very, very, very small. Real encryption systems use much longer blocks (hundreds of letters), and much larger keys. Also, they use other transformational techniques besides multiplication and division. But the ideas are exactly the same, and so it is safe to think of encryption as working by the algorithm just discussed.

In the algorithm above, the words "multiply," "products," and "divides" are in quotes because they are not the only operations that can be used for encryption. All that is needed is for an operation to have an inverse: divide is the inverse of multiply. So, there are many encryption algorithms.

Private key encryption works very well, and it is used a lot. But, there is one small problem: The sender and receiver have to agree on the key, which means they need to communicate somehow.

But, for online communication, agreeing on a key could be a showstopper, because the sender and receiver don't usually meet face-to-face. Thanks to a great mathematician and several enterprising computer scientists, the problem has been solved!

Public Key Encryption

The solution: Publish the key. Really! See Figure 10.4 for a schematic diagram. If the receiver publishes the key on his Web site, the sender can grab it, and encrypt the message. Then she sends the encrypted message to the receiver. He uses his key to decrypt it, and read her message. Slick, right? *public key encryption*

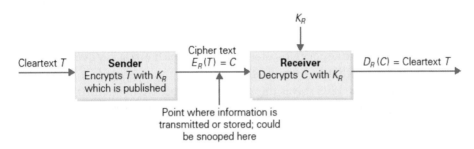

FIGURE 10.4 Public key cryptosystem. The sender uses the receiver's public key K_R to encrypt the cleartext, and only the receiver is able to decrypt it to recover the cleartext.

Well . . . couldn't the "bad guys" go to the Web site, too, get the key, grab the transmission, and decrypt it? They have the same access to the key that the sender and receiver do. True . . . but it's not just any key.

It's a public key, and it has some very astonishing properties. The public key is two special prime numbers multiplied together. (If you've forgotten, a prime number is evenly divisible only by itself and 1. Like 13.)

In a *public key cryptosystem* (*PKC*), the receiver publishes the special key, K. Then, the following occurs: *public key cryptosystem (PKC)*

1. The sender breaks up the message into blocks as before.

2. The sender cubes each block—yup, raises it to the third power—and divides by K, the special public key, keeping only the remainders—the stuff that's left after division.

3. The remainders are transmitted.

4. The receiver raises each remainder to a high power determined by the prime numbers and known only to him.

5. The receiver divides each by K, too, and saves only the remainders, which are—surprisingly—the original blocks!

6. The receiver assembles the message.

It's a little more complicated than our multiplication encryption algorithm on the previous page, and it's a tough process to do with a calculator. But computers are pretty good with the math!

Even so, it doesn't seem like this would work, because in Steps 2 and 5, after dividing by the magic key K, the main part of the number is tossed, and only the remainder is kept. It's kind of like baking bread, slicing it up, tossing the slices, and keeping the crumbs. How could this possibly work?

Thanks to Leonard Euler (OY• ler), we know that the prime numbers and the cubing in Step 2 have wonderful properties that make the six-step public key cryptosystem work. We won't go into the math, but two computer scientists—Whitfield Diffie and Martin Hellman—recognized that these properties would make a public key encryption technology work. Then, three more computer scientists—Ron Rivest, Adi Shamir, and Len Adleman—developed one of the popular PKC algorithms, *RSA*, which is outlined in the six steps above and illustrated in Figure 10.4.

RSA algorithm

In summary, public key cryptosystems let people exchange a key over an unprotected channel, and that key can be the private key that is used in the simpler private key protocols. PKC solves the key exchange problem—getting the private key to the other person—and once that's done, the simpler private key algorithm works fine.

Factoring Is Hard

How do we know that PKC systems work? Looking at Euler's formula—but you don't have to—mathematicians will tell you that K, the magic public key, is just two prime numbers, p and q, multiplied together. They'll say, correctly, that it is possible to figure out those two numbers—a process called factoring—from the published key. Maybe in theory, but in practice, probably not.

Although computer scientists are not certain, most believe that factoring is a very tough computation; that is, if the numbers p and q are large—maybe 60 digits apiece—it is impractical to factor them no matter how big and bad your computer is. So, the PKCs just use big prime numbers, and no one has figured out how to factor them fast. That fact is what keeps the PKC process safe.

Back to the Coffee Shop

Our discussion started with you in a coffee shop planning to use the wireless connection. We said that wireless uses radio signals, so every computer in the coffee shop can listen to the signals. So, the first question:

Q1: Does the coffee shop wireless use encryption?

Many "free Wi-Fi" hot spots do not. You can tell when your modem tells you that a wireless connection is available; it will name the wireless security protocol. If it doesn't say anything—if it doesn't ask for a password when you first use it—then there isn't any, and all of your signals are going to everyone as cleartext. If you're reading the news with your browser and *there are no other apps running on your machine*, who cares? If you're planning on using any other application, it may be a problem. This brings us to the second question:

Q2: When do I need to encrypt my wireless signals?

Most experts will tell you, "Always!", and it *is* good advice, but the coffee shop may not be using encryption, and you *do* want to read your email, which you must log into with your password. Will someone snoop that? Luckily, even if your wireless connection isn't encrypted, your application may be. On the Web, for example, when the URL begins with https, the "s" means secure. This technology is the *secure socket layer* (*SSL*), which is often indicated by a lock icon somewhere in the browser window. So, for example, your free email account is likely to use this kind of secure communication. This is probably good enough to read email at the coffee shop even without any better encryption. And finally, our third question:

secure socket layer (SSL)

Q3: If the coffee shop doesn't need secure wireless, do I need it for my wireless router?

Absolutely! First, you will use your own system for more secure transactions like banking. Second, many of us live near others who could piggyback onto your unsecured system. They are happy for you to pay their Internet video streaming charges. Third, even if your neighbors are not going to use your Internet, they can install software that allows them to watch everything you do, like typing passwords. Many applications do not use SSL when asking for your password. So, absolutely, you need to install a security barrier with your router.

Secure wireless technology has been under attack in recent years, with many systems—WEP and WEP2—being completely compromised. Today, WPA2—Wi-Fi Protected Access 2—is solid and recommended

✓ SECTION 10.3 ASSESSMENT

1. Using Julius Caesar's original encryption mode, decrypt the following message.

 `L ORYH SURJUDPPLQJ!`

2. Suppose you reply back to the message sent in the encrypting example where you were asked to "`MEET @ 9`". You reply back:

 `101257 042640 099645 087997`

 What message did you send?

3. Describe the difference between public key and private key encryption.

10.4 Recovering from System Failure and Computer Malware

A risk assessment plan minimizes risk but is not a guarantee against a system failure. Thus, a plan must be in place to recover from a system failure or breach.

Key Point

Recovering from a system failure takes patience and some pre-planning. If the failure involves data loss, the fastest way to recovery is to re-install data and software from a backup. To implement this procedure, you must have a regular back-up plan in place *before* the failure occurs. Once the data is lost or corrupted, it is too late to implement a backup plan. Thinking ahead and documenting the steps in a written plan is best practice for reducing security risks.

If the security breach involves lost or stolen hardware, have a plan in place that allows administrators to disable logons and delete sensitive data from the missing device. Software can be pre-installed on the missing device that allows you to perform these operations from a remote location.

There are millions of known computer viruses and thousands more pop up each day. If you are infected by a virus, use the proper virus removal tool to quarantine or delete the virus. Educating yourself on how to recognize and avoid viruses is the best prevention against them.

Understanding Malware

malware

Malware is an acronym for malicious software. Viruses are a type of malware. Although the term "virus" is often used to categorize all forms of malicious code, there is a distinction between various types. Following are the four categories of malware:

virus

- A *virus* is a program that intends to disrupt or destroy your computer files and data.

worm

- A *worm* is a program that is often embedded in an email attachment. It reproduces itself and can send a copy to everyone on your contact list, thereby propagating and moving on its own.

spyware

- *Spyware* is a program installed on your computer, usually without your permission. It is used to gather personal information and track browsing habits. Spyware is often attached to "free" software.

Trojan

- A *Trojan* is an unasked-for "gift"—like the horse of ancient Greece— that is a malicious program performing unauthorized activities. Trojans arrive with downloads of seemingly benign software, like "sharing" software from sites with "free stuff" such as music or wallpaper.

These are the principle ways malware gets into your computer.

What Does Malware Do?

Malware is a term used to cover a wide variety of threatening software. Some forms of malware simply track your Website browsing habits or download unwanted advertising. Others are more malicious. The three worst activities are the following:

backdoors

- *Backdoors* are software that "pokes a hole" in the computer, creating an access path allowing the attackers who produced the malware to run any program they want on your computer without being stopped by your computer's defenses. Such computers are usually set up to participate in a botnet.

- *Trojans* are software capable of so many unauthorized activities they're classified by type. Trojan keyloggers record every key you type, looking for passwords and other private information; Trojan FakeAVs pretend to be antivirus software, but they extort money from users to "fix" the problem it creates; and Trojan bankers watch for banking and credit card activity to capture account numbers and passwords. These are just a few of the types of Trojans; there are about two dozen others.

- *Rootkits* are software that infects your computer and then fights back rootkits
 against its security systems! If you manage to stop the infection, a rootkit
 can restart itself, copy itself, or even move itself. Rootkits purposely conceal
 themselves, which often makes removal nearly impossible.

The first thing that these malicious systems do is to lower the security defenses of
the computer so they don't get detected or caught.

✓ SECTION 10.4 ASSESSMENT

1. If you have a system failure that involves data loss, what should you do?

2. A laptop has been stolen. What should you do to recover from the security
 breach?

3. A computer has been infected with a virus. What should you do?

10.5 Prevention Strategies

*The best line of defense in preventing malicious security attacks is paying attention
to what files we open and what Websites and links we visit.*

**Key
Point**

The biggest problem—in fact, almost the only problem—in computer security is
us. Using common sense and thinking before we act goes a long way in preventing
security issues. There are few things that are truly "free." Consider the experiment
done in June 2013 by Coner Myhrvold.

His experiment: Using ten extremely popular search terms, he Googled each.
Then he clicked on the first ten search hits with Firefox running on a freshly
installed version of Windows for each. When he got to each site, he installed what-
ever "free stuff" it offered. He then analyzed what was sent and installed on his
computer. His results are summarized in Table 10.1.

TABLE 10.1 **Results for search terms from Myhrvold's "Free Stuff" experiment.**

Keywords	Results	Infected Files	Threats Detected by Lavasoft Ad-Aware
"free wallpaper"	2/6	11	Adware, Adware Installer, unwanted programs, miscellaneous
"free screensaver"	8/10	191	Hijacker, Adware, Adware Installer, unwanted programs, cookies, miscellaneous
"free games"	2/10	45	Adware, Adware Installer, cookies
"free game cheats"	0/1	0	N/A
"free word unscrambler"	0/10	0	N/A
"free e-cards"	0/10	0	N/A
"free lyrics"	5/10	608	Adware, Adware Installer, toolbar, cookies
"free music downloads"	5/10	835	Trojan, Adware, Adware Installer, toolbar, browser, plug-in, miscellaneous

The first column shows the search terms—definitely popular. Next is the num-
ber of links leading to downloads, out of the total landing pages with links. Third
is the count of infected files received, and the final column tells what they were
infected with. Notice he got 835 infected files from 5 free music sites! Also, two
malware files were installed: a backdoor (Hijacker) and a Trojan. But Myrhvold
summarized the real problem:

"Adware such as iLivid wreaked havoc on my PC speed and performance despite the fact that I installed several free programs [. . .] that promised the exact opposite. *Post install, my computer was effectively unusable.* Just opening the Web browser took several minutes because of the slate of adware running startup and background processes."

Safe Computing Checklist

Among the points security specialists continually make is that we will be safe if we just pay attention to what we're doing and understand the risks that go with it. Here are their most important bits of advice:

- **Turn off Bluetooth when not in use.** Bluetooth wireless is subject to many vulnerabilities, including nearby parties listening to calls and placing calls through your device. If you must use it, turn it *completely* off—not just "invisible" mode—when you're not in a conversation.

- **Keep your phone and other computers locked.** It may seem like you are always holding your phone, but you do put it down occasionally, making it possible for someone else to pick it up. Keeping it locked is a tiny hassle considering the personal data you have stored on it. . . or, considering the chance of loss or theft, do you want your sensitive information stored there in the first place?

- **Do not automatically click on email attachments.** Email attachments such as .jpg files are basically data and are generally safe, but many other files also contain program code. Malware can be embedded in the file's program code. When you open such files, the code runs and a worm or virus can be released. Table 10.2 is a list of file types that could potentially contain malware or viruses. Make sure they come from a reliable source before opening.

- **Never enter sensitive information in a pop-up.** Pop-ups are the main way malware gathers information. Most pop-ups are a nuisance, so turning them off entirely isn't a bad idea; that setting can be found in your Internet browser's Tools > Settings.

- **Thinking of getting something for nothing? Think again. . . .** As the story about Coner Myhrvold's experiment indicates, downloading free stuff can be extremely risky. But, we all like freebees. The security advice: Don't download until you've done your homework and have convinced yourself you're getting something of value from a legitimate site.

- **Know where you're going.** When you're surfing, it's always possible for Web links to appear to be connecting you to one place, when they're actually sending you somewhere else. Clicking a link provided to you in an email or in social media may actually link you to another site. If you are unfamiliar with the source, rather than clicking the link, copy/paste the blue anchor text into your Web browser. This avoids you being surreptitiously redirected to another site.

- **Be somewhat skeptical.** Social engineering (phishing) takes many forms, but there is just one goal: to get you to voluntarily give up your private information. This can be a form of data or identity theft. Be aware and pay attention to the Website you are actually on by viewing the URL of the site.

- **Use extreme care when visiting notorious sites.** Music sharing, sports gambling, and pornography sites are notorious as sources of "electronic infection." Minimizing visits minimizes risk.

TABLE 10.2 File extensions that can carry malware, primarily for Windows OS.

The file extension is the letter sequence following the last dot in the file name. Beware of files that have two extensions such as **data.txt.exe**. The two extensions are oftentimes a way to make a malicious file look safe. The last extension is the actual file type that the operating system will recognize.

.386	Virtual Device Driver (Windows 386 enhanced mode)	.fon	Font file	.ocx	Microsoft Object Linking
.3gr	VGA Graphics Driver/configuration files	.hlp	Help file	.pcd	Corel Adaptec CD Creator image file
.add	Adapter Driver file	.hta	HTML program	.pif	Shortcut to MS-DOS program
.ade	Microsoft Access project extension	.inf	Setup information	.reg	Registration entries
.asp	Active Server Page	.ins	Internet Naming Service	.scr	Screen saver
.bas	Microsoft Visual Basic class module	.isp	Internet communication settings	.sct	Windows Script Component
.bat	Batch file	.js	JavaScript file	.shb	Shell Scrap object
.chm	Compiled HTML Help file	.jse	JavaScript encoded-script file	.shs	Shell Scrap object
.cmd	Microsoft Windows NT command script	.lnk	Shortcut	.url	Internet shortcut
.com	Microsoft MS-DOS program	.mdb	Microsoft Access program	.vb	Visual Basic Script file
.cpl	Control Panel extension	.mde	Microsoft Access MDE database	.vbe	Visual Basic Script-encoded file
.crt	Security certificate	.msc	Microsoft Common Console document	.vbs	Visual Basic Script file
.dbx	Database Index	.msi	Microsoft Windows Installer package	.vxd	Microsoft Windows Virtual Device Driver
.dll	Dynamic Link Library	.msp	Microsoft Windows Installer patch	.wsc	Windows Script Component
.exe	Program file	.mst	Microsoft Windows Installer Transform file	.wsf	Windows Script File
				.wsh	Windows Script Host Settings file

10.6 Computer Crimes and the Law

Computer crime is on the rise. There are many laws at both the state and federal level to punish those who commit computer crimes. As technology continually changes, these laws are also ever changing.

 Key Point

A *computer crime* is any act that either maliciously targets a computer system, or uses a computer to commit a crime. Computer crimes are punishable by probation, fines, or jail sentencing. Following are five categories of computer crimes:

computer crime

- Computer hacking
- Identity theft
- Child pornography
- Cyber bullying
- Data theft

Types of Crimes

computer hacking

- *Computer hacking* is the unauthorized entry into a computer system for malicious reasons. Hacking may involve the stealing of sensitive data, altering or deleting data, or causing harm to the computer infrastructure. Most states have laws that prohibit computer hacking. Hacking is also prohibited under the Federal Computer Fraud and Abuse Act (CFAA).

 The largest retail hacking incident took place in 2013 when hackers infiltrated Target's system and stole credit card information and personal data from over 40 million loyal customers. The challenge for law enforcement is that it is usually dealing across international boundaries. The Target incident, for example, was linked to hackers in Russia.

identify theft
computer fraud

- *Identify theft* is the act of posing as someone else for fraudulent reasons. If identity theft is committed with the use of a computer, it is a computer fraud. Today, companies and Internet sites track large quantities of data about persons who use their products or visit their Websites. The security breaches of large companies which store consumer data, social media, Internet shopping, and storage of personal data all contribute to the rise of identity theft.

child pornography

- Possessing *child pornography* on a computer is a felony under federal law. Additionally, all 50 states have laws against child pornography. Child pornography is sexually explicit photos or videos of persons under the age of eighteen years old.

cyber bullying

computer abuse

- *Cyber bullying* is the act of threatening, stalking, or harassing someone through social media or over the Internet. Bullying someone with the use of a computer is a form of computer abuse. More and more states are adopting laws against cyber bullying. These laws are geared towards protecting minors and have gained widespread attention. A notorious incident was that of Rebecca Sedwick of Florida. In 2013, Rebecca committed suicide at the age of 12 after classmates harassed her on social media. Some students even urged her to commit suicide.

data theft

- *Data theft* is the stealing or collection of personal data from someone without his or her consent. While developing an application, one of your tasks may be to collect, manage, and store user data. It is important to understand the laws based around privacy. Privacy is the right of people to freely choose what data and under what circumstances they choose to share with others. It is good practice to ask for and document users' consent before collecting and storing personal information. Many sites and apps require acknowledgement of the company privacy policy. To protect your privacy, it is important to take the time to read and understand the policy. You can explore the privacy policy of U.S. government Websites at www.usa.gov/policies.

Tip
If you believe you have been a victim of identity theft, go to the Federal Trade Commission's Web site for instructions on what to do.
www.consumer.ftc.gov/features/feature-0014-identity-theft

While there are many state and federal laws that are aimed at prosecuting computer crimes and fraud, the *Computer Fraud and Abuse Act (CFAA)* covers a wide variety of crimes. The CFAA is a federal law and carries a penalty of up to $250,000 and 20 years in jail. If the crime involves illegal transfer of money or property and the Internet is used across state boundaries, a person can be convicted under the federal Wire Fraud Act.

Computer Fraud and Abuse Act (CFAA)

Note

You can listen to an interview concerning the alarming rate of cyber-crime and the Target security breach at http://www.npr.org/2014/01/13/262185937/how-the-hackers-did-it-a-discussion-about-targets-data-breach.

IT Careers

According to the U.S. Bureau of Labor Statistics, demand for security analysts is expected to grow by 18 percent through the year 2024. You can learn more about computer jobs and jobs in security at http://www.bls.gov/ooh/computer-and-information-technology/home.htm.

✓ Section **10.6** Assessment

1. Define computer crime and cite some examples.
2. What federal law prohibits computer hacking?
3. What law prohibits illegal interstate transfer of money or property over the Internet?
4. What factors influence the rise of computer crime?

10.7 Privacy Rights

Privacy is the right of people to choose freely under what circumstances and to what extent they will reveal themselves and their behavior to others.

Key Point

This definition emphasizes first that it is the person who decides the "circumstances" and the "extent" to which information is revealed, not anyone else. The person has the control. Second, it emphasizes that the range of features over which the person controls the information embodies every aspect of the person—themselves and their behaviors. Adopting such an inclusive definition is essential for covering situations of importance.

Enjoying the Benefits of Privacy

Now that we have the definition, what are the threats to privacy? There are only two basic threats: government and business. Historically, the governmental threat—a regime spying on its citizens— worries people the most, probably because when it happens the consequences are very serious. The business threat is a more recent worry, and its IT aspects even newer still. There are two types of business threats: surveillance of employees and the use of business-related information, including transaction information, for other purposes.

governmental threat

business threat

Voluntary Disclosure

In principle, a person can enjoy perfect privacy by simply deciding not to reveal anything to anyone; that is, to be a hermit, though that probably would mean living alone on a remote island, surviving on coconuts and clams. But most of us interact with many people and organizations—businesses, employers, and governments—to whom it is in our interest to reveal private information. That is, we freely choose to reveal information in exchange for real benefits.

- We tell our doctors many personal facts about ourselves so they can help us stay healthy.

- We allow credit card companies to check our credit record in exchange for the convenience of paying with a card.

- We permit our employer to read email we send at work, understanding that we are using the employer's computer, Internet connection, and time; that the email system is there for us to use on the job; and that we have no need or intent to send personal email.

- We reveal to the government our religion—though not in the United States—our parents' names and birthplaces, our race and ethnicity, and so on for the purposes of enjoying the rights of citizenship.

How private can we be when we reveal so much about ourselves, our attitudes, and our behavior? There must be clear guidelines adopted for handling private information, so that we have standards by which to judge whether the trust is warranted. For that, we have the Fair Information Practices principles.

Organization for Economic Cooperation and Development (OECD)

Fair Information Practices

In 1980 the Organization for Economic Cooperation and Development (OECD)—an organization of (currently) 34 countries concerned with international trade—developed an eight-point list of privacy principles that became known as the Fair Information Practices. They have become a widely accepted standard, forming a reasonably complete solution to the problem of keeping information private while at the same time revealing appropriate information to businesses and governments. We all have an interest in these principles becoming law. The principles also give a standard that businesses and governments can meet as a "due diligence test" for protecting citizens' rights of privacy, thereby protecting themselves from criticism or legal action. The OECD principles, listed in Table 10.3, are a practical implementation of privacy protection in the presence of computer technology.

Who Is Protected?

In 1995, in a landmark advancement for privacy, the European Union (EU) issued the European Data Protection Directive, a benchmark law incorporating the OECD principles. In the next few years, the member countries adopted it. Many non-EU countries, such as Australia, Canada, Hong Kong, and New Zealand, have also adopted laws based on OECD principles.

Europe's adoption of these standards is important because one provision in the EU directive requires that data about EU citizens be protected by the standards of the law even when it leaves their country. Non-EU countries that want information on EU citizens must show that they have privacy laws consistent with the OECD principles.

TABLE 10.3 A brief explanation of the OECD's Fair Information Practices guidelines.

Guideline	Explanation
Limited Collection	There should be limits to the personal data collected; data should be collected by fair and lawful means, and with the knowledge and consent of the person whenever possible.
Purpose	The purposes for collecting personal data should be stated when it is collected; the uses should be limited to those purposes.
Quality	The data should be relevant to the purpose of collection; it should be accurate, complete, and up-to-date.
Use Limitation	Personal data should not be disclosed or used for purposes other than stated in the Purpose Principle, except with the consent of the individual or by the authority of law.
Security	Personal data should be protected by reasonable security measures against risks of disclosure, unauthorized access, misuse, modification, destruction, or loss.
Openness	There should be general openness of policies and practices about personal data collection, making it possible to know of its existence, kind, and purpose of use, as well as the contact information for the data controller.
Participation	An individual should be able to (a) determine if the data controller has information about him or her, and (b) discover what it is. If the request is denied, the individual should be allowed to challenge the denial.
Accountability	The data controller should be accountable for complying with these principles.

Switzerland, a non-EU country, applied and was approved. The United States applied and was not. What sorts of laws protect U.S. privacy?

The United States has no OECD-like law. Its few privacy laws speak to specific situations. This is a hit-or-miss approach that is known as sectoral, meaning that it applies to different sectors of society. For example, the Health Insurance Portability and Accountability Act (HIPAA) protects an American's personally identifiable health information. Automobile registration information is also private by a specific law, as is the privacy of video rental titles by another specific law.

Most sectors—social media, to pick one—are not covered by privacy laws, and without broad OECD-like coverage, the EU isn't likely to approve the United States. This is a huge headache for multinational companies doing business with OECD countries. In order to accommodate the laws of other countries, they must establish a *safe harbor*, meaning that the company complies with OECD standards for citizens of EU countries.

A famous case concerning the right to privacy centered around the public exposure of the collection of data by the U.S. National Security Agency (NSA).

In June 2013 Edward Snowden—an analyst for the U.S. National Security Agency (NSA)—revealed that the U.S. government was collecting complete metadata records from telephone carriers. (Metadata is data about data, such as when a call was made, the number it was to, and so on; it doesn't include the content.) Further, using a surveillance program called PRISM, Snowden said the NSA was gathering data of Americans' online activity from Facebook, Microsoft, Google, and other large tech companies. This development took Americans by surprise, but it was also a shock overseas, because the records included calls and data from countries with OECD privacy laws, such as Germany.

Health Insurance Portability and Accountability Act (HIPAA)

U.S. National Security Agency (NSA)

Edward Snowden

Patriot Act

The Patriot Act was signed into law after the September 11, 2001 (9/11) terrorist attack on the World Trade Center Towers in New York City. The intent was to provide government with access to information that could lead to the capture of terrorists or prevention of future attacks.

Snowden's exposure of government activities has created much controversy over the Patriot Act.

In June 2015, The Patriot Act was extended into law. However, a section of the law was changed stopping the NSA from collecting phone records from citizens not involved in a terrorist crime. This section of the law, known as The USA Freedom Act, was signed into law by President Obama.

USA Freedom Act

This is an area of the law that continues to be scrutinized. You can follow the latest developments at the Electronic Privacy Information Center (www.epic.org/privacy/) and the Electronic Freedom Foundation (www.eff.org).

✓ SECTION 10.7 ASSESSMENT

1. Define privacy.
2. Explain the purpose of the Organization for Economic Cooperation and Development (OECD).
3. What is the Patriot Act?
4. What is the USA Freedom Act?
5. If you are writing a software application that collects and stores private user data, what should you do to comply with privacy laws?

10.8 Understanding Cookies

 Key Point *While most cookies are not harmful to your computer, understanding what cookies are and learning how to control the use of cookies helps reduce security risks.*

Cookies are a standard computer science concept originally used by Netscape engineers to connect the identity of a client across a series of independent client/server events. Here's the problem cookies solve.

Figure 10.5 illustrates the Web server's view of the client/server relationship. Imagine this is your bank's server and that you are paying bills online, which makes you a client. The server is helping many clients at once, and to know who's who, the server stores a cookie—a record containing seven fields of information that uniquely identify a customer's session—on your computer. *Cookies* are exchanged between the client and the server on each transmission of information, allowing the server to know which of the many client computers is sending information.

cookies

Though cookies serve a useful purpose—and most of us want to enable cookies so we can bank online—*third-party cookies* are a key way Web surfing behavior is tracked. The first two parties are you and the Web site you're visiting; the third party is a company—often an ad agency hired by the server company to place ads —that records where you've visited, based on the history you left as recorded in their database built with third-party cookies.

Generally, accepting cookies makes for more effective use of the Web, but it is wise to block third-party cookies (in your browser's privacy settings) if you haven't set the Do Not Track flag.

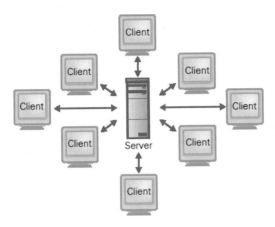

FIGURE 10.5 Server's view of the client/server relationship.

✓ SECTION 10.8 ASSESSMENT

1. Explain how cookies can be helpful.
2. For added security, what types of cookies should you block?

Chapter 10 — Review and Assessment

KEY TERMS

biometrics 272
CIA triad 270
cloud storage 272
computer abuse 290
computer crime 285
computer fraud 286
Computer Fraud and Abuse Act (CFAA) 287
computer hacking 286
cookie 290
cyber bullying 286
data communication system 274
data theft 286
encryption 275
Ethernet 273
fiber optics 273

firewall 274
identify theft 286
keylogger 276
malware 282
Patriot Act 290
private key encryption 278
public key encryption 279
risk assessment 270
security risk 270
smart chip ID 272
USA Freedom Act 290
Wi-Fi Protected Access (WPA) 275
Wi-Fi Protected Access II (WPA2) 275
Wired Equivalent Privacy (WEP) 275

CHAPTER SUMMARY

1. *Risk assessment* is the process of defining potential risks, identifying and implementing ways to reduce risks, and planning for security failures.

2. The three goals of a security plan are to keep sensitive data *confidential*, maintain data *integrity*, and insure the *availability* of the computer system.

3. The *physical facilities*, *hardware*, *software*, and *data communication system* are all components of a computer information system that are susceptible to security risks.

4. *Encryption* and *authentication* are two methods used to secure computer information systems.

5. *Malware* stands for malicious software and can be in the form of a *virus*, *Trojan*, *worm*, or *spyware*.

6. Install anti-virus software as a preventative measure. In the event of a malware security breach, install additional software to remove the malware.

7. *Computer hacking*, *identity theft*, *child pornography*, *cyber bullying*, and *data theft* are forms of computer crimes.

8. Computer crimes, fraud, and abuse are prohibited under both federal and state laws. Persons convicted of a crime involving a computer may serve probation, jail time, or be charged a penalty fee.

9. Follow *privacy laws* when collecting user information. Make company privacy policy available to software system users. Obtain consent to collect data.

CHAPTER ASSESSMENT

For each of the next four questions, create a two-column table. Use the following template.

Type of security risk	Ways to reduce the risk

1. Identify three security risks for the *physical facility* component of a computer system. Identify a way to control or minimize each risk.

2. Identify three security risks for the *hardware* component of a computer system. Identify a way to control or minimize each risk.

3. Identify three security risks for the *data communications* component of a computer system. Identify a way to control or minimize each risk.

4. Identify three security risks for the *software* component of a computer system. Identify a way to control or minimize each risk.

5. Identify and define five categories of computer crimes. Explain the state and federal laws, and penalties associated with each.

6. Define four categories of malware. What procedures would you use to recover from a malware infection?

APPLIED LEARNING

1. The process of identifying risks and creating an assessment plan can be applied to many things in life. Identify an activity or scenario in your life that has potential risks. It may help you by brainstorming possible "*what if*" questions. Here are two examples. *What if* a fire broke out in my home? *What if* my car broke down on an isolated road? There are many possible outcomes to these questions. Estimating the likelihood of, or quantifying, the risk helps put things in perspective, and helps you plan ahead.

 Identify a scenario in your life that has risks. Using the five-stage process in Figure 10.1, create a written assessment plan.

2. You are working on a team project to develop an airline ticketing application. The application allows passengers to book airplane flights over the Internet. The data is stored at the main headquarters on internal servers. Working in small teams, identify four computer components that may be susceptible to a security risk and create an action plan to minimize the risks.

3. Many companies offer free cloud storage such as Apple, Google, and Microsoft. Research the various services. Write a set of logical instructions describing how to open a cloud storage account. Exchange instructions with a team partner. Following each other's instructions, open a cloud storage account. Provide verbal feedback to your team partner on the set of instructions. (Are they easy to follow? Are there any missing steps?) Revise your instructions based upon the feedback.

NETBEANS TUTORIAL

Objectives

- Learn how to install NetBeans.

- Write a program using NetBeans Integrated Development Environment (IDE).

A.1 Installing NetBeans

NetBeans is a free Integrated Development Environment (IDE) supported by Oracle. It is available for download at Oracle's Website.

You need to install both the **NetBeans IDE** and the **Java Development Kit** (**JDK**) to complete the exercises in this book. You can find both applications at this Website: http://www.oracle.com/technetwork/java/javase/downloads/index.html.

Download the *Standard Edition* and choose the operating system that matches your computer. You can download them separately as shown in Figure A.1.

Java SE Downloads

FIGURE A.1 Java Standard Edition and NetBeans IDE Download Interface.

Alternatively, you can download and install them together in a bundle as shown in Figure A.2.

Java SE and NetBeans Cobundle (JDK 8u73 and NB 8.1)		
Product / File Description	File Size	Download
Linux x86	281.84 MB	⬇ jdk-8u73-nb-8_1-linux-i586.sh
Linux x64	277.82 MB	⬇ jdk-8u73-nb-8_1-linux-x64.sh
Mac OS X	340.95 MB	⬇ jdk-8u73-nb-8_1-macosx-x64.dmg
Windows x86	298.3 MB	⬇ jdk-8u73-nb-8_1-windows-i586.exe
Windows x64	305.27 MB	⬇ jdk-8u73-nb-8_1-windows-x64.exe

FIGURE A.2 Bundle download of JDK and NetBeans.

Once you have downloaded and installed these two programs, you will be ready to create your first application in Java using NetBeans.

A.2 Writing a Program Using NetBeans

This application will display "Hello World!" to the user screen. Following are the steps to create a program:

1. **Create a project using NetBeans IDE.**

 In the NetBeans IDE, you can write, test, build, and run your code.

 The first step is to create a project to store your code.

2. **Compile your code and save it into a class file**.

Once you have written your code, you can compile it. Java uses a programming language compiler called javac. Javac translates your English-like code into machine language.

3. **Run the program**.

Run your application to test.

Create a project using NetBeans IDE

1. Locate the **NetBeans IDE program** on your operating system and start it.

2. Choose **New Project…Java Application** as illustrated in Figure A.3.

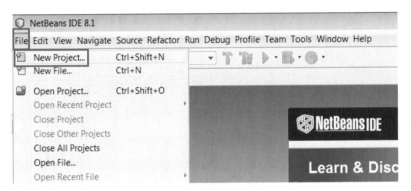

FIGURE A.3 Choose: File, New Project.

3. Choose **Java…Java Application Project**. Choose **Next>** as shown in Figure A.4.

FIGURE A.4 Choose: Java, Java Application Project window.

4. Name your project `Hello World App` and make all selections exactly as shown in Figure A.5. Click **Finish**.

FIGURE A.5 Project Name and Location window.

5. The IDE window is divided into three sections (Figure A.6). The following describes the three sections:

- The *Projects window* is where you can navigate through all the components of your project. The components can be expanded or contracted by clicking on the '+' or '-' symbols.

- The *Source Editor window* is where you will write your code.

- The *Navigator window* is where you can navigate between elements within a class.

FIGURE A.6 IDE Window Sections.

6. Choose **Tools | Java Platforms**. The **JDK (default)** should be listed on the left-hand side of the platform manager window, as shown in Figure A.7. If you do not see it, click **Add Platform**, navigate to your JDK install directory, and click **Finish**. You will know if it was added correctly if it appears in the platform manager window.

FIGURE A.7 Java Platform Manager window.

7. Write the code. Refer back to Figure A.5 and note that the **Create Main Class** checkbox is selected. This default option creates some basic code for you that is common to most classes.

 ■ Find the program comment section at the beginning of the code. Add a comment by changing the existing comment section.

   ```
   /**
    * Hello World program using Java
    * @author your name goes here
    */
   ```

 ■ Replace the line of code:

   ```
   // TODO code application logic here
   ```

 with

   ```
   System.out.println("Hello World!");
   ```

 Java is 'case sensitive' so type the code in as shown. In other words, "A" and "a" are not the same in Java. System.out.printLn is not the same as system. out.println.

8. Choose **File | Save**.

Compile your code and save it into a class file

Choose **Run | Build Project** to build your machine code. This is referred to as *bytecode*. If your project does not have errors, you will see results in your output window similar to Figure A.8. If you see the **BUILD SUCCESSFUL** message, your code ran properly. Congratulations! You have just created a Java program!

```
hello.world.app.HelloWorldApp
Output - Hello_World_App (clean,jar)
    Created dir: C:\NetBeansProjects\Hello World App\build
    Updating property file: C:\NetBeansProjects\Hello World App\build\built-jar.properties
    Created dir: C:\NetBeansProjects\Hello World App\build\classes
    Created dir: C:\NetBeansProjects\Hello World App\build\empty
    Created dir: C:\NetBeansProjects\Hello World App\build\generated-sources\ap-source-output
    Compiling 1 source file to C:\NetBeansProjects\Hello World App\build\classes
    compile:
    Created dir: C:\NetBeansProjects\Hello World App\dist
    Copying 1 file to C:\NetBeansProjects\Hello World App\build
    Nothing to copy.
    Building jar: C:\NetBeansProjects\Hello World App\dist\Hello_World_App.jar
    To run this application from the command line without Ant, try:
    java -jar "C:\NetBeansProjects\Hello World App\dist\Hello_World_App.jar"
    jar:
    BUILD SUCCESSFUL (total time: 1 second)
```

FIGURE A.8 Output window showing a successful build.

If the build output shows that the **BUILD FAILED**, you probably have a syntax error in your code. Errors are displayed in the Output window. You can click on an error in the output window to jump directly to the line of code that caused the error. Troubleshoot your error and try to run the program again. *Hint: Check for spelling errors and make sure you are using the correct upper and lower case letters.*

When you build your project, a program file is created on your computer. You can see where the new file is located by going to the Files tab in the navigation window. Figure A.9 shows the expanded *Hello World App* node and the file that is created. Java bytecode uses a **.class** file extension. Additionally, you can browse the NetBeans project folder on your hard drive and find the *HelloWorldApp.class* file.

FIGURE A.9 Files window.

Run the program

Run your application by clicking the green arrow on the toolbar. Alternatively, from the IDE menu choose **Run | Run Main Project**. Your results should resemble Figure A.10.

FIGURE A.10 Results of Hello World!

ECLIPSE TUTORIAL

Objectives

- Learn how to install Eclipse.
- Write a program using Eclipse Integrated Development Environment (IDE).

B.1 Installing Eclipse

Eclipse is a free Integrated Development Environment (IDE) you can use to build your applications.

> **Note**
>
> If you are working in a school lab, check with your instructor. Eclipse may be pre-installed, or your school may require specific installation guidelines. Additionally, your instructor may prefer that all labs be performed in NetBeans. (See Supplement A.)

Step 1: Download and install the Java SE Development Kit (JDK)

You must install the JDK before installing the Eclipse software. You can download the JDK from the following Website: http://www.oracle.com/technetwork/java/javase/downloads/index.html. Download the *Standard Edition* and choose the operating system that matches your computer. After the download is complete, double-click the file to start the installation process.

Step 2: Download and install Eclipse.

You can download the Eclipse software from http://www.eclipse.org/downloads/. Choose the operating system that matches your computer. Once the download is complete, double-click the file to start the installation process and choose all default options.

Once you have downloaded and installed these two programs, you will be ready to create your first application in Java using Eclipse.

B.2 Writing a Program Using Eclipse

This application will display "Hello World!" to the user screen. Following are the steps to create a program:

1. **Create a project using Eclipse.**

 In the Eclipse IDE, you can write, test, build, and run your application.

 The first step is to create a project to store your code.

2. **Create a class file and write your code.**

 Add a class to the newly created project and write the code.

3. **Compile and Run the program.**

 Compile your code into machine *bytecode* and run your application to test the results.

Create a project using Eclipse

1. Locate the **Eclipse IDE program** on your computer and start it.

2. Choose **File, New, Java Project** as illustrated in Figure B.1. Click the **Next** button.

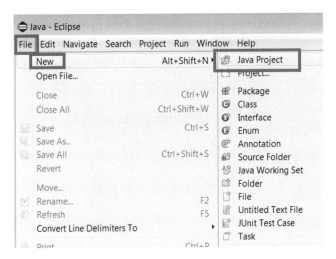

FIGURE B.1 Choose: File, New, Java Project.

3. Name your project `Hello World App` as shown in Figure B.2. Leave the default names for Project Location and Project Folder. (*Your instructor may provide an alternate location for your files.*) Click **Finish**.

FIGURE B.2 Specify the Project Name and Project Location.

Create a class file and write your code

1. From the IDE menu choose **File | New | Class**.

2. Name your class `Hello`. Check the *Public static void main(String[] args)* option, and click **Finish**.

These steps are illustrated in Figure B.3.

FIGURE B.3 Create the Java Class.

3. Now you are ready to write the code.

- Replace the line of code:

  ```
  // TODO Auto-generated method stub
  ```

 with

  ```
  System.out.println("Hello World!");
  ```

Java is case sensitive, so you will need to be mindful of your upper and lower case characters and type in the code exactly as shown in step 3. For instance, "A" and "a" are not the same in Java.

`System.out.printLn` is not the same as `system.out.println`.

4. Choose **File | Save.**

Compile and Run the program

1. From the IDE menu choose **Run | Run**. Your results will display in the Console window and should resemble Figure B.4.

FIGURE **B.4** Results of Hello World!

USING PACKAGES

Objectives

- Understand the value of using packages.
- Add program code to create a package.

C.1 Packages are Used to Organize and Group Classes

As an example, you can group together the classes and programming exercises in this textbook in a series of packages named chapter1, chapter2, chapter3, etc.

To use packages, include the following line of code:

```
package packagename;
```

Place this line of code directly after the initial comment block.

Chapter 2, Listing 2.1 creates a Welcome class. To organize the Welcome class into a package named Chapter1, use the following code.

```
/** Use package for the class */
package chapter1;
  public class Welcome {
public static void main(String[] args) {
System.out.println("Welcome to Java!");
  }
}
```

A package corresponds to a file folder. If you are using NetBeans or Eclipse, the folder is automatically created for you when you run the code. In other words, after running the code above, a folder named chapter1 is created on your storage device. Having all related classes grouped together in a file package makes it easy to locate files.

If you are not using an IDE such as NetBeans or Eclipse, you may have to manually create a directory and name it chapter1.

SUPPLEMENT

D

ALGORITHMIC THINKING

Objectives

■ Explain similarities and differences among algorithms, programs, and heuristic solutions.

■ List the five essential properties of an algorithm.

■ Use the *Intersecting Alphabetized List* algorithm to:

 • Follow the flow of the instruction execution

 • Follow an analysis explaining why an algorithm works

■ Demonstrate algorithmic thinking by being able to:

 • Explain the importance of alphabetical ordering for solutions

 • Explain the importance of the barrier abstraction for correctness

Key
Point

D.1 Algorithm Basics

An algorithm is a precise, systematic method for producing a specified result.

algorithm

As we've learned, computers must be given instructions for everything they do, so all they do is run algorithms. We normally call them programs, which are algorithms customized to do a specific task. Naturally, programmers and software developers care a lot about algorithms. But, they matter to the rest of us, too. Many of the problems we must solve personally are solved by algorithms, from describing how to achieve a clever effect in video editing to correcting mistakes in a term paper. Algorithms are solutions. And the best part is that by writing out the method carefully, some other agent—another person or a computer—can do the work. Of course, that is the reason computers are such powerful and useful tools.

In this supplementary chapter, we familiarize ourselves with algorithms and become more adept at reading them, writing them, and evaluating them. We start by learning about Jean-Dominique Bauby, a man whose hospital care required the use of algorithms. Next, we review algorithms we already know—how we learn them and how we use them. After that, we consider some defining characteristics of algorithms. Then, we study an algorithm we use every day; because it is an "industrial-strength" algorithm, it illustrates how an algorithm can exist in different forms, and why we prefer some algorithms over others. Finally, we consider how we know an algorithm does what it claims. Again, a simple illustration makes the point.

Jean-Dominique Bauby

Algorithms

In this section, we begin with simple, intuitive examples to continue our earlier discussion of algorithms. You already know that algorithms are important in our study. Now you'll find out they're even more familiar than you might have realized.

Writing One Letter at a Time

The book (and movie) *The Diving Bell and the Butterfly* tells the true story of a French man who became paralyzed from his chin down. He couldn't write. He couldn't talk. He couldn't even swallow. All he could do was turn his head a few degrees and blink his left eyelid. But he could think. And amazingly, he wrote the book about himself just by blinking his left eyelid!

The man, Jean-Dominique Bauby, wrote in *The Diving Bell and the Butterfly* that to be so paralyzed was like wearing the heavy suit and metal helmet deep sea divers wore in the days before SCUBA gear. He suffered from a condition called Locked-In Syndrome: His body was useless but his mind was active. He compared his thoughts to a butterfly, flitting quickly from one topic to the next. The idea became the title of his book.

Before he was paralyzed, Bauby was editor-in-chief at the fashion magazine *Elle* and an accomplished writer. So, it is not surprising that he wrote a book. What is surprising is that simply by blinking his left eye, he was able to communicate well enough to write at all. His problem—writing by blinking—will give us a situation to study algorithms.

Homemade Algorithms

Whenever Bauby wanted to say something, he had to spell it out letter by letter. To assist him, his nurses and visitors would say the alphabet, or point to the letters of the alphabet listed on a card in the order shown in Figure D.1. When they got to the right letter, he blinked. Then, they would go on to the next letter, starting over with the alphabet (see Figure D.1). It is a slow process. Try it!

E	S	A	R	I	N	T	U	L
O	M	D	P	C	F	B	V	
H	G	J	Q	Z	Y	X	K	W

FIGURE D.1 Alphabet listing shown to Jean-Dominque Bauby. When the nurse points to the correct letter, he blinks his left eyelid.

This process is an algorithm invented by his nurses. It illustrates important points about algorithms:

- We use and invent algorithms all the time to solve our problems; it doesn't take a degree in computer science to create algorithms.

- Although the algorithm doesn't seem to compute in the popular imagination of computing—where are the numbers, the mathematical formulas? —it does; it creates the content for a document, namely Bauby's book.

- The agent running the algorithm is not a computer. It's a nurse, and Bauby is the user. Often the agent that "runs" the algorithm is a person rather than a computer.

- As we are about to see, there are better and worse variations of this algorithm.

These observations emphasize the point that an algorithm is not an exotic creation requiring years of study and deep scientific knowledge, but rather a familiar concept that we use all the time without realizing it or thinking about it.

Many Questions; Fewer Questions

One way that the process was sped up was "word completion," in which the attendant said the word she guessed Bauby was trying to spell. This familiar autocomplete technique—for example, URL completion on the Web and word completion when texting—can save a lot of effort if you're blinking letters. However, there is an additional way to speed up blink-communication.

Frequency Order. Notice that the letters in Table D.1 are not listed in alphabetical order. You might guess that because Bauby is French, the order **e s a r i n t u l o m d p c f b v h g j q z y x k w** is how the French say the alphabet, but it's not. Like all people who use the Latin alphabet, the French use the standard **a b c** . . . sequence, too. The letters in the photograph are given in **frequency order** for French. That is, the letters are listed by how often they are used in written French—most to least. So, e is the most frequently used letter in French, **s** is next most frequent, then **a**, **r**, **i**, and so forth.

Asking—or pointing to—the letters in frequency order is smart, because it means that Bauby's assistant usually tried fewer letters. There is no guarantee, of course. The frequency ordering is an average, found by counting the number of times each letter occurs on thousands and thousands of pages of French text. Not every collection of French words has the same frequency, but it works pretty well. Let's give an example.

How Good Is Frequency Order? The famous French saying, "the more things change, the more they stay the same," *Plus ça change, plus c'est la même chose*, can be communicated by the algorithm just described. We illustrate how well the frequency ordering works by counting how many letters a person must ask to communicate the saying compared to communicating it using the normal alphabetical ordering. How do they compare?

To begin, we start with the first word, *plus*. To find **p**, we ask **e s a r i n t u l o m d p**, and determine that **p** is located after pointing to 13 letters. Next, we look for **l**, asking **e s a r i n t u l**, so l takes 9 letters. We find that **u** takes 8, and **s** is the second letter.

So, to communicate the first word, *plus*, requires us to ask $13 + 9 + 8 + 2 = 32$ letters. A computer program can finish the process for us, and finds that the total for the whole sentence is 247.

Now, we run the same experiment using the normal alphabetical order **a b c** Repeating the process from before, we ask **a b c d e f g h i j k l m n o p** to find that in this order **p** is letter 16, **l** is 12, **u** is 21, and **s** is 19. So, communicating **plus** using the normal alphabetical ordering takes $16 + 12 + 21 + 19 = 68$, which is more than twice the 32 letters needed when using the French frequency ordering. The computer program finds that for the whole sentence the normal alphabetical order requires 324 tries.

So, asking in frequency order required 247 letters compared to 324 for alphabetical order. Claude Mendibil and the other people assisting Bauby were very smart to use the frequency ordering. It saved him many, many blinks, which shortened the time it took to write *The Diving Bell and the Butterfly*. Such ideas are used in text compression.

Writing the book was a *computation* in which Bauby was the user and the assistant pointing to or asking the letters was the "agent," the person or thing following the instructions. In this case, the instructions were simple: Repeatedly ask the alphabet in frequency order, and each time Bauby blinks, write down the letter.

✓ SECTION D.1 ASSESSMENT

1. For yes/no questions, Bauby and the nurses used the rule one blink for "no" and two blinks for "yes." The presence/absence of a blink is enough to indicate one bit of information, so his 1-blink/2-blink protocol for yes/no seems wasteful—it could have been no-blink/1-blink. Can you figure out the practical reason why this wouldn't work for encoding his answer?

2. How many letters must you speak to communicate *merci* using the French frequency ordering: **e s a r i n t u l o m d p c f b v h g j q z y x k w**?

3. How many letters must you speak to communicate *merci* using the normal alphabetical ordering: **a b c d e f g h i j k l m n o p q r s t u v w x y z**?

4. Show that frequency order is not always faster by computing how many letters are needed to spell *abacus* using the English frequency ordering: **e t a o i n s h r d l u c m f w y p v b g k q j x z** and the normal alphabetical ordering.

D.2 A Closer Look

We have just seen an algorithm—a precise, systematic method for producing a specified result—in action. The process of constructing words and sentences by asking the letters one at a time is an algorithm.

🔑 **Key Point**

Letter Search algorithm

The *Letter Search* algorithm for Bauby presented here is clear enough for people to follow—you spelled out *merci*—but it is not yet precise enough for a computer. As you know, computers are clueless. For a method to be precise enough for a computer to follow, *everything* needs to be spelled out. Programmers make algorithms perfectly precise for computers by writing them in a programming language. That's how the count for the whole quote was determined. People *do* have a clue, so many things can be left out of the explanation; for example, after finding a letter, a computer has to be told to go back to the beginning of the letter sequence to start looking for the next letter. People figure that out by themselves.

Algorithms Versus Programs

The variations on the *Letter Search* algorithm illustrate an important point. Both letter search using frequency order (lsfreq) and letter search using alphabetical order (lsalpha) are examples of programs. Programs are algorithms that have been specialized to a specific set of conditions and assumptions, and are (usually) written in a specific programming language. The original explanation of an assistant asking the letters and Bauby blinking at the right moment was a *Letter Search* algorithm. lsfreq and lsalpha both use the *Letter Search* algorithm, but each has been specialized to a different sequence. This doesn't seem like a big difference, and it's not. We could write a letter search program that inputs the letter sequence to follow before it starts. It would be a different program from lsfreq or lsalpha, but it would still use the *Letter Search* algorithm.

So, programs are algorithms, and now you know the small difference between the two. In most cases, however, we do not need to make the distinction and can use the terms interchangeably.

In our discussion of the *Letter Search* algorithm, we focused on the two different orders of asking letters—frequency and alphabetic. This is typical. Every computational task has many ways of being solved. Computer professionals spend much of their time figuring out how well a solution works, or how to improve it. And it's important that they find a fast solution: When you're waiting for a computer to finish its task, you don't want to wait longer than necessary.

Experience with Algorithms

Because programs are algorithms and all of the applications you use daily are programs, you obviously use algorithms all the time. But, you regularly learn algorithms, too.

> **Tip**
>
> *Algorithm* is a strange word. (It's an anagram of logarithm!) It comes from the name of a famous Arabic textbook author, Abu Ja'far Mohammed ibn Mûsâ al-Khowârizmî (780–840 ad). He was a Persian scientist, mathematician, and astronomer, but he didn't invent the word "algorithm." The end of his name, al-Khowârizmî, means native of Khowârism (today it is Khiva, Uzbekistan). Over the centuries, references to his famous book corrupted the end of his name into *algorithm*.

Inventing Algorithms

Most of the algorithms you know you developed yourself, simply by thinking through what is required to achieve your goal. For example, think of all of the things you know how to do with your phone, or with complex applications like video editing software. When someone asks your help with a "How do I . . ." question, you will likely answer with an algorithm. For your answer to be successful, it is important that your algorithm have a few basic properties.

D.3 Writing Algorithms

Key Point

We want our algorithms to be successful. Because they are written for someone or something else to follow, it is important that they be precise.

An algorithm must have five properties:

- Input specified
- Output specified
- Definiteness
- Effectiveness
- Finiteness

Input Specified. The *input* is the data to be transformed during the computation to produce the output. We specify the type of data, the amount of data, and the form of the data that the algorithm expects.

input

Output Specified. The *output* is the data resulting from the computation, the intended result. Often the output description is given in the name of the algorithm, as in "Algorithm to compute a batting average." As with input, we must specify the type, amount, and the form the output will have. A possible output for some computations is a statement that there is no output—that is, there is no possible solution.

output

Definiteness. Algorithms must specify every step and the order to perform them. *Definiteness* means specifying the sequence of operations for transforming the input into the output. Details of each step must be spelled out, including how to handle errors. Definiteness ensures that if the algorithm is performed at different times or by different agents (people or computers) using the same data, the output is the same.

definiteness

Effectiveness. It must be possible for the agent to execute the algorithm mechanically without any further input, special talent, clairvoyance, creativity, help from Superman, and so on. Whereas definiteness specifies which operations to do, in what order, and when, *effectiveness* means that they are doable.

effectiveness

Finiteness. An algorithm must have *finiteness*; it must eventually stop, either with the right output or with a statement that no solution is possible. If no answer comes back, we can't tell whether the agent is still working on an answer or is just plain "stuck." Finiteness is not usually an issue for noncomputer algorithms because they typically don't repeat instructions. But, as you will see, computer algorithms often repeat instructions with different data.

finiteness

Query Evaluation

To discuss key ideas about algorithms, let's begin with an algorithm you probably use every day: the Google query evaluation algorithm.

A *query processor* makes an ordered list of the pages that hit on the keywords of your search query. Query evaluation makes that list; ordering that list so it is most convenient for you is a separate task and not considered here. Figure D.1 shows the query evaluation algorithm invented by Sergey Brin and Larry Page, and presented in their original paper, *The Anatomy of a Large-Scale Hypertextual Web Search Engine*.

query processor

The first thing we notice about this algorithm is that it is not written in a programming language. It uses "normal" English—specifically, "tech speak" English. So, for example, the term "doclist" is the list of URLs associated with each keyword. The term "rank" means "page rank"; "seek" means to go to a position in a list (stored as a file on a disk). If we read the whole paper, we would know what "short barrels" and "full barrels" are, but even without those definitions, tech speak is easier to understand than, say, ancient Greek.

 Note
When the Brin/Page algorithm was finally written in a programming language, it doubtless took tens of thousands of lines of code, explaining why humans prefer this seven-step description.

1. Parse the query.

2. Convert words into wordIDs.

3. Seek to the start of the doclist in the short barrel for every word.

4. Scan through the doclists until there is a document that matches all the search terms.

5. Compute the rank of that document for the query.

6. If we are in the short barrels and at the end of any doclist, seek to the start of the doclist in the full barrel for every word and go to step 4.

7. If we are not at the end of any doclist go to step 4.

Sort the documents that have matched by rank and return the top k.

FIGURE D.1 Original query evaluation algorithm developed by Brin and Page to find the hits for a Google search; from their original paper, The Anatomy of a Large-Scale Hypertextual Web Search Engine (infolab.stanford.edu/~backrub/google.html).

The paper presents its algorithm in tech speak first because only computers prefer to read code, and secondly, because the actual program would be too detailed for their purpose of explaining to people how query evaluation is supposed to go; they left out a lot of details that a computer would need to be told.

Here is the first fact about algorithms that is illustrated by query evaluation:

> **Algorithmic Fact 1.** Algorithms can be specified at different levels of detail. It is only necessary that the agent know the terms and operations used in the specification, and that they be within the agent's capability to perform (that is, effective).

The Brin/Page algorithm is written for technically trained people who have read the paper up to "Figure D.1," so it meets the criterion. When you explain video editing or other complicated operations to your friends, you use terms you know they know and operations you know they can perform.

Programs are usually written in a programming language (PL), which is compiled into assembly language (AL), which is assembled into binary form. All three —PL, AL, and binary—are different forms of the same thing. Each one is more detailed than its predecessor, and is understandable to anyone or anything fluent in that language.

 Note

English or any natural language is a very imprecise way to give an algorithm. Among its sources of imprecision are pronouns—he, she, they, them, and so on—and among them "it" is the worst, because we can't always be sure what it refers to. (The only pronoun Brin and Page used in their algorithm is the "royal we.") Using nouns instead of pronouns won't win any writing awards, but your algorithm will be more understandable.

Intersecting Lists

Algorithms always use *functions*—operations that the agent already knows how to perform—to simplify the algorithmic description. For example, Step 4 of the Brin/Page algorithm states, "Scan through the doclists until there is a document that matches all the search terms." They don't give instructions for performing a "scan through," but it's an operation that is critical to their solution; they assumed the agent's capability includes knowing how to do this right. Notice that this is not a case of an undefined word. "Scan" has its obvious meaning, but when it is necessary to match items on each list, the exact operation of the scan matters a lot.

The functionality Brin/Page assumed in their algorithm was Step 3, moving through the lists in a particular way.

> **Algorithmic Fact 2.** Algorithms always build on functionality previously defined and known to the agent.

In our case, readers of the Brin/Page paper would know that the most efficient way to "scan through" looking for matches is to alphabetize the lists and proceed as specified in the *Intersecting Alphabetized Lists* (IAL) algorithm.

IAL

Let's be clear about what their readers knew by giving an example of an algorithm that should *not* be used.

How Not to Match

Another way to implement "scan" to find the needed matches—we call it No Alphabetized Lists (NAL)—starts with any lists and works like an odometer. (The lists can be alphabetized or not; the algorithm will ignore the ordering.) It places the arrow pointers at the start of each list, and then advances the pointer of one of the lists all the way to the end looking for a match at each step; it then advances the next list one position, and repeats what it has done up to this point. (Think of the odometer as starting at 00000 and finding the 10 hits, 00000, 11111, . . . , 99999.) This is an algorithm. It checks every combination of URLs, and so it finds the identical information that the IAL does. But it's MUCH slower.

NAL

How much slower? An example will convince you that it's a lot slower. Consider five 10-item lists. The IAL moves the pointer past each item of each list once, giving a worst-case number of steps as

IAL: $10 + 10 + 10 + 10 + 10 = 50$

(We don't know what order the pointers will be advanced in, but it doesn't matter when we're only counting up how many advancements there are: At most, there are ten for each list.)

But the non-alphabetized lists solution repeatedly visits the same items. Because it works like an odometer, our sample lists will require as many steps as sweeping through a five-digit odometer:

NAL: $10 \times 10 \times 10 \times 10 \times 10 = 100,000$

Both solutions work. One solution is very efficient compared to the other.

So, when Brin and Page said "scan through the doclists," they knew that readers would use the IAL approach to find each match.

Summarizing the comparison between IAL and NAL, we have:

> **Algorithmic Fact 3.** Different algorithms can solve the same problem differently, and the different solutions can take different amounts of time.

The feature that makes IAL better than NAL is obviously the alphabetical order. It allows us to skip many, many checks for matching that would fail.

Different Solutions

An important point to emphasize is that the IAL and NAL algorithms are *not* different versions of the same solution. They are *different solutions* that solve one problem differently. This is clear because they each require a different form of the input and rely on that input's characteristics. For the IAL, the doclists must be alphabetized. The NAL doesn't care if the doclists are alphabetized or not because it ignores the order when it runs. Using the added information allows the IAL to bypass unproductive tests.

The difference in running times for the IAL and NAL algorithms also points to the fact that they are different solutions: Different forms of the same algorithm will have the same running time.

D.4 Understanding Why IAL Works

The way to know that an algorithm works is to know why it works.

We (and computer scientists generally) believe that the IAL solution is good in the sense of being clear and simple, and we've just argued that it is efficient. There is one main remaining question: How do we know that the algorithm works? That is, how do we know if it finds all of the hits?

Sometimes when we develop an algorithm to solve a problem, the solution doesn't have any loops in it. This makes it particularly easy to test—run it and see if the result is right. Done. But, most algorithms have loops and so they need a little bit of analysis to be sure they are right. Specifically, it is not enough to run it on an input; trying the program might reveal an error, but it might not. If the error involves a larger problem—and therefore, more looping—the small problem may work fine. Programs containing loops cannot be verified exhaustively, that is, by trying all cases, because there are infinitely many. We must be smarter.

A Strategy

Discovering why an algorithm works might seem difficult, but usually it is not. As its creator, we will know why because we gave the algorithm the "correct" properties when we developed it.

So, our strategy for "knowing why it works" is as follows:

- Find one or more properties that ensure the algorithm works.

- Explain, using the program, why they make it work.

In the case of the Intersecting Alphabetized Lists problem, we need to be sure that if there are hits to be found, the algorithm will find them. (If there are no hits, then Step 2 will always fail, meaning the algorithm "works" in that case.) So, we assume that one or more hits are among the URLs in the lists we are given. That means that the same URL is in all of the lists.

Explaining Why IAL Works

The small example in Figure D.2 of the IAL at work shows the algorithm applied to six lists in columns A through F. Notice how Step 3, advance-the-arrow-of-the-earliest-URL in any list, causes the arrows to move down the list until they all reach the same URL, Hit.com.

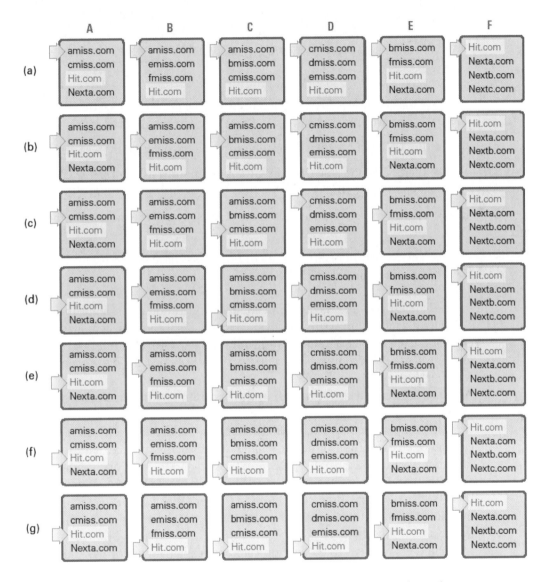

FIGURE D.2 Progress of the Intersecting Alphabetized List computation for six keywords. For columns A through F, the activity described by each row is: (a) initial configuration, (b) pass amiss.com, (c) pass bmiss.com, (d) pass cmiss.com, (e) pass dmiss.com, (f) pass emiss.com, (g) pass fmiss.com.

By definition, that is a hit. If this example were longer, then the next step would show all of the pointers advancing together to the next item after Hit.com in their lists.

Figure D.2 illustrates how we can organize our thinking about the correctness of the IAL algorithm.

Notice that the highlighted URLs of a hit—both Hit.com and Nextb.com—each make a ragged line across the lists.

We say the hit forms a "barrier" because, by being in every list, it stretches all the way across the lists; there are no gaps. These "hit barriers" have four properties:

- If a URL is a hit, then it must be part of a barrier, that is, in each list.

- If a URL is not a hit, then the URL is not in some list, and so the URL can't be part of a barrier.

- After a hit is recorded, all of the arrows "cross" the barrier on the next step.

- The algorithm begins as if all of the arrows have just "crossed" a barrier, which we can call the *0th barrier*.

The barriers give us a way to think about the operation of the algorithm.

When the algorithm begins, all of the arrows are at the first item, having just crossed the 0th barrier. The arrows will advance, one URL at a time, and *all of the arrows will stay between two barriers: the one they just crossed and the next one, which is the hit they are looking for next.*

As we think about the operation of the algorithm, we imagine the arrows like members of a very strange marching band, each stepping forward when it's their turn, stopping when they reach the barrier, marching in place waiting for the others, and when they are all at the barrier, they all step across at once. They repeat the same behavior inside the barrier they just crossed and the next one. And so forth.

So, that's it. The arrows move forward between a pair of barriers. If there are no hits, the "barriers" are simply the start and the end. When they all get to a barrier, the hit is recorded and they all cross together, repeating the same protocol with the next pair of barriers.

Computer scientists often develop elaborate explanations for why their algorithms work, but, we've seen that it's not too hard to know why an algorithm works just by informal discussion. That's good enough for us.

Summary on Correctness

Anyone who creates an algorithm needs to know why it works. This involves finding the algorithm's correctness-preserving properties and explaining why they do the job. The explanation is always customized to the algorithm. Most of the time, we only need to explain this to ourselves, but we must always be able to do it if someone like a user asks, "Why does it work?"

Supplement D — Review and Assessment

CHAPTER SUMMARY

1. We use algorithms daily, and we continually create them as we instruct other people in how to do a task.

2. Everyday algorithms can sometimes be unclear because natural language is imprecise.

3. Algorithms have five fundamental properties.

4. Algorithms can be given at different levels of detail depending on the abilities of the agent.

5. Problems can be solved by different algorithms in different ways.

6. Algorithms always work—either they give the answer or say no answer is possible—and they are evaluated on their use of resources such as space and time.

7. The *Intersecting Alphabetized Lists* (IAL) algorithm is used in Web searching and is preferred over other solutions.

8. Properties of the *Intersecting Alphabetized Lists* algorithm are used to explain why it works.

REVIEW QUESTIONS

1. An algorithm is a(n)

 a. list of general nonspecific steps to produce an output.

 b. logarithm.

 c. systematic method for producing a specified result.

 d. math problem.

2. Algorithms are used by

 a. only computers.

 b. only humans.

 c. various agents.

 d. no one, they are not real.

3. Algorithms must always

 a. produce output.

 b. produce output or state that there is no solution.

 c. produce input or state that there is no solution.

 d. state that there is no solution.

4. Algorithms are guaranteed to work

 a. 99.9 percent of the time.

 b. 100 percent of the time.

 c. depends on the computers they are running on.

 d. 50 percent of the time.

5. When writing an algorithm in a natural language it is helpful to use _____ instead of _____.

 a. programming language, natural language

 b. nouns, pronouns

 c. abbreviations, actual words

 d. nouns, adjectives

6. If an algorithm is performed with the same data, at different times with different agents the output will be

 a. the same.

 b. different.

 c. sometimes different and sometimes the same.

 d. impossible to tell.

7. How many algorithms can solve one specific problem?

 a. only one

 b. many

 c. It depends on the type of algorithm.

SHORT ANSWER

1. Programs containing _____ cannot be verified exhaustively.

2. A program is an algorithm that has been _____.

3. Algorithms must be _____; they eventually stop with the right output or a statement that no solution is possible.

4. Algorithms must be definite. They must specify ordered steps, including details on how to _____.

5. The steps in algorithms must be _____ so that the agent is able to follow them.

EXERCISES

1. This chapter describes how Jean-Dominique Bauby wrote a book by blinking. Explain what he was doing in terms of PandA concepts as he is being presented the alphabet.

2. What is the Web searching process called if not an algorithm?

3. State whether the following properties hold for the placeholder technique. Be sure to include details to support your answer.

 a. input

 b. output

 c. definiteness

 d. effectiveness

4. Explain how detailed an algorithm needs to be.

5. The IAL requires the agent to advance the arrow for the alphabetically earliest URL. Show that the IAL is effective by explaining how an agent would know which list has the "alphabetically earliest" URL, and so must have its arrow advanced.

6. What makes IAL (intersect an alphabetized list) faster than NAL (no alphabetized lists)?

7. Give the steps for checking your email inbox.

8. Explain the five proprieties of your algorithm for Exercise 7 (input specified, output specified, definiteness, effectiveness, and finiteness).

9. Develop an algorithm for brushing your teeth. Then explain the correctness of your algorithm, detailing why it works.

10. Why is it not enough to make sure an algorithm works by running it on a few inputs? How can you ensure that an algorithm will always produce the correct output or state that there is no solution for the given input?

UNDERSTANDING VARIABLE SCOPE

Objectives

- Explain variable scope.
- Understand local variable scope.
- Determine the scope of variables within a loop.

E.1 The Scope of Variables

The scope of a variable is the part of the program where the variable can be referenced.

scope of variables
local variable

Chapter 3 introduced the scope of a variable. This section discusses the scope of variables in detail. A variable defined inside a method is referred to as a *local variable*. The scope of a local variable starts from its declaration and continues to the end of the block that contains that variable. A local variable must be declared and assigned a value before it can be used.

A parameter is actually a local variable. The scope of a method parameter covers the entire method. A variable declared in the initial-action part of a `for`-loop header has its scope in the entire loop. However, a variable declared inside a `for`-loop body has its scope limited in the loop body from its declaration to the end of the block that contains the variable, as shown in Figure E.1.

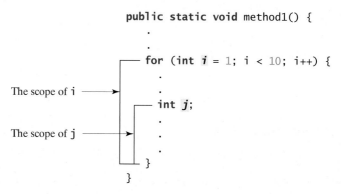

FIGURE E.1 A variable declared in the initial action part of a `for`-loop header has its scope in the entire loop.

You can declare a local variable with the same name in different blocks in a method, but you cannot declare a local variable twice in the same block or in nested blocks, as shown in Figure E.2.

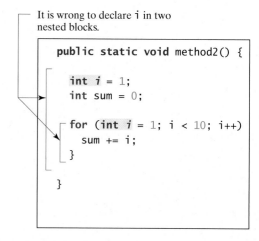

FIGURE E.2 A variable can be declared multiple times in nonnested blocks, but only once in nested blocks.

Caution

Do not declare a variable inside a block and then attempt to use it outside the block. Here is an example of a common mistake:

```java
for (int i = 0; i < 10; i++) {
}

System.out.println(i);
```

The last statement would cause a syntax error, because variable i is not defined outside of the for loop.

✓ SECTION E.1 ASSESSMENT

1. Define variable scope.
2. What is a local variable?
3. What is the scope of a local variable?
4. Fix the code below so the value of i is printed to the console.

```java
for (int i = 0; i < 10; i++) {
}

System.out.println(i);
```

NESTED LOOPS

Objectives

- Understand how to construct a nested loop.
- Evaluate nested loop examples.

F.1 Nesting Loops

Key Point

A loop can be nested inside another loop.

nested loop

Nested loops consist of an outer loop and one or more inner loops. Each time the outer loop is repeated, the inner loops are reentered, and started anew.

Listing F.1 presents a program that uses nested **for** loops to display a multiplication table.

LISTING F.1 MultiplicationTable.java

```
1   public class MultiplicationTable {
2     /** Main method */
3     public static void main(String[] args) {
4       // Display the table heading
5       System.out.println("            Multiplication Table");
6
7       // Display the number title
8       System.out.print("    ");
9       for (int j = 1; j <= 9; j++)
10        System.out.print("    " + j);
11
12      System.out.println("\n——————————————————————————————————————");
13
14      // Display table body
15      for (int i = 1; i <= 9; i++) {
16        System.out.print(i + " | ");
17        for (int j = 1; j <= 9; j++) {
18          // Display the product and align properly
19          System.out.printf("%4d", i * j);
20        }
21        System.out.println();
22      }
23    }
24  }
```

table title — line 5
outer loop — line 15
inner loop — line 17

```
            Multiplication Table
        1   2   3   4   5   6   7   8   9
  ------------------------------------------------
1 |     1   2   3   4   5   6   7   8   9
2 |     2   4   6   8  10  12  14  16  18
3 |     3   6   9  12  15  18  21  24  27
4 |     4   8  12  16  20  24  28  32  36
5 |     5  10  15  20  25  30  35  40  45
6 |     6  12  18  24  30  36  42  48  54
7 |     7  14  21  28  35  42  49  56  63
8 |     8  16  24  32  40  48  56  64  72
9 |     9  18  27  36  45  54  63  72  81
```

The program displays a title (line 5) on the first line in the output. The first **for** loop (lines 9–10) displays the numbers 1 through 9 on the second line. A dashed (–) line is displayed on the third line (line 12).

The next loop (lines 15–22) is a nested **for** loop with the control variable i in the outer loop and j in the inner loop. For each i, the product i * j is displayed on a line in the inner loop, with j being 1, 2, 3, …, 9.

Note

Be aware that a nested loop may take a long time to run. Consider the following loop nested in three levels:

```
for (int i = 0; i < 10000; i++)
  for (int j = 0; j < 10000; j++)
    for (int k = 0; k < 10000; k++)
      Perform an action
```

The action is performed one trillion times. If it takes 1 microsecond to perform the action, the total time to run the loop would be more than 277 hours. Note that 1 microsecond is one millionth (10^{-6}) of a second.

✓ SECTION F.1 ASSESSMENT

1. How many times is the `println` statement executed?

```
for (int i = 0; i < 10; i++)
  for (int j = 0; j < i; j++)
    System.out.println(i * j)
```

2. Show the output of the following programs. (*Hint*: Draw a table and list the variables in the columns to trace these programs.)

```
public class Test {
  public static void main(String[] args) {
    for (int i = 1; i < 5; i++) {
      int j = 0;
      while (j < i) {
        System.out.print(j + " ");
        j++;
      }
    }
  }
}
```
(a)

```
public class Test {
  public static void main(String[] args) {
    int i = 0;
    while (i < 5) {
      for (int j = i; j > 1; j--)
        System.out.print(j + " ");
      System.out.println("****");
      i++;
    }
  }
}
```
(b)

```
public class Test {
  public static void main(String[] args) {
    int i = 5;
    while (i >= 1) {
      int num = 1;
      for (int j = 1; j <= i; j++) {
        System.out.print(num + "xxx");
        num *= 2;
      }

      System.out.println();
      i--;
    }
  }
}
```
(c)

```
public class Test {
  public static void main(String[] args) {
    int i = 1;
    do {
      int num = 1;
      for (int j = 1; j <= i; j++) {
        System.out.print(num + "G");
        num += 2;
      }

      System.out.println();
      i++;
    } while (i <= 5);
  }
}
```
(d)

MULTIDIMENSIONAL ARRAYS

Objectives

- Give examples of representing data using two-dimensional arrays.

- Declare variables for two-dimensional arrays, create arrays, and access array elements in a two-dimensional array using row and column indexes.

- Program common operations for two-dimensional arrays (displaying arrays, summing all elements, finding the minimum and maximum elements, and random shuffling).

- Pass two-dimensional arrays to methods.

- Write a program for grading multiple-choice questions using two-dimensional arrays.

- Solve the closest-pair problem using two-dimensional arrays.

- Check a Sudoku solution using two-dimensional arrays.

- Use multidimensional arrays.

G.1 Introduction

Data in a table or a matrix can be represented using a two-dimensional array.

Chapter 7 introduced how to use one-dimensional arrays to store linear collections of elements. You can use a two-dimensional array to store a matrix or a table. For example, the following table that lists the distances between cities can be stored using a two-dimensional array named `distances`.

problem

Distance Table (in miles)

	Chicago	Boston	New York	Atlanta	Miami	Dallas	Houston
Chicago	0	983	787	714	1375	967	1087
Boston	983	0	214	1102	1763	1723	1842
New York	787	214	0	888	1549	1548	1627
Atlanta	714	1102	888	0	661	781	810
Miami	1375	1763	1549	661	0	1426	1187
Dallas	967	1723	1548	781	1426	0	239
Houston	1087	1842	1627	810	1187	239	0

```
double[][] distances = {
  {0, 983, 787, 714, 1375, 967, 1087},
  {983, 0, 214, 1102, 1763, 1723, 1842},
  {787, 214, 0, 888, 1549, 1548, 1627},
  {714, 1102, 888, 0, 661, 781, 810},
  {1375, 1763, 1549, 661, 0, 1426, 1187},
  {967, 1723, 1548, 781, 1426, 0, 239},
  {1087, 1842, 1627, 810, 1187, 239, 0},
};
```

G.2 Two-Dimensional Array Basics

An element in a two-dimensional array is accessed through a row and column index.

How do you declare a variable for two-dimensional arrays? How do you create a two-dimensional array? How do you access elements in a two-dimensional array? This section addresses these issues.

Declaring Variables of Two-Dimensional Arrays and Creating Two-Dimensional Arrays

The syntax for declaring a two-dimensional array is:

```
elementType[][] arrayRefVar;
```

or

```
elementType arrayRefVar[][]; // Allowed, but not preferred
```

As an example, here is how you would declare a two-dimensional array variable `matrix` of `int` values:

```
int[][] matrix;
```

or

```
int matrix[][]; // This style is allowed, but not preferred
```

You can create a two-dimensional array of 5-by-5 `int` values and assign it to `matrix` using this syntax:

```
matrix = new int[5][5];
```

Two subscripts are used in a two-dimensional array, one for the row and the other for the column. As in a one-dimensional array, the index for each subscript is of the `int` type and starts from `0`, as shown in Figure G.1a.

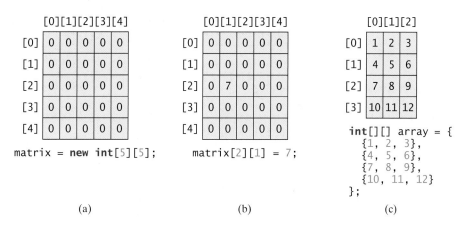

FIGURE **G.1** The index of each subscript of a two-dimensional array is an `int` value, starting from `0`.

To assign the value `7` to a specific element at row-index `2` and column-index `1`, as shown in Figure G.1b, you can use the following syntax:

```
matrix[2][1] = 7;
```

Caution

It is a common mistake to use `matrix[2, 1]` to access the element at row `2` and column `1`. In Java, each subscript must be enclosed in a pair of square brackets.

You can also use an array initializer to declare, create, and initialize a two-dimensional array. For example, the following code in (a) creates an array with the specified initial values, as shown in Figure G.1c. This is equivalent to the code in (b).

```
int[][] array = {
  {1, 2, 3},
  {4, 5, 6},
  {7, 8, 9},
  {10, 11, 12}
};
```

(a)

Equivalent

```
int[][] array = new int[4][3];
array[0][0] = 1; array[0][1] = 2; array[0][2] = 3;
array[1][0] = 4; array[1][1] = 5; array[1][2] = 6;
array[2][0] = 7; array[2][1] = 8; array[2][2] = 9;
array[3][0] = 10; array[3][1] = 11; array[3][2] = 12;
```

(b)

Obtaining the Lengths of Two-Dimensional Arrays

A two-dimensional array is actually an array in which each element is a one-dimensional array. The length of an array `x` is the number of elements in the array, which can be obtained using `x.length`. `x[0]`, `x[1]`,..., and `x[x.length-1]` are arrays. Their lengths can be obtained using `x[0].length`, `x[1].length`,..., and `x[x.length-1].length`.

For example, suppose `x = new int[3][4]`, `x[0]`, `x[1]`, and `x[2]` are one-dimensional arrays and each contains four elements, as shown in Figure G.2. `x.length` is 3, and `x[0].length`, `x[1].length`, and `x[2].length` are 4.

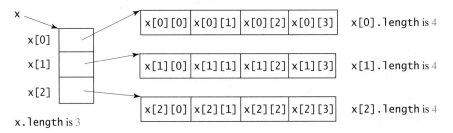

FIGURE G.2 A two-dimensional array is a one-dimensional array in which each element is another one-dimensional array.

Ragged Arrays

ragged array

Each row in a two-dimensional array is itself an array. Thus, the rows can have different lengths. An array of this kind is known as a *ragged array*. Here is an example of creating a ragged array:

```
int[][] triangleArray = {
  {1, 2, 3, 4, 5},
  {2, 3, 4, 5},
  {3, 4, 5},
  {4, 5},
  {5}
};
```

As you can see, `triangleArray[0].length` is 5, `triangleArray[1].length` is 4, `triangleArray[2].length` is 3, `triangleArray[3].length` is 2, and `trian-gle-Array[4].length` is 1.

If you don't know the values in a ragged array in advance, but do know the sizes—say, the same as before—you can create a ragged array using the following syntax:

```
int[][] triangleArray = new int[5][];
triangleArray[0] = new int[5];
triangleArray[1] = new int[4];
triangleArray[2] = new int[3];
triangleArray[3] = new int[2];
triangleArray[4] = new int[1];
```

You can now assign values to the array. For example,

```
triangleArray[0][3] = 50;
triangleArray[4][0] = 45;
```

> **Note**
> The syntax `new int[5][]` for creating an array requires the first index
> to be specified. The syntax `new int[][]` would be wrong.

✓ SECTION G.2 ASSESSMENT

1. Declare an array reference variable for a two-dimensional array of `int`
 values, create a 4-by-5 `int` matrix, and assign it to the variable.

2. Can the rows in a two-dimensional array have different lengths?

3. What is the output of the following code?

```
int[][] array = new int[5][6];
int[] x = {1, 2};
array[0] = x;
System.out.println("array[0][1] is " + array[0][1]);
```

4. Which of the following statements are valid?

```
int[][] r = new int[2];
int[] x = new int[];
int[][] y = new int[3][];
int[][] z = {{1, 2}};
int[][] m = {{1, 2}, {2, 3}};
int[][] n = {{1, 2}, {2, 3}, };
```

G.3 Processing Two-Dimensional Arrays

Nested for loops are often used to process a two-dimensional array.

Suppose an array `matrix` is created as follows:

```
int[][] matrix = new int[10][10];
```

The following are some examples of processing two-dimensional arrays:

1. *Initializing arrays with input values.* The following loop initializes the array
 with user input values:

```
java.util.Scanner input = new Scanner(System.in);
System.out.println("Enter " + matrix.length + " rows and " +
  matrix[0].length + " columns: ");
for (int row = 0; row < matrix.length; row++) {
  for (int column = 0; column < matrix[row].length; column++)
  {
    matrix[row][column] = input.nextInt();
  }
}
```

2. *Initializing arrays with random values.* The following loop initializes the array with random values between 0 and 99:

```java
for (int row = 0; row < matrix.length; row++) {
  for (int column = 0; column < matrix[row].length; column++)
  {
     matrix[row][column] = (int)(Math.random() * 100);
  }
}
```

3. *Printing arrays.* To print a two-dimensional array, you have to print each element in the array using a loop like the following:

```java
for (int row = 0; row < matrix.length; row++) {
  for (int column = 0; column < matrix[row].length; column++)
  {
     System.out.print(matrix[row][column] + " ");
  }

  System.out.println();
}
```

4. *Summing all elements.* Use a variable named total to store the sum. Initially total is 0. Add each element in the array to total using a loop like this:

```java
int total = 0;
for (int row = 0; row < matrix.length; row++) {
  for (int column = 0; column < matrix[row].length; column++)
  {
     total += matrix[row][column];
  }
}
```

5. *Summing elements by column.* For each column, use a variable named total to store its sum. Add each element in the column to total using a loop like this:

```java
for (int column = 0; column < matrix[0].length; column++) {
  int total = 0;
  for (int row = 0; row < matrix.length; row++)
    total += matrix[row][column];
  System.out.println("Sum for column " + column + " is "
    + total);
}
```

Find the row with the largest sum

6. *Which row has the largest sum?* Use variables maxRow and indexOfMaxRow to track the largest sum and index of the row. For each row, compute its sum and update maxRow and indexOfMaxRow if the new sum is greater.

```java
int maxRow = 0;
int indexOfMaxRow = 0;

// Get sum of the first row in maxRow
for (int column = 0; column < matrix[0].length; column++) {
  maxRow += matrix[0][column];
}
```

```
for (int row = 1; row < matrix.length; row++) {
  int totalOfThisRow = 0;
  for (int column = 0; column < matrix[row].length; column++)
    totalOfThisRow += matrix[row][column];

  if (totalOfThisRow > maxRow) {
    maxRow = totalOfThisRow;
    indexOfMaxRow = row;
  }
}

System.out.println("Row " + indexOfMaxRow
  + " has the maximum sum of " + maxRow);
```

7. *Random shuffling.* Shuffling the elements in a one-dimensional array was introduced in Section 7.2. How do you shuffle all the elements in a two-dimensional array? To accomplish this, for each element `matrix[i][j]`, randomly generate indices `i1` and `j1` and swap `matrix[i][j]` with `matrix[i1][j1]`, as follows:

```
for (int i = 0; i < matrix.length; i++) {
  for (int j = 0; j < matrix[i].length; j++) {
    int i1 = (int)(Math.random() * matrix.length);
    int j1 = (int)(Math.random() * matrix[i].length);

    // Swap matrix[i][j] with matrix[i1][j1]
    int temp = matrix[i][j];
    matrix[i][j] = matrix[i1][j1];
    matrix[i1][j1] = temp;
  }
}
```

✓ SECTION G.3 ASSESSMENT

1. Show the output of the following code:

```
int[][] array = {{1, 2}, {3, 4}, {5, 6}};
for (int i = array.length - 1; i >= 0; i--) {
  for (int j = array[i].length - 1; j >= 0; j--)
    System.out.print(array[i][j] + " ");
  System.out.println();
}
```

2. Show the output of the following code:

```
int[][] array = {{1, 2}, {3, 4}, {5, 6}};
int sum = 0;
for (int i = 0; i < array.length; i++)
  sum += array[i][0];
System.out.println(sum);
```

G.4 Passing Two-Dimensional Arrays to Methods

Key Point *When passing a two-dimensional array to a method, the reference of the array is passed to the method.*

You can pass a two-dimensional array to a method just as you pass a one-dimensional array. You can also return an array from a method. Listing G.1 gives an example with two methods. The first method, `getArray()`, returns a two-dimensional array, and the second method, `sum(int[][] m)`, returns the sum of all the elements in a matrix.

LISTING G.1 PassTwoDimensionalArray.java

```
 1  import java.util.Scanner;
 2
 3  public class PassTwoDimensionalArray {
 4    public static void main(String[] args) {
 5      int[][] m = getArray(); // Get an array
 6
 7      // Display sum of elements
 8      System.out.println("\nSum of all elements is " + sum(m));
 9    }
10
11    public static int[][] getArray() {
12      // Create a Scanner
13      Scanner input = new Scanner(System.in);
14
15      // Enter array values
16      int[][] m = new int[3][4];
17      System.out.println("Enter " + m.length + " rows and "
18        + m[0].length + " columns: ");
19      for (int i = 0; i < m.length; i++)
20        for (int j = 0; j < m[i].length; j++)
21          m[i][j] = input.nextInt();
22
23      return m;
24    }
25
26    public static int sum(int[][] m) {
27      int total = 0;
28      for (int row = 0; row < m.length; row++) {
29        for (int column = 0; column < m[row].length; column++) {
30          total += m[row][column];
31        }
32      }
33
34      return total;
35    }
36  }
```

get array

pass array

getArray method

return array

sum method

```
Enter 3 rows and 4 columns:
1 2 3 4  ↵Enter
5 6 7 8  ↵Enter
9 10 11 12  ↵Enter

Sum of all elements is 78
```

The method `getArray` prompts the user to enter values for the array (lines 11–24) and returns the array (line 23).

The method `sum` (lines 26–35) has a two-dimensional array argument. You can obtain the number of rows using `m.length` (line 28) and the number of columns in a specified row using `m[row].length` (line 29).

✓ SECTION G.4 ASSESSMENT

1. Show the output of the following code:

```java
public class Test {
  public static void main(String[] args) {
    int[][] array = {{1, 2, 3, 4}, {5, 6, 7, 8}};
    System.out.println(m1(array)[0]);
    System.out.println(m1(array)[1]);
  }

  public static int[] m1(int[][] m) {
    int[] result = new int[2];
    result[0] = m.length;
    result[1] = m[0].length;
    return result;
  }
}
```

G.5 Case Study: Grading a Multiple-Choice Test

Key Point

The problem is to write a program that will grade multiple-choice tests.

Suppose you need to write a program that grades multiple-choice tests. Assume there are eight students and ten questions, and the answers are stored in a two-dimensional array. Each row records a student's answers to the questions, as shown in the following array.

Grade multiple-choice test

Students' Answers to the Questions:

```
          0 1 2 3 4 5 6 7 8 9
Student 0  A B A C C D E E A D
Student 1  D B A B C A E E A D
Student 2  E D D A C B E E A D
Student 3  C B A E D C E E A D
Student 4  A B D C C D E E A D
Student 5  B B E C C D E E A D
Student 6  B B A C C D E E A D
Student 7  E B E C C D E E A D
```

The key is stored in a one-dimensional array:

Key to the Questions:

```
      0 1 2 3 4 5 6 7 8 9
Key   D B D C C D A E A D
```

Your program grades the test and displays the result. It compares each student's answers with the key, counts the number of correct answers, and displays it. Listing G.2 gives the program.

LISTING G.2 GradeExam.java

```
 1  public class GradeExam {
 2    /** Main method */
 3    public static void main(String[] args) {
 4      // Students' answers to the questions
 5      char[][] answers = {
 6        {'A', 'B', 'A', 'C', 'C', 'D', 'E', 'E', 'A', 'D'},
 7        {'D', 'B', 'A', 'B', 'C', 'A', 'E', 'E', 'A', 'D'},
 8        {'E', 'D', 'D', 'A', 'C', 'B', 'E', 'E', 'A', 'D'},
 9        {'C', 'B', 'A', 'E', 'D', 'C', 'E', 'E', 'A', 'D'},
10        {'A', 'B', 'D', 'C', 'C', 'D', 'E', 'E', 'A', 'D'},
11        {'B', 'B', 'E', 'C', 'C', 'D', 'E', 'E', 'A', 'D'},
12        {'B', 'B', 'A', 'C', 'C', 'D', 'E', 'E', 'A', 'D'},
13        {'E', 'B', 'E', 'C', 'C', 'D', 'E', 'E', 'A', 'D'}};
14
15      // Key to the questions
16      char[] keys = {'D', 'B', 'D', 'C', 'C', 'D', 'A', 'E', 'A', 'D'};
17
18      // Grade all answers
19      for (int i = 0; i < answers.length; i++) {
20        // Grade one student
21        int correctCount = 0;
22        for (int j = 0; j < answers[i].length; j++) {
23          if (answers[i][j] == keys[j])
24            correctCount++;
25        }
26
27        System.out.println("Student " + i + "'s correct count is " +
28          correctCount);
29      }
30    }
31  }
```

2-D array (line 5)

1-D array (line 16)

compare with key (line 23)

```
Student 0's correct count is 7
Student 1's correct count is 6
Student 2's correct count is 5
Student 3's correct count is 4
Student 4's correct count is 8
Student 5's correct count is 7
Student 6's correct count is 7
Student 7's correct count is 7
```

The statement in lines 5–13 declares, creates, and initializes a two-dimensional array of characters and assigns the reference to answers of the char[][] type.

The statement in line 16 declares, creates, and initializes an array of char values and assigns the reference to keys of the char[] type.

Each row in the array answers stores a student's answer, which is graded by comparing it with the key in the array keys. The result is displayed immediately after a student's answer is graded.

G.6 Case Study: Finding the Closest Pair

This section presents a geometric problem for finding the closest pair of points.

Key Point

Given a set of points, the closest-pair problem is to find the two points that are nearest to each other. In Figure G.3, for example, points (1, 1) and (2, 0.5) are closest to each other. There are several ways to solve this problem. An intuitive approach is to compute the distances between all pairs of points and find the one with the minimum distance, as implemented in Listing G.3.

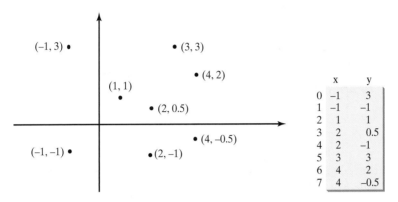

FIGURE G.3 Points can be represented in a two-dimensional array.

LISTING G.3 FindNearestPoints.java

```
1  import java.util.Scanner;
2
3  public class FindNearestPoints {
4    public static void main(String[] args) {
5      Scanner input = new Scanner(System.in);
6      System.out.print("Enter the number of points: ");
7      int numberOfPoints = input.nextInt();
8
9      // Create an array to store points
10     double[][] points = new double[numberOfPoints][2];
11     System.out.print("Enter " + numberOfPoints + " points: ");
12     for (int i = 0; i < points.length; i++) {
13       points[i][0] = input.nextDouble();
14       points[i][1] = input.nextDouble();
15     }
16
17     // p1 and p2 are the indices in the points' array
18     int p1 = 0, p2 = 1; // Initial two points
19     double shortestDistance = distance(points[p1][0], points[p1][1],
20       points[p2][0], points[p2][1]); // Initialize shortestDistance
21
22     // Compute distance for every two points
23     for (int i = 0; i < points.length; i++) {
24       for (int j = i + 1; j < points.length; j++) {
25         double distance = distance(points[i][0], points[i][1],
26           points[j][0], points[j][1]); // Find distance
27
```

number of points

2-D array

read points

track two points
track shortestDistance

for each point i
for each point j
distance between i and j
distance between two points

update shortestDistance

```
28              if (shortestDistance > distance) {
29                p1 = i; // Update p1
30                p2 = j; // Update p2
31                shortestDistance = distance; // Update shortestDistance
32              }
33            }
34          }
35
36        // Display result
37        System.out.println("The closest two points are " +
38          "(" + points[p1][0] + ", " + points[p1][1] + ") and (" +
39          points[p2][0] + ", " + points[p2][1] + ")");
40      }
41
42      /** Compute the distance between two points (x1, y1) and (x2, y2)*/
43      public static double distance(
44          double x1, double y1, double x2, double y2) {
45        return Math.sqrt((x2 - x1) * (x2 - x1) + (y2 - y1) * (y2 - y1));
46      }
47    }
```

```
Enter the number of points: 8  ⏎Enter
Enter 8 points: -1 3  -1 -1  1 1  2 0.5  2 -1  3 3  4 2 4 -0.5  ⏎Enter
The closest two points are (1, 1) and (2, 0.5)
```

The program prompts the user to enter the number of points (lines 6–7). The points are read from the console and stored in a two-dimensional array named `points` (lines 12–15). The program uses the variable `shortestDistance` (line 19) to store the distance between the two nearest points, and the indices of these two points in the `points` array are stored in `p1` and `p2` (line 18).

For each point at index `i`, the program computes the distance between `points[i]` and `points[j]` for all `j > i` (lines 23–34). Whenever a shorter distance is found, the variable `shortestDistance` and `p1` and `p2` are updated (lines 28–32).

The distance between two points `(x1, y1)` and `(x2, y2)` can be computed using the formula $\sqrt{(x_2 - x_1)^2 + (y_2 - y_1)^2}$ (lines 43–46).

The program assumes that the plane has at least two points. You can easily modify the program to handle the case if the plane has zero or one point.

multiple closest pairs

Note that there might be more than one closest pair of points with the same minimum distance. The program finds one such pair. You may modify the program to find all closest pairs in Programming Exercise G.8.

Tip

input file

It is cumbersome to enter all points from the keyboard. You may store the input in a file, say **FindNearestPoints.txt**, and compile and run the program using the following command:

```
java FindNearestPoints < FindNearestPoints.txt
```

G.7 Case Study: Sudoku

The problem is to check whether a given Sudoku solution is correct.

This section presents an interesting problem of a sort that appears in the news-paper every day. It is a number-placement puzzle, commonly known as *Sudoku*. This is a very challenging problem. To make it accessible to the novice, this section presents a simplified version of the Sudoku problem, which is to verify whether a Sudoku solution is correct.

Sudoku is a grid divided into smaller boxes (also called *regions* or *blocks*), as shown in Figure G.4a. Some cells, called *fixed cells*, are populated with numbers from 1 to 9. The objective is to fill the empty cells, also called *free cells*, with the numbers 1 to 9 so that every row, every column, and every box contains the numbers 1 to 9, as shown in Figure G.4b.

Sudoku

fixed cells

free cells

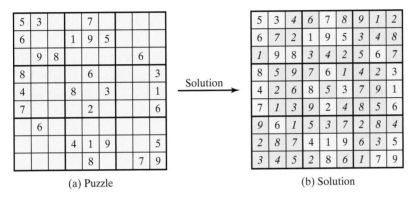

(a) Puzzle Solution → (b) Solution

FIGURE G.4 The Sudoku puzzle in (a) is solved in (b).

For convenience, we use value 0 to indicate a free cell, as shown in Figure G.5a. The grid can be naturally represented using a two-dimensional array, as shown in Figure G.5b.

representing a grid

5	3	0	0	7	0	0	0	0
6	0	0	1	9	5	0	0	0
0	9	8	0	0	0	0	6	0
8	0	0	0	6	0	0	0	3
4	0	0	8	0	3	0	0	1
7	0	0	0	2	0	0	0	6
0	6	0	0	0	0	0	0	0
0	0	0	4	1	9	0	0	5
0	0	0	0	8	0	0	7	9

```
int[][] grid =
  {{5, 3, 0, 0, 7, 0, 0, 0, 0},
   {6, 0, 0, 1, 9, 5, 0, 0, 0},
   {0, 9, 8, 0, 0, 0, 0, 6, 0},
   {8, 0, 0, 0, 6, 0, 0, 0, 3},
   {4, 0, 0, 8, 0, 3, 0, 0, 1},
   {7, 0, 0, 0, 2, 0, 0, 0, 6},
   {0, 6, 0, 0, 0, 0, 2, 8, 0},
   {0, 0, 0, 4, 1, 9, 0, 0, 5},
   {0, 0, 0, 0, 8, 0, 0, 7, 9}
  };
```

(a) (b)

FIGURE G.5 A grid can be represented using a two-dimensional array.

To find a solution for the puzzle, we must replace each 0 in the grid with an appropriate number from 1 to 9. For the solution to the puzzle in Figure G.5, the grid should be as shown in Figure G.6.

```
A solution grid is
  {{5, 3, 4, 6, 7, 8, 9, 1, 2},
   {6, 7, 2, 1, 9, 5, 3, 4, 8},
   {1, 9, 8, 3, 4, 2, 5, 6, 7},
   {8, 5, 9, 7, 6, 1, 4, 2, 3},
   {4, 2, 6, 8, 5, 3, 7, 9, 1},
   {7, 1, 3, 9, 2, 4, 8, 5, 6},
   {9, 6, 1, 5, 3, 7, 2, 8, 4},
   {2, 8, 7, 4, 1, 9, 6, 3, 5},
   {3, 4, 5, 2, 8, 6, 1, 7, 9}
  };
```

FIGURE G.6 A solution is stored in `grid`.

Once a solution to a Sudoku puzzle is found, how do you verify that it is correct? Here are two approaches:

- Check if every row has numbers from 1 to 9, every column has numbers from 1 to 9, and every small box has numbers from 1 to 9.

- Check each cell. Each cell must be a number from 1 to 9 and the cell must be unique on every row, every column, and every small box.

The program in Listing G.4 prompts the user to enter a solution and reports whether it is valid. We use the second approach in the program to check whether the solution is correct.

LISTING G.4 CheckSudokuSolution.java

```java
 1  import java.util.Scanner;
 2
 3  public class CheckSudokuSolution {
 4    public static void main(String[] args) {
 5      // Read a Sudoku solution
 6      int[][] grid = readASolution();
 7
 8      System.out.println(isValid(grid) ? "Valid solution" :
 9        "Invalid solution");
10    }
11
12    /** Read a Sudoku solution from the console */
13    public static int[][] readASolution() {
14      // Create a Scanner
15      Scanner input = new Scanner(System.in);
16
17      System.out.println("Enter a Sudoku puzzle solution:");
18      int[][] grid = new int[9][9];
19      for (int i = 0; i < 9; i++)
20        for (int j = 0; j < 9; j++)
21          grid[i][j] = input.nextInt();
22
```

read input

solution valid?

read solution

```
23      return grid;
24    }
25
26    /** Check whether a solution is valid */
27    public static boolean isValid(int[][] grid) {
28      for (int i = 0; i < 9; i++)
29        for (int j = 0; j < 9; j++)
30          if (grid[i][j] < 1 || grid[i][j] > 9
31              || !isValid(i, j, grid))
32            return false;
33      return true; // The solution is valid
34    }
35
36    /** Check whether grid[i][j] is valid in the grid */
37    public static boolean isValid(int i, int j, int[][] grid) {
38      // Check whether grid[i][j] is unique in i's row
39      for (int column = 0; column < 9; column++)
40        if (column != j && grid[i][column] == grid[i][j])
41          return false;
42
43      // Check whether grid[i][j] is unique in j's column
44      for (int row = 0; row < 9; row++)
45        if (row != i && grid[row][j] == grid[i][j])
46          return false;
47
48      // Check whether grid[i][j] is unique in the 3-by-3 box
49      for (int row = (i / 3) * 3; row < (i / 3) * 3 + 3; row++)
50        for (int col = (j / 3) * 3; col < (j / 3) * 3 + 3; col++)
51          if (row != i && col != j && grid[row][col] == grid[i][j])
52            return false;
53
54      return true; // The current value at grid[i][j] is valid
55    }
56  }
```

check solution

check rows

check columns

check small boxes

```
Enter a Sudoku puzzle solution:
9 6 3 1 7 4 2 5 8  ↵Enter
1 7 8 3 2 5 6 4 9  ↵Enter
2 5 4 6 8 9 7 3 1  ↵Enter
8 2 1 4 3 7 5 9 6  ↵Enter
4 9 6 8 5 2 3 1 7  ↵Enter
7 3 5 9 6 1 8 2 4  ↵Enter
5 8 9 7 1 3 4 6 2  ↵Enter
3 1 7 2 4 6 9 8 5  ↵Enter
6 4 2 5 9 8 1 7 3  ↵Enter
Valid solution
```

The program invokes the `readASolution()` method (line 6) to read a Sudoku solution and return a two-dimensional array representing a Sudoku grid.

The `isValid(grid)` method checks whether the values in the grid are valid by verifying that each value is between 1 and 9 and that each value is valid in the grid (lines 27–34).

isValid method

isValid method

The `isValid(i, j, grid)` method checks whether the value at `grid[i][j]` is valid. It checks whether `grid[i][j]` appears more than once in row `i` (lines 39–41), in column `j` (lines 44–46), and in the 3 × 3 box (lines 49–52).

How do you locate all the cells in the same box? For any `grid[i][j]`, the starting cell of the 3 × 3 box that contains it is `grid[(i / 3) * 3][(j / 3) * 3]`, as illustrated in Figure G.7.

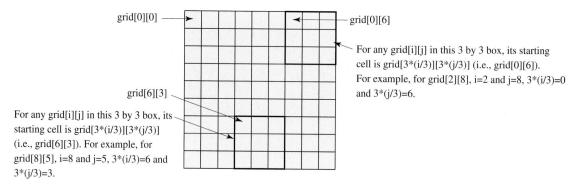

FIGURE G.7 The location of the first cell in a 3 × 3 box determines the locations of other cells in the box.

With this observation, you can easily identify all the cells in the box. For instance, if `grid[r][c]` is the starting cell of a 3 × 3 box, the cells in the box can be traversed in a nested loop as follows:

```
// Get all cells in a 3-by-3 box starting at grid[r][c]
for (int row = r; row < r + 3; row++)
    for (int col = c; col < c + 3; col++)
        // grid[row][col] is in the box
```

input file

It is cumbersome to enter 81 numbers from the console. When you test the program, you may store the input in a file, say **CheckSudokuSolution.txt**, and run the program using the following command:

```
java CheckSudokuSolution < CheckSudokuSolution.txt
```

G.8 Multidimensional Arrays

Key Point

A two-dimensional array consists of an array of one-dimensional arrays and a three-dimensional array consists of an array of two-dimensional arrays.

In the preceding section, you used a two-dimensional array to represent a matrix or a table. Occasionally, you will need to represent *n*-dimensional data structures. In Java, you can create *n*-dimensional arrays for any integer *n*.

The way to declare two-dimensional array variables and create two-dimensional arrays can be generalized to declare *n*-dimensional array variables and create *n*-dimensional arrays for *n* > = 3 For example, you may use a three-dimensional array to store exam scores for a class of six students with five exams, and each exam has two parts (multiple-choice and essay). The following syntax declares a three-dimensional array variable **scores**, creates an array, and assigns its reference to **scores**.

```
double[][][] scores = new double[6][5][2];
```

You can also use the short-hand notation to create and initialize the array as follows:

```
double[][][] scores = {
  {{7.5, 20.5}, {9.0, 22.5}, {15, 33.5}, {13, 21.5}, {15, 2.5}},
  {{4.5, 21.5}, {9.0, 22.5}, {15, 34.5}, {12, 20.5}, {14, 9.5}},
  {{6.5, 30.5}, {9.4, 10.5}, {11, 33.5}, {11, 23.5}, {10, 2.5}},
  {{6.5, 23.5}, {9.4, 32.5}, {13, 34.5}, {11, 20.5}, {16, 7.5}},
  {{8.5, 26.5}, {9.4, 52.5}, {13, 36.5}, {13, 24.5}, {16, 2.5}},
  {{9.5, 20.5}, {9.4, 42.5}, {13, 31.5}, {12, 20.5}, {16, 6.5}}};
```

`scores[0][1][0]` refers to the multiple-choice score for the first student's second exam, which is `9.0`. `scores[0][1][1]` refers to the essay score for the first student's second exam, which is `22.5`. This is depicted in the following figure:

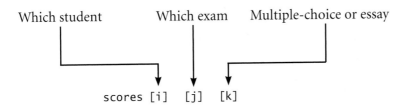

A multidimensional array is actually an array in which each element is another array. A three-dimensional array consists of an array of two-dimensional arrays. A two-dimensional array consists of an array of one-dimensional arrays. For example, suppose `x = new int[2][2][5]`, and `x[0]` and `x[1]` are two-dimensional arrays. `X[0][0]`, `x[0][1]`, `x[1][0]`, and `x[1][1]` are one-dimensional arrays and each contains five elements. `x.length` is 2, `x[0].length` and `x[1].length` are 2, and `X[0][0].length`, `x[0][1].length`, `x[1][0].length`, and `x[1][1].length` are 5.

G.9 Case Study: Guessing Birthdays

You may recall from Chapter 5 that you can find out the date of the month when your friend was born by asking five questions. Each question asks whether the day is in one of the five sets of numbers. Expanding on the Chapter 5 example, Listing G.6 GuessBirthdayUsingArray.java stores the five sets of numbers in a three-dimensional array.

The birthday is the sum of the first numbers in the sets where the day appears. For example, if the birthday is 19, it appears in Set1, Set2, and Set5. The first numbers in these three sets are 1, 2, and 16. Their sum is 19.

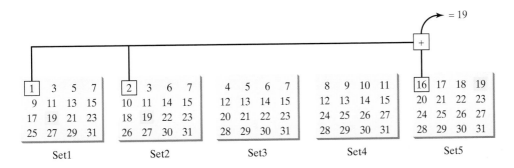

Listing G.6 shows the code, followed by a sample run using the birthday of 19. A **for** loop is used to retrieve the user's five answers. Refer back to Chapter 5 for a discussion on the mathematics behind the game.

LISTING G.6 GuessBirthdayUsingArray.java

three-dimensional array

Set i

add to day

```java
 1  import java.util.Scanner;
 2
 3  public class GuessBirthdayUsingArray {
 4    public static void main(String[] args) {
 5      int day = 0; // Day to be determined
 6      int answer;
 7
 8      int[][][] dates = {
 9        {{ 1,  3,  5,  7},
10         { 9, 11, 13, 15},
11         {17, 19, 21, 23},
12         {25, 27, 29, 31}},
13        {{ 2,  3,  6,  7},
14         {10, 11, 14, 15},
15         {18, 19, 22, 23},
16         {26, 27, 30, 31}},
17        {{ 4,  5,  6,  7},
18         {12, 13, 14, 15},
19         {20, 21, 22, 23},
20         {28, 29, 30, 31}},
21        {{ 8,  9, 10, 11},
22         {12, 13, 14, 15},
23         {24, 25, 26, 27},
24         {28, 29, 30, 31}},
25        {{16, 17, 18, 19},
26         {20, 21, 22, 23},
27         {24, 25, 26, 27},
28         {28, 29, 30, 31}}};
29
30      // Create a Scanner
31      Scanner input = new Scanner(System.in);
32
33      for (int i = 0; i < 5; i++) {
34        System.out.println("Is your birthday in Set" + (i + 1) + "?");
35        for (int j = 0; j < 4; j++) {
36          for (int k = 0; k < 4; k++)
37            System.out.printf("%4d", dates[i][j][k]);
38          System.out.println();
39        }
40
41        System.out.print("\nEnter 0 for No and 1 for Yes: ");
42        answer = input.nextInt();
43
44        if (answer == 1)
45          day += dates[i][0][0];
46      }
47
48      System.out.println("Your birthday is " + day);
49    }
50  }
```

A three-dimensional array **dates** is created in Lines 8–28. This array stores five sets of numbers. Each set is a 4-by-4 two-dimensional array.

The loop starting from line 33 displays the numbers in each set and prompts the user to answer whether the birthday is in the set (lines 41–42). If the day is in the set, the first number (**dates[i][0][0]**) in the set is added to variable **day** (line 45).

Following is a sample run of Listing G.6:

line#	day	answer	output
35	0		
44		1	
47	1		
53		1	
56	3		
62		0	
71		0	
80		1	
83	19		
85			Your birthday is 19!

✓ SECTION G.9 ASSESSMENT

1. Declare an array variable for a three-dimensional array, create a $4 \times 6 \times 5$ **int** array, and assign its reference to the variable.

2. Assume **int[][][] x = new char[12][5][2]**, how many elements are in the array? What are **x.length**, **x[2].length**, and **x[0][0].length**?

3. Show the output of the following code:

```
int[][][] array = {{{1, 2}, {3, 4}}, {{5, 6},{7, 8}}};
System.out.println(array[0][0][0]);
System.out.println(array[1][1][1]);
```

Supplement G — Review and Assessment

CHAPTER SUMMARY

1. A two-dimensional array can be used to store a table.

2. A variable for two-dimensional arrays can be declared using the syntax: `elementType[][] arrayVar`.

3. A two-dimensional array can be created using the syntax: `new elementType[ROW_SIZE][COLUMN_SIZE]`.

4. Each element in a two-dimensional array is represented using the syntax: `arrayVar[rowIndex][columnIndex]`.

5. You can create and initialize a two-dimensional array using an array initializer with the syntax: `elementType[][] arrayVar = {{row values}, . . . , {row values}}`.

6. You can use arrays of arrays to form multidimensional arrays. For example, a variable for three-dimensional arrays can be declared as `elementType[][][] arrayVar`, and a three-dimensional array can be created using `new elementType[size1][size2] [size3]`.

PROGRAMMING EXERCISES

> **Note**
> Exercises preceded by a star (*) are challenging.
> Exercises preceded by two stars (**) are more challenging.
> Exercises preceded by three stars (***) are most challenging.

*1. (*Sum elements column by column*) Write a method that returns the sum of all the elements in a specified column in a matrix using the following header:

```
public static double sumColumn(double[][] m, int columnIndex)
```

Write a test program that reads a 3-by-4 matrix and displays the sum of each column. Here is a sample run:

```
Enter a 3-by-4 matrix row by row:
1.5 2 3 4  ↵Enter
5.5 6 7 8  ↵Enter
9.5 1 3 1  ↵Enter
Sum of the elements at column 0 is 16.5
Sum of the elements at column 1 is 9.0
Sum of the elements at column 2 is 13.0
Sum of the elements at column 3 is 13.0
```

*2. (*Sum the major diagonal in a matrix*) Write a method that sums all the numbers in the major diagonal in an $n \times n$ matrix of `double` values using the following header:

```
public static double sumMajorDiagonal(double[][] m)
```

Write a test program that reads a 4-by-4 matrix and displays the sum of all its elements on the major diagonal. Here is a sample run:

```
Enter a 4-by-4 matrix row by row:
1 2 3 4.0  ↵Enter
5 6.5 7 8  ↵Enter
9 10 11 12  ↵Enter
13 14 15 16  ↵Enter
Sum of the elements in the major diagonal is 34.5
```

*3. (*Sort students on grades*) Rewrite Listing G.2, GradeExam.java, to display the students in increasing order of the number of correct answers.

**4. (*Compute the weekly hours for each employee*) Suppose the weekly hours for all employees are stored in a two-dimensional array. Each row records an employee's seven-day work hours with seven columns. For example, the following array stores the work hours for eight employees. Write a program that displays employees and their total hours in decreasing order of the total hours.

	Su	M	T	W	Th	F	Sa
Employee 0	2	4	3	4	5	8	8
Employee 1	7	3	4	3	3	4	4
Employee 2	3	3	4	3	3	2	2
Employee 3	9	3	4	7	3	4	1
Employee 4	3	5	4	3	6	3	8
Employee 5	3	4	4	6	3	4	4
Employee 6	3	7	4	8	3	8	4
Employee 7	6	3	5	9	2	7	9

5. (*Algebra: add two matrices*) Write a method to add two matrices. The header of the method is as follows:

```
public static double[][] addMatrix(double[][] a, double[][] b)
```

In order to be added, the two matrices must have the same dimensions and the same or compatible types of elements. Let c be the resulting matrix. Each element c_{ij} is $a_{ij} + b_{ij}$. For example, for two 3×3 matrices a and b, c is

$$\begin{pmatrix} a_{11} & a_{12} & a_{13} \\ a_{21} & a_{22} & a_{23} \\ a_{31} & a_{32} & a_{33} \end{pmatrix} + \begin{pmatrix} b_{11} & b_{12} & b_{13} \\ b_{21} & b_{22} & b_{23} \\ b_{31} & b_{32} & b_{33} \end{pmatrix} = \begin{pmatrix} a_{11}+b_{11} & a_{12}+b_{12} & a_{13}+b_{13} \\ a_{21}+b_{21} & a_{22}+b_{22} & a_{23}+b_{23} \\ a_{31}+b_{31} & a_{32}+b_{32} & a_{33}+b_{33} \end{pmatrix}$$

Write a test program that prompts the user to enter two 3×3 matrices and displays their sum. Here is a sample run:

```
Enter matrix1: 1 2 3 4 5 6 7 8 9 ↵Enter
Enter matrix2: 0 2 4 1 4.5 2.2 1.1 4.3 5.2 ↵Enter
The matrices are added as follows
1.0 2.0 3.0     0.0 2.0 4.0     1.0 4.0 7.0
4.0 5.0 6.0  +  1.0 4.5 2.2  =  5.0 9.5 8.2
7.0 8.0 9.0     1.1 4.3 5.2     8.1 12.3 14.2
```

**6. (*Algebra: multiply two matrices*) Write a method to multiply two matrices. The header of the method is:

```
public static double[][]
    multiplyMatrix(double[][] a, double[][] b)
```

To multiply matrix a by matrix b, the number of columns in a must be the same as the number of rows in b, and the two matrices must have elements of the same or compatible types. Let c be the result of the multiplication. Assume the column size of matrix a is n. Each element c_{ij} is $a_{i1} \times b_{1j} + a_{i2} \times b_{2j} + \ldots + a_{in} \times b_{nj}$. For example, for two 3×3 matrices a and b, c is

$$\begin{pmatrix} a_{11} & a_{12} & a_{13} \\ a_{21} & a_{22} & a_{23} \\ a_{31} & a_{32} & a_{33} \end{pmatrix} \times \begin{pmatrix} b_{11} & b_{12} & b_{13} \\ b_{21} & b_{22} & b_{23} \\ b_{31} & b_{32} & b_{33} \end{pmatrix} = \begin{pmatrix} c_{11} & c_{12} & c_{13} \\ c_{21} & c_{22} & c_{23} \\ c_{31} & c_{32} & c_{33} \end{pmatrix}$$

where $c_{ij} = a_{i1} \times b_{1j} + a_{i2} \times b_{2j} + a_{i3} \times b_{3j}$

Write a test program that prompts the user to enter two 3×3 matrices and displays their product. Here is a sample run:

```
Enter matrix1: 1 2 3 4 5 6 7 8 9 ↵Enter
Enter matrix2: 0 2 4 1 4.5 2.2 1.1 4.3 5.2 ↵Enter
The multiplication of the matrices is
  1 2 3       0 2.0 4.0      5.3 23.9 24
  4 5 6   *   1 4.5 2.2  =   11.6 56.3 58.2
  7 8 9       1.1 4.3 5.2    17.9 88.7 92.4
```

*7. (*Points nearest to each other*) Listing G.3 gives a program that finds
 two points in a two-dimensional space nearest to each other. Revise
 the program so that it finds two points in a three-dimensional space
 nearest to each other. Use a two-dimensional array to represent the
 points. Test the program using the following points:

```
double[][] points = {{-1, 0, 3}, {-1, -1, -1}, {4, 1, 1},
   {2, 0.5, 9}, {3.5, 2, -1}, {3, 1.5, 3}, {-1.5, 4, 2},
   {5.5, 4, -0.5}};
```

 The formula for computing the distance between two points (x1, y1,
 z1) and (x2, y2, z2) is $\sqrt{(x_2 - x_1)^2 + (y_2 - y_1)^2 + (z_2 - z_1)^2}$.

**8. (*All closest pairs of points*) Revise Listing G.3, FindNearestPoints.
 java, to display all closest pairs of points with the same mini-
 mum distance. Here is a sample run:

```
Enter the number of points: 8 ↵Enter
Enter 8 points: 0 0 1 1 -1 -1 2 2 -2 -2 -3 -3 -4 -4 5 5
↵Enter
The closest two points are (0.0, 0.0) and (1.0, 1.0)
The closest two points are (0.0, 0.0) and (-1.0, -1.0)
The closest two points are (1.0, 1.0) and (2.0, 2.0)
The closest two points are (-1.0, -1.0) and (-2.0, -2.0)
The closest two points are (-2.0, -2.0) and (-3.0, -3.0)
The closest two points are (-3.0, -3.0) and (-4.0, -4.0)
Their distance is 1.4142135623730951
```

***9. (*Game: play a tic-tac-toe game*) In a game of tic-tac-toe, two players
 take turns marking an available cell in a 3 × 3 grid with their respec-
 tive tokens (either X or O). When one player has placed three tokens
 in a horizontal, vertical, or diagonal row on the grid, the game is over
 and that player has won. A draw (no winner) occurs when all the
 cells on the grid have been filled with tokens and neither player has
 achieved a win. Create a program for playing tic-tac-toe.

 The program prompts two players to enter an X token and O token
 alternately. Whenever a token is entered, the program redisplays
 the board on the console and determines the status of the game
 (win, draw, or continue). Here is a sample run:

```
------------------
|   |   |   |   |
------------------
|   |   |   |   |
------------------
|   |   |   |   |
------------------
Enter a row (0, 1, or 2) for player X: 1 ↵Enter
Enter a column (0, 1, or 2) for player X: 1 ↵Enter

------------------
|   |   |   |   |
------------------
|   | X |   |   |
------------------
|   |   |   |   |
------------------
Enter a row (0, 1, or 2) for player O: 1 ↵Enter
Enter a column (0, 1, or 2) for player O: 2 ↵Enter

------------------
|   |   |   |   |
------------------
|   | X | O |   |
------------------
|   |   |   |   |
------------------
Enter a row (0, 1, or 2) for player X:

      . . .

------------------
| X |   |   |   |
------------------
| O | X | O |   |
------------------
|   |   | X |   |
------------------
X player won
```

*10. (*Largest row and column*) Write a program that randomly fills in 0s and 1s into a 4-by-4 matrix, prints the matrix, and finds the first row and column with the most 1s. Here is a sample run of the program:

```
0011
0011
1101
1010
The largest row index: 2
The largest column index: 2
```

**11. (*Game: nine heads and tails*) Nine coins are placed in a 3-by-3 matrix with some face up and some face down. You can represent the state of the coins using a 3-by-3 matrix with values 0 (heads) and 1 (tails).

Here are some examples:

```
0 0 0     1 0 1     1 1 0     1 0 1     1 0 0
0 1 0     0 0 1     1 0 0     1 1 0     1 1 1
0 0 0     1 0 0     0 0 1     1 0 0     1 1 0
```

Each state can also be represented using a binary number. For example, the preceding matrices correspond to the numbers

000010000 101001100 110100001 101110100 100111110

There are a total of 512 possibilities, so you can use decimal numbers 0, 1, 2, 3, . . . , and 511 to represent all states of the matrix. Write a program that prompts the user to enter a number between 0 and 511 and displays the corresponding matrix with the characters H and T. Here is a sample run:

```
Enter a number between 0 and 511: 7  ↵Enter
H H H
H H H
T T T
```

The user entered 7, which corresponds to 000000111. Since 0 stands for H and 1 for T, the output is correct.

*12. (*Locate the largest element*) Write the following method that returns the location of the largest element in a two-dimensional array.

```
public static int[] locateLargest(double[][] a)
```

The return value is a one-dimensional array that contains two elements. These two elements indicate the row and column indices of the largest element in the two-dimensional array. Write a test program that prompts the user to enter a two-dimensional array and displays the location of the largest element in the array. Here is a sample run:

```
Enter the number of rows and columns of the array: 3 4  ↵Enter
Enter the array:
23.5 35 2 10  ↵Enter
4.5 3 45 3.5  ↵Enter
35 44 5.5 9.6  ↵Enter
The location of the largest element is at (1, 2)
```

**13. (*Explore matrix*) Write a program that prompts the user to enter the length of a square matrix, randomly fills in 0s and 1s into the matrix, prints the matrix, and finds the rows, columns, and diagonals with all 0s or 1s. Here is a sample run of the program:

```
Enter the size for the matrix: 4  ↵Enter
0111
0000
0100
1111
All 0s on row 1
All 1s on row 3
No same numbers on a column
No same numbers on the major diagonal
No same numbers on the sub-diagonal
```

*14. (*Sort two-dimensional array*) Write a method to sort a two-dimensional array using the following header:

public static void sort(**int** m[][])

The method performs a primary sort on rows and a secondary sort on columns. For example, the following array

{{4, 2},{1, 7},{4, 5},{1, 2},{1, 1},{4, 1}}

will be sorted to

{{1, 1},{1, 2},{1, 7},{4, 1},{4, 2},{4, 5}}.

*15. (*Shuffle rows*) Write a method that shuffles the rows in a two-dimensional **int** array using the following header:

public static void shuffle(**int**[][] m)

Write a test program that shuffles the following matrix:

int[][] m = {{1, 2}, {3, 4}, {5, 6}, {7, 8}, {9, 10}};

*16. (*Central city*) Given a set of cities, the central city is the city that has the shortest total distance to all other cities. Write a program that prompts the user to enter the number of the cities and the locations of the cities (coordinates), and finds the central city and its total distance to all other cities. Here is a sample run:

```
Enter the number of cities: 5  ↵Enter
Enter the coordinates of the cities:
  2.5 5 5.1 3 1 9 5.4 54 5.5 2.1  ↵Enter
The central city is at (2.5, 5.0)
The total distance to all other cities is 60.81
```

*17. (*Even number of 1s*) Write a program that generates a 6-by-6 two-dimensional matrix filled with 0s and 1s, displays the matrix, and checks if every row and every column have an even number of 1s.

*18. (*Game: find the flipped cell*) Suppose you are given a 6-by-6 matrix filled with 0s and 1s. All rows and all columns have an even number of 1s. Let the user flip one cell (i.e., flip from 1 to 0 or from 0 to 1) and write a program to find which cell was flipped. Your program should prompt the user to enter a 6-by-6 array with 0s and 1s and find the first row *r* and first column *c* where the even number of the 1s property is violated (i.e., the number of 1s is not even). The flipped cell is at (*r*, *c*). Here is a sample run:

```
Enter a 6-by-6 matrix row by row:
1 1 1 0 1 1  ↵Enter
1 1 1 1 0 0  ↵Enter
0 1 0 1 1 1  ↵Enter
1 1 1 1 1 1  ↵Enter
0 1 1 1 1 0  ↵Enter
1 0 0 0 0 1  ↵Enter
The flipped cell is at (0, 1)
```

*19. (*Check Sudoku solution*) Listing G.4 checks whether a solution is valid by checking whether every number is valid in the board. Rewrite the program by checking whether every row, every column, and every small box has the numbers 1 to 9.

*20. (*Markov matrix*) An $n \times n$ matrix is called a *positive Markov matrix* if each element is positive and the sum of the elements in each column is 1. Write the following method to check whether a matrix is a Markov matrix.

```
public static boolean isMarkovMatrix(double[][] m)
```

Write a test program that prompts the user to enter a 3×3 matrix of double values and tests whether it is a Markov matrix. Here are the sample runs:

```
Enter a 3-by-3 matrix row by row:
0.15 0.875 0.375  ↵Enter
0.55 0.005 0.225  ↵Enter
0.30 0.12 0.4  ↵Enter
It is a Markov matrix
```

```
Enter a 3-by-3 matrix row by row:
0.95 -0.875 0.375  ↵Enter
0.65 0.005 0.225  ↵Enter
0.30 0.22 -0.4  ↵Enter
It is not a Markov matrix
```

*21. (*Row sorting*) Implement the following method to sort the rows in a two-dimensional array. A new array is returned and the original array is intact.

```
public static double[][] sortRows(double[][] m)
```

Write a test program that prompts the user to enter a 3 × 3 matrix of double values and displays a new row-sorted matrix. Here is a sample run:

```
Enter a 3-by-3 matrix row by row:
0.15 0.875 0.375  ⏎Enter
0.55 0.005 0.225  ⏎Enter
0.30 0.12 0.4  ⏎Enter

The row-sorted array is
0.15 0.375 0.875
0.005 0.225 0.55
0.12 0.30 0.4
```

*22. (*Column sorting*) Implement the following method to sort the columns in a two-dimensional array. A new array is returned and the original array is intact.

```
public static double[][] sortColumns(double[][] m)
```

Write a test program that prompts the user to enter a 3 × 3 matrix of double values and displays a new column-sorted matrix. Here is a sample run:

```
Enter a 3-by-3 matrix row by row:
0.15 0.875 0.375  ⏎Enter
0.55 0.005 0.225  ⏎Enter
0.30 0.12 0.4  ⏎Enter

The column-sorted array is
0.15 0.0050 0.225
0.3  0.12   0.375
0.55 0.875  0.4
```

23. (*Strictly identical arrays*) The two-dimensional arrays m1 and m2 are *strictly identical* if their corresponding elements are equal. Write a method that returns true if m1 and m2 are strictly identical, using the following header:

```
public static boolean equals(int[][] m1, int[][] m2)
```

Write a test program that prompts the user to enter two 3×3 arrays of integers and displays whether the two are strictly identical. Here are the sample runs:

```
Enter list1: 51 22 25 6 1 4 24 54 6  ↵Enter
Enter list2: 51 22 25 6 1 4 24 54 6  ↵Enter
The two arrays are strictly identical
```

```
Enter list1: 51 25 22 6 1 4 24 54 6  ↵Enter
Enter list2: 51 22 25 6 1 4 24 54 6  ↵Enter
The two arrays are not strictly identical
```

24. (*Identical arrays*) The two-dimensional arrays m1 and m2 are *identical* if they have the same contents. Write a method that returns `true` if m1 and m2 are identical, using the following header:

public static boolean equals(**int**[][] m1, **int**[][] m2)

Write a test program that prompts the user to enter two 3 × 3 arrays of integers and displays whether the two are identical. Here are the sample runs:

```
Enter list1: 51 25 22 6 1 4 24 54 6  ↵Enter
Enter list2: 51 22 25 6 1 4 24 54 6  ↵Enter
The two arrays are identical
```

```
Enter list1: 51 5 22 6 1 4 24 54 6  ↵Enter
Enter list2: 51 22 25 6 1 4 24 54 6  ↵Enter
The two arrays are not identical
```

***25.** (*Algebra: solve linear equations*) Write a method that solves the following system of linear equations:

$$a_{00}x + a_{01}y = b_0 \qquad x = \frac{b_0 a_{11} - b_1 a_{01}}{a_{00}a_{11} - a_{01}a_{10}} \qquad y = \frac{b_1 a_{00} - b_0 a_{10}}{a_{00}a_{11} - a_{01}a_{10}}$$
$$a_{10}x + a_{11}y = b_1$$

The method header is

public static double[] linearEquation(**double**[][] a,
double[] b)

The method returns `null` if $a_{00}a_{11} - a_{01}a_{10}$ is 0. Write a test program that prompts the user to enter a_{00}, a_{01}, a_{10}, a_{11}, b_0 and b_1, and displays the result. If $a_{00}a_{11} - a_{01}a_{10}$ is 0, report that "The equation has no solution."

***26.** (*Geometry: area of a triangle*) Write a method that returns the area of a triangle using the following header:

public static double getTriangleArea(**double**[][] points)

The points are stored in a 3-by-2 two-dimensional array `points` with `points[0][0]` and `points[0][1]` for (`x1`, `y1`). The method returns `0` if the three points are on the same line.

The formula for computing the area of a triangle is

$$s = (\text{side1} + \text{side2} + \text{side3})/2;$$

$$\text{area} = \sqrt{s(s - \text{side1})(s - \text{side2})(s - \text{side3})}$$

Write a program that prompts the user to enter three points of a triangle and displays the triangle's area. Here are two sample runs:

```
Enter x1, y1, x2, y2, x3, y3: 2.5 2 5 -1.0 4.0 2.0 ⏎Enter
The area of the triangle is 2.25
```

```
Enter x1, y1, x2, y2, x3, y3: 2 2 4.5 4.5 6 6 ⏎Enter
The three points are on the same line
```

*27. (*Geometry: polygon subareas*) A convex 4-vertex polygon is divided into four triangles, as shown in Figure G.9.

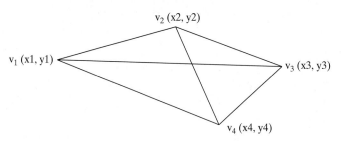

FIGURE G.9 A 4-vertex polygon is defined by four vertices.

Write a program that prompts the user to enter the coordinates of four vertices and displays the areas of the four triangles in increasing order. Here is a sample run:

```
Enter x1, y1, x2, y2, x3, y3, x4, y4:
  -2.5 2 4 4 3 -2 -2 -3.5 ⏎Enter
The areas are 6.17 7.96 8.08 10.42
```

*28. (*Geometry: rightmost lowest point*) In computational geometry, often you need to find the rightmost lowest point in a set of points. Write the following method that returns the rightmost lowest point in a set of points.

```
public static double[]
        getRightmostLowestPoint(double[][] points)
```

Write a test program that prompts the user to enter the coordinates of six points and displays the rightmost lowest point. Here is a sample run:

```
Enter 6 points: 1.5 2.5 -3 4.5 5.6 -7 6.5 -7 8 1 10 2.5 ⏎Enter
The rightmost lowest point is (6.5, -7.0)
```

****29.** (*Guess the capitals*) Write a program that repeatedly prompts the user to enter a capital for a state. Upon receiving the user input, the program reports whether the answer is correct. Assume that **50** states and their capitals are stored in a two-dimensional array, as shown in Figure G.10. The program prompts the user to answer all states' capitals and displays the total correct count. The user's answer is not case-sensitive.

```
Alabama        Montgomery
Alaska         Juneau
Arizona        Phoenix
...            ...
...            ...
```

FIGURE G.10 A two-dimensional array stores states and their capitals.

Here is a sample run:

```
What is the capital of Alabama? Auburn ⏎Enter
The correct answer should be Montgomery
What is the capital of Alaska? Juneau ⏎Enter
Your answer is correct
What is the capital of Arizona? ...
...
The correct count is 35
```

APPENDICES

Appendix A
Java Keywords

Appendix B
The ASCII Character Set

Appendix C
Operator Precedence Chart

Appendix D
Number Systems

Appendix E
Java Quick Reference

Appendix F
Java Modifiers

Appendix G
Special Floating-Point Values

Appendix H
Regular Expressions

Appendix I
Enumerated Types

Appendix J
Bitwise Operators

JAVA KEYWORDS

The following fifty keywords are reserved for use by the Java language:

abstract	double	int	super
assert	else	interface	switch
boolean	enum	long	synchronized
break	extends	native	this
byte	final	new	throw
case	finally	package	throws
catch	float	private	transient
char	for	protected	try
class	goto	public	void
const	if	return	volatile
continue	implements	short	while
default	import	static	
do	instanceof	strictfp*	

The keywords **goto** and **const** are reserved, even though they are not currently used in Java.

The literal values **true**, **false**, and **null** are not keywords, but they are reserved words. In other words, they cannot be used as identifiers in your program.

APPENDIX B

THE ASCII CHARACTER SET

Tables B.1 and B.2 show ASCII characters and their respective decimal and hexadecimal codes. The decimal or hexadecimal code of a character is a combination of its row index and column index. For example, in Table B.1, the letter **A** is at row 6 and column 5, so its decimal equivalent is 65; in Table B.2, letter **A** is at row 4 and column 1, so its hexadecimal equivalent is 41.

TABLE B.1 ASCII Character Set in the Decimal Index

	0	1	2	3	4	5	6	7	8	9
0	nul	soh	stx	etx	eot	enq	ack	bel	bs	ht
1	nl	vt	ff	cr	so	si	dle	dc1	dc2	dc3
2	dc4	nak	syn	etb	can	em	sub	esc	fs	gs
3	rs	us	sp	!	"	#	$	%	&	'
4	(	)	*	+	,	-	.	/	0	1
5	2	3	4	5	6	7	8	9	:	;
6	<	=	>	?	@	A	B	C	D	E
7	F	G	H	I	J	K	L	M	N	O
8	P	Q	R	S	T	U	V	W	X	Y
9	Z	[	\	]	^	_	`	a	b	c
10	d	e	f	g	h	i	j	k	l	m
11	n	o	p	q	r	s	t	u	v	w
12	x	y	z	{	\|	}	~	del		

TABLE B.2 ASCII Character Set in the Hexadecimal Index

	0	1	2	3	4	5	6	7	8	9	A	B	C	D	E	F
0	nul	soh	stx	etx	eot	enq	ack	bel	bs	ht	nl	vt	ff	cr	so	si
1	dle	dc1	dc2	dc3	dc4	nak	syn	etb	can	em	sub	esc	fs	gs	rs	us
2	sp	!	"	#	$	%	&	'	(	)	*	+	,	-	.	/
3	0	1	2	3	4	5	6	7	8	9	:	;	<	=	>	?
4	@	A	B	C	D	E	F	G	H	I	J	K	L	M	N	O
5	P	Q	R	S	T	U	V	W	X	Y	Z	[	\	]	^	_
6	`	a	b	c	d	e	f	g	h	i	j	k	l	m	n	o
7	p	q	r	s	t	u	v	w	x	y	z	{	\|	}	~	del

APPENDIX C

OPERATOR PRECEDENCE CHART

The operators are shown in decreasing order of precedence from top to bottom. Operators in the same group have the same precedence, and their associativity is shown in the table.

Operator	Name	Associativity
()	Parentheses	Left to right
()	Function call	Left to right
[]	Array subscript	Left to right
.	Object member access	Left to right
++	Postincrement	Left to right
--	Postdecrement	Left to right
++	Preincrement	Right to left
--	Predecrement	Right to left
+	Unary plus	Right to left
-	Unary minus	Right to left
!	Unary logical negation	Right to left
(type)	Unary casting	Right to left
new	Creating object	Right to left
*	Multiplication	Left to right
/	Division	Left to right
%	Remainder	Left to right
+	Addition	Left to right
-	Subtraction	Left to right
<<	Left shift	Left to right
>>	Right shift with sign extension	Left to right
>>>	Right shift with zero extension	Left to right
<	Less than	Left to right
<=	Less than or equal to	Left to right
>	Greater than	Left to right
>=	Greater than or equal to	Left to right

Operator	Name	Associativity
instanceof	Checking object type	Left to right
==	Equal comparison	Left to right
!=	Not equal	Left to right
&	(Unconditional AND)	Left to right
^	(Exclusive OR)	Left to right
\|	(Unconditional OR)	Left to right
&&	Conditional AND	Left to right
\|\|	Conditional OR	Left to right
?:	Ternary condition	Right to left
=	Assignment	Right to left
+=	Addition assignment	Right to left
-=	Subtraction assignment	Right to left
*=	Multiplication assignment	Right to left
/=	Division assignment	Right to left
%=	Remainder assignment	Right to left

APPENDIX D

NUMBER SYSTEMS

Introduction

Computers use binary numbers internally, because computers are made naturally to store and process 0s and 1s. The binary number system has two digits, 0 and 1. A number or character is stored as a sequence of 0s and 1s. Each 0 or 1 is called a *bit* (binary digit).

binary numbers

In our daily life we use decimal numbers. When we write a number such as 20 in a program, it is assumed to be a decimal number. Internally, computer software is used to convert decimal numbers into binary numbers, and vice versa.

decimal numbers

We write computer programs using decimal numbers. However, to deal with an operating system, we need to reach down to the "machine level" by using binary numbers. Binary numbers tend to be very long and cumbersome. Often hexadecimal numbers are used to abbreviate them, with each hexadecimal digit representing four binary digits. The hexadecimal number system has 16 digits: 0–9 and A–F. The letters A, B, C, D, E, and F correspond to the decimal numbers 10, 11, 12, 13, 14, and 15.

hexadecimal number

The digits in the decimal number system are 0, 1, 2, 3, 4, 5, 6, 7, 8, and 9. A decimal number is represented by a sequence of one or more of these digits. The value that each digit represents depends on its position, which denotes an integral power of 10. For example, the digits 7, 4, 2, and 3 in decimal number 7423 represent 7000, 400, 20, and 3, respectively, as shown below:

$$\boxed{7 \mid 4 \mid 2 \mid 3} = 7 \times 10^3 + 4 \times 10^2 + 2 \times 10^1 + 3 \times 10^0$$

$$10^3 \ 10^2 \ 10^1 \ 10^0 = 7000 + 400 + 20 + 3 = 7423$$

The decimal number system has ten digits, and the position values are integral powers of 10. We say that 10 is the *base* or *radix* of the decimal number system. Similarly, since the binary number system has two digits, its base is 2, and since the hex number system has 16 digits, its base is 16.

base
radix

If 1101 is a binary number, the digits 1, 1, 0, and 1 represent 1×2^3, 1×2^2, 0×2^1 and 1×2^0 respectively:

$$\boxed{1 \mid 1 \mid 0 \mid 1} = 1 \times 2^3 + 1 \times 2^2 + 0 \times 2^1 + 1 \times 2^0$$

$$2^3 \ 2^2 \ 2^1 \ 2^0 = 8 + 4 + 0 + 1 = 13$$

If 7423 is a hex number, the digits 7, 4, 2, and 3 represent $7 \times 16^3, 4 \times 16^2, 2 \times 16^1$, and 3×16^0 respectively:

$$\boxed{7 \mid 4 \mid 2 \mid 3} = 7 \times 16^3 + 4 \times 16^2 + 2 \times 16^1 + 3 \times 16^0$$

$$16^3 \; 16^2 \; 16^1 \; 16^0 = 28672 + 1024 + 32 + 3 = 29731$$

Conversions Between Binary and Decimal Numbers

binary to decimal

Given a binary number $b_n b_{n-1} b_{n-2} \ldots b_2 b_1 b_0$ the equivalent decimal value is

$$b_n \times 2^n + b_{n-1} \times 2^{n-1} + b_{n-2} \times 2^{n-2} + \; \ldots \; + b_2 \times 2^2 + b_1 \times 2^1 + b_0 \times 2^0$$

Here are some examples of converting binary numbers to decimals:

Binary	Conversion Formula	Decimal
10	$1 \times 2^1 + 0 \times 2^0$	2
1000	$1 \times 2^3 + 0 \times 2^2 + 0 \times 2^1 + 0 \times 2^0$	8
10101011	$1 \times 2^7 + 0 \times 2^6 + 1 \times 2^5 + 0 \times 2^4 + 1 \times 2^3 + 0 \times 2_2 + 1 \times 2^1 + 1 \times 2^0$	171

decimal to binary

To convert a decimal number d to a binary number is to find the bits b_n, b_{n-1}, $b_{n-2}, \ldots, b_2, b_1$ and such that

$$d = b_n \times 2^n + b_{n-1} \times 2^{n-1} + b_{n-2} \times 2^{n-2} + \; \ldots \; + b_2 \times 2^2 + b_1 \times 2^1 + b_0 \times 2^0$$

These bits can be found by successively dividing d by 2 until the quotient is 0. The remainders are $b_0, b_1, b_2, \ldots, b_{n-2}, b_{n-1}$, and b_n

For example, the decimal number 123 is 1111011 in binary. The conversion is done as follows:

Tip
The Windows Calculator, as shown in Figure D.1, is a useful tool for performing number conversions. To run it, search for *Calculator* from the *Start* button and launch Calculator, then under *View* select *Scientific*.

FIGURE D.1 You can perform number conversions using the Windows Calculator.

Conversions Between Hexadecimal and Decimal Numbers

Given a hexadecimal number $h_n h_{n-1} h_{n-2} \ldots h_2 h_1 h_0$, the equivalent decimal value is

hex to decimal

$$h_n \times 16^n + h_{n-1} \times 16^{n-1} + h_{n-2} \times 16^{n-2} + \ldots + h_2 \times 16^2 + h_1 \times 16^1 + h_0 \times 16^0$$

Here are some examples of converting hexadecimal numbers to decimals:

Hexadecimal	Conversion Formula	Decimal
7F	$7 \times 16^1 + 15 \times 16^0$	127
FFFF	$15 \times 16^3 + 15 \times 16^2 + 15 \times 16^1 + 15 \times 16^0$	65535
431	$4 \times 16^2 + 3 \times 16^1 + 1 \times 16^0$	1073

To convert a decimal number d to a hexadecimal number is to find the hexadecimal digits $h_n, h_{n-1}, h_{n-2}, \ldots, h_2, h_1$, and h_0 such that

decimal to hex

$$d = h_n \times 16^n + h_{n-1} \times 16^{n-1} + h_{n-2} \times 16^{n-2} + \ldots + h_2 \times 16^2$$
$$+ h_1 \times 16^1 + h_0 \times 16^0$$

These numbers can be found by successively dividing d by 16 until the quotient is 0. The remainders are $h_0, h_1, h_2, \ldots, h_{n-2}, h_{n-1}$, and h_n

For example, the decimal number 123 is 7B in hexadecimal. The conversion is done as follows:

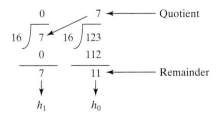

Conversions Between Binary and Hexadecimal Numbers

hex to binary

To convert a hexadecimal to a binary number, simply convert each digit in the hexadecimal number into a four-digit binary number, using Table D.1.

TABLE D.1 Converting Hexadecimal to Binary

Hexadecimal	Binary	Decimal
0	0000	0
1	0001	1
2	0010	2
3	0011	3
4	0100	4
5	0101	5
6	0110	6
7	0111	7
8	1000	8
9	1001	9
A	1010	10
B	1011	11
C	1100	12
D	1101	13
E	1110	14
F	1111	15

For example, the hexadecimal number 7B is 1111011, where 7 is 111 in binary, and B is 1011 in binary.

binary to hex

To convert a binary number to a hexadecimal, convert every four binary digits from right to left in the binary number into a hexadecimal number.

For example, the binary number 1110001101 is 38D, since 1101 is D, 1000 is 8, and 11 is 3, as shown below.

Note
Octal numbers are also useful. The octal number system has eight digits, 0 to 7. A decimal number 8 is represented in the octal system as 10.

Here are some good online resources for practicing number conversions:

- http://forums.cisco.com/CertCom/game/binary_game_page.htm
- http://people.sinclair.edu/nickreeder/Flash/binDec.htm
- http://people.sinclair.edu/nickreeder/Flash/binHex.htm

✓ Appendix D Assessment

1. Convert the following decimal numbers into hexadecimal and binary numbers:

 100; 4340; 2000

2. Convert the following binary numbers into hexadecimal and decimal numbers:

 1000011001; 100000000; 100111

3. Convert the following hexadecimal numbers into binary and decimal numbers:

 FEFA9; 93; 2000

JAVA QUICK REFERENCE

Console Input

```
Scanner input = new Scanner(System.in);
int intValue = input.nextInt();
long longValue = input.nextLong();
double doubleValue = input.nextDouble();
float floatValue = input.nextFloat();
String string = input.next();
String line = input.nextLine();
```

Console Output

```
System.out.println(anyValue);
```

Conditional Expression

```
boolean-expression ? expression1 :
  expression2

y = (x > 0) ? 1 : -1

System.out.println(number % 2 == 0 ?
  "number is even" : "number is odd");
```

Primitive Data Types

byte	8 bits
short	16 bits
int	32 bits
long	64 bits
float	32 bits
double	64 bits
char	16 bits
boolean	true/false

Arithmetic Operators

+	addition
-	subtraction
*	multiplication
/	division
%	remainder
++var	preincrement
--var	predecrement
var++	postincrement
var--	postdecrement

Assignment Operators

=	assignment
+=	addition assignment
-=	subtraction assignment
*=	multiplication assignment
/=	division assignment
%=	remainder assignment

Relational Operators

<	less than
<=	less than or equal to
>	greater than
>=	greater than or equal to
==	equal to
!=	not equal

Logical Operators

&&	short circuit AND
\|\|	short circuit OR
!	NOT
^	exclusive OR

if Statements

```
if (condition) {
  statements;
}

if (condition) {
  statements;
}
else {
  statements;
}

if (condition1) {
  statements;
}
else if (condition2) {
  statements;
}
else {
  statements;
}
```

switch Statements

```
switch (intExpression) {
  case value1:
    statements;
    break;
  ...
  case valuen:
    statements;
    break;
  default:
    statements;
}
```

loop Statements

```
while (condition) {
  statements;
}

do {
  statements;
} while (condition);

for (init; condition;
  adjustment) {
  statements;
}
```

Frequently Used Static Constants/Methods

```
Math.PI
Math.random()
Math.pow(a, b)
Math.abs(a)
Math.max(a, b)
Math.min(a, b)
Math.sqrt(a)
Math.sin(radians)
Math.asin(a)
Math.toRadians(degrees)
Math.toDegress(radians)
System.currentTimeMillis()
Integer.parseInt(string)
Integer.parseInt(string, radix)
Double.parseDouble(string)
Arrays.sort(type[] list)
Arrays.binarySearch(type[] list, type key)
```

Array/Length/Initializer

```
int[] list = new int[10];
list.length;
int[] list = {1, 2, 3, 4};
```

Multidimensional Array/Length/Initializer

```
int[][] list = new int[10][10];
list.length;
list[0].length;
int[][] list = {{1, 2}, {3, 4}};
```

Ragged Array

```
int[][] m = {{1, 2, 3, 4},
             {1, 2, 3},
             {1, 2},
             {1}};
```

Text File Output

```
PrintWriter output =
  new PrintWriter(filename);
output.print(...);
output.println(...);
output.printf(...);
```

Text File Input

```
Scanner input = new Scanner(
  new File(filename));
```

File Class

```
File file =
  new File(filename);
file.exists()
file.renameTo(File)
file.delete()
```

Object Class

```
Object o = new Object();
o.toString();
o.equals(o1);
```

Comparable Interface

```
c.compareTo(Comparable)
c is a Comparable object
```

String Class

```
String s = "Welcome";
String s = new String(char[]);
int length = s.length();
char ch = s.charAt(index);
int d = s.compareTo(s1);
boolean b = s.equals(s1);
boolean b = s.startsWith(s1);
boolean b = s.endsWith(s1);
boolean b = s.contains(s1);
String s1 = s.trim();
String s1 = s.toUpperCase();
String s1 = s.toLowerCase();
int index = s.indexOf(ch);
int index = s.lastIndexOf(ch);
String s1 = s.substring(ch);
String s1 = s.substring(i,j);
char[] chs = s.toCharArray();
boolean b = s.matches(regex);
String s1 = s.replaceAll(regex,repl);
String[] tokens = s.split(regex);
```

ArrayList Class

```
ArrayList<E> list = new ArrayList<>();
list.add(object);
list.add(index, object);
list.clear();
Object o = list.get(index);
boolean b = list.isEmpty();
boolean b = list.contains(object);
int i = list.size();
list.remove(index);
list.set(index, object);
int i = list.indexOf(object);
int i = list.lastIndexOf(object);
```

printf Method

```
System.out.printf("%b %c %d %f %e %s",
  true, 'A', 45, 45.5, 45.5, "Welcome");
System.out.printf("%-5d %10.2f %10.2e %8s",
  45, 45.5, 45.5, "Welcome");
```

APPENDIX F

JAVA MODIFIERS

Modifiers are used on classes and class members (constructors, methods, data, and class-level blocks), but the `final` modifier can also be used on local variables in a method. A modifier that can be applied to a class is called a *class modifier*. A modifier that can be applied to a method is called a *method modifier*. A modifier that can be applied to a data field is called a *data modifier*. A modifier that can be applied to a class-level block is called a *block modifier*. The following table gives a summary of the Java modifiers.

Modifier	Class	Constructor	Method	Data	Block	Explanation
`(default)`*	√	√	√	√	√	A class, constructor, method, or data field is visible in this package.
`public`	√	√	√	√		A class, constructor, method, or data field is visible to all the programs in any package.
`private`		√	√	√		A constructor, method, or data field is only visible in this class.
`protected`		√	√	√		A constructor, method, or data field is visible in this package and in subclasses of this class in any package.
`static`			√	√	√	Define a class method, a class data field, or a static initialization block.
`final`	√		√	√		A final class cannot be extended. A final method cannot be modified in a subclass. A final data field is a constant.
`abstract`	√		√			An abstract class must be extended. An abstract method must be implemented in a concrete subclass.
`native`			√			A native method indicates that the method is implemented using a language other than Java.

*Default access doesn't have a modifier associated with it. For example: `class Test {}`

Modifier	Class	Constructor	Method	Data	Block	Explanation
`synchronized`			√		√	Only one thread at a time can execute this method.
`strictfp`	√		√			Use strict floating-point calculations to guarantee that the evaluation result is the same on all JVMs.
`transient`				√		Mark a nonserializable instance data field.

The modifiers default (no modifier), `public, private`, and `protected` are known as *visibility* or *accessibility modifiers* because they specify how classes and class members are accessed.

The modifiers `public`, `private`, `protected`, `static`, `final`, and `abstract` can also be applied to inner classes.

SPECIAL FLOATING-POINT VALUES

Dividing an integer by zero is invalid and throws `ArithmeticException`, but dividing a floating-point value by zero does not cause an exception. Floating-point arithmetic can overflow to infinity if the result of the operation is too large for a `double` or a `float`, or underflow to zero if the result is too small for a `double` or a `float`. Java provides the special floating-point values `POSITIVE_INFINITY`, `NEGATIVE_INFINITY`, and `NaN` (Not a Number) to denote these results. These values are defined as special constants in the `Float` class and the `Double` class.

If a positive floating-point number is divided by zero, the result is `POSITIVE_INFINITY`. If a negative floating-point number is divided by zero, the result is `NEGATIVE_INFINITY`. If a floating-point zero is divided by zero, the result is `NaN`, which means that the result is undefined mathematically. The string representations of these three values are `Infinity`, `-Infinity`, and `NaN`. For example,

```java
System.out.print(1.0 / 0); // Print Infinity
System.out.print(-1.0 / 0); // Print -Infinity
System.out.print(0.0 / 0); // Print NaN
```

These special values can also be used as operands in computations. For example, a number divided by `POSITIVE_INFINITY` yields a positive zero. Table G.1 summarizes various combinations of the /, *, %, +, and - operators.

TABLE G.1 Special Floating-Point Values

x	y	x/y		x%y		
Finite	0.0	infinity	0.0	NaN	Finite	Finite
Finite	infinity	0.0	0.0	x	infinity	infinity
0.0	0.0	NaN	0.0	NaN	0.0	0.0
infinity	Finite	infinity	0.0	NaN	infinity	infinity
infinity	infinity	NaN	0.0	NaN	infinity	infinity
0.0	infinity	0.0	NaN	0.0	infinity	0.0
NaN	Any	NaN	NaN	NaN	NaN	NaN
Any	NaN	NaN	NaN	NaN	NaN	NaN

Note
If one of the operands is NaN, the result is NaN.

REGULAR EXPRESSIONS

Often you need to write the code to validate user input such as to check whether the input is a number, a string with all lowercase letters, or a social security number. How do you write this type of code? A simple and effective way to accomplish this task is to use the regular expression.

A *regular expression* (abbreviated *regex*) is a string that describes a pattern for matching a set of strings. Regular expression is a powerful tool for string manipulations. You can use regular expressions for matching, replacing, and splitting strings.

regular expression

Matching Strings

Let us begin with the `matches` method in the `String` class. At first glance, the `matches` method is very similar to the `equals` method. For example, the following two statements both evaluate to `true`.

matches

```
"Java".matches("Java");
"Java".equals("Java");
```

However, the `matches` method is more powerful. It can match not only a fixed string, but also a set of strings that follow a pattern. For example, the following statements all evaluate to `true`.

```
"Java is fun".matches("Java.*")
"Java is cool".matches("Java.*")
"Java is powerful".matches("Java.*")
```

"Java.*" in the preceding statements is a regular expression. It describes a string pattern that begins with Java followed by any zero or more characters. Here, the substring .* matches any zero or more characters.

Regular Expression Syntax

A regular expression consists of literal characters and special symbols. Table H.1 lists some frequently used syntax for regular expressions.

TABLE H.1 Frequently Used Regular Expressions

Regular Expression	Matches	Example
x	a specified character x	Java matches Java
.	any single character	Java matches J..a
(ab\|cd)	ab or cd	ten matches t(en\|im)
[abc]	a, b, or c	Java matches Ja[uvwx]a
[^abc]	any character except a, b, or c	Java matches Ja[^ars]a
[a-z]	a through z	Java matches [A-M]av[a-d]
[^a-z]	any character except a through z	Java matches Jav[^b-d]
[a-e[m-p]]	a through e or m through p	Java matches [A-G[I-M]]av[a-d]
[a-e&&[c-p]]	intersection of a-e with c-p	Java matches [A-P&&[I-M]] av[a-d]
\d	a digit, same as [0-9]	Java2 matches "Java[\\d]"
\D	a non-digit	$Java matches "[\\D][\\D]ava"
\w	a word character	Java1 matches "[\\w]ava[\\w]"
\W	a non-word character	$Java matches "[\\W][\\w]ava"
\s	a whitespace character	"Java 2" matches "Java\\s2"
\S	a non-whitespace char	Java matches "[\\S]ava"
p*	zero or more occurrences of pattern p	aaaabb matches "a*bb" ababab matches "(ab)*"
p+	one or more occurrences of pattern p	a matches "a+b*" able matches "(ab)+.*"
p?	zero or one occurrence of pattern p	Java matches "J?Java" Java matches "J?ava"
p{n}	exactly n occurrences of pattern p	Java matches "Ja{1}.*" Java does not match ".{2}"
p{n,}	at least n occurrences of pattern p	aaaa matches "a{1,}" a does not match "a{2,}"
p{n,m}	between n and m occurrences (inclusive)	aaaa matches "a{1,9}" abb does not match "a{2,9}bb"

Note
Backslash is a special character that starts an escape sequence in a string. So you need to use \\d in Java to represent \d.

Note
Recall that a *whitespace character* is ' ', '\t', '\n', '\r', or '\f'. So \s is the same as [\t\n\r\f], and \S is the same as [^ \t\n\r\f].

Note

A word character is any letter, digit, or the underscore character. So \w is the same as [a-z[A-Z][0-9]_] or simply [a-zA-Z0-9_], and \W is the same as [^a-zA-Z0-9_].

Note

The last six entries *, +, ?, {n}, {n,}, and {n, m} in Table H.1 are called *quantifiers* that specify how many times the pattern before a quantifier may repeat. For example, A* matches zero or more A's, A+ matches one or more A's, A? matches zero or one A's, A{3} matches exactly AAA, A{3,} matches at least three A's, and A{3,6} matches between 3 and 6 A's. * is the same as {0,}, + is the same as {1,}, and ? is the same as {0,1}.

quantifier

Caution

Do not use spaces in the repeat quantifiers. For example, A{3,6} cannot be written as A{3, 6} with a space after the comma.

Note

You may use parentheses to group patterns. For example, (ab){3} matches ababab, but ab{3} matches abbb.

Let us use several examples to demonstrate how to construct regular expressions.

Example 1

The pattern for social security numbers is xxx-xx-xxxx, where x is a digit. A regular expression for social security numbers can be described as

 [\\d]{3}-[\\d]{2}-[\\d]{4}

For example,

 "111-22-3333".matches("[\\d]{3}-[\\d]{2}-[\\d]{4}") returns true.
 "11-22-3333".matches("[\\d]{3}-[\\d]{2}-[\\d]{4}") returns false.

Example 2

An even number ends with digits 0, 2, 4, 6, or 8. The pattern for even numbers can be described as

 [\\d]*[02468]

For example,

 "123".matches("[\\d]*[02468]") returns false.
 "122".matches("[\\d]*[02468]") returns true.

Example 3

The pattern for telephone numbers is (xxx) xxx-xxxx, where x is a digit and the first digit cannot be zero. A regular expression for telephone numbers can be described as

```
\\([1-9][\\d]{2}\\) [\\d]{3}-[\\d]{4}
```

Note that the parentheses symbols (and) are special characters in a regular expression for grouping patterns. To represent a literal (or) in a regular expression, you have to use \\(and \\).
For example,

```
"(912) 921-2728".matches("\\([1-9][\\d]{2}\\) [\\d]{3}-[\\d]
    {4}") returns true.
```

```
"921-2728".matches("\\([1-9][\\d]{2}\\) [\\d]{3}-[\\d]{4}")
    returns false.
```

Example 4

Suppose the last name consists of at most 25 letters and the first letter is in uppercase. The pattern for a last name can be described as

```
[A-Z][a-zA-Z]{1,24}
```

Note that you cannot have arbitrary whitespace in a regular expression. For example, [A-Z][a-zA-Z]{1, 24} would be wrong.
For example,

```
"Smith".matches("[A-Z][a-zA-Z]{1,24}") returns true.
"Jones123".matches("[A-Z][a-zA-Z]{1,24}") returns false.
```

Example 5

Java identifiers are the names that identify the elements such as classes, methods, and variables in a program.

- An identifier must start with a letter, an underscore (_), or a dollar sign ($). It cannot start with a digit.

- An identifier is a sequence of characters that consists of letters, digits, underscores (_), and dollar signs ($).

The pattern for identifiers can be described as

```
[a-zA-Z_$][\\w$]*
```

Example 6

What strings are matched by the regular expression "Welcome to (Java|HTML)"? The answer is Welcome to Java or Welcome to HTML.

Example 7

What strings are matched by the regular expression "A.*"? The answer is any string that starts with letter A.

Replacing and Splitting Strings

The `matches` method in the `String` class returns `true` if the string matches the regular expression. The `String` class also contains the `replaceAll`, `replaceFirst`, and `split` methods for replacing and splitting strings, as shown in Figure H.1.

java.lang.String	
+matches(regex: String): boolean	Returns true if this string matches the pattern.
+replaceAll(regex: String, replacement: String): String	Returns a new string that replaces all matching substrings with the replacement.
+replaceFirst(regex: String, replacement: String): String	Returns a new string that replaces the first matching substring with the replacement.
+split(regex: String): String[]	Returns an array of strings consisting of the substrings split by the matches.
+split(regex: String, limit: int): String[]	Same as the preceding split method except that the limit parameter controls the number of times the pattern is applied.

FIGURE H.1 The `String` class contains the methods for matching, replacing, and splitting strings using regular expressions.

The `replaceAll` method replaces all matching substring and the `replaceFirst` method replaces the first matching substring. For example, the following code

```
System.out.println("Java Java Java".replaceAll("v\\w", "wi"));
```

displays

```
Jawi Jawi Jawi
```

The following code

```
System.out.println("Java Java Java".replaceFirst("v\\w", "wi"));
```

displays

```
Jawi Java Java
```

There are two overloaded `split` methods. The `split(regex)` method splits a string into substrings delimited by the matches. For example, the following statement

```
String[] tokens = "Java1HTML2Perl".split("\\d");
```

splits string `"Java1HTML2Perl"` into `Java`, `HTML`, and `Perl` and saved in `tokens[0]`, `tokens[1]`, and `tokens[2]`.

In the `split(regex, limit)` method, the `limit` parameter determines how many times the pattern is matched. If `limit <= 0`, `split(regex, limit)` is same as `split(regex)`. If `limit > 0`, the pattern is matched at most `limit - 1` times. Here are some examples:

```
"Java1HTML2Perl".split("\\d", 0); splits into Java, HTML, Perl
"Java1HTML2Perl".split("\\d", 1); splits into Java1HTML2Perl
"Java1HTML2Perl".split("\\d", 2); splits into Java, HTML2Perl
"Java1HTML2Perl".split("\\d", 3); splits into Java, HTML, Perl
"Java1HTML2Perl".split("\\d", 4); splits into Java, HTML, Perl
"Java1HTML2Perl".split("\\d", 5); splits into Java, HTML, Perl
```

Note

By default, all the quantifiers are *greedy*. This means that they will match as many occurrences as possible. For example, the following statement displays JRvaa, since the first match is aaa.

```
System.out.println("Jaaavaa".replaceFirst("a+", "R"));
```

You can change a qualifier's default behavior by appending a question mark (?) after it. The quantifier becomes *reluctant*, which means that it will match as few occurrences as possible. For example, the following statement displays JRaavaa, since the first match is a.

```
System.out.println("Jaaavaa".replaceFirst("a+?", "R"));
```

APPENDIX I

ENUMERATED TYPES

Simple Enumerated Types

An enumerated type defines a list of enumerated values. Each value is an identifier. For example, the following statement declares a type, named MyFavorite-Color, with values RED, BLUE, GREEN, and YELLOW in this order.

```
enum MyFavoriteColor {RED, BLUE, GREEN, YELLOW};
```

A value of an enumerated type is like a constant and so, by convention, is spelled with all uppercase letters. So, the preceding declaration uses RED, not red. By convention, an enumerated type is named like a class with first letter of each word capitalized.

Once a type is defined, you can declare a variable of that type:

```
MyFavoriteColor color;
```

The variable color can hold one of the values defined in the enumerated type MyFavoriteColor or null, but nothing else. Java enumerated type is *type-safe*, meaning that an attempt to assign a value other than one of the enumerated values or null will result in a compile error.

The enumerated values can be accessed using the syntax

```
EnumeratedTypeName.valueName
```

For example, the following statement assigns enumerated value BLUE to variable color:

```
color = MyFavoriteColor.BLUE;
```

Note that you have to use the enumerated type name as a qualifier to reference a value such as BLUE.

As with any other type, you can declare and initialize a variable in one statement:

```
MyFavoriteColor color = MyFavoriteColor.BLUE;
```

An enumerated type is treated as a special class. An enumerated type variable is therefore a reference variable. An enumerated type is a subtype of the Object class and the Comparable interface. Therefore, an enumerated type inherits all the methods in the Object class and the compareTo method in the Comparable interface.

Additionally, you can use the following methods on an enumerated object:

- `public String name();`
 Returns a name of the value for the object.

- `public int ordinal();`
 Returns the ordinal value associated with the enumerated value. The first value in an enumerated type has an ordinal value of 0, the second has an ordinal value of 1, the third one 3, and so on.

Listing I.1 gives a program that demonstrates the use of enumerated types.

LISTING I.1 `EnumeratedTypeDemo.java`

define an enum type

declare an enum variable

get enum name

get enum ordinal

compare enum values

```
 1  public class EnumeratedTypeDemo {
 2    static enum Day {SUNDAY, MONDAY, TUESDAY, WEDNESDAY, THURSDAY,
 3      FRIDAY, SATURDAY};
 4
 5    public static void main(String[] args) {
 6      Day day1 = Day.FRIDAY;
 7      Day day2 = Day.THURSDAY;
 8
 9      System.out.println("day1's name is " + day1.name());
10      System.out.println("day2's name is " + day2.name());
11      System.out.println("day1's ordinal is " + day1.ordinal());
12      System.out.println("day2's ordinal is " + day2.ordinal());
13
14      System.out.println("day1.equals(day2) returns " +
15        day1.equals(day2));
16      System.out.println("day1.toString() returns " +
17        day1.toString());
18      System.out.println("day1.compareTo(day2) returns " +
19        day1.compareTo(day2));
20    }
21  }
```

```
day1's name is FRIDAY
day2's name is THURSDAY
day1's ordinal is 5
day2's ordinal is 4
day1.equals(day2) returns false
day1.toString() returns FRIDAY
day1.compareTo(day2) returns 1
```

An enumerated type `Day` is defined in lines 2–3. Variables `day1` and `day2` are declared as the `Day` type and assigned enumerated values in lines 6–7. Since `day1`'s value is `FRIDAY`, its ordinal value is 5 (line 11). Since `day2`'s value is `THURSDAY`, its ordinal value is 4 (line 12).

Since an enumerated type is a subclass of the `Object` class and the `Comparable` interface, you can invoke the methods `equals`, `toString`, and `comareTo` from an enumerated object reference variable (lines 14–19). `day1.equals(day2)` returns true if `day1` and `day2` have the same ordinal value. `day1.compareTo(day2)` returns the difference between `day1`'s ordinal value to `day2`'s.

Alternatively, you can rewrite the code in Listing I.1 into Listing I.2.

LISTING I.2 `StandaloneEnumTypeDemo.java`

```
1  public class StandaloneEnumTypeDemo {
2    public static void main(String[] args) {
3      Day day1 = Day.FRIDAY;
4      Day day2 = Day.THURSDAY;
5
6      System.out.println("day1's name is " + day1.name());
7      System.out.println("day2's name is " + day2.name());
8      System.out.println("day1's ordinal is " + day1.ordinal());
9      System.out.println("day2's ordinal is " + day2.ordinal());
10
11     System.out.println("day1.equals(day2) returns " +
12       day1.equals(day2));
13     System.out.println("day1.toString() returns " +
14       day1.toString());
15     System.out.println("day1.compareTo(day2) returns " +
16       day1.compareTo(day2));
17   }
18 }
19
20 enum Day {SUNDAY, MONDAY, TUESDAY, WEDNESDAY, THURSDAY,
21   FRIDAY, SATURDAY}
```

An enumerated type can be defined inside a class, as shown in lines 2–3 in Listing I.1, or standalone as shown in lines 20–21 in Listing I.2. In the former case, the type is treated as an inner class. After the program is compiled, a class named EnumeratedTypeDemo$Day.class is created. In the latter case, the type is treated as a standalone class. After the program is compiled, a class named Day.class is created.

Note
When an enumerated type is declared inside a class, the type must be declared as a member of the class and cannot be declared inside a method. Furthermore, the type is always `static`. For this reason, the `static` keyword in line 2 in Listing I.1 may be omitted. The visibility modifiers on inner class can also be applied to enumerated types defined inside a class.

Tip
Using enumerated values (e.g., `Day.MONDAY`, `Day.TUESDAY`, and so on) rather than literal integer values (e.g., 0, 1, and so on) can make a program easier to read and maintain.

Using `if` or `switch` Statements with an Enumerated Variable

An enumerated variable holds a value. Often your program needs to perform a specific action depending on the value. For example, if the value is `Day.MONDAY`, play soccer; if the value is `Day.TUESDAY`, take piano lesson, and so on. You can use an `if` statement or a `switch` statement to test the value in the variable, as shown in (a) and (b).

```
if (day.equals(Day.MONDAY)) {
   // process Monday
}
else if (day.equals(Day.TUESDAY)) {
   // process Tuesday
}
else
   ...
```

(a)

Equivalent

```
switch (day) {
   case MONDAY:
      // process
Monday
      break;
   case TUESDAY:
      // process
Tuesday
      break;
   ...
}
```

(b)

In the `switch` statement in (b), the case label is an unqualified enumerated value (e.g., MONDAY, but not Day.MONDAY).

Processing Enumerated Values Using a Foreach Loop

Each enumerated type has a static method `values()` that returns all enumerated values for the type in an array. For example,

```
Day[] days = Day.values();
```

You can use a regular for loop in (a) or a foreach loop in (b) to process all the values in the array.

```
for (int i = 0; i < days.length; i++)
   System.out.println(days[i]);
```

(a)

Equivalent

```
for (Day day: days)
   System.out.println(day);
```

(b)

Enumerated Types with Data Fields, Constructors, and Methods

The simple enumerated types introduced in the preceding section define a type with a list of enumerated values. You can also define an enumerated type with data fields, constructors, and methods, as shown in Listing I.3.

LISTING I.3 `TrafficLight.java`

```
 1  public enum TrafficLight {
 2     RED ("Please stop"), GREEN ("Please go"),
 3     YELLOW ("Please caution");
 4
 5     private String description;
 6
 7     private TrafficLight(String description) {
 8        this.description = description;
 9     }
10
```

```
11     public String getDescription() {
12        return description;
13     }
14  }
```

The enumerated values are defined in lines 2–3. The value declaration must be the first statement in the type declaration. A data field named `description` is declared in line 5 to describe an enumerated value. The constructor `TrafficLight` is declared in lines 7–9. The constructor is invoked whenever an enumerated value is accessed. The enumerated value's argument is passed to the constructor, which is then assigned to `description`.

Listing I.4 gives a test program to use `TrafficLight`.

LISTING I.4 `TestTrafficLight.java`

```
1  public class TestTrafficLight {
2     public static void main(String[] args) {
3        TrafficLight light = TrafficLight.RED;
4        System.out.println(light.getDescription());
5     }
6  }
```

An enumerated value `TrafficLight.red` is assigned to variable `light` (line 3). Accessing `TrafficLight.RED` causes the JVM to invoke the constructor with argument "please stop". The methods in enumerated type are invoked in the same way as the methods in a class. `light.getDescription()` returns the description for the enumerated value (line 4).

Note

The Java syntax requires that the constructor for enumerated types be private to prevent it from being invoked directly. The private modifier may be omitted. In this case, it is considered private by default.

BITWISE OPERATORS

To write programs at the machine-level, often you need to deal with binary numbers directly and perform operations at the bit-level. Java provides the bitwise operators and shift operators defined in Table J.1.

TABLE J.1 Bitwise Operators

Operator	Name	Example (using bytes in the example)	Description
&	Bitwise AND	10101110 & 10010010 yields 10000010	The AND of two corresponding bits yields a 1 if both bits are 1.
\|	Bitwise inclusive OR	10101110 \| 10010010 yields 10111110	The OR of two corresponding bits yields a 1 if either bit is 1.
^	Bitwise exclusive OR	10101110 ^ 10010010 yields 00111100	The XOR of two corresponding bits yields a 1 only if two bits are different.
~	One's complement	~10101110 yields 01010001	The operator toggles each bit from 0 to 1 and from 1 to 0.
<<	Left shift	10101110 << 2 yields 10111000	The operator shifts bits in the first operand left by the number of bits specified in the second operand, filling with 0s on the right.
>>	Right shift with sign extension	10101110 >> 2 yields 11101011 00101110 >> 2 yields 00001011	The operator shifts bit in the first operand right by the number of bits specified in the second operand, filling with the highest (sign) bit on the left.
>>>	Unsigned right shift with zero extension	10101110 >>> 2 yields 00101011 00101110 >>> 2 yields 00001011	The operator shifts bit in the first operand right by the number of bits specified in the second operand, filling with 0s on the left.

The bit operators apply only to integer types (`byte`, `short`, `int`, and `long`). A character involved in a bit operation is converted to an integer. All bitwise operators can form bitwise assignment operators, such as =, |=, <<=, >>=, and >>>=.

GLOSSARY

0 based A number in or index of objects where the first element starts at the index of 0.

algorithm Statements that describe how a problem is solved in terms of the actions to be executed, and specifies the order in which these actions should be executed. Algorithms can help the programmer plan a program before writing it in a programming language.

Application Program Interface (API) A set of classes and interfaces that can be used to develop Java programs.

argument A value that is passed to a method when the method is invoked.

assembler A program that translates assembly-language programs into machine code.

assembly language A low-level programming language in which a mnemonic is used to represent each of the machine language instructions.

assignment operator (=) Assigns a value to a variable.

assignment statement A simple statement that assigns a value to a variable using an assignment operator (=). When a value is assigned to a variable, it replaces the previous value of the variable, which is destroyed.

attribute A variable that stores a value for an object.

back-end application Part of a software design that handles the data and operations that communicate with the server.

biometrics The process of measuring a person's biological features for the purpose of identification. Examples are fingerprint scanners, retina scanners, voice recognition, or facial recognition.

bit A binary digit 0 and 1.

block A sequence of statements enclosed in braces ({}).

boolean data type A primitive data type for Boolean values (true or false).

Boolean expression An expression that evaluates to a true or false value.

Boolean value True or false.

break statement A program statement used to exit out of the current loop.

bugs Logic errors.

bus A system that connects all the components of the computers together.

business constraints Often involve project scheduling, budgeting, and security guidelines of a project.

business ethics Moral principles applied to business issues and actions.

byte A unit of storage. Each byte consists of 8 bits. The size of hard disk and memory is measured in bytes. A megabyte is roughly a million bytes.

byte type A primitive data type that represents an integer in a byte. The range of a byte value is from

-2^7 (-128) to 2^7-1 (127).

bytecode The result of compiling Java source code. Bytecode is machine-independent and can run on any machine that has a Java running environment.

bytecode verifier A program in the JVM that checks the validity of the bytecode and ensures that the bytecode does not violate Java's security restrictions.

career A chosen field of work in which you try to advance over time by gaining responsibility and earning more money.

case sensitive A characteristic of a programming language where uppercase and lowercase letters are read as different items.

casting The process of converting a primitive data type value into another primitive type.

CD-R A compact disc for read-only permanent storage; the user cannot modify its contents once they are recorded.

CD-RW A compact disc that can be used like a hard disk; that is, you can write data onto the disc, and then overwrite that data with new data.

central processing unit (CPU) A small silicon semiconductor chip with millions of transistors that executes instructions.

char type A primitive data type that represents a Unicode character.

CIA triad A principle used to define the three key components of computer security: Confidentiality, Integrity, and Availability,

class An encapsulated collection of data and methods that operate on data. A class may be instantiated to create an object that is an instance of the class.

class diagram A type of illustration used to describe the components of a class.

class loader A program used to load object classes into memory.

cloud storage A storage system in which data is stored across multiple servers and various locations, and is accessible from multiple devices.

cluster A group of similar items.

comment Comments document what a program is and how it is constructed. They are not programming statements and are ignored by the compiler. In Java, comments are preceded by two slashes (//) in a line or enclosed between /* and */ in multiple lines.

compiler A software program that translates source code (e.g., Java source code) into a machine language program.

computer crime Any act that either maliciously targets a computer system, or uses a computer to commit a crime.

computer abuse Bullying someone with the use of a computer.

computer fraud The act of using a computer to gain unlawful use of data or the computer system. Identity theft is an example of computer fraud.

Computer Fraud and Abuse Act (CFAA) A federal law that carries a penalty of up to $250,000 and 20 years in jail.

computer hacking The unauthorized entry into a computer system for malicious reasons.

concatenation The process of joining two or more strings together.

conditional operator Used in an expression that requires three operands and is represented by the symbol "?".

console Refers to the input and output device of a computer.

constant A variable declared final in Java. A local constant is a constant declared inside a method.

constraints Limitations on a project; typically falls into two categories of either a business constraint or a technical constraint.

constructor A special method for initializing objects when creating objects using the `new` operator. The constructor has exactly the same name as its defining class.

`continue` statement A program statement used to jump to the next iteration of a loop.

cookie Small text files that store sets of name-value pairs on the disk in the client's computer. Cookies can be used for session tracking.

core The part of the processor that performs the reading and executing of instructions.

cyber bullying The act of threatening, stalking, or harassing someone through social media or over the Internet.

dangling `else` ambiguity Describes a common mistake where an `else` clause is mismatched to an `if` clause.

data communication system The structure that communicates and transmits data back and forth from client to server.

data field A variable that stores a value for an object.

data structure A format for organizing and storing data. An array is an example of a data structure.

data theft The stealing or collection of personal data from someone without his or her consent.

data type Used to define variables to indicate what kind of value the variable can hold.

debugging To find errors in a program.

declare variable Defines a variable with a data type.

decrement operator (−−) Subtracts one from a numeric variable or a `char` variable.

default constructor If a class does not define any constructors explicitly, a `no-arg` constructor with empty body is assumed. This is called a default constructor.

divide and conquer Also known as stepwise refinement, used to decompose a large program into subproblems.

dot operator An operator used to access members of an object. If the member is static, it can be accessed through the class name using the dot operator.

double type A primitive data type to represent double precision floating-point numbers with 14 to 15 significant digits of accuracy.

do-while loop A loop construct that begins with the keyword do.

drive Device for operating a medium, such as a disk or a CD.

DVD Stands for digital versatile disc or digital video disc; used to store data.

encapsulation Hiding the details of a class.

encoding Representing a character using a binary code.

encoding scheme A set of rules that govern how a computer translates characters into data the computer can actually work with.

encryption The process of applying an algorithm to convert data into an unreadable form during data transmission.

escape character The backslash (\\) is called an escape character.

escape sequence A special notation, consists of a backslash (\\) followed by a character or a combination of digits.

Ethernet cabling A type of hardware wiring where data is transmitted through electrical pulses over thin strands of copper wiring.

ethics A set of beliefs about what is right and what is wrong.

event-driven programming A type of programming style where code is written in blocks of procedures and functional units, but these blocks of code are associated with particular events that may occur.

expression Represents a computation involving values, variables, and operators, which evaluates to a value.

extensibility The ability to extend, or add to, a template.

fall-through behavior In a switch statement, if once a case is matched, the statements starting from the matched case are executed until a break statement or the end of the switch statement is reached. This phenomenon is referred to as the fall-through behavior.

fiber optics A type of hardware made up of tiny, glass threads where data is transmitted through light pulses.

final keyword A modifier that specifies a constant.

firewall A piece of hardware or software that controls the incoming and outgoing traffic to a computer system.

float type A primitive data type to represent single precision floating-point numbers with 6 to 7 significant digits of accuracy. The double type is used to represent double precisions with 14 to 15 significant digits of accuracy.

floating-point number A number that includes a fractional part.

flowchart A diagram that describes an algorithm or process, showing the steps as boxes of various kinds, and their order by connecting these with arrows.

for loop A loop construct that begins with the keyword `for`.

format specifier Specifies how an item should be displayed. An item may be a numeric value, a character, a Boolean value, or a string.

front-end application Part of a software design that provides the user interface.

Gantt chart A horizontal bar chart that shows a graphical illustration of a schedule.

gigabyte (GB) About 1 billion bytes.

gigahertz The clock speed of a computer is now usually stated in gigahertz.

hard disk Used for permanently storing data and programs.

hardware The physical aspect of the computer that can be seen.

hertz The unit of measurement of clock speed.

high-level language A classification of programming languages that is English-like and easy to learn.

identifier A name of a variable, method, class, interface, or package.

identify theft The act of posing as someone else for fraudulent reasons.

`if` statement A type of selection statement: A one-way `if` statement executes an action if and only if the condition is true.

increment operator $(++)$ Adds one to a numeric variable or a `char` variable.

incremental code and testing A programming methodology that develops and tests programs incrementally. This approach is efficient and productive. It helps eliminate and isolate errors.

incremental development and testing A programming methodology that develops and tests a program incrementally. This approach is efficient and productive. It helps eliminate and isolate errors.

index An integer value used to specify the position of an element in the array. In Java, the array index begins at 0.

infinite loop A loop that runs indefinitely due to a bug in the loop.

information hiding A situation in which the details of the implementation are encapsulated in the method and hidden from the client who invokes the method.

inheritance Defining a new class by extending an existing class.

initialize variables Variables often have initial values. You can declare a variable and initialize it in one step.

instance method A method that must be invoked from a specific object.

instantiation The process of creating an object of a class.

int type A primitive data type to represent an integer in the range from -2^{31} (-2147483648) to $2^{31}-1$ (2147483647).

integer overflow When a variable is assigned a value that is too large (in size) to be stored, it causes overflow.

integrated development environment (IDE) Software that helps programmers write code efficiently. IDE tools integrate editing, compiling, building, debugging, and online help in one graphical user interface.

interpreter Software for interpreting and executing the intermediate code, such as Java bytecode.

IPO Stands for Input, Process, and Output.

issue tracking system A system for documenting issues and resolutions to manage the progress of a project. The tracking system can be as simple as a spreadsheet, or an integrated development environment (IDE) that includes project management features.

iteration One time execution of the loop body.

Java Development Toolkit (JDK) Defines the Java Application Programming Interface (API) and contains a set of command line utilities, such as javac (compiler) and java (interpreter).

Java Virtual Machine (JVM) A machine that runs Java byte-code. It is called virtual because it is usually implemented in software rather than in hardware.

javac command The command to invoke the compiler to compile a Java source code program from the command line.

keylogger A piece of software or hardware that tracks and logs the activity on a computer.

keyword (or reserved word) A word defined as part of Java language, which has a specific meaning to the compiler and cannot be used for other purposes in the program.

kilobyte (KB) About 1,000 bytes.

lazy operator Same as short-circuit operator.

leader A type of manager who knows how to use available resources to help others achieve their goals.

library Describes the set of classes available in the Application Program Interface (API).

local area network (LAN) The LAN is commonly used in business, universities, and government organizations.

logic error A type of error that occurs when a program does not perform the way it was intended to.

long type A primitive data type to represent an integer in the range from -2^{63} to $2^{63}-1$.

loop A control structure that repeats executions of a block of statements.

loop body The part of the loop that contains the statements to be repeated.

low-level language A computer language that is close to machine language, such as assembly language.

machine language A set of primitive instructions built into every computer. The instructions are in the form of binary code, so you have to enter binary codes for various instructions.

main method The starting method for executing a program.

malware An acronym for malicious software. Viruses are a type of malware.

megabyte (MB) Roughly 1 million bytes.

megahertz One million hertz.

memory Internal storage consisting of an ordered sequence of bytes for storing programs and data.

method A block of code that performs a specific task.

method abstraction A technique in software development that hides detailed implementation. A process of-separating the use of a method from its implementation. The client can use a method without knowing how it is implemented.

method signature The combination of the name of a method and the list of its parameters.

million bits per second (mbps) A measurement of speed for transferring data.

modular code Makes the code easy to maintain, debug, and reuse.

modular design The practice of dividing your application into smaller, re-useable units that work together as a whole.

motherboard A circuit case that connects all of the parts of a computer together.

network interface card (NIC) A hardware device to connect a computer to a local area network (LAN).

new operator A keyword used to create objects in Java.

no-arg constructor A constructor without arguments.

null A literal of a reference variable that does not reference any concrete object.

object Can be created from a class using the class's constructor.

objective A short-term goal used to keep a project on track for completion; also means fairly, without emotion or prejudice.

object-oriented programming (OOP) An approach to programming that involves organizing objects and their behavior into classes of reusable components.

off-by-one error A common error where a step in the loop is executed one more, or one less, time than it should have executed.

operating system (OS) A program that manages and controls a computer's activities (e.g., Windows, Linux, Solaris).

operator associativity Defines the order in which operators will be evaluated in an expression if the operators have the same precedence order.

operator precedence Defines the order in which operators will be evaluated in an expression.

operators Operations for primitive data type values. Examples of operators are +, -, *, /, and %.

override Create a method in a subclass that supercedes a method that has been previously declared in a superclass.

parameter A variable that is defined in the method header.

Patriot Act Signed into law after the September 11, 2001 (9/11) terrorist attack on the World Trade Center Towers in New York City. The intent was to provide government with access to information that could lead to the capture of terrorists or prevention of future attacks.

PERT chart Shows project tasks, the order in which they must be completed, and the time requirements.

postdecrement Refers to the syntax such as x-- where the -- operator is placed after a variable.

postincrement Refers to the syntax such as x++ where the ++ operator is placed after a variable.

posttest loop The condition is checked after the loop body is executed.

predecrement Refers to the syntax such as --x where the -- operator is placed before a variable.

preincrement Refers to the syntax such as ++x where the ++ operator is placed before a variable.

pretest loop The continuation condition is checked before the loop body is executed.

primitive data type The most basic data types available in a programming language. In Java, the primitive data types are byte, short, int, long, float, double, boolean, and char.

priorities Tasks which must be completed first.

private key encryption A type of cryptography where the secret key is known only by the sender and the receiver of data.

problem A difficulty that you must resolve before you can make progress.

Procedural Language Units of programming code are grouped together into what is called a "procedure" or "function."

program A set of computer instructions that perform logical operations.

programming The process for writing a program.

programming languages Specific types of code languages used by software developers to communicate instructions to a computer.

programming paradigm Describes the way in which software is designed, such as object-oriented, procedural, or structural.

programming style Describes the way in which software is designed. Also referred to as a programming paradigm.

project management A process used to take a project from conception to completion.

property A variable that stores a value for an object.

pseudocode A set of instructions or algorithm that is written in an easily readable format and not in a particular programming language.

public key encryption A type of cryptography that uses two keys and is known to everyone.

quality assurance The process of monitoring a project to ensure the software design plan is followed and the expected results are achieved.

RAM Random-access memory. Named because the bytes in the memory can be accessed in any order.

reference type A data type that is a class or an interface.

relational operators A programming language construct used to compare two values. In Java they are: <, >, >=, ==, and !=.

requirements specification A formal process that seeks to understand the problem that the software will address and to document in detail what the software system needs to do.

risk assessment The process of identifying and planning for factors that can negatively affect the security of a system.

round-off error The difference between the calculated approximation of a number and its exact mathematical value.

runtime error Errors that cause a program to terminate abnormally.

security risk A person, object, or situation that poses a threat to the safety of something.

selection statement A statement that uses an `if` or a `switch` statement to control the execution of the program.

sentinel value A special input value that signifies the end of the input.

short type A primitive data type that represents an integer in the range from -2^{15} (-32768) to $2^{15}-1$ (32767).

short-circuit operator Evaluation that stops when the result of the expression has been determined, even if not all the operands are evaluated. The evaluation involving **&&** or **||** are examples of short-circuit evaluation.

single-dimensional array A common data structure that organizes data into a single row or column.

smart chip ID Cards and badges with this technology include a computerized chip that holds credentials and are read by a computer device to determine security clearance.

software The invisible instructions that control the hardware and make it work.

software development lifecycle A framework used for planning the stages of developing software. Examples of stages are: requirements specification, analysis, design, implementation, testing, deployment, and maintenance.

software license A legally binding agreement between the software producer and the user.

source code A human-readable set of instructions written in a programming language such as Java.

specific import Specifies a single class in the import statement. For example, `import java.util.Scanner` imports Scanner from package java.util.

statement A unit of code that represents an action or a sequence of actions.

statement terminator The semicolon is the statement terminator symbol in Java.

`static` method A non-instance method.

stepwise refinement When writing a large program, you can use the "divide and conquer" strategy, also known as stepwise refinement, to decompose it into subproblems. The subproblems can be further decomposed into smaller, more manageable problems.

storage devices Used to permanently store programs and data.

`string` object A sequence of characters stored in a single entity. Strings are objects in Java.

Structured Programming style A type of programming paradigm where code is written in a meaningful, logical order.

stub A simple, but not a complete version of the method. The use of stubs enables you to test invoking the method from a caller.

subjective Affected by existing opinions, feelings, and beliefs.

supplementary Unicode Those characters that go beyond the original 16-bit Unicode limit.

`switch` statement Executes statements based on the value of a variable or an expression.

syntax error Errors that are caused by an incorrect sequence of characters or spelling and is detectable at compile-time.

system design To design a process for obtaining the output from the input. This phase involves the use of many levels of abstraction to break down the problem into manageable components and design strategies for implementing each component.

team A group of two or more people who work together to achieve a common goal.

technical constraints Often beyond the control of the programmer. For instance, a hardware or network configuration may place constraints on the application's performance. Also called environmental constraints.

terabyte (TB) About 1 trillion bytes.

tracing program A method of reviewing how a program works.

transistors Tiny electric switches for processing information.

`trim()` method Returns a new string by eliminating whitespace characters from both ends of the string.

two-dimensional array A data structure where information is organized in columns and rows.

Unicode A code system for international characters managed by the Unicode Consortium. Java supports Unicode.

Unified Modeling Language (UML) A graphical notation for describing classes and their relationships.

unique address A specific location in memory that is used to locate and store data.

UNIX epoch January 1, 1970 Greenwich mean time (GMT) is known as the Unix epoch because 1970 was the year when the Unix operating system was formally introduced.

Unstructured Programming Style A type of programming style where code is written in sequentially ordered lines and includes GOTO statements.

USA Freedom Act A section of the Patriot Act that was changed stopping the NSA from collecting phone records from citizens not involved in a terrorist crime.

value type Stores a variable's values in physical memory.

value-returning method Terminology used when a method returns a value.

variable Variables are used to store data and computational results in the program.

void method A type of method where a value is not returned to the caller.

while loop A loop construct that begins with the keyword `while`.

Wi-Fi Protected Access (WPA) Formerly adopted by the industry as a standard in 2003; meant to improve the older WEP encryption policy.

Wi-Fi Protected Access II (WPA2) Was adopted as an industry standard in 2006, and provides a higher level of security than its WPA predecessor.

wildcard import Imports all the classes in a package and is denoted by an asterisk (*). As an example, `import java.util.*` imports all classes from `package java.util`.

Wired Equivalent Privacy (WEP) The oldest of the three types of wireless encryption. Although it is widely used, it provides the least amount of protection.

work ethics Moral principles, or beliefs and behaviors about what is right and wrong in a work environment.

INDEX